DATE DUE

JAN 3 0 1995	
FEB 1 3 1995	
FEB 2 7 1995	
MAR 1 4 1995	

BRODART   Cat. No. 23-221

PLAS

PITT
LATIN
AMERICAN
SERIES

Rebirth of the Paraguayan Republic

Rebirth of the Paraguayan Republic
The First Colorado Era, 1878–1904

HARRIS GAYLORD WARREN
with the assistance of Katherine F. Warren

University of Pittsburgh Press

Published by the University of Pittsburgh Press, Pittsburgh, PA 15260
Copyright © 1985, University of Pittsburgh Press

Feffer and Simons, Inc., London

Manufactured in the United States of America

Library of Congress Cataloging in Publication Data

Warren, Harris Gaylord, 1906–
   Rebirth of the Paraguayan Republic.

   (Pitt Latin American series)
   Bibliography: p. 349
   Includes index.
   1. Paraguay—History—1870–1938.   I. Warren,
Katherine F.   II. Title.
F2688.W375   1985   989.2′06   84–19528
ISBN 0–8229–3507–4

For Grandchildren
Sharon and Douglas
Kevin and Jason

Contents

Tables

Maps

Preface

The division of a country's history into periods, especially if those periods are relatively short, is a convenient if somewhat misleading device, misleading because significant historial continuities are easily slighted in the effort to construct an accurate, intregrated account. I have attempted to minimize this danger in writing the history of Paraguay from the watershed years of 1869–1870 to the Colorado defeat in 1904. In the first decade of this thirty-five-year span, studied in *Paraguay and the Triple Alliance,* Paraguayans gradually recovered basic national bearings, struggled with outstanding success against the machinations of Argentina and Brazil, adopted a liberal constitution, and entered actively on the way to laissez-faire capitalism under guidance of the emerging Colorado party. Colorado political control and Colorado economic policies were firmly established under presidents Bareiro, Caballero, and Escobar who dominated the country from 1878 to 1890. Colorado political supremacy was increasingly threatened by intransigent Liberals who finally succeeded in their revolution of 1904. By that time the Colorados had institutionalized their economic objectives, an achievement the Liberals were unable, or unwilling, to change significantly before the Chaco War engulfed the country.

Reborn under Colorado guidance, the Paraguayan Republic was greatly changed from the Paraguay of the three dictators who ruled from 1815 to 1869–1870. Under them the state owned nearly all the land, operated many estancias, monopolized trade, and permitted none of the political and economic freedoms associated with laissez-faire capitalistic democracy. Under the Colorados, freedom of entrepreneurs to exploit natural resources and the available labor supply was zealously promoted by the state to create a modern capitalist society. The function of government was to provide the legal framework within which the broad economic goal could be accomplished.

The first Colorado era in Paraguay has hitherto lacked a comprehensive history based primarily on archival sources. No resident Paraguayan would add to his popularity by publishing an unvarnished history of the Colorado era in which General Bernardino Caballero figured so prominently.[1] This hero of the Paraguayan War is second only to Francisco Solano López in the Colorado—indeed in the national—pantheon of heroes. As every researcher in modern Paraguay knows too well, access to pertinent unpublished personal and official sources is so severely limited as to be pratically impossible. Consequently, one must go to foreign archives, to London, Washington, Buenos Aires, and Rio de Janeiro especially, for most of the reliable sources. Reliable published materials for the period are very scanty, indeed. This is especially true of newspapers, only short runs of which are available in most cases. Except for copies preserved in foreign archives, time and insects have ravaged most of what remain. For those that are available, grateful acknowledgment is made to Señor Carlos Alberto Pusineri Scala, director of the Casa de la Independencia in Asunción and an historian-anthropologist of great expertise. Confronted by so many difficulties, why does the scholar persist in devoting so much of a short life to the study of a very small country buried in the heart of South America? There is much truth in the comment of a brilliant young Paraguayan historian, Juan Carlos Herken Krauer: "Paraguay is not a country—it is an obsession."

For support in pursuing this obsession, I am deeply indebted to the American Philosophical Society for grants from the Penrose Fund and to the many archivists and librarians in three continents who were uniformly gracious, patient, and helpful in meeting my many requests. I am especially grateful to Dr. Marta Gonçalves, chief of the Arquivo Histórico, Ministério das Relações Exteriores, Itamaraty, Rio de Janeiro; to my daughter, Mrs. William D. Elliott, and to my son, Dr. Gordon H. Warren, for providing copies of fugitive materials; and to Mr. Thomas Whigham of Stanford University for his aid in the use of the Godoi Collection at the University of California, Riverside. Sr. Juan Carlos Herken Krauer sent me a copy of his carefully researched "El Paraguay entre 1869 y 1913: Contribuciones a la historia económica regional del Plata." Published in 1984, this study is a most valuable addition to literature on the Colorado era.

Rebirth of the Paraguayan Republic

Prelude: The Heritage of War

The War of the Triple Alliance was for Paraguay a disaster of such magnitude as to defy complete understanding. More than one-half of the country's population perished during the long conflict with Argentina, Brazil, and Uruguay from 1865 to 1870. Epidemic diseases swept unhindered through the civilian population fatally weakened by malnutrition and outright starvation. Military hospitals were overcrowded and unsanitary, grossly undermanned, and woefully short of medical supplies. The thousands who perished in battle and from disease, starvation, and execution were a fearful price to pay for Paraguay's release from a half century of dictatorship.

The country's physical wealth suffered far less than its people, although much of it was destroyed or abandoned. Agricultural production had practically ceased by 1869; a once thriving cattle industry disappeared; the short railway was wrecked and its rolling stock was unusable; vacant farmsteads fell into decay, and scores of villages were ghostly reminders of more prosperous days. Allied armies demolished the iron works at Ibicuy (or Ybicuí), the shipyard and arsenal at Asunción, and the telegraph line to Humaitá. These public works had been constructed by foreign technicians under Carlos Antonio López, the *obrero máximo* (very great builder). Grandiose buildings—a national theater, the oratorio, and the government palace—were still unfinished in Asunción when Francisco Solano López challenged the armed might of Brazil, Argentina, and Uruguay. Appalling ineptitude on both sides needlessly prolonged the war which finally was nearly over when the Allies occupied Asunción in January 1869. But it was not until March 1, 1870, that Brazilian cavalry finally destroyed the pitiful remnants of Paraguay's army at Cerro Corá, and legend has it that there the marshal-president, Francisco Solano López, exclaimed, "Muero con mi patria!" as he died on the muddy banks of a small stream. Paraguay was not dead, although the conquerors did practically nothing to revive the shattered country.

Paraguay benefited from the traditional antagonism between Argentina and Brazil as the Allies prepared to enforce terms of the Triple Alliance treaty of May 1, 1865. Brazil was in a very favored position. Uruguay had dropped out of the war long before its end, and Argentina had been forced to withdraw many units to quell rebellious provincial caudillos. Brazil's fleet controlled the rivers and its victorious army had overwhelming superiority over Argentina's contingent. President Domingo Faustino Sarmiento wisely ordered Argentine troops to occupy Villa Occidental, capital of the Chaco, leaving eastern Paraguay to the Brazilians. Argentina's princely territorial demands included all of what is now the Paraguayan Chaco, and the move across the River Paraguay to Villa Occidental provided a strong military presence in the disputed area while avoiding possible clashes with Brazilian troops.

One of Brazil's fears was Argentina's dream of reconstituting the old Viceroyalty of Río de la Plata, an event that would reunite Argentina, Uruguay, and Paraguay. With this concern always present, it was not at all strange that Brazil refused to support Argentina's extreme territorial demands, no matter how clearly granted by the Triple Alliance treaty.

Allied concern over Paraguay was almost entirely political. Before Paraguay could sign treaties with the Allies, a government must be created. Brazil's representative, José Maria da Silva Paranhos, Visconde do Rio Branco, controlled this process. His was the difficult task of restraining Argentina, reconciling Paraguayan factions, and guiding the formation of a credible government. Neither General Julio de Vedia, the Argentine commander, nor Rio Branco had orders or possessed the means to relieve the starving and diseased war survivors who crowded into Asunción. Paraguayans returning to their ruined country quickly formed rival political clubs, foreshadowing creation of the Liberal and Colorado parties and of the factions that developed in each of them. Prominent among leaders of the emerging Liberals were the brothers Decoud, especially José Segundo and Juan José, whose father had commanded the Paraguayan Legion. This unit, formed by Paraguayan exiles in Buenos Aires, had played a minor role in the Argentine army. A principal associate of the Decouds was Benigno Ferreira, a skillful politician who had left the Legion to serve under an Argentine general. Dr. Facundo Machaín, a brilliant young lawyer who had been educated in Chile, commanded the respect of all Liberals. Juan Silvano Godoi, who was going to school in Argentina when the war began, was an impetuous and daring schemer whose unbridled ambition far exceeded his political ability. All these Liberals were young men, most of them in their twenties, who had been nurtured on the writings of Voltaire, Montesquieu, Rousseau, and Jefferson, and had at least dabbled in the classics. Although hatred of the López clan was the principal bond that held the Legion together, many of its members soon made common cause with the lopiztas, an amorphous group of conservatives, war veterans fiercely loyal to the memory of López, government officials and a few diplomats returned from abroad. Their most prominent leader was Cándido Bareiro, a López agent who had returned to Asunción in 1869. These rival groups published newspapers and contended for influence in the political organization of Paraguay. (For the Colorado party, see chapter 5.)

With Rio Branco directing events, the Allies set up a Triumvirate as the provisional government, a move that precipitated intense activity among the Colorados and the Liberals. Rio Branco's choice to head the Triumvirate was the ex-sergeant Cirilo Antonio Rivarola. Scion of a prominent family, Rivarola was a brave man whose moderate ability was unequal to the task of surviving the devious intrigues that kept Paraguay's political scene in constant turmoil. After a year of bickering, Argentina and Brazil finally agreed on a preliminary treaty that all parties signed on June 20, 1870, and the Triumvirate could proceed with efforts at reconstruction. Having no resources and receiving almost no aid from the Allies, Rivarola accomplished very little as the extent of war's catastrophe revealed itself.

A provisional government having been organized, the next step in political reconstruction was the election of delegates to a constitutional convention that would draft a charter to guide the creation of a permanent government. In the contest for delegates to the convention of 1870, Liberals won a numerical advantage but were outmaneuvered by Bareiro's followers. Godoi, one of the *convencionales*, persuaded the convention to replace Rivarola with Facundo Machaín as provisional president, only to have Bareiro undo his scheme promptly with a coup that had Allied approval. Bareiristas then removed Liberals from control of the convention but kept the Decouds and Machaín to write the constitution. The convention finished its work quickly, elected Rivarola as constitutional president, and on November 25, 1870, a Te Deum in the cathedral celebrated the installation of Paraguay's new government.

Rivarola was only slightly more effective as president than he had been as a triumvir, but he tried valiantly. During his first few months in office, a Brazilian favorite, Juan Bautista Gill, emerged as a powerful politician. His questionable conduct in office precipitated a series of events that caused Rivarola to dissolve Congress and to order new elections, after which he promised to resign and to allow the new Congress to elect a president. The Allies made no attempt to interfere with these blatantly unconstitutional moves. The new Congress was duly elected, and Rivarola, true to his promise and thinking that he had Gill's support, submitted his resignation and retired to his country estate. Much to his chagrin, Congress accepted the resignation and replaced him with Vice-President Salvador Jovellanos in December 1871. The Rivarola regime had been badly shaken by plots and a revolt in November led by two war heroes, General Bernardino Caballero and Colonel Patricio Escobar, who were destined to dominate the first Colorado era.

To negotiate a general treaty with Paraguay, Brazil replaced Rio Branco with João Mauricio Wanderley, Barão de Cotegipe. Argentina's envoy was Dr. Manuel Quintana, a brilliant lawyer-politician whose best arguments could not persuade Cotegipe to honor territorial commitments of the Triple Alliance treaty. Cotegipe proceeded to negotiate a treaty with Paraguay by which Brazil gained all its territorial objectives. He then returned to Brazil, leaving Juan Bautista Gill without his main support in the struggle for power with Benigno Ferreira, the strongman of the Jovellanos cabinet. Ferreira soon forced Gill into exile. Two scandalous loans floated in London in 1871 and 1872 netted Paraguayan politicians about $400,000 in gold and burdened the country with a debt of £1,562,000, a debt that weighed heavily on Paraguay throughout the Colorado era.

The years 1872–1874 were tumultuous as revolts masterminded by Bareiro enlisted the support of Caballero, Escobar, Gill, and Rivarola in a successful attempt to force Ferreira from power. Although Gill had played a minor role in the revolt, he had Brazilian support in the election of 1874 and became president for the term ending in November 1878. Gill sincerely wished to see the end of Brazilian occupation, a goal made possible by signing the Machaín-Irigoyen treaty with Argentina in 1876. Since Argentina and Paraguay agreed to submit their Chaco dispute to arbitration, Brazil hastened to evacuate its troops. Delighted with this development, President Gill turned his considerable talents to dealing with the awesome social and economic problems which had defied solution. However, he had only a few months to enjoy his new freedom from the Brazilian presence. A plot by Juan Silvano Godoi resulted in his murder on April 12, 1877, giving him the dubious honor of being the only Paraguayan president to be assassinated while in office. Vice-President Higinio Uriarte completed the term, and then gave way to Cándido Bareiro.

Part I

THE COLORADOS' PARAGUAY

"It is impossible not to feel pity for this unfortunate but singularly interesting country, which, from no fault of its own, but rather from adversity and the long reigns of tyranny, has been so suddenly plunged from its former position of an influential, rich, and rising Republic, to its present comparatively unknown state. However, it cannot be denied that with peace and the steady-increasing prosperity, and with enlightened and liberal statesmen (such as the present Government) to promote the welfare of the people, in encouraging foreigners to come out by offering them reliable securities, by settling pending claims, by showing themselves to be in earnest, and thus, finally, bringing their country to the favourable notice of Europe, Paraguay has every reason to hope that she will regain her former prosperity and rank among the great South American Republics."

Arthur G. Vansittart
Buenos Aires, November 15, 1882

1

The Land, the People, the Towns

The Colorados inherited a Paraguay greatly reduced in area by the Brazilian and Argentine treaties of 1872 and 1876 and with its claim to the Chaco Boreal challenged by both Argentina and Bolivia. The Paraguayans, except for a few fringe settlements like Villa Occidental (later renamed Villa Hayes) on the right bank of the Río Paraguay, lived east of the Indian-infested, forbidding Chaco. Often called a paradise by poorly informed writers whose exaggerated description bore little resemblance to reality, eastern Paraguay could not be developed without a tremendous amount of work and a continuing struggle against natural forces. Although Spanish colonization had begun in 1537, Paraguay in the 1870s was still an undeveloped country whose small population was grouped into struggling villages and towns or scattered widely in less than one-half of the area east of the river.

The Land

The total area occupied by Paraguay could not be determined accurately or even approximately until ownership of the Chaco Boreal had been settled, and this was not done until the boundary was agreed upon in 1938, after Paraguay had won the bloody Chaco War (1932–1935) against Bolivia. Eastern Paraguay was 61,719 square miles of savannah, swamp, and forest, approximately equal to the area ceded to Brazil and Argentina after the Paraguayan War. The Chaco Boreal extended northwestward toward Bolivia. Although Paraguay eventually obtained title to 95,328 square miles of this area, there was no Bolivian-Paraguayan boundary during the first Colorado era.[1] Not until the 1890s was there any serious or extensive effort by Paraguay to develop the neighboring Chaco. Except for the few occupied spots on the right bank, the Colorados' Paraguay was the 39,500,160 acres lying east of the river.

Most of Paraguay was very poorly known as late as 1890. The French geographer-explorer, Emmanuel de Bourgade la Dardye, found many errors in existing maps because of difficulties presented by the terrain: "The vast virgin forests extending through the east and north have presented an obstacle to travellers before which they have recoiled. Beyond the valley that reaches from Asunción to Villa Encarnación, except for a few roads that have been opened for the purpose of exploring the forests of yerba-maté, there are hardly any highways of communication, almost all transport being conducted along the rivers, upon the banks of which the population is mainly concentrated."[2]

The two great rivers, the Paraguay and the Paraná, served as boundaries for most of eastern Paraguay. At the southwestern tip of the country, the Paraguay flows into the Paraná at an altitude of 180 feet above sea level some eight hundred miles north of Buenos Aires. this is the lowest point in Paraguay and contrasts sharply with a couple of hills northeast of Asunción which exceed two thousand feet. The swampy, thinly populated Ñeembucú Plain in the southwest is drained by the meandering Tebicuary River. To the north, in a belt of hills and fertile valleys formed by volcanic upheavals, most of the Paraguayans lived in villages and on small farms. Low conical hills dot the basaltic plain that extends east to the Paraná Plateau. The hills within Asunción rise to three hundred feet or more above the river. North of this central hill belt is the extensive central lowland that continues across the Rio Apa into Brazil's Mato Grosso. The Paraná Plateau comprises one-third of the country from the Encarnación area in the southeast to the Brazilian border on the north.[3]

Affluents of the Paraguay drain most of the country. Except when they flow down from the Paraná Plateau, Paraguayan rivers are shallow, meandering streams. Only the Paraguay itself is navigable by craft larger than rafts and *chatas* (low-lying barges, sometimes armed with a small caliber cannon). Nevertheless, the Tebicuary in the south, and the Manduvirá, Jejuí-guazú, Ypané, and Aquidabán north of Asunción were important transportation routes in a country where roads were practically nonexistent. Except for the Río Monday and Río Acaray systems, nearly all the rivers that flow eastward or southward to the Paraná are short streams of little economic significance.

In attempting to attract immigrants, many nineteenth-century writers greatly exaggerated the fertility of Paraguay's soil. Misled by the great expanse of dense tropical forests, the exuberant and varied vegetation that flourished in a generally mild climate, they composed extravagant rhapsodies. Of eastern Paraguay's less than 40 million acres, about 30 percent, or 12 million acres, can support intensive agriculture if scientific practices are followed, a condition met poorly if at all in the nineteenth century. More than one-half of the area of very good soils is in the forested Alto Paraná region, which was very sparsely inhabited. Only about 400,000 acres of rich land lie in the central area where the largest cities, Asunción and Villa Rica, scores of villages, and a large number of small farms (or *chacras*) were located. Altogether, about one-half of eastern Paraguay can be culti- vated with expectation of fair results. Application of proper fertilizers is necessary to provide such essential minerals as phosphorous, cal- cium, and magnesium.[4]

Eastern Paraguay has few metallic minerals, a frustrating fact in view of the abundance of such resources in neighboring Brazilian states. There is some iron ore near Ybicuí, about forty kilometers south of Paraguarí, which was capably exploited under the direction of English engineers imported by Carlos Antonio López. A few other important deposits were largely ignored. Sandstone, limestone, gran- ite, clays, talc, and glass sand are abundant in several areas. Excellent bricks and tiles were produced in the Villa Hayes area of the Chaco and at scores of kilns in eastern Paraguay, especially at Areguá and Villa Rica. Many industries using marble, limestone, basaltic stone, sandstone, and other minerals could be established, but there was almost no capital for such enterprises until well into the twentieth century.

Paraguay's wealth was primarily vegetable, and nature had been lavish in endowing the country with a bewildering variety of plants, ranging from microscopic organisms to gigantic trees that reached heights of more than one hundred twenty feet. Travelers to Paraguay invariably noted the lush vegetation that blanketed the palm- studded savannahs, covered the hills with forests, and grew with wild abandon in the great swamps of the southwest. South and southeast of Asunción there were large areas of good grazing land, and even the swampy Ñeembucú Plain could support large herds of cattle. The variety of flora made Paraguay a great laboratory for the botanist and naturalist.

Magnificent forests covered about one-half of eastern Paraguay, and large stands of quebracho, palm, and other varieties relieved the monotony of the Chaco. Probably the most imposing and richest tropical, or pseudotropical, forest occupied much of the plateau from Encarnación north to the Río Acaray. Agricultural colonists in this area were required to expend a great amount of labor, first to clear the forest and then to prevent its encroachment on their fields. Large stands of native yerba (*Ilex paraguayensis*) occurred in many areas and formed the basis for numerous Paraguayan fortunes.[5]

The climate of eastern Paraguay generally is described as being

Map 1. Eastern Region of the Republic of Paraguay
Adapted from Adolf N. Schuster, *Paraguay* (Stuttgart, 1929), p. 16.

subtropical. Masses of hot, humid air from the north blanket the country in the summer, while cold air from the south can make the winters miserable. There are no mountain barriers to the flow of these air masses. Paraguay's summer, roughly from November through March, brings periods when the temperature rises above 100°. These miserably hot and humid days generally end with torrential rains that bring temporary relief. For a short time after a heavy rain there may be some pleasant weather before the oppressive heat again closes in. Annual precipitation in eastern Paraguay averages fifty-five inches in Asunción, fifty-nine inches in Villa Rica, and sixty-seven inches in Encarnación. Most of the rain falls in the summer months, although there is no well defined rainy season.

Paraguayan winters, while usually not severe, can be cold enough to cause considerable discomfort. Temperatures range from about 30° to over 90° F., with averages in the sixties. Frost occurs every year somewhere in the country, generally on the Paraná Plateau. The threat of frost in May, June, July, and August is very real. In 1878 there were sixteen days of frost in these months, three in 1880, and ten in 1881 when ice formed in rural areas and coffee trees suffered severe damage. Despite the obvious climatic shortcomings of very heavy rains, frequent droughts, extreme heat, stifling humidity, and raw winter days, nineteenth-century observers generally agreed with the secretary of the British legation in Buenos Aires who stated in his very thorough report of 1882 that "it may be safely said that the climate of Paraguay, on the whole, is a healthy one, and can be compared very favourably with that of any other country in South America."[6]

Nature often is harsh in Paraguay. Heavy rains frequently cause floods both east and west of the Río Paraguay. Rivers overflow their banks and create broad swamps, or *esteros*, cut new channels, and leave behind numerous oxbow lakes. These lakes and stagnant pools provide ideal breeding places for swarms of mosquitoes and contribute to the prevailing high humidity. A torrential rain is reason enough for people to stay home despite the importance of a scheduled event. Many an unwary pedestrian has been stranded on a street corner in Asunción as flooded streets become swift-flowing streams. Fortunately, enterprising men provide moveable sidewalk "bridges" and accept small gratuities from grateful pedestrians who prefer not to remove their shoes and hosiery in order to wade across the streets, or to wait for the flood to subside. In rural areas, small, easily forded creeks and rivulets turn into boiling torrents. Unless built on high ground, the farmer's hut or little house becomes isolated in a muddy sea, and the thatched roof often fails to shed the downpour.

Severe droughts occur with sufficient frequency to cause great agricultural losses. To these visitations are added swarms of locusts whose depredations increase the general misery. Resulting crop failures cause widespread hunger as plantings of maize, beans, and mandioca are destroyed. The three disastrous winter droughts of 1889, 1893, and 1897 contributed significantly to the financial problems of three Colorado presidents and coincided with economic depressions. The drought of 1889 caused such severe distress that both the national government and individuals sent relief to the hungry. *Jefes políticos* (local party leaders endowed with minor executive and police powers) were charged with distributing both money and food to the needy in their districts.[7] Four years later the Brazilian minister reported: "As a result of the prolonged drought that has also occurred in this country, a general despondency prevails in the interior, because of the pitiful condition of the crops. Serious future consequences are feared, not only for agriculture but also for animal husbandry."[8] In 1897, when for four months there was almost no rain, nearly all crops died and locusts devoured what did survive. The government cancelled import duties on maize which the Banco Agrícola bought in large quantities to distribute at cost. The British consul, W. J. Holmes, reported that this drought had serious economic effects:

> There has been no improvement in the trade and commerce of this consular district during the year 1897. On the contrary, a succession of bad seasons and other misfortunes seriously interfered with trade and caused an almost general failure of crops. A cold and almost rainless winter was followed by an exceptionally hot and almost rainless summer. Wells and springs were dried up—in many places are dry still—and the crops, when they did not fail entirely, gave but a scanty yield. To add to the distress brought about by unpropitious seasons, large swarms of locusts made their appearance about the middle of September, first at Villa del Pilar and afterward in other parts of the country. . . . The agricultural classes—who at the best of times lead more or less hand-to-mouth existence—having in consequence of these visitations little or no produce to sell and, indeed, barely enough to live on, were without money to purchase either seed for sowing or other necessaries. Country traders and shopkeepers consequently were unable to dispose of their stocks, and the wholesale merchants in Asunción, in their turn, were not only obliged to put up with reduced sales, but could not obtain payment of the sums due to them by their country customers.[9]

Low water reduced traffic on the Paraguay and Paraná rivers, and large numbers of chatas loaded with yerba were left stranded on interior streams. Steamers from Buenos Aires could approach no closer than Angostura, thirty-two miles below the capital. This drought, one of the longest on record, continued to September 1898. Indeed, there was inadequate rainfall from 1894 to 1898, and for the seven years ending in 1898, locust infestations practically ruined agriculture.[10]

The People

Determining the size of Paraguay's population has always been an exercise in frustration. The difficulties and pitfalls encountered by the demographer were graphically described by a careful investigator:

> The estimates that have been made as to the aggregate population of Paraguay are of the most conflicting character. Scarcely any writers agree in their statements, and amongst the numerous returns that have been put forth, not a few have been wilfully or carelessly misleading, whilst others are in flagrant violation of every law which governs such statistics everywhere. If a summary recently published in a local review could be accepted, it would be certain that Paraguay must have experienced some strange convulsions of the ordinary conditions of human reproduction—entire families being obliterated by sterility, and others being multiplied with the fecundity of a rabbit-warren.[11]

There was only one comprehensive count between 1785 and 1872, that of 1846, the results of which remained generally unknown until Dr. John Hoyt Williams unearthed about twenty thousand pages of documents in the Archivo Nacional in Asunción. This census yielded 238,862 persons in eastern Paraguay. On the basis of this count, Williams estimates that the population might have been about 400,000 when the Paraguayan War began in 1864. At the close of the war, the Allies estimated the population at about 176,000 natives and 56,000 foreigners. All estimates merely guessed at the number of Indians in the Chaco and east of the Paraguay River. Excluding Indians and the occupation forces, a figure of 232,000 may be assumed to be fairly accurate for 1872. In 1876 a large number of foreigners left when the Brazilians evacuated their troops, but no one knows how many. Again, assuming an annual increase of about 3 percent, which seems reasonable, there were about 200,000 people in eastern Paraguay in 1880, considerably fewer than the 346,048 reported by the government in 1879.[12] A Brazilian consul-general estimated the 1884 population at 320,000, including 19,600 foreigners (see table 1). The Mulhalls, leading Argentine publishers, reported a total of 180,000, including 3,000 foreigners, in 1885. A census of sorts in 1900 estimated the population at 635,571, including some 80,000 Chaco Indians.[13] From these questionable data, it is possible for the daring to conclude that the population of eastern Paraguay during the first Colorado era increased from less than 300,000 in 1880 to nearly 600,000 in 1900, a figure that approximates an annual increase of 3 percent.

A large majority of Paraguayans lived in small towns, villages, and on ranchos (small farms) scattered throughout the country. The largest center of population was Asunción, which numbered about

Table 1

Estimated Foreign Population of Paraguay in 1884

Country of Origin	Number	Country of Origin	Number
Italy	8,500	Germany	500
Spain	8,000	England	100
France	800	Argentina	100
Brazil	800	Uruguay	100
Portugal	600	Others	100

Source: Pedro Ribeiro Moreira, "Relatorio commercial e politico do anno findo de 1884," RCBA-0 238/3/7.

18,000 in 1880. Outside of the capital, only Villa Rica (Villarrica), the center of a rich agricultural area, was of any considerable importance. Even this very old city had only 13,000 people in 1880. Concepción, northern center of the yerba trade, was third with about 11,000. San Pedro, north of Asunción at the mouth of the important Río Jejuí, was fourth in size with about 10,000. Encarnación, the terminus of the Paraguay Central Railway to the southeast, was destined to become relatively important, but its population was insignificant until after 1900 (see table 2). Villages of a few hundred people were numerous and by 1904 had become a dominant demographic feature. Paraguay was still very thinly inhabited at the end of the Colorado era. Nevertheless, the trend toward urbanization was well under way. Fifteen years after the Colorado era ended, William Lytle Schurz observed accurately: "If a line were drawn in a slightly southeastern direction from the Apa to the Alto Paraná, passing through Horqueta, San Estanislao, and Colonia Hohenau, the country to the east of this line would include the most undeveloped portion of the Republic, except, of course, the interior of the Chaco. There are probably not more than 25,000 inhabitants in all this region, which comprises considerably over half the area of eastern Paraguay. For all practical purposes, most of this country is farther from the capital than is Buenos Aires."[14]

The Paraguayan War left the surviving population with a great disparity between the sexes. Although all figures for the postwar period are inaccurate, the Allies in 1872 reported that of Asunción's 17,350 civilians, 11,066 were females. This ratio of females to males may have held for much of the country. The official census of 1879 showed 230,000 females and 116,000 males, or about two to one, a much more likely state of affairs than the frequently repeated nonsense that there were ten or more females to every male. By 1900, the normal balance between the sexes had been restored, but during

Table 2

Principal Centers of Population, 1879 and 1897

City or Village	1879	1897
Asunción	16,000	45,000
Villa Rica	12,600	19,000
Concepción	10,700	10,000
San Pedro	9,700	8,000
Luque	8,800	9,000
San Estanislao	7,400	7,500
Itauguá	6,900	7,100
Itá	6,300	6,500
Paraguarí	5,300	5,700
Humaitá	3,800	3,700
Pilar	3,700	3,722
Yaguarón	3,400	3,600

Sources: H. G. and E. T. Mulhall, *Handbook of the River Plate,* (5th ed., 1885), p. 626; Meulemans, *La République du Paraguay,* p. 3.

most of the Colorado era females undoubtedly outnumbered males. The problem was further exacerbated by the tendency of males to seek employment in neighboring Brazilian and Argentine provinces. Although Colorado governments made efforts from time to time to promote the immigration of industrious Europeans, they had little success in competing with countries that offered greater stability and more attractive political and economic conditions.

Principal Cities and Towns

Viewed from the vantage point of Cerro Tacumbú, a hill to the southwest, Asunción was a picturesque city of closely packed houses with roofs of red tile, bordering sandy streets lined with orange trees except in the central area where the lack of trees was painfully noticeable. One could see the few large buildings near the river and a variety of craft anchored in the bay protected by the Banco San Miguel, and the muddy Río Paraguay bordering the Chaco. The view was enchanting to Ernst Mevert who noted that many houses facing the streets were built around flower-filled patios where a central well provided water for family use.[15] A British observer noted that "dense orange groves surround the numerous 'Quintas' which encircle the town whilst in the far west of the picture the Chaco is discerned and to the south rises the Peak of Lambaré."[16]

The general appearance of Asunción changed so little during the

Colorado era that one who might have left the town when Caballero seized power in 1880 could have returned fifty years later without finding any need for reorientation. The Colorados added no imposing buildings to those left by the López family. The Cabildo, where Congress met, the unfinished Oratorio, now the Panteón Nacional de los Héroes, with its imposing dome, the cathedral, railway station, López Palace, customs house, and National Theater remained as principal landmarks. The English journalist W. F. Mulhall from Buenos Aires had little to say that was complimentary about either private dwellings or public buildings: The López Palace was "out of all proportion with the size of the town. . . . The majority of buildings in Asunción are extravagant luxuries, out of place in their narrow surroundings and too big for Asunción. . . . These ruins of past greatness, glaring at the wretched buildings all around, looking down on the poverty-stricken people that wander under their rumbling pillars, tottering arcades, and dangling rafters, are unique. They are not grand, rather the reverse, but they must have appeared colossal to a people living in primitive dwellings." The whole effort at grandeur was a spurious brick-and-mortar attempt to copy the granite of France.[17]

The marketplace, extremely busy for a short time after daybreak, provided both color and odors in the downtown area. In the 1890s, this market was still a threat to public health, a focus of infection "that continually omits its unhealthy odors and contaminates the entire neighborhood."[18] Housed in a large building with colonnaded walls, the market was the gathering place for scores of barefooted women who had risen before dawn to carry their baskets of corn, beans, peas, short cigars, mandioca, meat, chipá (buns or cakes made of mandioca flour and cheese), fruits, and other produce to market. The shopper could also buy mate, ñandutí (spiderweb) lace, leather goods, and small bundles of firewood. At the end of the century an American found it strange that "notwithstanding the large forests, the firewood of Asunción is sold in little bundles at the markets. A bundle costs five cents, and the average housekeeper buys her wood from day to day, and carries it home along with her vegetables and meat."[19] Although the more affluent sellers occupied stalls, most of the women sat on the ground with their goods arranged before them.

Asunción had plenty of hotels to serve the traveler. Best of all was the Hispano Americano, formerly the mansion of Benigno López, on Calle Palma, noted for its "handsome glass-covered patio, beautifully adorned with stuccoed columns that produce the most agreeable effect." Transients of modest means preferred the Hotel Crimea or the Oriental.[20]

Reflecting increased business activity resulting in part from public land sales, Asunción grew considerably from 1885 to 1890. Home building and rental units failed to meet the demand for housing; two new hotels provided some relief but living costs were high, especially for foreigners who demanded more than the natives. Some Paraguayans joined critical foreigners in deploring the condition of their city. After nine years of Colorado rule, one editor complained that nothing had been done to improve the capital:

> The foreigners who come to visit this capital have good reason to accuse us of being a forsaken disorderly city, and especially because the central and most heavily populated area is the filthiest and most neglected part of the city.
>
> Outsiders and natives immediately notice the high and unsightly weeds along the main streets that elicit justified condemnation of the indolent city government that does not require inhabitants and every proprietor to clean their property to the edge of the sidewalk on every street.[21]

A traveler in 1888 commented on the beautiful trees and flowers that were allowed to grow untended in the plazas which were without benches for the visitor. The unadorned city, more than a decade after Caballero had seized power, had not been improved. The major old buildings were in disrepair or remained unfinished, although a new theater was being built to replace the skeletal remains of the ambitious theater planned by the Italian architect Alejandro Ravizza. An influx of European influence would yet make Asunción an important metropolis. However, by 1913 Asunción had changed little. The red tiled roofs, barred windows opening on the street, the Andalusian patio, and other features of Moorish origin, had not disappeared. Homes in the more traditional Western European style were being built as the city thrust outward.[22]

A sympathetic visitor from Buenos Aires believed that one week was plenty to spend in the capital. The majority of tourists returned by the steamer that had brought them on a leisurely trip up the winding Paraná and Paraguay rivers, "bearing with them impressions which mainly depend on the social surroundings into which they have been thrown. A few may have enjoyed themselves, but the greater number go back with the conviction that Asunción is a wretched place, half in ruins, intolerably hot, miserably dull and destitute of all interest, and they are right to a certain extent."[23] Two decades later, a semiofficial publication indulged in extravagant praise of Asunción as a flower garden of paradise for the ill to convalesce and for the tourist to revel in the "mixture of primitive and civilized."[24]

A real estate boom in the mid 1880s caused land prices to double in a few months. Both foreign and native speculators made small fortunes as rural residents succumbed to the lure of the capital, and a small flow of immigrants more than doubled the city's population in two decades and outran the ability of the *municipalidad* (city government) to provide needed services. The city's shortcomings were obvious: unpaved and unlighted streets, irregular sidewalks, poor drainage, no central water or sewage systems, inadequate public transportation, and a very indifferent police force.

Starting with relics of the López era, the Colorados achieved more in planning than in construction of public monuments. The López Palace, finally finished in 1888 except for painting, provided quarters for the president and other officials, but several agencies had to share the old unfinished theater. In the 1890s, several new buildings were completed, and plans were drawn for repairing and enlarging existing structures. The Public Works Commission enlisted the services of José Segundo Decoud, Emilio Aceval, and other prominent citizens when it was created in 1887, and despite limited income did manage to contract for dredging the harbor and repairing many public buildings. This commission planned wisely, and eventually its projects for an insane asylum, new wharves, bridges and roads, a new port, park and street improvements, schools, and completion of the Oratorio, were realized.[25] Economic depressions, almost chronic during the Colorado era, caused many needed projects to be postponed. Despite various efforts to provide a central water supply, such as the concession to Ricardo Antonio Gonçalves in 1893, Asunción depended upon wells, cisterns, springs, and windmills until well after World War II.

The capital's streets were in a deplorable condition when the Colorados came to power. In fact, they showed little improvement from the time of the dictator Francia and deteriorated badly during the Allied occupation. At the end of 1878, the Brazilian chargé observed that "gas lighting, sewers, running water, drains, etc., improvements which always go with civilization of a people, are all unknown in Paraguay, which for many years to come will be without them, such is the state of misery and of prostration in which the city exists."[26] Gradual improvement in lighting increased the sense of security in pedestrians who rarely ventured out at night except in groups large enough to repel would-be footpads. The 350 kerosene lamps that provided dim light in 1870 had been increased to 1,000 by 1896 and gave employment to a score of men who replenished the kerosene, cleaned the globes, and lighted the lamps at dusk. Hopeful enterprisers who obtained concessions for gas lights in 1872 and 1886 were unable to carry out their plans. Concessions for arc lights were granted by 1900, but resulted in nothing more than a few lights by 1904.[27] President Escobar asked Congress to use $f2,000,000 from land sales for public works. High on the list was improvement of the capital's all but impassable streets and construction of bridges and roads in the interior to facilitate transportation of agricultural products.[28]

Travel on Asunción's streets was always an adventure for the daring—and still is. Because much of the city was sixty or more feet above the river, the streets sloped enough to create intermittent streams that came with every rain and left several inches of sand while washing away accumulated debris. Pedestrians were well advised to avoid the narrow sidewalks at night because they varied suddenly and unpredictably in height and were in constant disrepair. Congress on July 30, 1874, approved a contract with Sinforiano Alcorta, an Argentine enterpriser resident in Asunción, to pave some of the central area with granite. Several years later little progress had been made, and one editor noted that "the condition of our streets

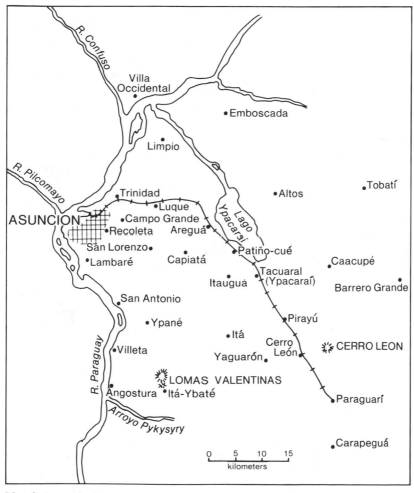

Map 2. Asunción Area

with their big puddles is shameful."[29] An Englishman who knew
Asunción well has left a graphic description of the city's streets:

> There are no public carriages in Asunción, and, indeed, no other vehi-
> cles than rough bullock carts. I believe that there is a State carriage
> stowed away somewhere, which is brought to light now and then, in
> order to convey a Foreign Minister to his official reception, and there
> may be two or three others, the property of rich Brazilians, which are
> used for journeys outside the town, but to drive in a carriage through
> the streets of Asunción, would be a feat which would certainly end in
> the collapse of all the springs, and probably in that of the occupants.
>
> A sort of red iron rock-stone is the foundation of the streets; where
> it is very hard, a point or a little hillock is formed; where it is softer, the
> ground is worn into a rut. There are natural springs almost
> everywhere, and rivulets running through the streets, which during
> heavy rains become torrents.[30]

City officials had little success in collecting taxes to pay for street
lighting, cleaning, improvements, and patrols to stop the stealing of
lights and to drive off the animals that wandered freely through the
city. With aid from Congress, they succeeded in paving some sixteen
thousand meters with stone from nearby quarries before the Liberals
took over in 1904, and by 1910 about forty thousand square meters of
wooden blocks and stone paving had been completed in the capital.[31]
The block pavement on Calle Palma was so well done that it was in
good condition thirty years later.

Two tramway companies were doing a big business in Asunción
by 1890, and a telephone company was operating successfully. The
first tramway was proposed by James Nelson Horrocks for a group of
English capitalists on April 1, 1871. Congress granted the concession,
and the first portion of the line, running for about thirteen blocks
from the port market to the railway station, began operating on
January 19, 1873. Cars drawn by horses and mules made nineteen
round trips daily between 6:40 A.M. and 8:30 P.M.[32] In the 1880s,
another tramway company, El Conductor Universal, built a line
running from the port to La Cancha Sociedad, an amusement park
and playing field on the northeast edge of the city. Dr. Francisco
Morra bought the Horrocks tramway and obtained a concession to
extend it to the Recoleta church and cemetery to the southeast. This is
the area of the present Villa Morra development. Morra's extension
began to operate on September 29, 1887. An English capitalist with
Argentine ranching experience, Campbell P. Ogilvie, bought the profitable tramway for £45,000 in 1889 and extended it to San Lorenzo
del Campo Grande, then ten miles from Asunción.[33] Traffic increased
through 1892, then fell off somewhat as streets improved, service
deteriorated, and personnel became insolent and incompetent. Altogether the Villa Morra Company had fourteen miles of track,
monopolized the tramway service, employed 1,770 men, used 150

horses and mules and five locomotives to haul forty-four passenger cars and twenty-three freight wagons. In 1898, 698,000 passengers rode the cars, a considerable decrease from the 1,500,000 riders in 1891.[34]

Hundreds of people went on outings to the Recoleta cemetery, a rather grim place for social amusements, but one that provided a fine view of the city. A spacious lawn in front of the plain church provided a playground for children while their elders cleaned the houselike mausoleums or decorated graves with lace and ribbons. A fine Italian restaurant beside the cemetery was a favorite place for fashionable breakfasts.

Foreign influence made such an impact on Asunción that some travelers refused to accept the small capital as typical of the country. Disliking the "European varnish" that was causing the city to lose "all of its original and striking features, the traveler who wanted to see the 'real' Paraguay had to visit the interior." Riding from the railhead at Paraguarí to Villa Rica in 1887, a distance of about forty miles, P. A. Freund and W. F. Mulhall of Buenos Aires preferred the crude comforts of farmers' huts to the attractions of Asunción. Entering Villa Rica at noon on a hot day, they found the streets deserted and were appalled by the number of houses in ruins. "Not a soul to be seen; not a dog stirring; not a sound to be heard, beyond the tramp of our horses' hoofs; no hotels, no inns: this in the midst of a thriving, industrious, and populous settlement."[35] The travelers should not have been surprised by such inactivity. After all, it was siesta time. Before the war, at least eighty commercial houses were doing business in the city, and "often one hundred bullock carts left for Tacuaral and Paraguay [Paraguarí] laden with tobacco, rice, maize, etc. Today [1887] there are not eight stores and not a dozen carts leave the town in a week. In every street you see the decay of past prosperity: old brick houses in ruins, roofs falling into pieces, new dwellings of small size and wretched appearance springing up alongside the massive walls of old days."[36] This hardly conforms to the picture of a "thriving, industrious, and populous settlement." Many buildings, including the old church, were in ruins but many substantial houses were being built, and the new church in the center of town was well kept and crowded with worshipers on Sundays and religious holidays.

Villa Rica, Paraguay's second city in size and importance, was founded in 1676 after having been moved from its original location in Guayrá in southwestern Brazil in the early seventeenth century to escape the raids of *mamelucos* (mestizos) from São Paulo. Temporarily located at other sites, the city was finally built on a pleasant plateau about six hundred feet above sea level. Surrounded by fertile fields, the city prospered and rivaled Asunción until the war nearly destroyed it. After the Paraguayan War, Villa Rica attracted foreign settlers. Most of the British immigrants to Paraguay settled there, and Australians founded two colonies nearby in the 1890s. The Paraguay Central Railway reached the city in 1889 and made its headquarters there for construction of the line to Pirapó, where the rails stopped in 1891. Linking Villa Rica with Asunción by rail brought great advantages to both cities, since the only other means of transportation were horses, ox carts, and the weekly stage from Paraguarí. Guaireños, as residents of Villa Rica are called, were renowned for their hospitality, and the city's girls and women were famous for their beauty. Legend has it that men who had to return to Asunción wept all the way to Paraguarí! At least, the hospitality of Captain Hunter Davidson was no myth. This American, a native of Maryland and an officer in the U.S. Navy, had cast his lot with the Confederacy. After the American Civil War he emigrated to Paraguay[37] and finally settled in Villa Rica, where he purchased and restored the crumbling mansion which "was built regardless of expense before the Paraguayan War by Sr. Luis Omens, perhaps the wealthiest man in the country at that time." Francisco Solano López has been charged with having seized the property of this millionaire whom he ordered to be killed. Davidson named the place Liberty Hall, and here in magnificent surroundings he entertained such visitors as Freund and Mulhall, who were ecstatic in describing the mansion's attractions. Only a few days at Liberty Hall were needed to cast a spell over the visitors, who forgot the "wretched looking houses, huts, hovels, and debris of crumbling dwellings," and succumbed to the "perfumed atmosphere, . . . esteemed and loved by people who are kind and simple—primitive in their attire and customs,—sons and daughters of nature: it is no wonder if these charms are magnetic, and foreigners yield to their attractions and settle forever in this beautiful arcadia."[38]

Villa Rica, about ninety-two miles by rail east of Asunción, marked the limit of what might be called "nuclear Paraguay." Other towns, varying in size from a few hundred to two or three thousand inhabitants, were clustered around the capital. Paraguarí, forty-five miles from Asunción, was the terminus of the railway for many years and gained importance as a center for the tobacco trade. Caacupé, fifteen miles north of Paraguarí, lay in beautiful country and was noted for the church that housed the revered Virgin of Caacupé, objective of the annual pilgrimage on December 8. Tobatí, some eleven miles north and northeast of Caacupé, was an isolated village typical of scores of agricultural communities. Luque, an Asunción suburb, was "famed for its tobacco, which is of so good a quality that it can compete with the best Bahia tobacco in the market."[39] This attractive village was the provisional capital when López ordered the evacuation of Asunción during the Paraguayan War. Itauguá, mid-

way between Asunción and Caacupé, was the famed center of *ñandutí*
lace making and also produced bricks and tiles of excellent quality.
When John N. Ruffin, the American consul, visited Itauguá in
January 1899, it was a thriving little city of about six thousand people
which supported two schools for boys and one for girls. Nearly every
house was a *ñandutí* "factory," where little girls six years of age and
old women of ninety worked at the quadrangular frames. A bakery,
tannery, brick kilns, and a tobacco warehouse provided employment.
The people were "hospitable, intelligent and appreciative . . . handsome, well dressed, beautiful, sociable and interesting."[40] Yaguarón,
founded by Jesuits in 1539, was the center for production of petit-
grain essence, an industry begun by the French botanist, Benjamín
Balanza, in 1876. Its magnificent colonial church contained a beautiful altar and pulpit. Itá, about seven miles northwest of Yaguarón,
produced various clay products of fine quality, as did Areguá on the
west shore of Lake Ypacaraí.

River towns on the left bank of the Paraguay, although lacking
port facilities, were relatively important as landings for boats bound
upstream from Buenos Aires, or going down from the Brazilian ports
in Mato Grosso. Villa del Pilar, about thirty miles north of the
Paraguay-Paraná conjunction, was the major port serving south-
western Paraguay. A thriving cattle industry developed in its hinterland during the Colorado era and attracted Argentine ranchers. Villa
Franca, another small port fifty miles north of Pilar, was also favored
by good grazing lands. The little port of Oliva, another twelve miles
upriver, was opposite some fine stands of timber in the Argentine
Chaco. More important was Villeta, sixty miles north of Oliva and a
few miles south of Asunción, which became a major exporter of logs
and other forest products. San Antonio, a small village between
Villeta and Asunción, was the site of industries begun by Edward
Augustus Hopkins during the presidency of Carlos Antonio López.
Here were gathered huge piles of oranges for shipment to Buenos
Aires. When a river boat tied up at the landing, some sixty women
formed a continuous line bearing on their heads baskets loaded with
the fruit which they dumped in bins aboard the craft.

Only five river towns north of Asunción merited attention. On the
Chaco side was Villa Hayes with a fair sawmill and about eight
hundred people, among whom were convicts condemned to forced
labor. Rosario, at the mouth of the arroyo Cuarepotí, was ninety miles
north of Asunción. Nearby was one of the many López estates. San
Pedro, near the mouth of the Río Jejuí-guazú, was a very well built
and attractive town through which chatas loaded with yerba came
from the interior. Concepción, two hundred sixty miles north of
Asunción, formerly "the emporium of Paraguay," was the last river
town of any importance before reaching the Apa, and recovered its

position as center of the yerba trade both for northern Paraguay and
Mato Grosso. Carlos Casado, who bought 3,000 leagues of Chaco land
in 1886, established Puerto Casado three years later on the right bank
of the Paraguay about eighteen miles south of the Apa. This marked
the beginning of rapid development and exploitation of the Chaco
fringe and the establishment of numerous little river ports between
Puerto Casado and Bahía Negra, a Paraguayan port on the Río
Paraguay about six hundred kilometers upriver from Asunción.

Paraguay was amply endowed with the natural resources to
support a moderately prosperous economy. That this did not occur
for so many decades was largely the fault of political rivalries and
wretched government that made other areas so much more attractive.

2

The Government

Paraguay's political troubles are blamed on a combination of weaknesses. General political incompetence, especially among the military leaders, has been decried by many perceptive writers who have observed the inadequacies of officials. An obvious defect in the political system was the lack of an efficient bureaucracy, of a body of minor officials, secretaries, and clerks to whom routine tasks could be delegated with some degree of confidence that they would be handled expeditiously. Commercial houses employed the few capable administrators available, and xenophobia prevented adequate use of foreigners. The situation was better toward the end of the century as the educational system improved. Still, Paraguay did not produce enough well-educated citizens to meet the demands of government.

The past weighed heavily on Paraguay. Its authoritarian colonial period with conflicts between Jesuits and hacendados, its three great dictators, and the devastating War of the Triple Alliance left deep scars and open wounds. Ignorance, poverty, fanaticism, corruption, *empleomanía* (lust for office), and party factionalism all contributed to the country's troubles. One suspects that the discipline imposed by *estancieros* (ranchers), *hacendados* (plantation owners), and the few large business entrepreneurs did much to prevent complete chaos.

A Frame Without Substance—the National Government

When Cándido Bareiro inaugurated the first Colorado era in Paraguay, he became president of a country whose government was rudimentary at best. The constitution of 1870 provided an excellent framework of government for a politically sophisticated, well-educated people, who could be served by a cadre of dedicated civil servants in a peaceful, prosperous country.[1] Postwar Paraguay met

27

none of these requirements. Something even more important for successful functioning of a constitutional republic was lacking: a broadly held faith in genuinely democratic processes and willingness to sacrifice selfish interests for the common welfare. Only imperfectly realized in the world's most successful republics, this faith was rarely encountered among Paraguayans whose political heritage was one of oppressive dictatorships. An intelligent but cynical observer, Brazil's consul general, noted in 1883: "Still, despite the rule of a government that desires to be liberal and constitutional, many years must pass before the people, certainly the most uncouth in America, can succeed in conquering their routinized and fanaticized spirit. I do not rule out as impossible a return to the miseries of former dictatorships."[2] In a later report, the same official asserted that the people were unable to understand the obligations or to make the sacrifices demanded by liberty. Accustomed to despotism, they longed for its return.[3] While this indictment is harsh, actions of the Colorados and, later, of the Liberals did much to verify it.

Although General Caballero had seized power in a ruthless military coup in 1880 to serve out the remainder of Bareiro's term, he stood for reelection only once. There were no two-term Colorado presidents. The constitution prohibited a president from being reelected until after the passage of two consecutive presidential terms; but this prohibition would not have bothered Caballero, who could easily have summoned a convention to amend the constitution. Fortunately, with the exception of Col. Juan A. Escurra, last in the Colorado succession, the seven elected presidents were capable if not brilliant men.

The Congress, made up of twenty-six deputies and thirteen senators, reflected the control of a Colorado political oligarchy kept in power by the simple expedient of preventing Liberals from voting.[4] Some very capable men served in every Congress. One may mention Cecilio Báez, Facundo Insfrán, Ramón Zubizarreta, Francisco C. Cháves, Ramón Lara Castro, Adolfo Riquelme, and many more. But there were also many who could at best be called semiliterate, whose knowledge of parliamentary procedure and their country's needs equaled their intelligence. No one could be elected to Congress without approval of the Caballero clique. Once nominated by this group, or by the Central Committee of the Colorado party after 1887, election was certain. Congress, therefore, was generally a rubber stamp for the executive. A Brazilian consul general reported accurately: "Any act by the executive, however absurd and scandalous it may be, immediately is confirmed by the chambers which in fact depend upon him, for they are named by him, and therefore the government does not meet with any [congressional] opposition."[5] This criticism, while justified in 1884, was not true of every Congress. When permitted to hold office, the few Liberals in Congress did present genuine opposition, and in the 1890s there were dissident Colorados who could not be silenced. Nevertheless, the majority always supported the executive. Many members of Congress took their duties lightly. Legislators absented themselves with or without valid reasons and frequently so many were away that a quorum could not be obtained. The Brazilian minister observed in 1895 that "Congress continued to be completely inactive, the occasion being very rare in which either the Chamber or the Senate has had a sufficient number to begin a session."[6] The salary of a member of Congress was about $f400 for a session, enough to be worthwhile without being exorbitant, but the desire for office was so pervasive that the Congress could have been filled even if the position had paid no salary. Eligio Ayala (1880–1930), a leading statesman of the twentieth century, clearly explained this mania for office. No matter how good as a poet, judge, writer, lawyer, or physician, a man lived in obscurity if he had no public post: "The modest sergeant who entertains the people of the city's suburbs with his comic dance Santa Fé, will not attract anyone's attention, he will not be admitted in 'society.' But if by virtue of a fortunate night conspiracy, in the morning he is invested with the role of minister, he will receive in the act the homage of students and professors, of merchants and industrialists, of intellectuals and bankers, and the [leading] families will open their doors and arms to him."[7]

The judicial system attracted some well-prepared lawyers, graduates of Argentine universities; but, except for the national courts in Asunción, poorly prepared magistrates presided over most of the country's tribunals. Justices of the peace in the eighty-four *partidos*, (small rural governmental units) generally knew nothing of the law and were notoriously corrupt. Even the Superior Tribunal of Justice, highest court in the land, did not escape scathing journalistic criticism.[8] Favoritism, corruption, incompetence, neglect of duty, and outrageous delays characterized all courts in the early 1870s.[9] Twenty years later, an American vice-consul sought a quick trial for a compatriot who had been charged with passing Confederate paper, for "without influence a man might remain indefinitely incarcerated in Paraguay without trial."[10] A noted essayist accused Paraguayan governments of condemning citizens without legal process. He asked: "Is this a republic? Is this a human society? So long as we have no right to defend ourselves openly, of seeing face to face whoever testifies against us, we shall be a horde, not a nation."[11]

Paraguay borrowed all but one of its basic codes, most of them from Argentina. The criminal code came from Spain. The penal code of 1887 was native; the rural code of 1887 (that replaced the Argentine code adopted in 1877) was a hodgepodge of Paraguayan law imposed on an Argentine base.[12] Paraguay did make feeble efforts to write its own codes. In accordance with an act of May 31, 1875, President Gill appointed a commission of very capable men to draft a civil code. This commission was brushed aside as Congress adopted the Argentine civil code on August 19, 1876. In 1903, President Escurra appointed Dr. Francisco C. Cháves, his minister of justice, to preside over a commission to revise Paraguay's codes, with the exception of the rural code which Dr. Venancio López was to revise. Neither the commission nor López completed the assignment.[13]

An obvious lack of Paraguayans capable of holding subordinate administrative positions caused all Colorado presidents to call on foreigners. President Juan G. González informed Congress in 1891 that a lack of skilled personnel among Colorados caused him to seek qualified men regardless of party affiliation. He appointed so many foreigners that Congress passed a bill requiring the heads of all offices to be Paraguayan citizens. President González promptly vetoed this shortsighted measure. Congress tried again in 1892 and again González vetoed the bill; this time Congress overrode the veto and by 1893 all foreigners had been replaced by "Paraguayans wholly incompetent."[14]

A common complaint of foreign consuls was the complete lack of reliable statistics. Although the Mesa de la Estadística General (General Statistical Office) was created in July 1885, the two volumes published by 1887 were worthless as sources of information for reports on commerce and population. The American consul in 1892 complained that "no statistics or data on Paraguay had been published by the government since 1889." Dr. William Stewart, the British consul who was also head of the Board of Health, informed his colleagues that information in previous reports was worthless, and he could provide no reliable statistics.[15] A few Paraguayans recognized the need for keeping records to provide a source for accurate statistics upon which critical economic and social policies could be based, but they could make no dent in the massive inadequacy resulting from Paraguayan administrative incompetence.

City and Rural Government

Rudimentary under Francia and the Lópezes, municipal and rural government improved little during the Colorado regime. In the capital as well as in towns and villages, government was poorly organized and poorly administered. A municipal commission appointed for Asunción in 1869 was abolished in 1870 and its duties distributed among a jefe político and other officers. Congress on February 10, 1872, established the Junta Económica-Administrativa (Economic Administrative Committee) as the ruling body for seven principal towns, including Asunción. Each council was composed of a president and three members appointed by the minister of the interior. The council was to collect funds, prepare budgets, administer finances, keep books, and make fortnightly reports to the ministry. From time to time additional councils were created for other towns. The council president doubled as mayor, a situation that often caused conflict with the departmental jefe político. Each council had a paid secretary, but none of the members received any compensation other than the questionable prestige that accompanied the position. Consequently, there were frequent resignations. The system proved to be so unsatisfactory that Congress revised the law after ten years to create *cuerpos municipales* (municipal councils) that retained basic features of the 1872 juntas. Except for Asunción, which had six *municipales titulares* (councilmen), two of whom were selected by the council as president and vice-president, each of the 1882 councils had four members. Councilmen were elected by popular vote for two-year terms, two from each of three districts in Asunción and at large in other towns. Both foreigners and citizens could vote in municipal elections.[16] Although they were endowed with ample powers of government, the twenty-nine councils created by the 1882 law enjoyed indifferent success. Asunción, however, did make considerable progress in public works, especially in street paving. On May 8, 1891, Congress replaced Asunción's cuerpo municipal with the *intendencia municipal* headed by an appointed *intendente* or mayor. The first to hold this position was a Frenchman, Francisco Casabianca, whose appointment probably helped to spark the antiforeign move in Congress.[17]

Tinkering with village and city government did very little to improve the quality of administration, law enforcement, public hygiene, education, and public works, all of which were badly neglected throughout the country except in Asunción which had the benefit and, at times, misfortune of being directly under the active oversight of the minister of the interior. Another exception was Villa Rica which, at the end of the century, was clearly the country's second city as the result of increasing prosperity and the contributions of dedicated citizens. Rural administration was very poor because it was generally impossible to find qualified men to accept government posts at the very low salaries paid for the positions.

The Armed Forces

Paraguay's armed forces were hardly sufficient to maintain internal order. President Caballero inherited an "army" of 57 officers and 550 men divided between cavalry and infantry armed with Remington rifles. The navy at Caballero's disposal was hardly formidable. Congress in 1881 authorized spending 10,000 pesos for modern arms and a gunboat. A screw steamer of 440 tons, the *Comercio de Rocha*, was purchased in 1882, fitted with four guns, renamed the *Pirapó*, and, under Captain Domingo A. Ortiz, was Paraguay's coast guard.[18] By 1892 the army still numbered only 600 men and the navy was still the aging *Pirapó*. In assessing South America's armed forces in 1893, the British minister observed that "Paraguay, owing to her unfortunate circumstances, pecuniary and other, need scarcely be seriously taken into account, at present. She has but one small gun-boat, and no army to speak of worthy of the name, though I believe they possess every martial quality, and especially that of obedience."[19] Although a national guard was organized under the act of August 22, 1898, very few men joined. Lack of a relatively large standing army did not prevent the Colorados from being able to crush the few armed revolts attempted by Liberals. Not until the popular revolt of 1904, when dissension among Colorados fatally weakened the party, were Liberals able to capture the government. Even then Liberals could not have won without the very poorly concealed aid of Argentina, which contributed money, ships, and matériel to ensure the Liberal triumph.

The Conditions of Government

Teodosio González, one of Paraguay's foremost lawyers, has called his country "the classic land of misgovernment and anarchy" caused by incapacity, negligence, and arbitrary rule by officials at all levels.[20] Paraguayans had the political institutions, at least on paper, to create a vital democracy. The constitution of 1870, which was to endure until 1940, was an admirable document in many ways, but where were the people to apply such a document? Asunción, Villa Rica, Concepción, and possibly Itauguá, Caacupé, and Pilar could have provided enough intelligent men to fill local governmental posts; but the smaller towns generally offered few choices for jefe político, chief of police, and other officers. The people who survived the war were ignorant of politics and went "in herds like cattle to drink, to cry, to fight, to dance, to fire skyrockets, to waste their time, their money and even their lives. . . . But the Paraguayan will resign himself to everything, satisfied with having upheld his [party] color, his opinion."[21] Rural authorities, especially the jefes políticos and justices of the peace, generally were political hacks of little distinction and less ability. There were exceptions, of course, like José del Rosario Miranda, who came from a small village and held important national positions. Men like Miranda usually left their drab villages in order to enjoy the glamor and excitement of life in Asunción. For the most part, rural functionaries were blind implements of the president or the minister of the interior, reflected the party's dictatorial power, and imposed their will ruthlessly.[22]

Critics were equally pessimistic about national executives, legislators, judges, and administrators. Bitter and disillusioned, one editor criticized government at all levels. There were legislators who knew nothing about lawmaking, administrators "with as much preparation as the fox for guarding the geese," judges ignorant of the law, and bankers who were frightened by the smallest calculation. Poncho-clad peasants who were trained to plant potatoes became deputies, ministers, judges, senators.[23] Extreme as these strictures may be, *La Democracia*, despairing for the country's future, editorialized: "One must really confess that there is no democratic life among this people: the Constitution is a lie, the teachings of youth in classrooms are lies, and finally every appeal to the feeling of patriotism by public authorities is a lie."[24] Even President Egusquiza, the most intelligent of the Colorado military presidents, admitted in 1898, the last year of his term, that constitutional guarantees had not been realized. Paraguayan society was still experiencing tremors incident to moving from despotism to democracy: "Neither a wise legislature nor an honest and active government can in an instant change the moral and intellectual condition of nations ... one does not with the stroke of a pen erase a hundred years of history."[25]

The very articulate essayist, Rafael Barrett, found in the past the reason for Paraguayan willingness to tolerate outrageous government. In a sympathetic, sensitive analysis he observed that "the roots of a nation, like those of a tree, are underground. They are the dead. The dead are alive. Past generations nourish present generations; our calamities are the ramifications of old calamities which can not be avoided or stopped or finished at their origin. Our past is terror, and in terror we go on living."[26] Dr. William Stewart, writing his unpublished "Historia" in 1908, arrived at essentially the same conclusion much earlier than Barrett did. He called *lopizmo* "the Judaic shibboleth of a political party," referring to the dictatorial methods of Colorado leaders before 1904. People had not the least idea of their rights under the constitution of 1870. He could see no progress toward political cooperation, he had no faith in elected officials. During the revolt of 1908 he wrote: "Can any man of sane judgment believe that a country that has been exposed for the last hundred years to the most calamitous form of government in the hands of leaders, the majority of whom did not know how to read or write—is capable of suddenly raising itself to a position that will permit it to exercise its full rights of autonomy, advantageously for it and for those who are interested in its well being? The thought is absurd."[27] One of those calamities was the lack of education, and Paraguayans had long been told that

liberty was a great evil among uneducated people. On this ground
Antonio Ildefonso Bermejo had defended the dictatorship of Carlos
Antonio López.[28]

The masses of people had very little education before the War of
the Triple Alliance, despite numerous assertions to the contrary.
Educational institutions begun after the war were poorly supported
and made little impact on the country until after the Colorado era.
Nevertheless, Paraguay was not without intellectuals, many of whom
had been educated abroad, capable of contributing significantly to
government. One writer has divided them into generations at
fifteen-year intervals, beginning in 1811, calling a generation those
who were prominent at a given time. Thus, the generation of 1871
included Benigno Ferreira, Facundo Machaín, and the brothers Decoud. This generation produced the constitution of 1870. For the next
group, that of 1886, Juan Silvano Godoi, Ignacio Ibarra, and Cecilio
Báez are given as examples. The generation of 1901, in many ways the
best in a century, included José de la Cruz Ayala, Adolfo Soler, Manuel
Gondra, Fulgencio R. Moreno, Blas Garay, Eduardo Schaerer, and
Eusebio Ayala, all of whom were active during the first Colorado
era.[29] Obviously, this division is arbitrary but it does call attention to
the steadily improving level of Paraguayan intellectual life.

Why haven't intellectuals played a larger role in Paraguayan
history? The answer lies partly in their inability to divorce themselves from the military. This was true of such nineteenth-century
intellectuals as José Segundo Decoud, Juan Crisóstomo Centurión,
and Benigno Ferreira, and of such twentieth-century leaders as
Moreno, Gondra, and the cousins Eligio and Eusebio Ayala. Intellectuals were unable to command a consensus or to overcome debilitating splintering in political parties. During the postwar occupation,
Brazilian policy determined who would be president. When dissidents appeared, invariably there was an intellectual-military team.
This dependence on the military subordinated the intellectual,
exaggerated the role of the military, and prevented a healthy con-
tinuity of ideals in Paraguayan politics.

Intellectuals were by no means above participating in bitter
factional struggles. Factions formed around strong leaders who
gained adherents because of principles, charisma, the promise of
jobs, the opportunity for graft, and the personal satisfaction of being
an official who could exercise power of some sort. Factionalism had
not been permitted under the three dictators of the first republic.
During the Francia and López regimes, dissidents kept their mouths
shut, sniped at the dictators from foreign havens, or lived out their
lives in jail if they escaped execution. Even after 1870, politics was a
very dangerous game. Arturo Bray, that master of flowing prose and
the brilliant essay, did not exaggerate:

Active politics is not only a ferocious task but one of loyalty and consequence. Whoever belongs to a party gives public notice of it and he risks his life in every confrontation or election. To participate in politics in these times was not surely to dream of a sinecure, a well paid office, but to be in permanent struggle and constant danger. The ideal is to defend it at gunpoint, and there is no place there for dudes and pampered babes. He who does not have audacity to suffer on his shoulder the naked blade of a heavy cavalry saber, had better withdraw and stay home; the non-political is then one who truly renounces the exercise of his civic rights, or feels no desire to govern his fellow citizens. But he who opts for descending to the ring, has to fight like a tiger with well tempered courage, muscles of steel and Spartan fortitude.[30]

Corruption among officials was taken for granted. This malfeasance ranged from petty bribery to grand larceny. Friends and relatives of officeholders considered favors as obligations, regardless of qualifications or concern for the public good.[31] Everyone, a journalist remarked, was out to make money: a doctor became a minister of justice, a shoemaker became a judge, a drunkard became a statesman. The editor of an anti-Colorado paper, with some exaggeration, asserted that all Paraguay's few rich men obtained their wealth "with the immoral favor of the public treasury." With the exception of a very few foreigners, all had been able to accumulate fortunes by diverting public funds to their own uses. With sure insight, the editor observed: "This proves, anyway, that the only certain way to find riches is at the seat of government, that he who separates himself from this center is exposed to misery; and, principally, that the national treasury, instead of serving to promote the common welfare, advances the interests of those who, abdicating honesty, gather in turn. How far we are from those times that we should remember when a Themistocles would die in poverty after having managed the richest treasure of the ancient world!"[32]

During the cabinet crisis of 1900, President Emilio Aceval despaired of finding a new minister of hacienda because the majority of public men were unscrupulous and venality was common. Finally, he selected a man whose principal qualifications were integrity and honesty. Toward the end of the Colorado era, the experienced Brazilian minister was completely cynical about the Congress, whose members were more interested in advancing their own fortunes than in promoting the public welfare. He complained that lack of consideration and appreciation for past assistance marked congressional treatment of economic affairs with Argentina and Brazil. Political leaders had recklessly wasted the country's resources, and their squandering of public funds could only result in national bankruptcy and untold misery for the masses. Emilio Aceval, shortly before his inauguration as president in November 1898, hoped that the "pernicious elements" in Congress could be eliminated in the next elections.[33] Unfortunately, Aceval's wish was unfulfilled.

The Electoral Process and Revolution

The entire electoral process, from registration of voters to recording the voice votes, was permeated by fraud. One could select any election and find well-substantiated charges of intimidation and violence wherever official candidates were challenged. Troops and police armed with pistols, rifles, and swords; thugs armed with machetes and knives; and election officials blind to the planned terror around them, made voting an act of heroism for members of the opposition. These were the conditions that caused formal organization of parties in 1887. Freedom of suffrage was no more than a meaningless phrase in an era when masses sold their votes to the highest bidder. Government control of the electoral process sometimes caused the opposition to boycott elections. In 1890, for example, Liberals debated whether it was worth while to vote in the congressional election to be held in February 1891. They finally decided to make the effort at selected polling places, and violence erupted wherever they showed in strength on election day. On that occasion, the Colorados did permit Liberals to elect two of the thirteen senators and five of the twenty-six deputies. A decade later, conditions had changed little, and again Liberals wondered if it would be worth while to contest the 1901 congressional election.[34]

Colorados certainly had no monopoly on these nefarious practices. When Liberals came to power after their successful revolution in 1904, they were in no hurry to bring about electoral reform. Adequate laws providing for a permanent civil register, the secret ballot, and other reforms finally were enacted in 1916 and 1918, but these changes could not prevent electoral fraud and did little to turn the Paraguayan away from accepting revolution as a valid political process.

An axiom of Latin American politics is that the government never loses an election unless it chooses to do so. Of course, there are exceptions in some countries but not in the Paraguay of the Colorados. The opposition, therefore, had four courses available: abstention, exile, joining the party in power, or revolution. While not recognized by the constitution as a way to bring about political change, revolution was always a possible resort of the defeated and the disgruntled. Francia and the Lópezes had crushed ruthlessly every revolutionary plot, real or fancied. After the Paraguayan War, rival politicians, aligned with either Brazil or Argentina, sought to gain power by revolution if they failed at the polls. Cecilio Báez proclaimed the justification for revolution as a political process: "Revolutions are sacred when their objective is to reestablish the rule of ignored law, to recover usurped power, to avenge great injustices, or to revindicate outraged national honor."[35] Every Paraguayan government for more than a century has had to maintain surveillance of exiles while at the same time being wary of Brazilian and Argentine intentions. Revolts have run the gamut from quixotic plots to full-scale invasions. Nearly all of them in the first Colorado era originated in Argentine territory and had the active support or benign acquiescence of Argentine governments.

Brazil and Argentina were major political poles, magnets to attract Paraguayan politicians. This polarity not only required Argentine and Brazilian leaders to be suspicious of one another but also prevented Paraguay from leading a truly independent political existence. During the Colorado era, Paraguay's two powerful neighbors generally refrained from overt involvement in Paraguayan politics. There were two notable exceptions: Brazil in 1894 planned and paid for a coup to prevent José Segundo Decoud from succeeding to the presidency, and Argentina in 1904 blatantly supported the Liberal revolt that ended Colorado dominance.

Some revolutionary plots appear to have been almost if not entirely Paraguayan in origin. This was true of the Liberal revolt of October 1891, and of the plotting against President Egusquiza in December 1895. There were so many factions that both Liberals and Colorados were accused by egusquicistas. If there really was a plot in 1895, premature publicity ended it. Even innocent gatherings, small or large, would be looked upon with suspicion by the *siutacionistas*, those holding power at the moment. However much statesmen and editors might deplore the fact, revolution was a very real part of the Paraguayan political way.

Part II

THE POLITICAL WAY

Politically, the postwar decade was a struggle between two loosely defined groups, many of whose members were governed by expediency rather than principle. The National Republicans, popularly called Colorados or Reds, and the Liberals, called Azules or Blues, began as defenders or vilifiers of the "martyred" Francisco Solano López. In these roles, they could be called *lopiztas* or anti-*lopiztas*. Although Brazil had been the principal instrument in the destruction of López and the first Paraguayan Republic, lopiztas curried Brazilian favor and were attracted to the Empire because it posed as Paraguay's champion in thwarting Argentine territorial ambitions. Brazil's statesmen had little preference for either Liberals or Colorados and judged all of them primarily by their attitude toward the Empire.

Paraguay clearly was the political preserve of Colorados during the three decades preceding the Liberal revolt of 1904. Theirs was a rule of men, not of laws. What has come to be known as *coloradismo*, or *caballerismo*, was far from being a body of political ideology. Coloradismo was political and economic opportunism, justified by its apologists on purely pragmatic grounds. Liberal opponents of the Colorados attacked specific acts and conditions for which they held their enemies responsible. They were disunited, powerless except for support given occasionally by Argentina or Brazil to keep recalcitrant lopiztas in order. Neither group could claim the constitution of 1870, since that document embodied an eclectic liberal philosophy completely foreign to the Paraguayan experience, a fact that bothered none of the Colorado presidents, least of all Cándido Bareiro.

3

Bareiro and the Colorado Triumph, 1878-1880

Cándido Bareiro, who had played so prominent a role during the first years of the postwar decade, was clearly Paraguay's most astute politician. That he could hold Bernardino Caballero and Patricio Escobar more or less in check testified to his political skill, and the ambitious José Segundo Decoud was sharp enough to realize that his time had not yet come. Bareiro could not escape from the shadow cast by the brutal murders of October 1877, which had left the highly respected Facundo Machaín and other prisoners dead in their cells, but there was no cohesive opposition to this leader of the emerging Colorados. No "liberal" club opposed the grossly misnamed Club Libertad which promoted the candidacy of Bareiro and Adolfo Saguier. Internal anarchy, rumors of invasion, and fears of revolt justified a state of siege until after Bareiro's inauguration in November 1878.

Bareiro, like every other Paraguayan president, inherited a bankrupt treasury, formidable debts, monumental claims, a disorganized country, an undependable congress, and political rivals ready to destroy him whenever circumstances permitted. Why, one may well ask, did anyone want the dubious honor of being president of Paraguay in 1878? An imaginative man could make profitable deals: there was much land available and no end of eager buyers, as Caballero and Escobar were to demonstrate. Customs receipts, small as they were, did represent a source of income. And, after all, not everyone could be the president of a country, even of a country desperately poor and struggling heroically to survive.

Bareiro–the Foremost Colorado

Founder of the Partido Colorado—this is the title that Bareiro had earned during the decade of Allied occupation, despite the fact that there were no formal party organizations until 1887. He had been the magnet to which were pulled the militaristic, conservative, undemocratic elements among politicians who jockeyed for power and prestige. Dr. Facundo Machaín, his principal opponent, was the most brilliant of the young liberals in whose ranks were enlisted the brothers Decoud—Adolfo, Juan José, and José Segundo—and such erratic firebrands as Juan Silvano Godoi, who often affected Chilean spelling and enjoyed combining his three names in various ways. An innocent beneificary of the murder of President Gill on April 12, 1877, Bareiro was the obvious choice to succeed the martyred president.

Bareiro was the first clearly identifiable Colorado, although some would reserve that dubious honor for Juan Bautista Gill. Caballero, hailed less than a century later as the founder of coloradismo, may have been popular with survivors of the war; but it was Bareiro, with the aid of José Segundo Decoud, who provided the brains for coloradismo at the beginning. Decoud, a realist, deserted the Liberals (see chapter 4). Bareiro's principles were not a philosophy. As a Liberal historian has written, "His, indeed, was the concept of political intolerance applied to all factions that opposed his will, his the proselyting work that founded and moulded the Colorado Party's basic tendencies since 1869."[1] Bareiristas had dominated the convention of 1870, but the liberal philosophy of the constitution it produced certainly was not coloradismo. Bareiro and his followers believed in violence to silence opponents, scorned freedom of the press, ignored civil liberties, regarded the public domain as the legitimate source of private wealth, made a mockery of elections, dominated Congress, swept opponents into jail by mass arrests, and depended upon the military to keep them in power. All these practices have persisted in Paraguayan history.

Bareiro's term got off to a slow start when a summer tempest kept the diplomatic corps indoors and postponed the scheduled celebration until November 28, three days late. Bareiro's short term in office was to be almost as tempestuous as the weather that marred the inaugural festivities. Surely he had no illusions about the difficulties ahead. He had shared in creating many of the conditions that would defy improvement, and a charitable view would be that death mercifully removed him from the scene before he was overwhelmed by the huge disaster that was Paraguay.

Bareiro's cabinet was reasonably popular, although popularity was not really significant. Bernardino Caballero in Interior and Patricio Escobar in War and Marine were logical choices. Juan Antonio Jara in Hacienda (treasury) brought little knowledge of government finance to his post. Dr. Benjamín Aceval in Foreign Affairs and José Segundo Decoud in Justice, Worship, and Public Instruction, were by far the most capable men in the cabinet.[2] The most influential newspaper of the day regarded Decoud as deceitful and, therefore, an unwise choice. Bareiro had appointed him in order to placate rivals and to avoid plots and civil disturbances. Perhaps Decoud was deceitful because in a very short tme he had abandoned his liberalism in order to join the winning side. Even Benigno Ferreira, the principal Liberal leader after the murder of Facundo Machaín, from his exile in Buenos Aires had accepted and then declined the post as comptroller general.[3] Buenos Aires was the safest place for Ferreira.

President Bareiro could gain considerable political advantage from the recovery of sovereignty over Villa Occidental, renamed Villa Hayes in honor of the U.S. president in whose name the area was awarded to Paraguay. Bareiro wisely named Aceval as head of the Paraguayan delegation to accept the transfer of authority over Villa Hayes on May 14, 1879, since it was Aceval who had argued Paraguay's case successfully.

There is no question about Bareiro's desire to be a good president. His first order to the jefes políticos was to enforce the laws strictly and to the justices of the peace to maintain personal safety. He was a "law-and-order" president, determined to restore confidence in the national government. Public officials must be honest, breaking sharply with the past, and would be required to give a strict accounting of funds entrusted to them.[4] Considering the treasury's condition, this was indeed a wise policy and, the cynic might add, unrealistic.

State of the Nation

Revolts and venal administration had left Paraguay's finances in shambles. Customs receipts were the only significant source of income. There were no taxes on property or estates of deceased persons. Still, the government required only modest revenues, and good administration could make the most of limited resources.

Paper money in circulation amounted to only $f109,506, and bonds of the defunct Asociación del Comercio Paraguayo were down to $f6,000.[5] Because no one knew how many internal debt certificates and payment orders were afloat, the minister of hacienda late in 1878 ordered all holders of these instruments to present them for validation. So many counterfeits were discovered that on April 29, 1879, another decree required a second validation as well as the surrender of paper money, which was to be burned.[6] To amortize the verified certificates, customs duties were raised 3 percent. Never bulging with resources while Bareiro was president, the treasury showed no encouraging trends. Its published monthly balances to June 30, 1880, varied from almost nothing to a high of $f151,637 in May 1879. Balances for the winter months of July, August, and September 1879, were particularly low, reflecting a great drop in trade.[7]

Paraguayan budgets for much of the Colorado era followed unique accounting practices. Congress received a salary budget from the president, leaving other expenses to be paid from funds appropriated as needed. The budget for 1880, for example, was a modest $f271,828, and Bareiro's salary was an equally modest $f500 monthly. Revenues were too low to meet even this insignificant figure, and previous legislation had allocated much of the government's income to specific purposes. The law of April 16, 1879, allotted the wharfage fee to such public works as completion of the Oratorio and the National Theater, construction of a building for Congress, completion and furnishing of the Government Palace, and founding an agricultural school in Villa Hayes.[8]

The customs law of 1880 provided for 30 percent or more duties on most imports. Additional duties of 4 percent were levied to support the Colegio Nacional, to cover deficits, and to pay costs of suppressing the 1879 revolt. Widespread smuggling made a mockery of customs laws and reduced anticipated revenue so much that Congress on June 8, 1880, authorized Segundo Machaín y Cía. to start a lottery that was expected to yield about $1,000 monthly to support the Charity Hospital. Bareiro and his ministers recognized the immorality of a lottery, especially in a country so miserably poor as Paraguay, even though Paraguayans are born gamblers, willing to sell their only shirts and *tupois* (a loosely fitting short cotton gown) to bet on a long shot. Desperate for money, the government issued $f120,000 in paper in July 1880, to pay salaries. To amoritze this issue, a council of merchants would oversee the allocation of export duties, wharfage fees, proceeds from stamped paper and commercial licenses.[9] Bareiro also asked Brazil for a loan of $150,000 to $200,000 in 1880 after a revolt, a severe drought and locust plague, and unpaid salaries left the treasury without a peso. The Brazilian chargé gave Bareiro a good recommendation, but the imperial government expressed deep regret that it could not guarantee such a loan. This was one disappointment that Bareiro did not face; he died before the answer arrived from Rio de Janeiro.

The nation also suffered from the lack of banking institutions. The Gill administration had killed the first efforts at commercial banking, and for several years there was no banking enterprise in the country. One Joaquín Obejero had been granted a concession in August 1878 to create the Banco del Paraguay. Obejero had deposited $f30,000 in government debt certificates as proof of his intent, but stock could not be sold and the effort failed. One more optimist appeared during Bareiro's short term. Alexander Francis Baillie, by now an old Paraguayan hand, represented a group of Englishmen headed by tramway owner James Nelson Horrocks, who proposed to create the Banco Anglo-Paraguayo and offered a guaranty of £1,000. All parties approved. At last, *La Reforma* exulted, Paraguay would have a bank. Congress granted the concession on June 5, 1880, then waited in vain for the bank to appear.[10]

Preoccupation with efforts to beat a path through the financial jungle did not preclude attempts to end factional politics. Unfortunately, many Colorados considered pacification to be synonymous with elimination of all principal opponents.

Murder and Revolution

Cirilo Antonio Rivarola had lost most of his political power when he resigned as president in December 1871. During the next seven years he wasted his resources in vain efforts to regain political influence. He figured in nearly every antigovernment plot, alternately and simultaneously sought aid from Brazil and Argentina, and maintained a base of operations on his estancia at Barrero Grande (now Eusebio Ayala). Lack of roads made this relatively remote ranch difficult to reach. Barrero Grande was Rivarola country, and nearly all its few inhabitants were loyal to their *caraí*, their leader. No matter who was president in Asunción—Jovellanos, Gill, Uriarte, or Bareiro—Rivarola ruled in Barrero Grande. He played an important role in starting the revolts of 1873–1874 which laid the foundation for Colorado rule; for his own convenience he cooperated with Caballero and Escobar, neither of whom he trusted. Brazil's selection of Juan Bautista Gill to follow Jovellanos was a serious blow to Rivarola, who sensed dimly if at all that to Brazilian statesmen all Paraguayan politicians were insignificant puppets to be manipulated at will while they kept an eye on Argentina.

After the evacuation of Allied troops from Asunción, presidents Uriarte and Bareiro, urged on by Escobar and Caballero, periodically sent raiding parties into Barrero Grande, hoping to catch Rivarola off guard. The former president did have a certain following in Asunción, Villa Rica, and various small towns; so long as he lived he appeared to be a threat to the Bareiro-Caballero-Escobar clique. Rivarola became tired of hiding in the hills of Caraguatay and unwisely accepted Bareiro's offer of protection if he were to come to Asunción. His plan probably was to seek reconciliation with the government he had helped to gain power and obtain a lucrative position or at least a foreign mission. Just what promises he received when he conferred with President Bareiro on December 31, 1878, will never be known. Despite the promised protection, Rivarola had the good sense to arrange to spend the evening with the Brazilian consul general, João Antônio Mendes Totta Filho. Someone, and suspicion naturally falls on Caballero and Escobar, had arranged for a deadly escort to fall in with the ex-president when he left Bareiro's home on that sultry New Year's Eve.

During the hot summer days, when the city lay smothered in a blanket of humid air, *asuncenos* kept their stores and homes open until well after 9:00 P.M. Rivarola walked along Calle Palma, the principal shopping street, in plain view of scores of people. When he reached the corner of 25 de Noviembre, now Independencia, six thugs attacked. Five of them plunged knives into Rivarola's body and the sixth struck him on the head with a machete. No one came to his aid. Bareiro's house and the police headquarters were but a block away, a police post less than 100 feet distant, yet no one reached the dying man for thirty minutes. Rivarola's companion, identified only as Major López, escaped with minor wounds and hid until daybreak when he sought asylum with the Brazilian chargé. Together they went to see Bareiro, who was terribly upset by the news and offered López sanctuary until he could return to Barrero Grande.[11]

Several weeks passed during which the search for Rivarola's murderers was fruitless. "It is strange," José de Almeida e Vasconcellos, the Brazilian chargé observed, "that no culprits have been found when the crime was committed by four to six persons in the most public street in the city, a few steps from the house of the President of the Republic, where there is always a guard, and before 10 P.M. when the shutters were open and many people were abroad in that area."[12] This atrocious murder could have been shrugged off had not public opinion been outraged. Scapegoats had to be found, so Col. Juan Alberto Meza, chief of the presidential guard, General Ignacio Genes, chief of police, and fifteen hirelings were arrested. Bareiro waited for the right time to bring the prisoners to trial. He still was not free from the power of Caballero, Escobar, and Meza, all notorious enemies of Rivarola. If he moved too quickly, he told Vasconcellos, he too would be assassinated. "What one concludes from this state of affairs," Vasconcellos reported, "is that this people cannot yet be governed except by an iron hand lest anarchy reign."[13]

Vasconcellos had been in Paraguay long enough to have lost his illusions about the country, still he was greatly disturbed when the courts freed all the conspirators on January 24, 1880, despite conclusive evidence of their guilt. The verdict came too late to help General Genes, who had died in jail. In reviewing the case, Vasconcellos provided a rare insight into Paraguay's criminal justice process. What could one expect, he asked with ill-concealed exasperation, in a semibarbarous country? Truly, "the democracy of the South American Republics is a genuine mockery thrown in the face of the whole world, since the omnipotence of government rules and never equality before the law, which is true democracy." A hundred jurors had been selected for the year; of these the three defense attorneys had rejected more than sixty, the majority of whom were more or less independent foreigners, so that the jury was composed of five young government employees, two foreigners, the comptroller general, and a Spanish lackey of Ricardo Brugada, one of the defense lawyers. The community expected severe punishment of the criminals, an outcome that General Caballero was determined to prevent. The judge who started the case, Col. Silvestre Aveiro, was dismissed for bias. Caballero made certain that his intimate friend and companion in arms, Colonel Meza, was absolved, "and since this was the one who ordered the crime perpetrated by members of the Squadron he commanded, it was necessary also to absolve the assassins, in order to keep them from denouncing him, as they would do naturally if they were condemned." Vasconcellos rightly concluded that the scandal would weigh heavily upon Bareiro's administration. The prosecutor, Don Próspero Gamboa, knew that it was useless to appeal the verdict and would himself be the target of assassination if he did. José Segundo Decoud, then minister of foreign affairs, was the only prominent cabinet member to emerge untainted from the miserable affair and was quick to condemn it.[14] At a time when Paraguayan finances were in such a distressed state, this scandal could only detract from the country's credit,[15] and probably influence Brazil against granting a much needed loan.

Another Godoi Revolt

President Bareiro sent a cheerful message to Congress in April 1879, unaware of the plotting led by Juan Silvano Godoi in Buenos Aires. Bareiro reported that the country was completely tranquil, with police and military forces reorganized and a functioning court system. Although the economy still lagged, agriculture and commerce had recovered from the damaging torrential rain. Negotiations were proceeding with Bolivia to settle the Chaco dispute, and Dr. Benjamín Aceval had returned from Washington with an arbitral victory over Argentina. Social conditions appeared to be improving and the church problem had been settled. Religious authority in Paraguay was in complete confusion after the war. Francisco Solano López had executed the bishop, foreign priests who had come in with the occupation forces aroused resentment among native clergymen, and Padre Fidel Maíz, a very popular priest, was condemned by papal officials in Rio de Janeiro and Buenos Aires because of his role as a judge in the López military court that condemned hundreds of prisoners to death. Paraguayans strongly resented the appointment of foreign administrators (vicars) of the church and the effort to defrock Padre Maíz. An agreement with the papacy in 1878 provided that the clergy present a list of three candidates for the bishopric, it being understood that the first name would be submitted to the pope as the Paraguayan choice. Padre Pedro Juan Aponte of Villa Rica headed the list and so became bishop of Paraguay on October 13, 1879. Bareiro made efforts to shake off the Caballero-Escobar shackles. He persuaded Escobar to resign by giving him a lease on a huge area of yerbales on the Alto Paraná. Vasconcellos expected that Caballero, too, would be eased out of office.[16]

Juan Silvano Godoi in Buenos Aires was plotting to end the peaceful state of affairs. Major planner of the assassination of President Gill on April 12, 1877, he had escaped to Argentina before the fatal day. Obviously with connivance of some Argentine officials, Godoi and other Paraguayan exiles in Buenos Aires financed the purchase of an armed merchant ship, the *Galileo*, upon which were loaded a large supply of munitions, uniforms, and some five hundred men. Juan Silvano and Nicanor Godoi sailed with the ship from Buenos Aires early in June. Héctor Francisco Decoud was among the plotters in Asunción who anxiously awaited the arrival of the *Galileo*.[17] Renamed *El Libertador*, the ship escaped detention by Argentine authorities at Rosario and Corrientes, then quickly captured Humaitá, Pilar, Villa Franca, and Villa Oliva.[18] These were easy conquests, meaningless because Godoi could not garrison the villages. Nevertheless, there was a very real threat to the capital which was only ninety kilometers north of Villa Oliva.

Bareiro and the Congress acted with commendable vigor by authorizing a loan of $50,000, declaring a state of siege, and mobilizing the National Guard. Bareiro sent Escobar with 2,000 men to confront the rebels by land and ordered the *Taraguy* to attack *El Libertador*. The Paraguayan warship sailed from Asunción on June 14 and sighted the rebel ship a day later. Just as the two vessels were about to clash, *El Libertador* hoisted the Argentine flag and very conveniently the Argentine *Resguardo* sailed between them.[19]

Although subordinate officials had cooperated with Godoi, their superiors in Buenos Aires were unhappy with the *Galileo*'s venture and the obviously inadequate preparations among rebel sympathizers in Paraguay. Deciding to disengage themselves from the fiasco, Argentine authorities ordered the *Resguardo*'s captain to release Godoi's prisoners and to transfer the rebels' large store of munitions to the Argentine ship. Prisoners on their own vessel, Godoi and his men had no choice but to allow the *Resguardo* to shepherd them downstream where they were released at Buenos Aires. Godoi, apparently, was allowed to keep the munitions and equipment that had been assembled by the Paraguayan Committee in Buenos Aires.[20]

The revolt had failed so miserably that Bareiro lifted the state of siege on July 5. His reassuring manifesto echoed the indignation expressed in *El Comercio* against such outrageous ventures. There were no prosecutions in Asunción. Perhaps Bareiro had in mind the murder of President Gill in 1877, of Facundo Machaín and Cirilo Antonio Rivarola. President Bareiro, civilian leader of the 1873–1874 revolts, drew the line at assassination: "It is not possible," he warned, "to found free governments on the victims bloodied by the dagger of the treacherous assassin." The rebellion was utterly senseless, and its immediate effects were to increase Bareiro's popularity as well as the national debt.[21]

A President Passes

Even the most charitable of judges would find little to praise in Bareiro's administration. To the turmoil of Rivarola's murder and Godoi's revolt were added charges of graft, continued financial distress, and unfulfilled concessions. Despite the need for immigration, Bareiro did little except sponsor acts to promote settlement of the Chaco, and one of these measures was the cause of great controversy. Congress made a princely grant in the northern Chaco to Francisco Javier Bravo on August 4, 1879,[22] a concession that smoothed the way for signing the Decoud-Quijarro Treaty on the following October 15 (see chapter 11). An enemy accused Bareiro of having accepted a bribe of £20,000 from Bravo, the money to be paid when the project had become a functioning enterprise.[23] Such accusations were so common among Paraguay's politicians that this one belongs in the "never proven" file.

Bareiro's message to Congress in April 1880 anticipated much better times. The country was at peace; general well-being was spreading despite the horrible weather of 1879, as could be seen by increased rural activity. Commerce, while suffering some paralysis, would improve as the people, realizing that laws alone could not remedy their troubles, turned to hard work. Again he reminded the country that the religious question was settled and the government, poor though it was, had sent two students to Rome to study for the priesthood. Bareiro believed that the Decoud-Quijarro Treaty was an outstanding diplomatic achievement that would end the Chaco dispute with Bolivia.[24]

Devout asuncenos crossed themselves apprehensively on the morning of September 4, 1880, when measured strokes of tolling bells sounded in the city. Quickly the news spread. At 10:00 A.M. a stroke had left President Bareiro dead at his desk. Charitably, the Brazilian chargé reported that this was an "irreparable loss for the country, so lacking in competent men for administration."[25] Mourning the sad event, *La Reforma* recalled Bareiro's promises: "I shall govern with the Constitution; I shall maintain peace and public order with a firm hand and I shall promote development of the national wealth with salubrious measures." The editor exaggerated a little in praising Bareiro for "moralizing" the administration and reestablishing the country's credit: "He was an austere citizen, a pure patriot, an eminent statesman worthy of the times of Cato and Cincinnatus. . . . Bareiro has died; but his example, his ideas, his aspirations will never die."[26]

The administration of Cándido Bareiro, cut short by death in less than two years, was a transition from the postwar decade, an introduction to the first Colorado era. There was no sharp break with the past to which Paraguay was bound firmly by historical continuities. The most important result of his death was the swift coup that stole the presidency from Adolfo Saguier, for it was this act that restored military dictatorship to Paraguay.

4

Bernardino
Caballero, 1880–1886

Bernadino Caballero was the most influential man in Paraguay during nearly all the Colorado era. Although his political dominance has been overemphasized in view of his inability to maintain a unified Colorado party or to prevent a move for accommodation or coalition with Liberals, there is considerable justification for blanketing the entire first Colorado era under the term *caballerismo*. Caballero had no well-defined political philosophy, no coherent economic, social, or political plan. For ideas he depended upon his own instincts and the advice of José Segundo Decoud. He was an opportunist who met problems as they appeared with temporary, Band-Aid solutions. He treated symptoms while ignoring underlying causes. If he was imbued with the despotic doctrines of the López tyranny under which he grew to manhood and won military fame, he was more of a benevolent caraí, or leader, a father figure to the unsophisticated Paraguayans who had survived the war. In their search for heroes, such Paraguayan superpatriots as the late Juan Emiliano O'Leary selected charismatic leaders of the past for canonization. Prominent among the chosen few are Francisco Solano López and two generals who served him faithfully, José Eduvigis Díaz and Bernadino Caballero. Paraguayan publicists and historians of our own time appear determined to eclipse all previous efforts to bury the real Caballero under an avalanche of extravagant adulation.

Caballero's Coup

Although Vice-President Adolfo Saguier certainly was no threat to Caballero, the death of President Bareiro offered a chance too good to miss for Caballero and his clique, who moved with amazing speed as soon as they learned that Bareiro was dead. The cabinet, and proba-

51

bly Father Fidel Maíz, urged Caballero to assume the presidency. The lucky general had no objections, so the coup went smoothly from the beginning when Minister of War and Marine Pedro Duarte summoned an unsuspicious Saguier to receive the allegiance of troops in the plaza facing the *policía*. Duarte honored Saguier by putting him in a cell and assuring the astonished vice-president that he would remain there until he signed his resignation. Saguier signed. Then the Permanent Commission, the watchdog for Congress when it was not in session, gave its consent and summoned Congress to meet in special session at 3:00 P.M. on September 4, 1880. Congress met, accepted Saguier's resignation, and elected Caballero as president.[1]

No Paraguayan political coup ever went more smoothly. The conspirators were ready with a proclamation which for cynicism has no equal in the country's history:

Manifesto to the People
The illustrious President of the Republic, D. Cándido Bareiro, has just died and in the duty of maintaining imminently threatened peace and order, I have taken command of the national forces until the Honorable Congress of the Nation can meet and adopt those measures warranted by the circumstances.
For this purpose all measures to guarantee order have been taken. I assume the responsibility willingly in the name of the salvation of the country and its institutions. The people may be assured that it will be my first duty to guarantee the lives and interests of all inhabitants of the Republic.
You may rest assured that my greatest desire is to fulfill the Constitution and the laws of the Nation.

Bernardino Caballero
Asunción, September 4, 1880

This pronouncement, issued immediately after Saguier's inspired resignation and before the Permanent Commission had called Congress into session, met with widespread approval, according to Caballero's apologists. The revolution of 1874 had finally succeeded in capturing the country for the military with congressional approval.[2] As Arturo Bray observed sarcastically, "It requires some effort to perceive what the dangers could be that threatened order and tranquillity, since Caballero was master of the barracks and no opposition party existed, not even an organized nucleus of citizens capable of disturbing the peace."[3]

The Brazilian foreign office received assurances that the new government would be friendly. Brazil's chargé reported favorably on events, although compelled to acknowledge that the coup was unconstitutional. He insisted that Saguier had no support in the country and his elevation to the presidency would have caused "an immediate conflagration in the entire Republic; on the other hand,

General Caballero is well liked by all." Caballero, he wrote, had no desire to be president but acceded to pressure from his friends in order to maintain peace.[4] If the chargé really believed this nonsense, he was too naive to be a diplomat. Brazil's old friend, Juan José Brizuela, was confident that Caballero would replace most of the cabinet with good lopiztas and that the government's policy would favor Brazil.[5] As could be expected, Paraguay's most influential paper gave its support: "We have complete and decided confidence in the situation, because it means for us peace, order, liberty, progress, and personal guarantees."[6]

Caballero the Golden

"Bernardino Caballero. Ocho sílabas de oro que suenan a gloria— Eight golden syllables that ring in glory."[7] To many Paraguayans, Bernardino Caballero is second only to Francisco Solano López as a national hero, and the remains of both lie in the Panteón Nacional. Caballero was much more likeable than López, much more a man of the people. Born in Ybicuí on May 20, 1839, he was little bothered by formal education. In his mid twenties when the war broke out in 1864, Caballero had achieved the rank of cavalry sergeant. However he came to the attention of López, and some of the stories about his meteoric rise are not complimentary, promotions came fast and he ended the war as a general. Although he fought in many bloody battles, he emerged unscathed and surrendered to the Brazilians after the final skirmish at Cerro Corá in 1870. The victors removed him to Rio de Janeiro with other prisoners. His comfortable life among the cariocas ended in 1871 when Viscount Rio Branco, who had taken a liking to him, sent him to Buenos Aires where he dictated his memoirs to the Viscount's son, the Baron Rio Branco of future fame.[8] This association produced a strong friendship between the Rio Brancos and Caballero and helps to explain Caballero's leaning toward Brazil in the Argentine-Brazilian struggle for influence in Paraguay.

Not by accident was Caballero a principal leader of the revolts of 1873–1874 and the winner of a cabinet position. President Gill sent him to London in 1874 in a vain attempt to negotiate a settlement of the disastrous postwar loans. Gill and Bareiro were such powerful rivals that Caballero, had he entertained presidential ambitions in 1874, would have needed Brazilian support, and the Brazilians were not then ready for Caballero to be president. Each of these rivals had his turn in the presidency, and when Bareiro died, Caballero was still young and vigorous, a handsome, bearded, blue-eyed blond abundantly endowed with much-admired machismo.

A prominent Paraguayan scholar, an acknowledged expert in colonial history and also a dedicated Colorado, finds in Caballero a nearly model statesman. It was Caballero who

> restored public peace and assured the general tranquility. . . . He understood that parties are forms of political cooperation to channel popular aspirations and avoid dictatorship. For that reason, he permitted the foundation of the Liberal party. For that reason, he himself founded the Colorado party two months later. He began a policy of tolerance and of cooperation with fellow citizens of different and opposing political opinions. He granted liberties to the opposition and to the press. During the era of rebirth that began with him, he never closed a press nor deported a single journalist.[9]

Caballero deserves very little of this praise. The country was at peace when he became president, and why eulogize him for allowing Paraguayans to exercise their constitutional rights? Freedom of the press was really something new in Paraguay, and Caballero did tolerate an astonishing amount of outrageously scurrilous journalism. Many newspapers were unrestrained in editorial excesses; cartoons often were perceptive and generally downright vicious. José Segundo Decoud, wise in the ways of Paraguayan journalists, probably counseled restraint in dealing with them. After all, their influence could not have been very extensive, and their diatribes were much too frenetic to be convincing.

Paraguay had no genius in the presidential chair. As the Brazilian chargé observed: "He is the first to recognize his ineptitude to exercise such lofty functions." The British minister, although agreeing that Caballero had little ability, called him "genial and kind hearted," devoted to Paraguay. He had not participated in the barbarities committed by López, and his presidency was "a guarantee for orderly and, unless measured by a much severer standard than generally prevails in South America, honest government."[10]

Caballero carried himself with dignity. His comportment was impeccable, like a Spanish grandee who could easily identify with the common man. Like other men in other times, he looked like a president whatever his weaknesses. Tactful and patient, he commanded both respect and loyalty. Caballero impressed another British minister as being a "straight forward man,—in appearance more like a German or an Englishman than a South American—and though not credited with any remarkable ability—is liked for his simple manners and geniality and respected for the great personal courage he displayed in the terrible Lopez war."[11] The greatest blemishes on Caballero's career were the murders of Machaín and Rivarola, crimes for which he has been held responsible by such writers as Arturo Bray, who asserts that nothing could "cleanse that smear of blood and mud from the golden epaulets of Bernardino Caballero. For that

reason, his political enemies—who are many and very relentless—
come to the point of discussing and denying his glory as a fighter,
while his admirers, also numerous, put him in the clouds. For some
[he is the] 'warrior of the Virgin sword' and 'general ostrich': for
others, 'the centaur of Ybycuí and rebuilder of our nationality.' "[12]

Caballero had the virtue of recognizing his own limitations, and
he therefore generally surrounded himself with wise counselors. He
did not rush headlong into impossible programs; his conservative
bent led him to sponsor projects most desired by the middle and
commercial classes. While there were incompetents in the government, their weaknesses were more than overcome by such men as
Decoud and Centurión.

The most capable man in the cabinet was José Segundo Decoud,
who had been a flaming Liberal in the early 1870s. Decoud's defection
to the caballeristas was pure opportunism. He could see easily that
the revolts of 1873–1874 had Brazilian acquiescence, if not support, so
he sailed with the tide. Decoud was born in Asunción on May 14, 1848,
and so was in his early thirties when he embraced caballerismo. He
had been editor of *La Regeneración*, had served in the Triumvirate
from its beginning in 1869 under Rivarola, and was a prominent
member of the constitutional convention in 1870. From 1879 to the
end of the century he was in every cabinet save one, and most of that
time was recognized as among the most influential men in the country. He was not universally liked or trusted, even among Colorados.
La Reforma had faith in all Bareiro's ministers except Decoud. Juan
Silvano Godoi, by no means a Colorado, called him amoral, a
schemer and troublemaker, a grafter who in 1871 had proposed
Paraguayan annexation to either Brazil or Argentina. More sound
was the judgment of the British minister to Argentina, who found
both Caballero and Decoud superior to their Argentine counter-
parts.[13] The American Minister, John Edmund Bacon, called Decoud
"ablest of the Paraguayans, the ablest & best informed man that I
have met in South America." Decoud spoke Spanish, English, French,
and German, had the largest private library in the Plata basin, and
was reputed to be the "ablest diplomatist in South America."[14]

Decoud may have supported Bareiro and Caballero because he
saw a chance to exert a modifying influence on caudillos who would
rule anyway. He must have been an unhappy man, haunted by
memories of the murders committed in October 1877 and the assassination of Rivarola. He could not have been unaware that those
atrocities were the work of the Caballero clique which he had defied
by accompanying Machaín's body to Buenos Aires for burial. After
this he was a devoted servant of his country, the noblest man by far
who served the Colorados, the most distinguished statesman in
Paraguay's long period of reconstruction. When he resigned from

Bernardino Caballero, about 1890.
Courtesy Ricardo Caballero Aquino.

José Segundo Decoud as Paraguayan delegate
to the Washington Conference, 1889.
Courtesy Columbus Memorial Library, Organization of American States.

President Aceval's cabinet in 1900, the Brazilian minister reported accurately: "In Snr. Decoud this government loses its real intellectual head and its right arm, the reason why all of the governments since 1870 have been unable to dispense with his services and his cooperation, despite the attacks and the serious accusation of 'annexationist' made against him."[15] When he died on March 4, 1909, after a long illness during which he was paralyzed for a year, *El Diario*'s editor wrote a fitting epitaph: "José Segundo Decoud signed the magna carta of our nationality, he founded the university, opened schools, solved important international problems, created colonies and devoted all of his energy to arousing the spirit of the Paraguayan people."[16]

Juan Crisóstomo Centurión y Martínez was one of the really bright lights in the Colorado regime and was responsible to an unrecognized degree for Caballero's success. An exceptionally handsome man, he cut a fine figure in uniform or mufti. Born in Itauguá in 1840, Centurión received his early education in Asunción, where Ildefonso Antonio Bermejo, one of the "civilizers" brought to Paraguay by Carlos Antonio López, was among his teachers. López selected the bright youngster as one of those sent to Europe at state expense for further education. Centurión studied abroad, mostly in England, for five years and there became a great admirer of Shakespeare, Milton, and other literary masters. He had the opportunity to study English life in its many aspects, to visit museums and other cultural institutions. Centurión concentrated on international law as preparation for a diplomatic post. Upon completion of his studies, he visited France and then dutifully returned to Asunción in 1863. The new president, Francisco Solano López, immediately made him a member of his personal cabinet of intimate advisers and inevitably he became involved in the War of the Triple Alliance. Wounded at Tuyutí, he was decorated with the National Order of Merit and promoted to captain. When López, obsessed with fears of conspiracy and treason, ordered the trial of hundreds of suspects at San Fernando, Centurión was one of the most severe judges of the "bloody tribunals." Remarkably, while in the midst of a terrific struggle, López did not forget education. He entrusted to Centurión the creation and conduct of a school to teach French, English, and Spanish. Centurión originated the idea of publishing the fascinating war journal *Cabichuí* and enlisted such talented clergymen as Fidel Maíz and Gerónimo Becchis for the task.[17] Faithful to López to the end, he fought at Itá-Ybaté and Ascurra, and was with his commander at Cerro Corá, where he suffered a painful face wound. His Brazilian captors made him walk the eleven-day journey to Concepción, took him to Asunción, and then to Rio de Janeiro. Released from surveillance, Centurión made his way to London where he married a beautiful Cuban. He moved with his wife to Cuba, where he practiced law, published his *Viaje nocturno* in New York (1877), and in 1878 returned to Asunción. In the Paraguayan capital he edited *La Reforma,* served as attorney general under Caballero and on the commission that created the Colegio Nacional. He served with Benjamín Aceval and Ramón Zubizarreta on the committee appointed in 1886 to revise the criminal code. Centurión joined Caballero in organizing the Colorado party on September 11, 1887. He served as minister of foreign affairs (1888–1890) under President Escobar and in this capacity produced a state paper that was a brilliant defense of Paraguay's title to the Chaco Boreal, a defense never improved upon by scores of later writers. This man of many talents became a senator in 1895 and held the post until his death on March 12, 1902.[18]

The presence of Decoud and Centurión among Colorado leaders failed to temper the judgment of the Brazilian consul general, who believed that Caballero's government was encumbered neither by intelligence nor a high degree of morality. He did admit, however, that by comparison with other South American governments and those of the postwar decade, Caballero's government was "one of the best possible, considering the social condition of the nation that still is incapable of understanding and meeting the heavy demands of liberty." If Caballero's regime lacked the virtues and patriotism of a free and progressive government, neither did it have the despotic tendencies of the great dictatorships. This was a fact "even more remarkable considering that almost all of the members of the executive branch do not belong to the new generation but matured under the oppressive military rule of López which has no parallel except in the darkest times of Byzantine decadence."[19]

The Provisional Presidency

Caballero's administration began vigorously in 1880. Among other achievements were establishing the Civil Register, starting the town of Villa Florida, inaugurating a messenger service from Paraguarí to Paso Santa María in southeastern Paraguay, and granting twenty-five leagues of government land to his wife, Doña Melchora Melgarejo de Caballero. Congress responded promptly to the proposals made in his annual message in April 1881. In June, the General Department of Immigration was created in the ministry of the interior.[20] Other laws in June authorized creation of a Banco Nacional and the private Banco del Paraguay. The Banco Nacional del Paraguay finally began its uncertain career on January 2, 1884, but soon was in serious trouble. The railway, too, gave the administration great concern, but Paraguay did not regain possession of it until 1886.[21] More successful was the effort to improve communications. The needed legislation was passed in September, 1881, and in November, Paraguay contracted to restore the telegraph line to Paso de Patria for $41,800.²²

Paraguay's economic recovery from the war needed such ambitious outlays, and Caballero went ahead with his proposals, probably anticipating income from land sales. The internal debt had declined from about $f800,000 to some $f647,000 in less than two years. As to the war debts, if Paraguay had taken them seriously, the country would have been crushed indefinitely. This was hardly the time to spend money on a gunboat, but an agent did acquire an aging Italian vessel at Montevideo which, as noted above, became the *Pirapó*.²³

These measures were accomplished by ignoring the English debt, although decline in the internal debt caused optimistic reports in Buenos Aires, where some people had great confidence that the Caballero regime was raising the country from the lethargy into which anarchy and misgovernment had plunged it. The budget for 1882 was set at $f285,275, while the country acknowledged debts of $23,426,293. The economic situation was not encouraging, despite Paraguay's appearance as an Arcadia to the British minister to Argentina. *La Reforma* admitted that if dependent solely on its own resources, Paraguay could not maintain itself. There was practically no army to defend its independence against a powerful enemy, and the country continued as an independent nation only because neither Brazil nor Argentina cared to pay the price of absorption.²⁴ Caballero, well aware of the Argentine-Brazilian standoff, prepared for the election of 1882.

Caballero was too good a politician to leave his election to chance. Recognizing the need for a popular mandate, a group of his supporters called a mass meeting on September 25, 1881, in the Teatro Nacional. While hardly a political convention, it was the nearest thing to one that had occurred since the war. The purpose was to organize the party of caballerismo, the party that would wait six years before formally organizing. The Club Libertad that emerged from this meeting appeared to be a resurrection of the group that had promoted Bareiro's candidacy and enjoyed the trappings of party organization: a central committee, president, vice-president, and secretary. There was no argument about candidates as the club endorsed Caballero for president and Juan Antonio Jara for vice-president.²⁵

Caballero faced enough serious problems in 1882 to cause wonder about the sanity of anyone who sought the presidency. The country was bankrupt, ridden with corruption, a pawn in the continuing Argentine-Brazilian game of power politics. The Brazilian chargé, a newcomer to Asunción, feared Argentine involvement in a revolt that in March 1882 was rumored to be in the making. General Patricio Escobar, highly respected in the interior, had appeared in Asunción on a visit. His yerbales (stands of yerba trees) on the Alto Paraná were thriving. The most prestigious firm in Asunción, Oribe y Cía., had invested 100,000 patacones (approximately equal to dollars) in the enterprise, which employed more than four hundred yerbateros (yerba gatherers). At about the same time came Adolfo P. Carranza, secretary of the Argentine legation, who served as chargé until Dr. Héctor Alvarez could take over as minister. There was no connection between Escobar and Carranza, but rumor had it that the brothers Saguier and other Paraguayans in Buenos Aires would cooperate with Escobar and various "friends" of Caballero to assassinate the president. The worried Brazilian chargé asked for another gunboat since the one in port was in bad shape and its crew depleted by desertions. The Brazilian foreign office expressed little concern.[26]

A somewhat more experienced diplomat, also a stranger to Paraguay, was Henrique Barros Cavalcanti de Lacerda, who became the Brazilian minister on April 19. Lacerda confirmed the rumor but not the plot. Escobar may have wanted to be vice-president and probably came to Asunción to test the political winds. Lacerda could believe that Argentina was up to something when President Julio Roca stopped off to visit the ruins at Humaitá when he was en route to Formosa, and then Dr. Alvarez arrived. These concidences did not presage a revolution. The only people with enough resources to revolutionize the country had too much to lose since they enjoyed political and economic perquisites dispensed by Caballero.[27] The election on September 25, 1882, went smoothly, as did the inauguration two months later.

Caballero—Constitutional President

Having been elected unanimously, Bernadino Caballero at last was the constitutional president of Paraguay. The country was peaceful. As he had informed Congress on April 1, 1882, anarchy had ended and the country could devote itself to reconstruction: "Yesterday our fields, fertile and populated in other times, were a sad and desolate desert, without the least sign or manifestation of life; today the home has been rebuilt on the wreckage, the family has begun to take form again, and everyone strives earnestly to promote his own welfare." Strict observance of the constitution was necessary to prevent society from becoming unhinged, a victim of the "savage and unrestrained impulses of despotism."[28] After having violated the constitution so blatantly less than two years before, Caballero was nothing if not brazen. His reference to the reformation of family life and resurrection of agricultural activity was sound, and his government was indeed "slowly raising the country from its prostration." There was no contest between political parties, "since all are content with the present situation and as to candidates for the future presidency, there are none other than the general himself whom all accept with enthusiasm," his friend and representative in Montevideo, Juan José Brizuela, informed the Brazilians.[29]

Caballero's administration achieved several notable successes in foreign affairs, thanks to José Segundo Decoud. Argentina renewed diplomatic relations and signed a new commercial treaty. Uruguay, in the Decoud-Kubly treaty of 1883, renounced war indemnities and two years later returned captured war trophies. Encouraged by this success, Decoud kept up pressure on Argentina and Brazil to cancel the war debts. While relations were cool with Argentina, the threat of an Argentine-Brazilian conflict over Misiones led to declarations of Paraguayan neutrality in such an event. Argentina, having discovered a larger channel in the Pilcomayo north of the 1876 boundary, tried unsuccessfully to reopen the boundary question. Negotiations with Bolivia over the Chaco continued, and Paraguay strengthened its claim by selling huge areas of that territory at nominal prices. In 1885, Decoud negotiated a settlement with the English bondholders.[30]

Domestic achievements make an imposing list. There was considerable improvement in education, especially in Asunción. Congress authorized schools of agriculture, business, and arts in June 1882. The National University had its beginning when the School of Law, attached to the Colegio Nacional, was created in July 1882. Congress also voted subsidies for students to be educated in Uruguay and Argentina. The Ateneo Paraguayo, founded on August 20, 1883, was not of Caballero's doing but it added luster to his regime. Anyone with a plan to better Paraguay enjoyed a warm welcome by Caballero. As a result, the government founded several agricultural colonies and encouraged general immigration. Business interests organized a chamber of commerce, a sign of increasing economic activity in Asunción. Toward the end of Caballero's term, on March 6, 1886, Congress repurchased the railway from Mendes, Patri y Cía. and laid plans to extend the line to Villa Rica. Fiscal improvement provided an impetus for nascent banks and encouraged foreign investment.[31]

Caballero, or whoever wrote his annual messages to Congress, was not reluctant to claim credit for the political calm prevailing in Paraguay.[32] On the surface, at least, there was scarcely a ripple. Decoud assured an English diplomat that there was no real opposition to the government, although a few malcontents in Congress criticized the regime for the sake of notoriety. In 1885, Caballero again noted that chaos had ended when the people became aware that their sacred rights would be protected, that justice would prevail, that the government would respect "the rights of the citizen within the inflexible orbit of the law." Progress, however slow, was evident. There were a few who looked for Utopia in a few days, who indulged in unprincipled propaganda to promote anarchy and to present the country "in the worst possible light."[33] This pointed reference to dissidents acknowledged the undercurrent of discontent which surfaced in such papers as *La Verdad Autógrafa*, in which "Prometeo" published acidulous editorials. A rival paper published equally exaggerated pieces praising Caballero for binding up the country's wounds, restoring vitality to commerce, and starting a stream of European immigration. Because of Caballero's immense popularity, this journalistic champion enthused, legal guarantees were meaningful and public powers worked in entire harmony.[34]

In his last message to Congress, Caballero ignored the political unrest seething in Asunción, Villa Rica, and the smaller towns. He found the country peaceful, the heat of political campaigns dissipated, and citizens working devotedly at tasks that would "place them in the best position to exercise freely their duties and rights in democratic life." Apparently oblivious to the irony of his words, he could say: "I have always believed that revolutions are justified only when their objective is the vindication of the trampled rights of a people." The revolution of 1873–1874, by inference, had "unanimous sympathy for a holy cause" and must not be confused with disturbances whose authors arrogantly identified patriotism and good government with their own advancement. He warned against seeking violent solutions to problems that required long periods of peace to resolve. As long as freedom of the press, of assembly and of suffrage existed, there would never be reason for extreme measures. He condemned electoral frauds as abominable and odious crimes that could end only in anarchy and despotism.[35] Caballero surely knew how the corruption, electoral frauds, and violence that he tolerated made a mockery of these fine sentiments. Inclusion of such sentiments in the annual message again leads one to believe that it was Decoud who was the author.

Caballero's praises followed him out of office as Colorado editors poured out columns of uncritical acclaim. False prosperity induced by land sales continued into the first months of Escobar's administration, and the official press constantly attributed the apparent well-being and political calm to the wisdom of Caballero. Newspapers in Montevideo and Buenos Aires echoed the same theme even while the political truce was coming to a violent end.[36] Beneficiaries of Caballero's coloradismo did not know it, but the Pax Caballero was dead.

5

Escobar and Party Formation, 1886–1890

Contemporaries regarded Escobar's presidency as a continuation of caballerismo. Policies and programs begun under Caballero were continued, financed by sales of the public domain. Economic prosperity, however, eluded the Colorados. The country lacked financial institutions that could withstand natural disasters. Dependent upon Platine markets and Argentine tariff policies, Paraguay's foreign trade was exceptionally vulnerable to economic fluctuations abroad. These conditions, coupled with the vagaries of nature, caused Escobar's term to end in depression and widespread misery.

Efforts by the Colorados to maintain a one-party government were completely unrealistic. Emergence of fairly cohesive political groups was apparent in the postwar decade, although *personalismo* rather than well defined political philosophies served to attract followers. Caballero, through brazen control of elections, had caused widespread opposition that inevitably would shatter the apparent political unity of coloradismo. Formal organization of the two major political parties was the most significant event during Escobar's tenure. Neither party had a disciplined core of supporters, but Colorados controlled the armed forces, the police, and government at all levels. Even with this powerful advantage, they could not prevent organization of an opposition party that eventually would drive them from power. A brief attempt to form a coalition slate in 1890 ended in mutual recrimination. When Escobar left office, political peace was as elusive as the goddess Yací whose refuge was the waning moon.

Heir to Caballero

Caballero had no doubt about the man he wanted to follow him in the presidency. It would be General Patricio Escobar, a brave, battle-scarred veteran who wanted nothing more than to spend the rest of his life accumulating enough wealth to live comfortably. By no means a blind follower of Caballero, Escobar agreed with considerable reluctance to become president, "the second link in forging the hegemony of caballerismo."[1] Unpretentious and with no apparent political qualifications, Escobar was greatly underrated. Dr. William Stewart, who knew him well, is supposed to have said that Escobar was so ignorant that he could not explain himself in any language, not even Guaraní.[2] Though certainly not loquacious, Escobar could and did express himself clearly and forcefully.

Patricio Escobar, generally pictured as the ever faithful companion of Caballero, was born on March 17, 1843, in San José, some 110 kilometers east of Asunción. Recruited as a private in the army in 1865, he rose through the ranks to become a colonel. He fought in many battles, was wounded frequently, and remained loyal to the marshal-president. It was Escobar who assembled the remnants of Paraguay's army after the disastrous defeats of late 1868. He continued to fight through the last battles, during which he suffered several more wounds. Captured by the Brazilians at Cerro Corá, he was one of the prominent officers whom the victors sent to Rio de Janeiro. Like Caballero and Centurión, he was much too prominent to be left in Paraguay while the Allies were setting up a puppet regime.[3]

Escobar was astute, cunning, crafty, and reticent, attributes that made him a master plotter and conspirator. He was an excellent judge of men, made no promises he could not keep, and kept those that he made. Less charismatic than Caballero, still he inspired loyalty and confidence among his followers. Like so many of his contemporaries, Escobar fathered numerous progeny. His wife, Ignacia Garcete, gave birth to nine sons, one of whom, Patricio Alejandrino, incurred the wrath of President Escurra in 1902 by joining an attempted revolt. Alejandrino eventually became a general.

Stern of visage and noble in bearing, Escobar possessed a natural dignity that set him apart as a man of importance. He was judicious and exercised remarkable self-control in the face of the most trying circumstances. Foreign diplomats credited him with being much more intelligent than Caballero, whom he supported and to whom he gave excellent advice. Much of the wisdom attributed to Caballero was pure Escobar, and both generals had the good sense to listen to such sage advisers as Centurión and Decoud.

The vice-presidential candidate, José del Rosario Miranda, had held important political posts. Born in Barrero Grande in 1832, he had an indifferent education. He, too, was a veteran of the Paraguayan War from which he emerged with the rank of major. The postwar Triumvirate made him jefe político of Caraguatay in 1869, and a year later that district sent him to the constituent convention that drafted the constitution of 1870. A member of the Gran Club del Pueblo, he had the skill and personality to attract support in the convention from both factions that contended for leadership. He was a good if not brilliant orator whose words commanded attention and caused him to be elected president of the convention. Unfortunately, he lacked the qualities necessary to maintain political leadership, but he was a capable subordinate. The Brazilian chargé judged him to be "indecisive and timid," a compliant man who would serve Escobar faithfully.[4] At various times he had served as president of the Superior Tribunal of Justice, minister of war and marine, minister of foreign affairs, deputy in Congress, minister to the Holy See, and was an organizer of the Club del Pueblo formed in 1885 to ensure Escobar's election. When Benjamín Aceval refused the vice-presidential nomination, Miranda accepted the post. And at the end of the presidential term in 1890, he entered the Senate where he served until 1896, then returned to Caraguatay where he died in 1903.[5]

Leaving nothing to chance, Caballero had a group called the Club del Pueblo formed in 1885 to support Escobar and Miranda. Among the members of this organization were men who within two years would form the Liberal party: Benjamín Aceval, Cecilio Báez, José María Fretes, Ignacio Ibarra, and many others. There was some objection to Escobar. José de la Cruz Ayala, the famous and revered "Alón" who was then editor of *El Heraldo*, and Héctor Francisco Decoud refused to support the Colorado candidates. In order to quiet Alón, Caballero had him drafted into the army, sent to the Chaco, and later exiled. This clumsy act of oppression cost the Colorados the support of many young intellectuals. The club held a mass meeting in the theater on July 26, 1885, and unanimously nominated Escobar and Miranda.[6] They were, of course, elected in September 1886, fraudulently, but nevertheless elected.

Promises and Achievements

Fine promises abounded in Escobar's inaugural address in November. His program included equitable distribution of the tax burden, careful use of revenues, aid to commerce, promotion of public works, and the creation of higher educational institutions for agriculture, the arts, and business. Aware that agriculture was the principal source of Paraguay's wealth, he would encourage its development and bring in immigrants to establish agricultural colonies. He would combat vagrancy and banditry, and seek a new penitentiary where criminals could be rehabilitated and returned to society as useful citizens. In foreign relations he would promote good relations with Bolivia.

Except for Benjamín Aceval as minister of foreign affairs, Escobar's cabinet inspired no confidence. Manuel A. Maciel, minister of justice, was reasonably competent; Juan Alberto Meza, minister of interior, had been involved in Rivarola's murder; Agustín Cañete in hacienda and Pedro Duarte as minister of war and marine were the cabinet's strong men and widely recognized as Caballero's henchmen. Escobar's cabinet appointments were generally so unpopular that the observant Brazilian chargé surmised that Caballero had dictated them in order to maintain a large measure of control, and expected Escobar to assert himself in due time.[7]

A brief review of events under Escobar will show him to have been a fairly good president. The two rival parties, Centro Democrático (Liberal) and the Asociación Nacional Republicana (Colorado) were organized formally without government interference. The small army, fully obedient to Caballero and Escobar, temporarily suspended harassment of Liberals. Greatest of all cultural events was opening the National University on December 31, 1889, with schools of law, medicine, and social sciences. A Superior Council of Education was created to oversee schools throughout the country. A law of September 21, 1887, established the National Library and Museum. Continuing the policy of promoting private investment, huge blocks of land in the Chaco were sold, especially to Carlos Casado del Alisal of Argentina, whose company flourished until the mid twentieth century. Proceeds from such sales were to go into public works, especially for extending the Paraguay Central Railway and for completing the Government (or López) Palace and the Oratorio de la Asunción, popularly called the Panteón Nacional, the National Theater, now the Municipal Theater, the Charity Hospital, and for repairing the cavalry barracks which became the present Escuela Militar.

The administration's experience in banking and finance were less than notable, although four banks began their shaky careers.[8] The view from Buenos Aires was favorable, as conservative papers praised railway construction, promotion of immigration, organization of banks, and increased opportunities for foreign capital.[9] The Argentine papers obviously were reflecting the report of Paraguay's minister of interior who in 1888 wrote that everything was calm, all laws were being obeyed, and "all persons without any exception may live on Paraguayan soil, protected by the guarantees provided for them by the Constitution."[10] A deepening economic crisis soon made a mockery of these claims as intensified political warfare reflected decreasing prosperity. Whether because of his government's achievements or as a gesture of friendship, the Provisional Government of Brazil bestowed the Grand Cross of the Order of the Cruzeiro on Escobar on January 4, 1890.[11]

A measure of Escobar's strength was his toleration of bitter and even vile journalistic criticism. Héctor F. Decoud in April 1884 founded *El Heraldo*,[12] a paper much more restrained than *El Látigo Inmortal* and *La Verdad Autógrafa* whose shrill accusations were countered by *La Democracia*, which was by no means subservient to the Colorados, and by *El Paraguayo*. In reviewing Escobar's first year, *El Látigo* charged that electoral frauds had been committed with official approval, that public lands had been squandered by Cañete—the same old Caballero practices.[13] *La Cotorra* showed no restraint as it asserted that Juan G. González and José Segundo Decoud were openly buying support for the election to be held early in 1888. The entire public administration, *La Cotorra* screamed, was corrupt, especially the judges who should be driving thieves from the public treasury and removing muggers and assassins from the streets. The editor called the respected Báez a charlatan, the president of the Superior Tribunal of Justice a nobody, and Agustín Cañete a great thief.[14] After the organization of political parties, *El Látigo* charged that Caballero's circle was composed of gauchos pretending to be politicians, sycophants who were supported by the worst elements of society. The editor, Plácido Casaús (or Casajús), wrote sarcastically: "They raise Don 2° to the skies: the foremost intelligence, the first Paraguayan, and they forget what is most important, the first Brazilian Sergeant, perhaps the first Paraguayan traitor."[15] As the United States was to learn, this maligned official was a first-rate diplomatist.

Resurrection and Death of the Hopkins Claim

Paraguay's principal business with the United States during the Colorado era was concerned with the old Hopkins claim and the "Case of the Missing Jewels," which were effectively disposed of during Escobar's term. The Hopkins claim originated in confiscation by Carlos Antonio López of property owned by the United States and Paraguay Navigation Company, of which Hopkins had been the principal mover with the backing of daring but gullible New England capitalists. Hopkins was also U.S. consul in Paraguay. A resourceful entrepreneur who later had much to do with public works in Argentina, he had the ability but not the temperament to make a great success of his various enterprises in Paraguay—provided, of course, that López would have permitted such competition with the state. Outrageously brash and arrogant, Hopkins caused the company to lose its entire investment in the Paraguayan venture.[16] To be rid of Hopkins, López canceled his exequatur and expelled him from the country.

The irascible Hopkins fumed and fussed for more than thirty

years, during which he constantly annoyed American officials with his wildly exaggerated claims. For a short time, fate appeared to be on his side. Lieutenant Thomas Jefferson Page, commanding an exploring expedition of the Plata River system, had sent the small *Water Witch* into the Paraná where it sailed too close to the Paraguayan shore and was fired on by a coastal battery on February 1, 1855. The helmsman was killed,[17] so both Hopkins and the United States had claims against Paraguay.

After López had shown little inclination to settle the claims, President Buchanan sent a naval expedition that eventually assembled twenty-three craft, some of which could barely stay afloat, to chastise Paraguay in 1858–1859. Judge James B. Bowlin was the commissioner with powers to treat with López. The Argentine caudillo, Justo José Urquiza, was president of the Argentine Confederation, which did not include Buenos Aires city and province. Military operations involving Paraguay and the northern part of the confederation might weaken Urquiza's hold, so he made a hasty trip to Asunción and persuaded López to be reasonable. Unknown to Bowlin, Hopkins, or apparently anyone other than López, Bowlin's secretary, the urbane, genteel, and devious Sam Ward, betrayed the mission by accepting a bribe from López. Some of the fleet proceeded as far as Corrientes, where Bowlin left it while he continued on to Asunción. After much discussion, Bowlin and López signed an agreement by which Paraguay agreed to settle the *Water Witch* affair for a payment of $10,000 and to submit the Hopkins claim to arbitration. Bowlin's instructions had been to obtain an indemnity, but the arbitration route seemed more acceptable. Hopkins's company was claiming $935,000, an utterly absurd figure that was probably between five and ten times the damages actually suffered. Although López was willing to settle for $250,000, Sam Ward persuaded him to submit the claim to arbitration. Ward, of course, was not doing this for nothing. The arbitration in 1860 resulted in an award that outraged Hopkins: Paraguay owed the company nothing![18]

President Buchanan refused to proclaim the decision because the arbitral commission had decided a question not submitted to it. The question was *how much* Paraguay owed the company, and not *if* it was liable for damages. This was, indeed, splitting hairs to micron dimensions. When Charles Ames Washburn went to Paraguay as U.S. commissioner in 1861, he tried unsuccessfully to reopen the case. Neither the elder López nor his son would consider the claim. There the dispute rested until Secretary of State Thomas F. Bayard instructed Judge John E. Bacon, American minister to Uruguay and Paraguay, to discuss the matter with José Segundo Decoud.[19] By this time Hopkins had the nerve to ask for $1 million, although he was willing to accept one-tenth of that amount. Bacon believed that Hopkins had a good case, but Decoud presented a counterclaim against which he had little defense.

Many foreigners had deposited jewels, specie, and other valuables with Washburn for safekeeping during the Paraguayan War. When Washburn escaped from Asunción with a naval escort from the USS *Wasp*, some of the valuables were left in a box in the legation. Amazingly, the box escaped the looting by Allied soldiers and eventually was sent to Rio de Janeiro where it was delivered to the American minister, James H. Partridge. An inventory showed $19,488 in hard cash and a considerable amount of jewelry.[20] Although owners of the valuables tried as early as 1870 to recover their property, they received no satisfaction from the United States. Decoud had raised the question with various American representatives, beginning with John C. Caldwell in 1881.[21] Caldwell ignored Decoud's inquiries. His successor, William Williams, started a search for the missing box, which eventually was traced from Rio de Janeiro to a Washington attic. When it was found in February 1884, it contained only a few worthless trinkets.[22] Partridge might have been able to tell what had happened to the contents had he not committed suicide soon after the discovery. Judge Bacon, therefore, had a difficult time with Decoud, who always raised the question of the missing jewels whenever the Hopkins claim was mentioned. Bacon had more success with Benjamín Aceval, Decoud's successor as minister of foreign affairs, who agreed that Paraguay should pay Hopkins $90,000 in gold. When Bacon arrived with Hopkins to accept the arrangement, the Brazilian minister thought it might be a good time to press for payment of the *polizas* (indemnification certificates) granted to citizens of Mato Grosso for war damages.[23] Although the Paraguayan Senate approved the Bacon-Aceval protocol, the Chamber of Deputies insisted that the United States make restitution for the missing jewels before considering any payment to Hopkins.

The delay in Congress infuriated Hopkins, whose postwar business ventures in Paraguay added to his disappointment. He demanded that the United States send a gunboat to Asunción to collect $200,000 in gold.[24] One has to question his good sense, if not his sanity. The whole sad business, from the expulsion of Hopkins, to the Bowlin expedition, to arbitration, to reopening the claim, had become a cause célèbre in Paraguay and no government could afford to bow before pressure from the United States. The missing box was finally sent to Montevideo in April 1888. There it rested in a bank for many years. Bacon did succeed in persuading Paraguay to try again for the $90,000 but Congress ignored the claim and that ended the matter. And the jewel box? Not until March 1926 was the nearly empty but famous box delivered to Asunción and into the custody of

U.S. Minister George L. Kreeck, who quickly turned it over to the Paraguayan government, thus ending the case of the missing jewels,[25] but the jewels are still missing.

It is apparent that U.S.-Paraguayan relations were not especially critical during the Colorado era, however annoying picayunish matters might be, like the attempt of a syndicate to collect on the worthless polizas. Somehow an American in Mato Grosso had been persuaded to acquire twenty-nine of the polizas with a face value of more than $542,000 which had grown to $1,079,862 by 1889 through compounding of unpaid interest. The American buyer was able to get rid of them to a syndicate of gullible investors in New York. Members of the syndicate included General W. W. Dudley, member of the legal firm of Dudley and Michener, Albert C. Cheney and his brother George, and two or three others whose anonymity should, in all charity, be protected. Referring to these "indemnity bonds," Albert Cheney, as trustee and for himself, asked Dudley's firm to try to collect.[26] The syndicate fared no better than did Hopkins. Far more important to the Escobar administration was the formal organization of political parties.

Factional Rivalries

Creation of the Caballero-Escobar military dictatorship, however benign it might be, caused deep disappointment among Liberals, many of whom had supported Godoi's quixotic revolt of 1879. There were no formal party organizations, but the terms *Colorado* and *lopizta* were practically synonymous, as were *Azul* and *Liberal*. The legionarios who had fought with the Allies were not necessarily liberal in attitude or philosophy. Many were simply personal enemies of López, and so it is not surprising to find many of them supporting caballerismo. Indeed, personalities rather than principles generally determined Paraguayan political alignment.

The two groups could agree on many points. Paraguay needed immigrants, a sound financial system, increased commerce, greater exploitation of its natural resources, internal peace and better law enforcement, more roads and bridges, an improved railway, nationwide telegraphic communication. An adequate school system, from the lowest grades to advanced technical and professional institutions, needed to be created, although a beginning had been made. There were some in both camps who opposed the sale of public lands for a pittance and the creation of huge holdings, especially in the Chaco, in the north of eastern Paraguay, and in the yerbales. Although they were vociferous in condemning Colorado land policy, they did little to reverse it when they won the chance in 1904.

Carlos Pastore, Paraguay's brilliant agricultural economist, sees party formation has having been hastened by the Colorado land sales that alienated large areas of public domain and aroused the opposition of intellectuals, campesinos, small merchants, and many cattle ranchers. Among the intellectuals were many young graduates of the Colegio Nacional, founded in 1878. Some of them became Colorados, others found employment as agents of foreign capitalists, and most of them became Liberals who repudiated the colonial economic system that appeared in new form under caballerismo. The ultimate prize of political victory was control of the land.[27]

Epifanio Méndez Fleitas, a dissident Colorado exiled by the dictatorial Stroessner regime during the second Colorado era (1954–) attempts to apply the Hegelian thesis—antithesis—thesis formula to Paraguayan politics. To this leader of the Movimiento Popular Colorado (MOPOCO), "coloradismo . . . is a reply to the historical-biological need derived from the war of 1865–70, as an *organ* of reconstruction and liberation of the country."[28] There was only one party, one ideology, and Cándido Bareiro was the precursor of its formalization. Benigno Ferreira, the legionario driven into exile after the revolts of 1873–1874, was an aberration far removed from the mainstream of Paraguayan life. Aberrations, too, were those who sold out to foreign powers, and those—including Alfredo Stroessner—whose iniquities, Méndez Fleitas insists, betray pristine coloradismo.

Caballero and Escobar certainly did not anticipate the philosophy of Méndez Fleitas, that coloradismo embodied or embraced all Paraguayan political ideology. They were men of action who would brook no opposition in Congress or at the polls. Their ideal of a monolithic state was difficult to realize in Paraguay, and stirrings of discontent occurred early in the Colorado era. Formerly regarded as stalwart caballeristas, three deputies in Congress unexpectedly broke the political truce on October 25, 1885. The minister of hacienda, Juan de la Cruz Giménez, was giving a report so contradictory and confused that Antonio Taboada began to ask embarrassing questions. Taboada's antecedents were impeccable. Son of a *convencional* (a member of the constitutional convention of 1870), born in Villa Rica on November 26, 1848, he entered the army in 1864 and had the good fortune to be captured with Colonel Antonio de la Cruz Estigarribia at Uruguayana. After the war he belonged briefly to the original Club del Pueblo to challenge the actions of Brazil's José Maria da Silva Paranhos, then helped to found the Gran Club del Pueblo. He served honorably under the Triumvirate and Rivarola, was a deputy in 1871, took part in the Tacuaral revolt of 1871 and in the Bareiro-Caballero revolts of 1873–1874. He became military commandant and jefe político of Villa Rica. A founder of the Club Libertad to support Caballero, he remained faithful and helped to found the renovated Club del Pueblo to elect Escobar. Sent to Congress from Villa Rica, he proved his independence and courage by calling the minister of hacienda an embezzler. Debate in Congress was furious when Taboada attacked Giménez. Among the deputies who supported Taboada were Ignacio Ibarra, editor of *La Democracia*, and José María Fretes. These deputies were on the parliamentary committee appointed to investigate Taboada's charges. Not for years had there been such a good show in Congress! Rowdy Colorado partisans packed the galleries on November 8 when questioning resumed, with two stalwart Colorados, José Segundo Decoud and Juan Gualberto González, defending Giménez.[29]

Factional rivalries were intensified preceding the congressional elections of February 1887. In Villa Rica, several prominent men formed the anti-Caballero Club Popular in December 1886. Marcelino Rodas, its president, Bernardino Rodón, and Antonio Taboada were its leaders. Rodas, also a veteran of the war, was a self-educated, self-made man who delighted in sartorial elegance. A large gold chain across his vest set off his summer whites and his somber winter garb. Some accounts attribute to him the choice of a blue kerchief as the Liberal symbol.[30] Colorados named Bernardino Caballero and Claudio Gorostiaga as candidates for the posts of senator and deputy from Villa Rica. To oppose this official slate, the Club Popular on December 16 nominated Esteban Gorostiaga and Antonio Taboada.

Both factions prepared for the election of February 13, 1887, which proved to be more corrupt than usual. In Villa Rica, troops and armed civilian caballeristas prevented their rivals from registering. Finally, the election was postponed because the justice of the peace, who was to conduct it, prudently went into hiding.[31] An Argentine traveler described the scene with a touch of humor: "Some elections were going on in the orthodox fashion and the police were galloping about all the time, armed with knives, swords, and revolvers: this intimidation, the reason for which I could not fathom as there is no female suffrage here and the only men I saw were policemen or foreigners. The Guyrenos [people of Villa Rica] frightened out of their wits, had barred their doors, and the town looked like a city of the dead."[32]

El Paraguayo, a progovernment paper, gloated over success in the February election. The "Lilliputian (read liberal)" party had lost everywhere, and the future was bright for the country. Caballero and Decoud were content with humble posts in Congress. Continuing in this vein, the editor pontificated: "There are two parties—one stands for good government and progressive development of commerce and industry, and seeks the rule of liberty as the secure base for social order. This is the Gran Partido Nacional, which, having overthrown a corrupt regime, has introduced progress and civilization." As to its opposition, the "flamante partido liberal" (upstart Liberal party) was made up only of self-seeking men. "Here we have the two parties; the one carries painted on its banner the winged horse of progress and the other the opposite symbol—THAT OF THE CRAB!!!"[33] The Gran Partido Nacional won without having to resort to bayonets and guns as did the "flamante partido liberal." It is a lie, *El Paraguayo* insisted brazenly, that Colorados won by the use of force. Did not henchmen of Esteban Gorostiaga and Taboada drive caballeristas from the polls in Villa Rica? Did not Liberals show up everywhere armed to the teeth? Where Liberals controlled the polls, they were guilty of outrageous frauds: Villeta returned 837 votes, more than its total male population; Villa Oliva had twenty-five qualified voters who cast 375 votes. Caballeristas admitted that eleven Liberal deputies had been elected but they refused to take their seats and forced a congressional investigation. The Committee on Elections made a scathing report, calling attention particularly to fraud in Luque, Villeta, San Lorenzo de la Frontera, and Limpio.[34] Since none of the election returns have been preserved, there is no way to check the accuracy of these charges. One may safely assume, however, that Liberals were no paragons of virtue during the election.

When Congress convened on April 1, 1887, the Gran Partido Nacional had a clear majority in the Senate. Four deputies remained to be certified or elected, including one from Villa Rica. The twenty-two certified deputies were evenly split between caballeristas and Liberals. Control of the Chamber of Deputies was crucial, since Escobar had defied Caballero by appointing two Liberals to his cabinet. If caballeristas won the Chamber, then Congress would do nothing until Escobar removed the two Liberals.[35] The Committee on Elections, controlled by caballeristas, certified the election of three Colorados to the disputed seats. Liberals decided that it was time to organize.

Formal Party Organization

The name Gran Partido Nacional was popularly used to include the caballeristas, or Colorados, and their opponents usually were referred to as Liberals, or the Liberal party. Neither group had a formal organization, a situation that changed quickly after the particularly violent election in Villa Rica, which had been postponed to June 22, 1887. In an asinine display of violence, government troops fired on voters, effectively driving Liberals from the polls. Many Liberals were arrested and then forced to ride to Paraguarí to take the train to Asunción where Colorados intended to throw them into jail. When the train stopped at Luque, crowds loaded the coaches with flowers. Widespread resentment against Escobar and Caballero soon won release for the prisoners, and the outraged Liberals prepared to formalize their association. Antonio Taboada called a group of forty friends to meet at his home in Asunción on July 2. This group called another and larger meeting for July 10 when 134 Liberals met and organized the Centro Democrático, which was to be the official name of the Liberal party until 1894.[36]

Members approved party statutes on July 24 and elected officers: Antonio Taboada, president; Pedro V. Gill, vice-president; José de la Cruz Ayala, secretary; and a board of directors which included Cecilio Báez, the party's leading theoretician. Many young intellectuals rallied to the party, and it is notable that not one legionario was among them. Many were veterans and at least one, José María Carillo, was a descendant of Carlos Antonio López; another was Eduardo Vera, aide to one of the war's great heroes, General Eduvigis Díaz.[37]

The founding of the Centro Democrático caused alarm in government circles. Its avowed purposes were to oppose big government and to protect the liberties guaranteed by the constitution of 1870, which included sanctity of elections. La Nación, a Colorado organ, scoffed at the idea of 32,447 literate Paraguayans out of a population of 199,431 being able to operate a democratic government. These specific figures are utterly amazing in view of the plain fact that Paraguay had never had an accurate census of any kind. As if frightened by ghosts of ages past, Colorado leaders moved quickly to formalize their own organization. Villa Rica is honored as the birthplace of the Liberal party; the Colorados selected Paraguarí. Several Colorados, prominent officials in the government and their supporters, met at General Caballero's home on August 25, 1887. The prominence of these leaders, La Nación editorialized smugly, gave assurance that the new center "would be under the sacred auspices of the liberty established by the laws and the Constitution."[38]

José Segundo Decoud and Juan Crisóstomo Centurión were the leading intellectuals among ninety-four men who signed the declaration that "they were resolved to form a political group for the praiseworthy object of concerning themselves seriously with all questions of political interest that might promote the prosperity and happiness of the country, and to propose measures to secure the public liberties sanctified by the fundamental charter of the country." A committee headed by Decoud and Centurión formulated the party's principles, which some two hundred men signed at the second meeting on September 2.[39] Among this group of lopiztas and antilopiztas were twenty-three former legionarios. Any attempt to equate Liberals with treason to Paraguay is ridiculous, but even today Colorados continue to wave this badly tattered and faded "bloody shirt." Organized as the Asociación Nacional Republicana, the new group was simply the old Partido Nacional, the amorphous Colorado party. Everyone was invited to the formal organization exercises held at the

Teatro Olimpo in Asunción on September 11. Caballero, of course, was the unanimous choice for president of the party.[40]

The newly organized Centro Democrático and Asociación Nacional Republicana rapidly attracted members. Political passions resulted in bloody clashes between Colorados and Liberals, even during the annual pilgrimage to the shrine of the Virgin of Caacupé on December 8. These disturbances annoyed Escobar, as did the questions from José Segundo Decoud, president of the Permanent Commission. Decoud made pointed inquiries about political warfare, the absurd Lynch land claims, (see chapter 12) the Bolivian port at Puerto Pacheco, and Argentine threats to increase tariff duties on Paraguayan yerba and tobacco. Escobar silenced Decoud at the end of 1887 by making him minister of foreign affairs to replace the Liberal Benjamín Aceval. At the same time Higinio Uriarte became minister of hacienda.[41] A correspondent reported that Paraguay's ignorant presidents, especially Caballero and Escobar, desperately needed the services of this "combination of Figaro and Bismarck," but despaired of the future so long as Meza and Cañete were active in the government.[42] Decoud, recognized as a possible presidential candidate, despised his colleague Colonel Meza, also a presidential aspirant. Escobar solved this problem in 1888 by replacing Decoud with Centurión, "a prudent man of conciliatory spirit."[43]

Gestures toward Coalition

Even by Paraguayan standards, the political campaign of 1888 was especially dirty. The literate population had plenty of newspapers to read, some of which warranted the highest award for irresponsible journalism. After Liberals formed the Centro Democrático, they published *El Independiente* which, while notoriously partisan, was more restrained than *El Látigo Inmortal* and *La Nación*, whose editors excelled in the use of invective. *La Nación* reviewed the list of Liberals and found that many were unemployed former officials, aspirants rejected for office, or ungrateful recipients of Caballero's favors, and predicted that the Centro, having no program, would vanish like a soap bubble.[44] Taking up the challenge, *El Látigo* insisted that the Centro was a reasonable, peaceful group that simply wanted to let everyone know what a rotten government Paraguayans endured and to remind them of their rights. In issue after issue, *El Látigo* praised the Centro Democrático for upholding constitutional rights and challenging the thieving Colorados whose ostensible leaders were puppets in the hands of José Segundo Decoud.[45]

Elections at the end of 1888 in Asunción certainly verified *El Látigo*'s wildest charges of fraud at the polls. The newly organized Liberals put up two candidates for senator and two for deputy. Registration was set for December 23, and Colorados used every device to ensure a Liberal defeat. Much to the astonishment of Colorados, some fifteen hundred defiant Liberals had gathered by 8:30 A.M. near the Church of the Encarnación to register. Colorados rushed in from other precincts to register but were denied access to the polls, which were surrounded by Liberals. Police then arrived, armed with Winchesters and Remingtons, and dispersed the Liberals with gunfire that killed four and wounded thirty-seven, while sixty-eight were marched off to jail. Mounted police, sabers in hand, chased fleeing Liberals through the streets. A Colorado candidate, Colonel Manuel Maciel, withdrew from the race to protest his party's violence.[46] All the Liberals could do was to return to their bitter journalistic warfare, prepare for an eventual revolution, or seek to form a coalition with the Colorados. As El Látigo remarked on January 1, 1889, "año nuevo, vida nueva." Part of the "new life" was highlighted on January 4 when a fire of unknown origin consumed the Church of the Encarnación.

The Centro Democrático lacked the military strength needed to challenge the Colorados successfully, but they could and did cause a distressing amount of turmoil. Colorado leaders did not relish continued violent confrontations that would seriously disrupt their program of land sales, negotiations with Bolivia, and the promising prosperity of such enterprises as La Industrial Paraguaya (see chapter 13). If the economic crisis of 1889 were to be dealt with successfully, a costly revolution must be avoided. Conciliation, therefore, appealed to both parties. Perhaps Taboada and Caballero individually or jointly urged the nonpolitical and highly respected Otoniel Peña to suggest conciliation. Perhaps Peña was representing the consensus of businessmen when in September 1889 he suggested that Colorados and Liberals eschew political warfare for the good of Paraguay. Caballero replied favorably. Taboada, recognizing the need for harmony during the critical economic situation, agreed but insisted that political parties were necessary to prevent the rise of despotism.[47]

Confronted by the undeniable fact of Colorado superiority and control of government forces, Liberal leaders agreed that in the election of September 1890 the presidential candidate would be a Colorado and the vice-presidential candidate a Liberal.[48] After lengthy discussions, the Comisión Directiva of each party agreed that Juan Gualberto González and Victor M. Soler would be the candidates, political offices would be distributed evenly, and a coalition ministry appointed. Opposition papers called the proposed coalition a big mistake, while the Colorado La Nación hailed the agreement and praised the Liberal manifesto which stated: "Revolution, in truth, is the recourse of people against intolerable situations, but it is neither the only nor the best way to conduct public affairs and to reestablish political and administrative morality."[49]

Taboada, too clever a politician to be deceived by the Colorados, kept in touch with Juan Silvano Godoi and Benigno Ferreira in Buenos Aires. Conciliation, he wrote, would be very advantageous for the Liberals but "everything depends on the good faith of the men of the opposite party."[50] Liberals might well have heeded the strident warnings of *El Látigo* which summoned good Paraguayans to oppose the Colorado tyranny that had destroyed law and morality. Mounting a screaming attack in type and cartoons, the paper charged Colorados, and especially Caballero, with corruption, thievery, oppression, and murder.[51]

As predicted by its opponents, the unstable coalition soon dissolved. When Liberal voters attempted to register at the cathedral on January 1, 1890, machete-wielding soldiers and municipal employees met them. Col. Juan Antonio Jara, jefe político of the capital, arrived at 9:30 A.M. and restored order. Apparently he did not know that the mayor of Asunción had ordered the attack. President Escobar promptly proclaimed his innocence. *El Látigo* lashed out furiously at the perfidious Colorados, comparing El Gaucho (Caballero) with the barbarous Guaycurus of the Chaco whose promises were nothing but a cover for treachery.[52] After several weeks of fruitless political maneuvering, Soler withdrew from the race on March 31. A week later, on Sunday, April 6, more than eight hundred Colorados met at Caballero's home to replace Soler and to answer Taboada's justified denunciation. Taboada called attention to Colorado violation of the Pact of Conciliation, both in Asunción and rural areas, which demonstrated their faithlessness, contempt for the constitution, and devotion to dictatorial methods. These were the crimes that had caused formation of the Centro Democrático in 1887 and which now ended the political truce and caused large numbers of Liberals to flee to neighboring countries. Freedom, Taboada proclaimed, had died during Escobar's presidency, administrative corruption had spread throughout the government, and Paraguayans had been reduced to despicable servilism.[53]

The Sunday gathering at Caballero's *quinta* (country home) accepted Soler's resignation, named Senator Rosendo Carísimo as vice-presidential candidate, and adopted a reply to the Liberals which was issued over Caballero's name. The Colorados in turn accused the Liberals of faithlessness, with never having intended to honor the pact, and blamed the Centro Democrático for the resumption of political warfare. The Centro replied with a refutation of Colorado allegations which showed the impossibility of reconciliation.[54]

Aware of the threat of revolution, President Escobar in his message to Congress gave Paraguayans a lesson in political science. Either Decoud or Centurión was probably the author, since the presidential message revealed a breadth of knowledge never associated with Escobar. Revolution, the message asserted, was justified as a means for a people to recover liberties suppressed by despotic rule. A nonviolent revolution which restores such rights is an illustration of human nature operating at the highest level, but seditious movements and insurrections are the efforts of ignorant and vulgar people who seek in violence the remedy for their complaints and realization of personal ambition. Since government belongs to all in a republic, the constitution offers ample room to exercise individual rights. Then, speaking directly to Paraguayans, he said: "A country . . . will never come to be completely free when its people are not industrious, when there is no spirit of initiative among them which brings together individual resources to carry out a useful enterprise, when little effort is devoted to the cultivation of mother earth to which is linked man's well-being—in a word, when they are not independent and expect everything from the largess of the government. There can be no liberty without independence, and there can be no independence without work, from which it follows that liberty is the legitimate daughter of work and enterprise."[55]

Escobar had reason to fear a revolution encouraged by Liberals who had fled to Argentina. Benigno Ferreira and Juan Silvano Godoi were cooperating with Liberals in Paraguay to cause a simultaneous uprising in several parts of the country. When a traitor or spy, identified as one of the Gondras, wrote to Escobar from Buenos Aires to warn him that a revolt was being prepared under Argentine protection, Centurión urged the Argentine minister of foreign affairs to be vigilant.[56] When Godoi learned that the Escobar government was bringing in arms and munitions, he sent an agent in an unsuccessful effort to hijack the shipment. By June 1890, while the economic situation worsened and trade all but ceased in Asunción, rumors of revolt had died down. Still Escobar took no chances. The shipment of munitions arrived safely and was used to arm an enlarged army and the steamer *Elena*, which was converted to a warship.[57] A conspirator gloated that the new recruits were all Liberals who would fade away into the first forest they came to if sent into the field. Nevertheless, early betrayal of their plans caused Liberals to delay the revolt, and Escobar made a big show of not believing the reports of various spies.[58]

Colorados were by no means unanimously in favor of Juan Gualberto González, and Carísimo lacked enthusiasm for the vice-presidential post. Dissident Colorados preferred Colonel Juan Alberto Meza as head of the ticket. When Meza announced his candidacy on July 12, Caballero and Escobar hosted a banquet at which they strongly endorsed the González-Carísimo slate, and in a published manifesto regretted efforts to split the party. After several conferences in August, Caballero persuaded Meza to withdraw. Rosendo Carísimo, however, refused to be a candidate so the Colorados replaced him with Marcos Morínigo.[59]

In the midst of this bickering, Her Majesty's minister to Argentina and Paraguay arrived to observe events. He was not favorably impressed: "It is really sad to listen to tales of dishonesty and peculation rampant in high places, although of course allowance must be made for exaggeration. Official laziness would also seem to be here carried to an extreme point, a shower of rain being enough to put a stop to all official proceedings." Nor was he especially cordial toward Centurión, "one of the most relentless of the 'fiscales' [prosecuting attorneys] of the deceased President López, and who sent many to torture and to death with apparently equal unconcern."[60] He regarded the political backbiting as a family quarrel, since both Meza and González were sons-in-law of Caballero.

Liberals boycotted the presidential election in September, so González and Morínigo faced no opposition. Caballero and Escobar maintained their popularity in the country, despite the economic stagnation and the threat of revolution. The next decade, however, would bring great changes as the pax Colorado disintegrated under the blows of factionalism and resumption of Argentine and Brazilian interference in domestic politics.

6

The Trials of González, 1890-1894

Juan Gualberto González presided precariously over a country whose economic problems appeared to be insurmountable. The quick flow of cash from land sales had ended, and such huge enterprises as Carlos Casado and La Industrial Paraguaya were in early stages of development. Natural disasters brought droughts, floods, and swarms of voracious locusts to discourage farmers. Immigration languished despite the founding of new colonies. The paper peso fluctuated widely, keeping gold at a high premium. Political factionalism doomed González to almost four years of frustration before Brazil financed the coup that sent him into exile.

Few presidents tried more earnestly than González to fulfill the inaugural oath. Desperately he tried to bring capable men into office; he organized a good cabinet, submitted needed reforms to Congress, and watched helplessly as all but one of the banks closed their doors. In the midst of political and economic troubles, Argentina raised its tariff on Paraguayan tobacco. The government had to default on external debt payments as commercial activities almost halted. However, there were positive factors at work that reflected renewed prosperity in Argentina. That country's excesses in paper money, foreign borrowing, unfavorable balance of trade, and wild land speculation had reached a climax in 1890. In Brazil, too, there was political and economic confusion. Paraguay's economic recovery was dependent upon events in its two great neighbors, and not until 1895 did the country appear to be moving toward relative prosperity.

Brave Beginnings

The usual pomp of a Te Deum in the cathedral, followed by parades, banquets, concerts, and dances in Asunción marked the inauguration of González and Morínigo on August 25, 1890. The cabinet appeared to be well chosen, balancing political factions and administrative ability. To José Tomás Sosa went the powerful post of interior; Dr. Venancio López, nephew of Francisco Solano and recently returned from Buenos Aires with a law degree, took over foreign affairs. This was a post that José Segundo Decoud should have had, but González put him in hacienda where he could struggle with the economic crisis. Dr. Benjamín Aceval headed justice, worship, and public instruction. The only military man in the cabinet, Col. Juan B. Egusquiza, became minister of war and marine. Appointments to the Superior Tribunal of Justice brought well qualified men to that important body.[1]

These appointments served notice that González was sincere in his desire for reconciliation of political factions, an impossible goal. What appeared to be a minor event revealed that factionalism would severely handicap the new administration. President Escobar had rewarded Juan Crisóstomo Centurión with the appointment as envoy to various European governments, but Centurión's Colorado enemies persuaded González to revoke the appointment, giving the state of the treasury as an excuse. A cut in the budget for pensions and salaries lent credence to the claim,[2] as did the persistent depression.

Decoud dealt promptly if ineffectively with the economic disaster. He had a program ready for Congress to consider before that august body of bemused politicians assembled. Most of the Decoud program centered on money and banking. The treasury needed metallic reserves, so customs duties must be paid in part in gold or its equivalent. To prevent wild fluctuations in the exchange rate, government would control that magic figure. To increase the circulating medium, Decoud wanted large issues of paper money, to be backed by mortgages, public lands, and the anticipated increase in gold reserves. To encourage agriculture, he proposed prizes for exceptional production and the construction of mills and factories to process raw materials.[3]

Decoud's program, which Congress approved in its entirety, could not cure Paraguay's multiple economic ills. Argentina had tried similar programs with disastrous results, and Decoud himself had formerly opposed such measures. His were inflationary moves that would result only in further economic decline. Tinkering with the customs reduced trade and promoted smuggling. Especially bad was the increase of duties on exports of yerba, tobacco, and hides.[4]

Paraguayans knew too little of history and very little of economics. Francia and Carlos Antonio López had accumulated gold stocks by selling surpluses abroad; private producers had been allowed to do the same thing on a limited scale. This is how the Paraguayan women acquired their stocks of beautiful gold jewelry and how the many *plateros* (jewelry makers) of Asunción acquired their raw materials. Gold could not be accumulated by government fiat.[5] Trade and production continued to lag, but the Paraguayans probably were more concerned with the congressional elections of 1893 and the following presidential election.

Liberal Revolts and Plots

González, plagued by chronic depression, also faced the constant threat of revolt by Liberals who were so outraged by systematic Colorado oppression that their leaders threatened to take up arms. The Brazilian minister sadly misjudged the Paraguayan political scene early in 1891. Reviewing conditions elsewhere in Latin America, he found only revolutions, plots, and rumors of impending revolts, while in Paraguay all was tranquil under a government that upheld the right of everyone to seek his own betterment.[6] Liberals had participated in the February 1891 elections; as usual Colorado terror and fraud at the polls defeated their candidates. At Ybicuí, José de la Cruz Ayala campaigned with an armed guard which a band of mounted Colorados ambushed. Many were killed or wounded in the attack. Ayala escaped to Argentina, where he died in 1893. Liberals outnumbered Colorados in many places but the Colorados used mobs and soldiers to disperse Liberal voters at Luque, Barrero Grande, Altos, Caazapá, and elsewhere. The jefe político led the mob that atacked Liberals in Ybicuí. No elections were held there nor in Quiquió since Colorados were in the minority.

Colorados showed amazingly little political acumen. Having permitted Liberals to elect two senators and three deputies, Congress refused to seat them and ordered new elections.[7] The outraged Liberals reacted with a manifesto that truthfully listed Colorado political and economic crimes: greedy men had ruined the country, freedom of suffrage was a joke, administration of justice was a mockery, public funds regularly enriched office holders, public lands had been squandered to enrich a few, jefes políticos were ignorant and arrogant, and farmers were being exploited.[8]

While González struggled with economic problems and Colorado factionalism, Liberals moved toward their first armed revolt. When Antonio Taboada, pleading weariness, resigned as party president on February 26, Maj. Eduardo Vera, the party's vice-president, succeeded him.[9] For many months the Liberal press attacked the Colorados. *La Democracia*, which had an unusually able staff of editors, joined the more strident *El Independiente* in providing publicity and opened its columns to Benigno Riquelme and other directors of the Centro Democrático as they rang the changes on Colorado corruption. When *La República* asserted that the Colorados did indeed have a national policy, *La Democracia* asked sarcastically if electoral fraud, criminal officials, economic disaster, and general malfeasance comprised such a policy.[10]

These attacks in the press were a planned prelude to revolt. Liberal leaders appointed a six-man revolutionary committee to do its planning. The supposedly tired Taboada undertook to marshal resources, including the steamer *Teniente Herreros;* Juan Bautista Rivarola was to gather arms for 700 men; Eduardo Vera and Pedro Pablo Caballero, nicknamed Caballerito, were to assemble recruits. If victorious, the rebels would establish a provisional government, order new presidential elections, and send Caballero, Escobar, and other Colorado leaders into exile.[11] Cecilio Báez wrote the manifesto for this first armed revolt by the Liberals. Recounting many cases of Colorado violence, the manifesto accused the situacionistas of gross mismanagement, thievery, cruelty, fraud, injustice, and usurpation of the government. Báez called the Colorados a "pandilla de caudillejos oscuros" (a gang of obscure, despicable caudillos) who had sold the country to foreigners, reduced Congress to a rubber stamp, and had corrupted the courts. Each Colorado president was indicted: Caballero was a usurper; Escobar had sold the Tacurupucú yerbales and had stolen the proceeds; and under González there was general misery while politicians looted the Banco Agrícola and depreciated the currency.[12]

The rebels planned carefully. Carbines and revolvers to arm upward of two hundred men were brought in and stored at the Resguardo, or customs guardhouse, an easy task since Rivarola was superintendent of customs. Small groups of men, who came discreetly from Villeta, Capiatá, and other country towns gathered at the homes of Taboada and Pedro Caballero. The revolt was to begin with attacks on the Resguardo and Capitanía (harbor-master's office) to obtain the weapons. These attackers would join 200 men under Vera who were to gather at the port and move on tram cars to assault the infantry and cavalry barracks. Pedro Caballero was to join this attack with 100 men, while Taboada waited in the Plaza Uruguaya with a reserve of 400 men. A score of rebels would attempt to seize Bernardino Caballero, then president of the Senate.[13]

Although the rebels fell far short of assembling the 700 men, their revolt began as planned at 7:00 P.M. on Sunday, October 18, 1891. President González had been warned but refused to believe that a rebellion was imminent. Bernardino Caballero took no chances and stationed a strong guard in his home, which drove off his would-be kidnappers. The rebels easily captured the Resguardo and Capitanía, then moved against the infantry and cavalry barracks. In each case most of the officers and men were absent on leave, but the remainder fought bravely despite the loss of their commanding officers. Major

Vera, hero of the Paraguayan War, and the young Liberal deputy Juan Pablo Machaín also died early in the fighting. Colonel Juan B. Egusquiza, minister of war, and Police Chief Juan A. Meza rallied loyal troops to repel the rebels. Fighting continued until about 4:00 P.M. on October 19. Completely routed, the rebels fled or attempted to hide. Several, including Cecilio Báez, took refuge in the Brazilian and Argentine legations; some escaped to the *Teniente Herreros* which took them to Formosa.[14]

Colorados crushed the revolt ruthlessly. González proclaimed a state of siege for thirty days, during which his police and soldiers captured 150 Liberals. Although jailed, most of the captives were treated leniently. All Liberals who held government posts were dismissed at once; the editors of opposition papers served short prison terms; and loyal troops dispersed rebel groups in rural areas.[15] Inclined to view the revolt lightly, an Argentine editor quickly changed his mind: "The Paraguayan Revolution was not such a nursery affair as at first supposed. There was a fight and several funerals after it."[16] There would be more funerals if the Colorados refused to change their ways drastically. Rumors of revolutionary plots, which continued for several months, assumed significance when a part of the infantry, protesting against bad treatment and lack of pay, mutinied on March 21, 1892. The mutineers were promptly jailed.[17] President González informed Congress that everything was under control and sternly lectured citizens who would disturb the peace while serious economic crises gripped the country.[18]

The president's lecture, ably seconded by editorials in *La República*, did not end the confusion. Armed bands committed so many crimes in areas close to Asunción that the government was forced to declare a state of siege and to send troops to crush the bandits.[19] Antonio Taboada and Pedro Caballero were directing the attacks from their Formosa refuge. Their followers assaulted police stations to obtain arms and soon were fighting vainly against the small Colorado army. Opposition papers continued their shrill attacks, charging that the Colorados were creating a *mazorca* (a gang of ruthless thugs) to crush the Liberals.[20] Revolutionary activity ended by September 1892, enabling González to lift the state of siege and turn his attention to political and economic problems.

Election of 1893

Paraguay had hardly recovered from the revolts of 1891 and 1892 when maneuvering for another election intensified personal and partisan rivalries. Thirteen deputies and four senators were to be elected on February 12, 1893. That Colorados would win all of the posts was evident; the real struggle was for influence in the presidential election of 1894. Both parties were badly fractioned. Dr. José Urdapilleta, editor of *La Democracia*, was correct in calling them embryonic groupings serving personal rather than national interests.[21] The Liberals by the end of 1892 had split into factions: Cívicos or moderates, and Radicals. Urdapilleta, a Cívico, urged accommodation with Egusquiza and the moderate Colorados. Soon so many Liberals and Colorados were identified as Cívicos that they were a de facto third party. Two principal Colorado factions were the *gonzalistas* and *caballeristas*. Escobar and his followers half-heartedly supported Caballero. Still another Colorado faction, led by Col. Juan Antonio Meza, also supported Caballero reluctantly. President González became closely identified with the Cívicos and began the policy of accommodation that became known as *egusquicismo*. Caballero still had presidential ambitions. The Brazilian minister regarded him as "the one in whom we can place the most confidence." He considered the Radical Liberals as pro-Argentine, opposed to the González policy of accommodation, and likely to seek power through revolution. Bickering politicians were ignoring the general welfare while the country slid deeper into chaos.[22]

Those who might turn to the press for guidance in the congressional election found little but polemics supporting strongly partisan viewpoints. *La Democracia*, ably edited by Urdapilleta, was more restrained than its colleagues but still reflected the moderate Liberal-Colorado, or Cívico, coalition. *El Independiente*, edited by the Bolivian Pedro Pablo Barba, supported the pro-Argentine Liberal Radicals, or Radical Liberals. In a charitable moment Barba called the González government the worst in Paraguayan history. Decoud and his followers bought the paper in February 1893 and reversed its policies. *La Prensa* in Buenos Aires opened its columns to Cecilio Báez and Enrique D. Parodi, whose anti-Brazilian articles *La Democracia* gladly reprinted. To combat this Liberal press, President González depended primarily upon *La República*. Caballeristas found support in *El Tiempo*, founded in 1891 and edited by Angel M. Molinas. Press-inspired rumors that Brazil and Paraguay had a secret alliance caused the Brazilian legation to publish a strong denial in *La Democracia*. Cecilio Báez, an accomplished polemicist, replied with a violent anti-Brazilian attack.[23]

Wrangling among Colorados continued as more candidates appeared than were needed for the official slate. Early in December 1892, *El Independiente* called upon conservative Colorados and Liberal Radicals to form a Unión Nacional to defeat the gonzalistas. At about the same time Antonio Taboada, a leader of the 1891 revolt, returned to Paraguay where he spent a few days in jail before being released on bond.[24] His presence was quickly shown in the Liberal manifesto of December which declared that participation in the coming election was useless, despite the undisputed fact that Liberals were in the majority. The real electoral battle, therefore, was between the gonzalistas, increasingly identified as Cívicos, and caballeristas. A rumor that Caballero would withdraw from politics was scotched by *El Tiempo* but caused fears that he might lead a coup against González. Rumors also had Caballero on the verge of announcing his candidacy for the 1894 presidential campaign.[25]

The congressional election on February 12, 1893, was anticlimactic. As expected, Liberals boycotted the polls and caballeristas abstained from voting in Asunción. Gonzalistas won easily but their victory hastened the Colorado downfall. Caballero obviously was not the arbiter of Paraguayan politics, although a recent writer has asserted that after he seized power in 1880, Caballero was "the absolute master and political director of the country until 1904."[26] Sadly, *La Democracia* commented on February 16: "One must honestly confess that there is no democratic life in this people; the Constitution is a lie; the teachings to youth in the classroom are lies; and, finally, all the expressions of patriotic sentiments by public authorities are lies." Shortly after it began publication in February 1893, *La Libertad* excoriated the gonzalistas: Cívicos had done nothing good under González; freedom of the press, so apparent during the rule of the generals, was seriously eroded; shadowy agricultural colonies were founded only to permit official grafting; the country suffered in the depths of misery; and persecution by political authorities had become one of the most disastrous plagues ever known in Paraguay.[27] Economically and politically these strictures had considerable justification, but they ignored the heritage of corruption, fiscal irresponsibility, and political oppression bequeathed by the generals so revered by caballeristas. Perhaps more important was failure to recognize the cultural renaissance begun by the postwar generation.

President González continued to receive blame for all of Paraguay's many troubles. Nearly every crop that survived the severe drought of 1892–1893 became food for a plague of locusts. Hunger and general misery prevailed in the country, where discouraged workers loafed on the ravaged land and ranchers saw their cattle reduced to staggering skeletons. Credit and commerce dried up with the land. Politics, too, had become a continuing crisis. González wanted his brother-in-law Decoud to succeed him as president, but Minister of War Juan Bautista Egusquiza was strongly favored by the Cívicos. Unknown to gonzalistas, reports from their ministers in Asunción were causing Brazil's leaders at Itamaraty, the foreign office in Rio de Janeiro, to consider an outrageous interference in Paraguayan affairs.[28]

Too Many Candidates

Three major controversies occupied the Paraguayans during the critical years of 1893 and 1894: the continuing argument with the
Paraguay Central Railway, the dispute with Bolivia over the Chaco
Boreal, and the presidential election of 1894. These were also the
years of increased activity in colonization, when Socialists founded
Nueva Australia and seceders from that colony founded Cosme, and
when other agricultural colonies began their uncertain careers. Discussions continued with Brazil and Argentina over the war debt; the
Mato Grosso frontier showed no signs of becoming peaceful; and
Argentina imposed heavy duties on Paraguayan products. Underlying all these domestic and international developments was the persistent economic depression, yet Paraguayan politicians and Brazil's
foreign office gave first priority to the 1894 presidential election.

Colorados and Liberals entered the campaign with the same
basic divisions that appeared before the congressional election in
February 1893. Generally, Colorados of all factions were called
situacionistas, or "ins" by their opponents, but there was no harmony
among them, and all of them were by no means "in." The old generals
attracted a numerous following, had no confidence in President González, and regarded General Egusquiza with suspicion. They could
not understand this conciliatory ex-legionario who had joined with
them to found the Asociación Nacional Republicana in 1887. Marcos
Morínigo, the vice-president, was a strong caballerista and adamant
in opposing accommodation with Liberals. While gonzalistas
claimed to represent the main stream of coloradismo, they were split
between support for Decoud and Egusquiza. Thus there were three
Colorado factions: caballeristas, gonzalistas, and egusquicistas, or
disidentes.[29]

Colorado confusion apparently presented Liberals with a great
opportunity, although many of their leaders were still in exile as a
result of the 1891 revolt. Manuel I. Frutos and Fernando A. Carreras
struggled to hold the party together despite the Cívico-Radical
schism. Several of the exiles returned in 1893 and 1894 without
bringing the factions closer together. Radicals emerged as the
stronger faction, with Cecilio Báez, Fabio Queirolo, and Alejandro
Audibert as leaders. Many Liberals put their faith in Dr. Benigno
Ferreira (1846–1920), who, as a brilliant young lawyer, had played
such a prominent role in the early 1870s. Intransigent defender of
Paraguay's territorial heritage, Ferreira incurred the displeasure of
Brazil, whose statesmen promoted the revolt of 1873–1874 to eliminate him from the Jovellanos government. Ferreira did not return
from his Buenos Aires exile until late in 1894, when he made a brief
visit.[30]

The most controversial of the several candidates was José Segundo Decoud. Clever, brilliant, and always the opportunist, Decoud had moved easily from Liberal to Colorado leadership in the 1870s. He was beyond question Paraguay's foremost diplomat.[31] Every president, from Cirilo Antonio Rivarola to Emilio Aceval, appointed him to high positions. He matched wits successfully with leading statesmen of several countries. After the failure of his financial measures under González, he spent many months as Paraguayan minister to Argentina while attempting to promote his presidential candidacy. Decoud had the support of the Argentine minister in Asunción, who regarded Caballero as a friend of Brazil and one who would have no scruples in helping whoever paid him best. *El Nacional* in Buenos Aires probed the political atmosphere and reported that Decoud could be the man to unite the Colorados. *La Libertad* replied that "there is a man whom the Paraguayan people detest with horror" and making him president would be the worst calamity in Paraguayan history.[32] The Brazilian minister reported that in the article in *El Nacional*, Decoud had dropped his mask, was seeking the aid of pro-Argentine Liberals, such as Taboada, Ferreira, Juan Silvano Godoi, and others who, having no influence in Asunción, would seek power through an alliance with Decoud.[33]

General Caballero, of course, was Decoud's principal opponent early in the game. A dedicated friend of Brazil, Caballero deserved that country's full support. By June 1893 Caballero appeared to have more public backing than any other candidate. After a large crowd of friends and supporters had celebrated Caballero's birthday on May 20, the old general returned the compliment with a banquet attended by all high officials. Nevertheless, González, continuing his opposition, stationed troops strategically to discourage an expected coup.[34] He insisted on Decoud, and when the latter returned from Buenos Aires in September 1893, rumors flew wildly: Egusquiza would resign to help Decoud; José Tomás Sosa, minister of interior, was General Escobar's choice; Dr. Benjamín Aceval would be a compromise candidate. While these and other rumors multiplied like mosquitoes in the marshes, Caballero remained silent.[35]

Egusquiza gained adherents as political maneuvering continued. Caballero had no fear of the minister of war, recently promoted to the rank of brigadier general, whose candidacy he regarded as a new effort by gonzalistas to assure Decoud's election. Liberals, seeking to take advantage of Colorado factionalism, reentered the political battle. Unfortunately, Radicals and Cívicos could not agree. Dr. Cecilio Báez, leader of the Radicals, persuaded Dr. Benjamín Aceval and Juan B. Gaona to enter the contest. Aceval, skillful in gaining support from various factions, was a friend of General Escobar, and Gaona, a wealthy and very influential businessman, was widely respected. Denying that Liberals had made a choice, *El Centinela* implored the party to close ranks and not select candidates who "changed their ponchos with every utterance."[36]

As it had in the congressional election of 1893, the press, except for the Liberal-leaning *La Democracia*, showed no restraint. Most vituperative of antigovernment organs were *El Centinela* and, as usual, *El Látigo Inmortal*. In the Easter season the former, with heavy sarcasm and no discernible literary merit, offered a prayer and a new creed:

> I believe in Juan Gualberto, almighty father, creator of banks with inconvertible paper money, and I believe in José Segundo his only son our lord, who was conceived by the work and grace of the political spirit. Born of the holy virgin patria, [José Segundo Decoud] suffered under the power of his evil ambition, was crucified, dead and buried morally for having taken up arms against his mother country; he descended into hell as a condemned sinner, and is now being raised from the dead for the common welfare. He will ascend to the presidency and will seat himself at the right hand of Father Juan; from here he will judge the living and the dead at his pleasure. I believe in the communion of the gonzalistas to seize everything, in the forgiveness of sinners, the resurrection of the mazorca and the life with hunger. Amen.[37]

El Centinela scornfully rejected other candidates as well. Everyone knew that Caballero was a notorious figure, that Egusquiza would even "gamble with the jewels of the Virgin of Caacupé." José Tomás Sosa was still worse, and Juan González Granado, mentioned as a compromise candidate, was worthless. These judgments would have been more respected had not the editor indulged in flurry after flurry of wild, unsubstantiated charges. *La Libertad*, supposedly "an organ of the people," began publication on March 1, 1893. A daily that combined Saturday and Sunday issues, this paper was subsidized by the Brazilian minister to promote Caballero's candidacy.[38] Another pro-Caballero paper was *La Patria*, which appeared in April 1894 under the direction of the old lopizta Gregorio Benítez and edited by the precocious Blas Garay. To counter these two papers, González had *La República* and *El Progreso*, the latter ably edited by Manuel Domínguez, Fulgencio R. Moreno, and Arsenio López Decoud, all of whom were to become prominent in Paraguayan letters and politics. When *La Libertad* prepared a biography of Caballero for sale, *El Centinela* charged that hordes of beggars roamed the streets and that a man who had a chicken stew was considered rich, but the people should rejoice "because the biography of General Caballero has been published and that bonanza treasure can be had for two pesos a copy. At two pesos the history of the great man is the cheapest thing that can be found, and of course what stomachs need most are biographies of generals."[39]

The need for compromise among the Colorados was obvious. Urdapilleta editorialized that neither Caballero nor Decoud was worthy of the presidency because neither had clean hands and both must share responsibility for Paraguay's economic misery. Egusquiza was emerging as the compromise candidate, since Caballero preferred him to Decoud, and Decoud preferred him to Caballero.[40] Other candidates were suggested but President González made it clear that if he could not have Decoud, Egusquiza must be the candidate. There was so much political traffic to and from the homes of Escobar and Caballero that the president feared a coup, so he increased the number of armed men visible in the capital.[41]

José Segundo Decoud was one of the very few Paraguayans who had a sense of history. In him were combined the idealist, the dreamer, and the pragmatist, the practical politician. He would have been less than human not to have wished for the presidency, but his excellent sense of the politically possible saved him from suffocation by unrealized ambition. His role was to be that of senior statesman, a major intellect in postwar Paraguay, whose public service was to be a guiding factor in the rebirth of the Paraguayan republic. When he returned to Asunción from Buenos Aires for a visit in September 1893, he realized the hopelessness of his candidacy. As La Democracia had predicted, Decoud withdrew from the race and swung his support to Egusquiza.[42] Decoud's move was a direct challenge to the caballeristas who, controlling the Comisión Directiva de la Asociación Nacional Republicana, had nominated Caballero and Col. Manuel A. Maciel on November 18. Caballero issued a manifesto in which he described the country's ills and agreed to serve if his party's December 17 convention called upon him. Uncommitted Liberals and neutrals then proposed that caballeristas and egusquicistas name delegates who would nominate Colorado candidates. Both Liberal factions rejected this move, which they interpreted as an effort to eliminate a Liberal from the race.[43]

The Brazilian minister feared that a revolution was imminent as rumors multiplied. He regarded Egusquiza as a mediocre man whose influence would fade when he resigned from the cabinet. With Decoud on their side, dissident Colorados called for a meeting in the Plaza Uruguaya on December 10 to nominate their candidates. On the appointed day, one week before the caballeristas were to meet, some four thousand men, most of them public employees, met and nominated Egusquiza and Dr. César Gondra, president of the Superior Tribunal of Justice. Liberals hastened plans to nominate Dr. Benjamín Aceval and to start a paper in his support. Rival Colorado factions appeared to be deadlocked early in 1894, with neither having enough strength to win without a revolution. Some neutrals continued their efforts to persuade Caballero and González to support a

noncontroversial candidate, while others tried to align Caballero
with the Liberals to support Aceval. The cloudy political situation
was expected to be clarified when Egusquiza resigned from the
cabinet, a move that would allow him to test the depth of his support.[44] Egusquiza was to be the beneficiary of entirely unexpected
support from Brazil.

The Cavalcanti Coup of 1894

Brazilian statesmen entertained a deep distrust for Decoud. They
remembered his service in the Paraguayan Legion, which had been
controlled by Argentina, they remembered his opposition during the
years of occupation, and they were easily convinced that he really
was in favor of annexing Paraguay to Argentina. Brazilian diplomats
in Asunción had no praise for Decoud, especially during the complicated political maneuvering in 1893 and 1894. Lins de Almeida, the
Brazilian minister, bombarded Itamaraty with alarming reports
about the threat of annexation and urged his government to forestall
any effort by Argentina to increase its influence.[45] Almeida's reports
caused so much concern among his superiors that they planned to get
rid of President González. They decided that the instrument should
be someone unfamiliar to the main actors in Asunción and chose Dr.
Amaro Cavalcanti, a noted economist, to replace Almeida. Surprised
and chagrined by his unexpected recall, Almeida nevertheless briefed
Cavalcanti thoroughly before presenting him to President González
on March 9, 1894.[46]

　　Both Argentina and Brazil were undergoing so much domestic
turmoil that one wonders why Paraguay appeared to be so important.
A likely explanation is that Floriano Peixoto, successor to Deodoro da
Fonseca as leader of the infant Brazilian republic, feared that Argentina might take advantage of Brazil's apparent weakness to
strengthen its hold on Paraguay. To prevent this development, Brazil
needed to guarantee that President González would not maneuver
Decoud into the presidency.

　　Cavalcanti's first reports merely supported Almeida's conclusions: Caballero, Escobar, and Morínigo were staunch friends of Brazil; González could not be trusted; and Egusquiza would pose no
threat to Brazil. With the presidential election only five months away,
Cavalcanti decided to use the broad powers granted him by Floriano,
who had placed at his disposal Brazilian gunboats "and whatever
pecuniary resources he might need." Promising to be discreet, Cavalcanti thought that it might be advisable to bring reinforcements from
the Mato Grosso flotilla as he prepared to engineer the overthrow of
González.[47]

Egusquiza, more deeply concerned as March wore on, feared that González would, indeed, impose Decoud through military force and with Argentine aid. Cavalcanti, when informed by Egusquiza of his fears, immediately asked Brazil's foreign minister, Dr. Alexandre Cassiano do Nascimento, that both the armed forces and promised money be made available for him to move quickly.[48] With Cassiano's assurance that he would have the needed resources, Cavalcanti was ready when González unwisely intensified his efforts to undermine Egusquiza. In response to his orders, *La República*, the official paper, dropped Egusquiza as the candidate and called for a noted statesman to lead the country. This poorly veiled advance notice from González led Cavalcanti to report that a coup to overthrow González probably would occur.[49]

Lured by promises of future favors and present enrichment, Caballero and Escobar agreed to Cavalcanti's plan. Three Brazilian gunboats in the harbor were a persuasive argument, as was the money with which Cavalcanti bribed the capital police, key officers, and leading members of Congress. Incredibly, these measures failed to arouse the president's suspicions. González was alone with his secretary at 11:15 A.M. on June 9 when members of Congress politely presented a note from General Egusquiza announcing that he was assuming the presidency until Congress could appoint a successor. The president, understandably disturbed, demurred until his visitors escorted him to the cavalry barracks where generals Caballero, Escobar, and Egusquiza presented him with a resignation to sign. González stubbornly refused to sign, so the generals put him on a boat bound for Buenos Aires. Cavalcanti had won in a completely bloodless coup that was a model for bold intervention in Paraguay's affairs. Congress met on June 10 to confirm Morínigo as acting president. Dutifully, the new chief executive appointed a pro-Egusquiza cabinet, and Cavalcanti asked to be relieved of his mission.[50]

Egusquiza had no difficulty in winning the election on August 20. Caballero had withdrawn from the race to support Egusquiza and Dr. Facundo Insfrán, one of Caballero's nephews. Cynics observed that this was part of Caballero's price for dropping out of the contest. Cavalcanti shrugged off accusations that he had engineered the coup, but too many people had been involved who could not be prevented from talking. In accounting for £17,288 he had received on July 3, 1894, Cavalcanti reported a balance of £518 which he suggested should be given to the Mato Grosso flotilla.[51]

Juan Gualberto González, exiled in Buenos Aires, had to be content with defending his administration in a lengthy manifesto that is a good summary of his achievements. When he became president, González asserted, Paraguay was suffering from the worst depression since 1870. Not a bank remained open, the price of gold was astronomical, land values had plummeted, businesses had closed, three years of drought and locust plagues had ruined agriculture, and Argentina had imposed crippling tariffs. Despite obstacles imposed by partisan politics, he had succeeded in beginning economic recovery. To support this claim, González cited an increase in customs revenues from less than $f2,000,000 in 1890 to nearly $f6,000,000 in 1893. The government had built bridges and roads, extended the railway for 115 kilometers, expanded tramway services, opened the telegraph line to Paso de Patria and connected with the Argentine line, completed the López Palace, refurnished public offices, built a new police building, begun a new jail, finished the old theater, completed the charity hospital, and begun such other works as rebuilding the Encarnación church in Asunción. Paraguay had participated in the Chicago World's Fair, which was preceded by an exhibit in the López Palace. González had revived old agricultural colonies and had established new ones to stop emigration caused by previous sales of public land. To do so, the government had been compelled to purchase lands so recently sold by Caballero and Escobar. In foreign affairs, González had negotiated eighteen treaties and had expanded diplomatic and consular representation.

Defending his political record, González proudly pointed to protection of the basic freedoms of assembly, political activity, and the press. Even after the revolt of 1891, the guilty leaders had been punished lightly. His was not a perfect government, to be sure, but concern for the public welfare had always been his guide. Political warfare among supporters of Caballero, Egusquiza, and Aceval had kept the country in turmoil. It was no secret that caballeristas preferred armed conflict to elections, thus requiring the government to take necessary precautions. He had forced Egusquiza to resign from the cabinet but, depending on his loyalty, had left all of Egusquiza's appointees in office.[52]

The trials of González were over, and General Juan Bautista Egusquiza was inaugurated without incident on November 25. The victim of Cavalcanti's coup had been a good president, convinced that the time had come for civilians to replace generals as presidents, and that Decoud was the best man qualified to guide Paraguay's recovery. Unfortunately, Brazil's exaggerated fears of Decoud, continuing economic distress, and Brazilian support of continued military leadership combined to produce the bloodless coup of 1894. Even without the presence of Cavalcanti, his blatant bribery and display of naval power, Caballero and Escobar probably would have deposed González, who was presiding over a government almost inevitably made bankrupt by their own policies in the 1880s. Cavalcanti, by switching

Brazil's support from Caballero to Egusquiza, may well have prevented a civil war between the generals and so made possible the experiment in political conciliation soon to be called *egusquicismo*. Cavalcanti's coup was the last Brazilian triumph in Paraguayan politics for many decades, and was self-deafeating, since Argentina's influence increased steadily.

7

Egusquiza and the Politics of Conciliation, 1894-1898

The master essayist Arturo Bray accurately analyzed the political situation when Egusquiza became president. An obscure commander in Misiones when González made him minister of war, Egusquiza repaid the favor by leading the troops who deposed González in the Cavalcanti coup of June 9, 1894. Educated in the "famous colegio of Concepción del Uruguay," Juan Bautista Egusquiza promised to be a new kind of president. He knew the time had come for Paraguay to change political direction, to complete the González policy of cooperation with Liberals. No fundamental difference separated the Colorados and the Liberals: each party was founded on the doctrine of democratic principles and the practice of popular suffrage, "on the common base of citizens' rights consecrated by our theoretically exemplary Constitution of 1870. Between the postulates of one and the other party there existed no doctrinaire differences." There was, therefore, no good reason why the parties should not cooperate—except the Paraguayan psychology: the older politicians refused to give way and the younger ones were impatient. They were like the "good campesino who customarily picks the fruit from the tree before it reaches its golden maturity, in his uncontainable desire to devour thoughtlessly; and those that he doesn't eat, he allows to rot until they fall by themselves, benefitting no one."[1]

Egusquiza believed that the Colorado party in twenty years of absolute government had given everything it could "without showing or demonstrating that instinct of progressive evolution in its men or in its methods which is an indispensable condition for a party to escape the rigors of decadence and dissolution."[2] The country needed a change. The old generals had failed to groom worthy successors. The same fate befell the Liberals a half century later. Egusquiza deliberately sought new blood and the assistance not only of perceptive Colorados but of the Liberal Cívicos.

Brave Promises and Futile Efforts

President Egusquiza may have appeared to be "one of the practical businessmen of Paraguay . . . with enthusiastic hope for the future for all things about him,"[3] but he faced a formidable task in attempting to save Paraguay from its sad state of prostration. A good omen was the signing on November 23, 1894, two days before the inaugural, of the Ichazo-Benítez Treaty with Bolivia, a treaty never ratified. The three generals—Caballero, Escobar, and Egusquiza—appeared to have the country under control, and the president began his term with a fairly good cabinet.[4] Caballero and Escobar would not play an important role in the administration, but, the Brazilian chargé warned, José Segundo Decoud remained a threat to Brazil. Argentina favored him and Brazil could no nothing about Argentine control over Paraguay's economy since, by means of customs duties, Buenos Aires could decree poverty or prosperity for the upriver country. This control would continue until Brazil built a railway to Paraguay.[5]

Egusquiza brought Liberals into Congress by permitting the party to elect two senators and four deputies in the 1895 congressional election. Sternly he prohibited Colorado opposition to these men at the polls. Small as it was, this gesture caused the Brazilian minister to believe that after twenty-four years of futile efforts, a form of constitutional life was beginning in Paraguay.[6] The president opened Congress on April 1, 1895, with a message glowing with confidence that "one of the most dependable signs of our present favorable situation is the gradual disappearance of the deep hatreds and passions that have divided and ruled the Paraguayan family since the war." There had been no complaints about fraud in the last elections, and he promised measures to remove cause for political warfare. Congress gave substance to this promise with a law of April 16 that granted amnesty to all who had been convicted or had fled because of political crimes.[7]

Henrique Carlos Ribeira Lisboa, the Brazilian envoy who knew the country well, found little cause for optimism when he compared Egusquiza's ebullience with Paraguayan social and economic decadence. Everything was primitive; lack of resources prevented needed improvements. Even near the capital, transport and communication were completely neglected. Many primary schools had been closed to save money. The railway was in a deplorable condition, with little hope for completion to Encarnación, and there was no prospect of building other lines. The few intelligent, capable men were discouraged and many emigrated to Argentina. Egusquiza knew well the real condition of Paraguay but preferred to conceal the truth in order to make a heroic effort to save his country from impending ruin.[8]

Hope for cooperation from Liberals in Congress was quickly

dispelled. Dr. Cecilio Báez, abrasive leader of the Radical Liberals, made himself a nuisance by stridently attacking Agustín Cañete, the strongest man in the cabinet and Caballero's personal representative. Cañete, as minister of hacienda, was involved in liquidating the Banco Nacional del Paraguay, and Báez accused him of conniving with the receivers to defraud depositors through the issue of new notes. Cañete had reduced the liquidating commission to two members, which was entirely legal. Colorados in Congress closed ranks to defeat the effort to impeach Cañete. Having won vindication, Cañete offered his resigation from the cabinet, where he also served as ad interim minister of foreign affairs. Immediately rumors were circulated that José Segundo Decoud would be appointed to the latter post. Like his predecessors, Egusquiza needed Decoud's services more than he needed to placate Liberals in Congress.[9] Disgusted by attacks on his character, Cañete insisted on resigning. Egusquiza and his advisers sought in one stroke to silence both Liberal and Colorado critics by naming Dr. Benjamín Aceval, who was generally considered above any hint of scandal, as minister of hacienda and Decoud as minister of foreign affairs. Decoud, so recently considered a prime enemy of Caballero in the Colorado party, was now regarded as the general's representative! These appointments drew praise from all important newspapers in Asunción.[10]

Brazilians needed to revise their assessment of José Segundo Decoud. Lisboa disagreed strongly with his two predecessors, Lins de Almeida and Amaro Cavalcanti, who firmly believed that Decoud would promote the annexation of Paraguay to Argentina. Although he could not determine the extent to which Decoud favored Argentina, it was easy to understand "that there should be on his part, as among all educated Paraguayans, a certain inclination in favor of Argentina. The similarity of origin, language, and customs is an entirely sufficient explanation for that preference. Besides, the fact that many Paraguayans receive their education and training in Buenos Aires, which ties them to a degree to Argentine society, would suffice." Showing himself an exceptionally able analyst, Lisboa observed that "the educated men of this country, and Snr. Decoud most of all, are fully convinced that Paraguay will be unable to take a single step on the way to progress if it be left to its own resources." As to Brazil and Argentina, three questions were posed: Which would provide immediate and effective aid if needed? Which has the greater interest in providing that aid? Which would give aid with the least risk to Paraguay? Obviously, Brazil would be able to offer more than Argentina and had good reason to do so. Paraguay, in a sense, lay athwart Brazil's route to Mato Grosso, "which the benefits of civilization can hardly penetrate so long as Paraguay remains in its present backward state." Argentine statesmen were very shortsighted. They hindered emigration to Paraguay and imposed crippling tariffs on its products, although the prosperity of Corrientes and, to a lesser extent, of Santa Fe and Entre Rios provinces was linked with Paraguayan prosperity. Obviously, too, aid from Argentina posed the greater threat to Paraguayan autonomy. Lisboa reached these conclusions after many conversations with his neighbor, José Segundo Decoud, and they were no different from opinions expressed by Decoud in 1882 to the Brazilian chargé, Henrique de Barros Cavalcanti. Lisboa concluded that Decoud was no threat to Brazil, to which he looked for economic aid. It was time to forget Decoud's journalistic attacks on Felippe José Pereira Leal in 1875.[11]

Something approaching prosperity appeared to be near as Paraguay recovered somewhat from the financial crises of the early 1890s. President Egusquiza earnestly attempted to create a political atmosphere within which economic confidence and progress could flourish, and for a time he appeared to be succeeding. He took measures to promote foreign trade, to improve the quality of yerba exported, to create a school of agriculture, and to tighten controls over exploitation of state-owned yerbales. The financial situation, always of great concern, appeared to be improving. The White-Aceval Agreement of 1895 provided for payment of bonds, held by English creditors for the most part, of £934,640. The internal debt of $f437,980 at the end of 1895 was very small, and the income of $f5,100,495 was encouraging. Egusquiza promised not to increase the $f5,000,000 of paper money then in circulation. The premium paid for gold declined steadily until in 1896 it stood at 570. The government compleed allotment of 500 square leagues to the Anglo-Paraguay Land Company in accordance with the Decoud settlement of 1885, and Congress was expected to authorize the assignment of duties on yerba exports to resume payment on the external debt. Plans for a new bank were under way.[12]

Surveyng the national scene for Congress in April 1896, President Egusquiza observed that complete peace reigned with no fear of disturbance. The government could devote its entire attention to the work of national reconstruction, a work in which Paraguayans needed to unite and put an end to anarchy. Parenthetically, one should remember that it was Egusquiza who had led in the overthrow of President González, a leader equally anxious for political conciliation. To show his faith in the patriotism of fellow politicians, Egusquiza had invited members of all parties to serve in the government with the only criterion being ability, not party membership.[13]

Egusquiza was too optimistic. The expected economic prosperity, with increased government revenue, proved to be so elusive that Congress authorized the issue of $8,000,000 in treasury bills in October 1896; and on July 1, 1897, the authorized amount of paper money in circulation was raised to $f10,000,000. Still Egusquiza could point to considerable agricultural progress: tobacco improved in quality, foreign experts were employed to teach modern methods of tobacco culture and marketing, and the number of cattle and horses increased steadily. Economic progress easily could have been more significant if such capitalists as Juan Bautista Gaona, José Urdapilleta, and Francisco Milleres—all former or actual bank presidents—had not been subject to Liberal attacks in Congress and the press.[14] Moreover, constant rumors of Liberal plots to rebel discouraged immigration and investment.

Another matter of considerable importance worried Egusquiza. The Argentine-Chilean dispute appeared to worsen in 1896. Fearing that war might result and that Paraguay might be involved, Egusquiza sent Juan Silvano Godoi on a mission to Rio de Janeiro to ask for arms and a guaranty of Paraguay's neutrality. Decoud denied publicly that Godoi was sent by the government, and the story was spread that he was representing Enrique Solano López, who was trying to gain recognition of claims to land north of the Apa.[15]

Search for Political Accommodation

There is no reason to doubt Egusquiza's desire for party harmony nor the determination of other politicians to prevent it. The casual foreign observer was not likely to be very enthusiastic about prospects for peaceful collaboration among Paraguay's snarling factions. Granville Stuart of Montana, the American minister to Paraguay and Uruguay, returned from a trip to Asunción early in 1897 to find another plot among Uruguayan politicians and a chance to compare the two countries to which he was accredited. Uruguay, he reported, "is a republic in name only, it being a military oligarchy of the most abritrary kind, and Paraguay is the same. Their Constitutions and laws are excellent, fully equal to our own; but the authorities violate both whenever they think it advantageous to do so, and there is no redress."[16] No redress but revolution, he might have added, and revolution was always a threatening cloud on the political horizon.

Many of the Liberals had opposed the González-Morínigo ticket in 1890, an opposition that led eventually to the abortive revolt of October 18, 1891, after continued refusal of the Colorados to risk honest elections. The failure of this revolt resulted in considerable bickering, especially after Taboada, Báez, Pedro P. Caballero, Adolfo Soler, and other leaders returned from exile in 1892 and 1893. Fabio Queirolo exercised a calming influence and Manual I. Frutos, hero of the Paraguayan War, led in reassembling party strength,[17] with Fernando A. Carreras as secretary. The more restless members, thinking about direct action, recalled Dr. Benigno Ferreira from Buenos Aires at the end of 1894. Taboada, Caballero, Soler, Queirolo, Báez, and Dr. Alejandro Audibert formed the nucleus of this group, although Queirolo had some difficulty in deciding between conciliation and revolution. Báez, Carreras, Taboada, and others were not happy with Ferreira, whose role in the 1872 loans had aroused suspicion, but they agreed to serve on the party directorate when a convention elected Ferreira as president of the party on February 23, 1895.[18]

The Liberal directorate failed to unite behind Ferreira. Queirolo, Báez, and Audibert were in part responsible for articles in *El Pueblo* in March 1895 which again raised the question of the 1872 loans. Ferreira resigned and Queirolo replaced him as head of the party. Other touchy issues included the railway question. Some members wanted to attack "The Enterprise," as the English railway company was called, which was then engaged in a long dispute with the government, while others considered the course imprudent—maybe because they were too closely involved in the whole business, as, indeed, were most Paraguayan politicians of any prominence. Báez, Carreras, and Emiliano González Navero appear not to have been in any way involved in accepting favors of any sort from the Paraguay Central Railway. These three eventually became the nucleus of the Radical Liberal leadership. Personalities had proved to be more important than policies or principles: "To the clash of temperaments was added that of personal interests and the party from that moment followed the individual fate of its men in conflict."[19]

Attacking Cañete and other Colorados in Congress in 1895 did not consume all Liberal energies. Throughout the year, and especially after the return of Benigno Ferreira from Buenos Aires, there was a remote possibility that Liberal factions would unite and start a revolution with Argentine aid. President Egusquiza was not especially skillful in administrative matters, but he knew how to handle military threats. When rumors of revolt increased in November 1895, he made military dispositions to counter any attack and was ready to declare martial law if necessary. Should a revolt come, the Liberals, despite their quarreling, were better organized than the old and decadent oligarchy which had ruled Paraguay for so long. A Liberal rebellion had indeed been planned for the end of November, although it had not gone beyond the talking stage. When a common soldier revealed the plot to Caballero, the leaders were arrested but not brought to trial because Egusquiza, following his conciliation policy, had loaded the courts with Liberals. Egusquiza was so uncertain of himself that he suspected Caballero and Escobar of being in the plot.[20]

Egusquiza rightly believed that the Cívico faction of the Liberals offered the best chance for collaboration. General Ferreira retained leadership of this group, which included four deputies and several men prominent in Paraguayan letters. Their press organ, *El Cívico*, appeared first on September 1, 1895, and continued publication into 1908.[21] Radicals, too, could muster an imposing array of talent under the leadership of Dr. Cecilio Báez. Among the Radicals were Ramón Lara Castro, brilliant and indefatigable defender of Paraguay's interests in the long argument with the Paraguay Central Railway; two future presidents, Eduardo Schaerer and Manuel Gondra; the famous lawyer, Dr. Alejandro Audibert; and a noted educator, Luís A. Riart.[22]

Cooperation from Liberals would be welcome but Egusquiza's principal concern was within his own party. General Caballero, although outmaneuvered in 1894, remained loyal to the party and in November 1896 vainly sought reconciliation with the Rojos Disidentes (Dissident Colorados) led by Santiago Gómez Sánchez.[23] The caballeristas still had strength that they could muster, as they were to show in the 1902 coup that resulted in a long eclipse of the Colorados. No leader appeared in 1897 or 1898 with the strength or ability to bring the liberal Colorados, led by Egusquiza, and the conservative Liberals, led by Ferreira, into an new party. Although the use of the terms *liberal* and *conservative* have little meaning at this point in Paraguayan politics, neither do *Cívico* and *Radical.* They are merely convenient labels by which to identify factional allegiance.

Godoi's Mission to Rio de Janeiro

Juan Silvano Godoi, or Juansilvano Godoi, as he often signed himself, was involved in every anti-Colorado revolt from 1877 to 1895, a period which he spent in exile in Buenos Aires. There he was an important member of the Paraguayan Committee, a highly respected and popular member of society, a noted bibliophile and art collector. Scion of an old and wealthy family, Godoi's position in Paraguayan society was enhanced by marriage to Bienvenida Rivarola. Their lovely, talented, and adored daughter Haidé presided like a princess over the Godoi mansion at Santa Fe 2583 in Buenos Aires during her mother's prolonged absences in Asunción. After Haidé's death from tuberculosis in 1897, the heartbroken Godoi packed up his pictures and library and returned to Asunción under an amnesty granted to political exiles. Amnesty was a splendid gesture, since it brought many dangerous men back to Asunción where they could be watched.

Among those who were happy to greet Godoi was Enrique Solano López, a son of Madame Elisa Alicia Lynch and Francisco Solano López, who had been accepted by a portion of Asunción's society and had achieved a degree of stature among Colorados. Since the early 1880s, Godoi had been assisting Enrique in his efforts to have the claims of Madame Lynch to huge areas of land in Brazil, Argentina, and Paraguay validated so that they could be sold. Part of the land

Enrique claimed lay north of the Rio Apa in the area ceded to Brazil and added to Mato Grosso. Here were rich expanses of yerbales which were being exploited by Matte Larangeira, the Brazilian company in fierce competition with La Industrial Paraguaya. Many high ranking politicians of both parties had invested in La Industrial, which also encountered competition from Matte Larangeira in yerbales west of the Paraná.

Except for having his claim registered in Corumbá, Enrique met with continuous frustration in his efforts to win a clear title to the Mato Grosso lands. He then enlisted the aid of President Egusquiza, with whom he entered into an interesting agreement. Egusquiza promised to help López press his Mato Grosso claims by sending a special envoy, who proved to be Juan Silvano Godoi, to treat directly with the president of Brazil. For his part, Enrique made a noble gesture: as soon as the Mato Grosso claims were settled with a satisfactory compensation, he would surrender the titles to all the lands his mother had acquired during the war, as well as the "present Government Palace, the University and Colegio Nacional." His claims to other properties would be settled by the courts. Egusquiza specified that he in no way bound himself to recognize the validity of Enrique's claims.[24]

Armed with letters from Egusquiza to Dr. Amaro Cavalcanti and President Prudente José de Moraes Barros, Godoi sailed for Rio de Janeiro in January, 1896. He also had instructions from Egusquiza to examine both Argentine and Brazilian Mausers and to advise which to buy. In Rio de Janeiro, Godoi enlisted the aid of Senator Rui Barbosa who precipitated an acrimonious debate in Congress without winning anything. When Godoi left Rio de Janeiro on March 9, 1896, Prudente de Moraes sent his card to wish him *feliz viagem*.[25] After his return, Godoi published his *Mi misión a Rio de Janeiro* (Buenos Aires, 1897) in which he accused José Segundo Decoud with having proposed annexation of Paraguay to Argentina. Godoi based his accusation on a letter from José Segundo to his brother Adolfo, dated January 21, 1878. This letter was indeed very interesting:

> I have nothing from you to answer, but I do not want this ship to sail without writing some lines to you suggesting an idea which, in my judgment, is of great transcendence. This deals with initiating a campaign to procure the union of Paraguay to the Argentine Republic by means of annexation. This thought, as you are not unaware, will meet at the outset serious opposition here as well as there [Buenos Aires]. But this is no reason to despair. I believe that a dignified and reasonable propaganda, describing the miserable condition of Paraguay and the impossibility of its maintaining an independent existence, will weigh heavily with the Argentine diplomats to bring about a successful conclusion to the project.
> It will be necessary for you to confer with Dr. [José] Urdapilleta

and Dr. [Fernando] Iturburu to invite them to support this idea. If they were so disposed, you could form an organized center of Paraguayans which, together with others that would be established in various parts and here, could thereupon begin the task. I believe meanwhile that you should keep absolutely silent in this matter.

I hope that you will send me your views about the proposal. The idea is not new in the Plata; but I think the time has come for it to take root. The times are bad. The danger of a general dissolution is imminent. Paraguay will not save itself in any other way. It seems to me that this is better than to indulge eternally in revolutions that will do nothing more than to bury the country deeper in chaos and anarchy.[26]

Before making his accusation, Godoi submitted several Decoud letters to a handwriting expert who certified that the 1878 letter was genuine.[27] However, subsequent copies of the original letter show clearly that the 1878 date had been altered to read 1891—a date much more convenient for Godoi's purposes, one of which was surely to embarrass the Colorados in the 1898 campaign. Godoi succeeded in raising a brief storm in political circles. Decoud offered his resignation as minister of foreign affairs, threatened to sue Godoi for libel, and asked that Congress appoint a committee to investigate the charge. The press, both Liberal and Colorado, was nearly unanimous in supporting Decoud. By the end of October 1897 the affair appeared to have been forgotten, but the Liberal minority resurrected it in April 1898. After a bitter debate, the deputies on May 5 voted against the resolution to impeach Decoud.[28]

The Election of 1898

Egusquiza had fulfilled his promise to permit some Liberals to be elected to Congress. He had allowed freedom of the press beyond reason as opposition editors exercised no self-restraint, with the exception of Ignacio Ibarra of *La Democracia*. Egusquiza warned Congress in 1897 that Paraguay's progress would be delayed when citizens wasted their time fighting one another; personal egos must be subjected to the country's welfare.[29] The president was also annoyed by the efforts of such young firebrands as Juan Emiliano O'Leary, who had joined in the campaign of Enrique Solano López to sanctify and to glorify his father. To Cecilio Báez this was an effort to place a heavenly halo on the head of the Devil himself. Enrique's followers succeeded in blowing into flame the poorly banked political fires. Excoriating members of the wartime Paraguayan Legion, which had to be part of the apotheosis effort, would arouse hostility among both major parties since powerful Colorados, such as Egusquiza, former President González, and José Segundo Decoud had been officers in the Legion. One could not condemn López without condemning his enemies.

Maneuvering for the 1898 presidential election began in earnest more than a year before the event, although the public appeared to be apathetic.[30] President Egusquiza had selected his minister of war, Emilio Aceval, as his successor; Aceval, too liberal for the old generals, would continue egusquicismo. Caballero and Escobar preferred Agustín Cañete or Caballero's nephew, the widely respected Dr. Facundo Insfrán who had founded Paraguay's School of Medicine in addition to serving in Congress. This split among the Colorado leaders caused a division in the party's Comisión Directiva. Many young men followed the example of Dr. Blas Garay, the brilliant young Colorado who returned early in 1898 from his mission to Spain, where he had been searching the Spanish archives to document Paraguay's claim to the Chaco Boreal, and rejected overtures from Liberal Cívicos and Colorado egusquicistas to support the caballeristas.[31]

Liberals, biding their time, knew that Colorados would easily win the contest so they resorted to journalistic attacks in an effort to widen the Colorado split. Condemning Egusquiza's choice, the Liberal press preferred Cañete as the one most *simpático* and worthy of being president. Caballero and Escobar were still powerful men, more prestigious than Egusquiza, but the president did keep control over the army. The three generals and other Colorado leaders conferred frequently without being able to come to an agreement on a candidate.[32]

Reduced political agitation at the end of January 1898 aroused fears that a storm was about to break. When Angel Martínez, minister of interior, acted suspiciously, Egusquiza asked him to resign and sent him to Buenos Aires for his health. Caballero and Escobar had left Asunción to determine sentiment in the interior, where Cañete was very popular. They returned in February and held a long conference with Egusquiza at which they agreed reluctantly to support Emilio Aceval. The old generals were suspicious of Aceval, a civilian who had the support of the Cívicos and the moderate Colorados. Industrialists, especially those opposed to Matte Larangeira, would aid Cañete, who was a shareholder in La Industrial Paraguaya. The Brazilian minister preferred Aceval but pointedly stayed away from him in order not to antagonize the Argentines, since Brazil's aid to Egusquiza in 1894 was well known. Aceval's election was important to Brazil, since the president could easily hamper free passage of products from Mato Grosso through Paraguay, and Matte Larangeira was very vulnerable. Argentina's minister, Lauro Cabral, was openly attempting to make Paraguay an ally, holding trade concessions as bait. However, Egusquiza and Aceval were cool toward Argentine blandishments. There were still annexationists in Paraguay to whom Cabral could appeal in his efforts to undermine Benigno Ferreira, who feared that the rise of an Argentine colossus would be a real menace to the smaller South American nations. With the April session of Congress rapidly approaching, the two parties finally selected their candidates. Liberals agreed on Dr. Alejandro Audibert and Rosendo Carísimo. Audibert was a good lawyer with congressional and judicial experience. Carísimo, a capitalist from Concepción, would appeal to supporters of La Industrial Paraguaya, but he was not a politician. The Colorados accepted Emilio Aceval and Andrés Héctor Carvallo, and at this Cañete resigned from the cabinet.[33]

In his message to Congress in April, Egusquiza remarked that the country was peaceful and the work of regeneration could continue. Paraguay as a nation had been nurtured under despotism, but democratic practices were slowly winning. Certain tremors were to be expected as the country passed from dictatorship to freedom. The constitutional guarantees of 1870 still had not been achieved, laws could not alone regenerate people: "Neither a wise legislature nor an honest and active government can in an instant change the moral and intellectual conditions of nations. One cannot erase a hundred years of history with a penstroke."[34]

Paraguayans needed the little excitement that was provided when a decrepit Spanish gunboat, denied refuge in Platine ports, sailed up the rivers to anchor at Asunción on May 25, 1898. This vessel, El Temerario, was one of the floating wrecks that Spain sent across the Atlantic to confront the new American navy in the Spanish-American War. The mercurial American consul, Dr. John N. Ruffin, wisely asked the advice of Brazil's Brasilio Itiberê da Cunha, dean of the diplomatic corps, who told him not to make a big issue of the event because there were many Spaniards in Asunción and President Egusquiza had enough problems without facing a demand that the poor old ship be given asylum.[35] Paraguayans generally appeared to be sympathetic to the United States, and the diplomatic corps, including the Spanish chargé, had called on Ruffin to express sympathy when the Maine went down at Havana. Ruffin was concerned because Decoud had assured the United States of Paraguay's strict neutrality in the war.[36] So far as the Department of State was concerned, El Temerario, if unarmed, could stay at Asunción until it finished rusting away. The gunboat's captain refused to surrender his guns and, after repairing some machinery, sailed north to anchor off the Río Apa where, so far as the record is concerned, ship and crew disappeared into history. Paraguayans could return with little enthusiasm to the election of their next president.

After getting rid of Martínez, Egusquiza made other cabinet changes in the midst of rumors that a revolt was about to occur. Some Liberals were always planning to rebel and no president could ever drop his guard. Itiberê da Cunha suggested that perhaps some of the "vessels from the Matto Grosso flotilla should be stationed at Asunción" to protect Brazilian interests. He would telegraph if they were needed. There was no revolt. Ferreira and the Argentine minister restrained the Liberals, who were not ready for their great stroke, and the three Colorado generals held their partisans in check. Liberals stayed away from the polls on September 25 when, to no one's surprise, Aceval and Carvallo were elected. Congress accepted the returns and on November 25, 1898, the last civilian Colorado president took office.[37]

The election of 1898 was the last victory for Juan Bautista Egusquiza, who owed so much to Brazil's Amaro Cavalcanti. During the 1890s, Brazilian statesmen continued to fear Argentine annexationism, although there was little reason to be so concerned. Argentina was represented by mediocre diplomats in Asunción until the appointment of Lauro Cabral and Alejandro Guesalaga reversed its policy of neglect. At the turn of the century, Argentina could count on the rivalry between Matte Larangeira and La Industrial Paraguaya, the increasing prosperity of Carlos Casado's Chaco enterprise, and turmoil on the Mato Grosso frontier to create a pro-Argentine sentiment despite the antiforeign campaign being waged by resurgent lopiztas. Argentina's influence in Paraguay was increasing steadily, while statesmen at Itamaraty appeared to be losing interest.

8

Aceval and the Failure of Conciliation, 1898–1902

With Aceval in the presidency, Paraguay at last had a civilian chief executive whose education and experience fully qualified him for the position. Unfortunately, the country was not yet ready politically to benefit from his talents. Aceval started with an excellent cabinet whose members could contribute significantly to ameliorating if not solving Paraguay's increasingly difficult problems. Partisan rivalries caused cabinet crises as Aceval vainly attempted to conciliate various factions while continuing the policy of egusquicismo. Economic difficulties were exacerbated by interruptions in trade caused by recurring epidemics of typhus.

The campaign to glorify Francisco Solano López easily found enthusiastic support among emotional university students as well as seasoned veterans of Paraguay's political wars. While a major cause of a rebirth of patriotic spirit, this bold effort to create a López cult distressed President Aceval, who correctly recognized it as posing a deadly threat to his policy of political conciliation. It was this policy that increased apprehension among Colorado leaders and gave them a foreboding of coming disaster, a disaster made inevitable by the coup that deposed Aceval and led directly to Liberal plans for the revolution of 1904.

Aceval, the president

Emilio Aceval and Andrés Héctor Carvallo took office with the usual fanfare of Te Deum, reception, and inaugural ball on November 25, 1898. The new president, far from being a nonentity, had been active in Paraguay's economic and political life. Born in Asunción on October 16, 1854, Aceval was still but a child when he became a soldier in 1867. He survived two wounds, obtained a good education after 1870,

106

and traveled in Europe and the United States before he returned to Asunción, where he was highly respected in business and professional circles. President of the Banco Nacional and an organizer of the Sociedad Colonizadora del Paraguay in 1888, Aceval was an experienced, capable, and honest administrator. In politics he was a moderate Colorado, a supporter of egusquicismo.[1] Consul Ruffin was lavish in his praise: "He is a man of high education and brilliant parts, being one of the most cultured and learned men in the Republic. As an orator he is one of the most forcible, graceful, eloquent and convincing south of the Gulf of Mexico and among the South American statesmen stands with the first."[2]

The cynical observer, remembering fine promises in previous Colorado inaugurals, might well have been skeptical of Aceval's program. The new president promised an honest and economical administration; he would encourage agriculture through pest control, irrigation, increased immigration, and promotion of foreign markets; he would improve education at all levels; in the realm of politics, he would continue Egusquiza's effort to promote genuine harmony. In short, he sought the welfare of all Paraguayans.[3] Aceval's choices for cabinet positions bore out his intentions. No more experienced and capable men could have been found than José Segundo Decoud in foreign affairs, José Urdapilleta in hacienda, Guillermo de los Ríos in interior, and Dr. José Caminos, physician-politician, in justice. Juan Antonio Escurra, a caballerista of very limited ability, became minister of war and marine.[4] Escurra was politically dangerous, and his appointment obviously was meant to placate the caballeristas.

Aceval faced monumental problems that became more and more difficult as his term progressed. In foreign affairs, he sought a new commercial treaty with Brazil that would restore reciprocity and correct the error that had imposed a tariff on goods entering Paraguay from Mato Grosso.[5] The Mato Grosso frontier was a lawless area that provided unlimited opportunity for smuggling, cattle rustling, and poaching in yerbales, and Aceval would have to be wary of becoming involved in the Mato Grosso disorders of 1901. Outbreaks of plague in Asunción, introduced from Argentina, caused both Brazil and Argentina to impose quarantines that practically ended trade for two years. The argument with Bolivia over the Chaco Boreal became more bitter. Propaganda of the lopiztas became more strident, cabinet crises occurred frequently, and neither caballeristas nor radical Liberals would cooperate with Aceval's conciliatory political objectives.

The usual New Year's reception to welcome 1899 was large and well attended by the small diplomatic and consular corps, officials, politicians, merchants, and others of Asunción's social elite who shared the general optimism which reflected internal peace, anticipation of a large harvest, increasing trade, and a decreasing gold premium. An ominous note was increased speculation in land, making it difficult for the government to carry out its agricultural colonization program.[6] Aceval's message to Congress on April 1 repeated his inaugural promises. Again he emphasized the desire for conciliation, for cooperation of all factions, and deplored the rantings of demagogues who would destroy the country which "had recovered from its past disasters and with unbreakable faith has turned completely to the task of rebuilding that will raise it from its ruins."[7]

Several significant achievements under Aceval mark him as a very good administrator and the only president since 1869 who approached greatness. To handle the debt, he created a Public Debt Administration; to strengthen the treasury, he ordered all public funds to be deposited in the Banco Agrícola; to collect taxes, he set up the Internal Revenue Office under a collector general; to end confusion in measurements, he caused Congress to adopt the metric system as of January 1, 1901. He improved primary instruction by creating a National Council of Education under a director general of schools, although his choice for the position, Enrique Solano López, proved to be unfortunate. To promote agriculture, he ordered a mortgage section to be established in the Banco Agrícola, improved roads and bridges, and ended the import duty on blooded cattle in order to improve Paraguay's herds. Industry benefited from liberal concessions, small subsidies to shipbuilders, construction of roads and bridges, and harbor works. A National Council of Hygiene in the ministry of interior considered the nation's health problems although without being able to ameliorate them significantly.[8]

Periodic quarantines against Paraguay because of bubonic plague had serious economic and political effects. After the Argentine ship *El Centauro* had introduced plague in Asunción, the Argentine government imposed a quarantine from November 1899 to May 1900 which cut off exports, reduced government revenues, and caused widespread hardship. Attempting to help Paraguay solve its health problems, Argentina sent a medical mission to Asunción in 1899 but had to recall it after a short stay in order to fight the plague in Rosario and Buenos Aires. The ports were open but a short time when Argentina again imposed a quarantine. These outbreaks of plague definitely were the result of trade with downriver ports, especially with Buenos Aires and Rosario.[9]

Cabinet Crises

Aceval became president because General Egusquiza was still stronger than generals Caballero and Escobar, whose followers, egusquicistas or caballeristas, refused to cooperate despite an official

statement that they had agreed patriotically to avoid sterile bickering and to unite in order to work for Paraguay's betterment. Unable to
retain support of the caballeristas, Aceval in 1900 made a bargain
with the Cívicos by which this Liberal faction gained two cabinet
posts. This accommodation failed to stabilize the fluid political situation, which was exacerbated by a continuing depression and dissatisfaction with Brazilian influence on the government.[10]

Political infighting, which prevented administrative stability
during Aceval's first year in office, intensified so seriously that it
threatened internal peace and the government's very existence. Opponents missed no opportunity to attack the government. They
blamed Aceval for Argentina's withdrawal of its medical mission and
for the quarantines that cut off foreign trade. Once fairly popular,
Aceval began to lose public confidence. The entire cabinet offered to
resign in mid January 1900 in order to give Aceval a chance to choose
ministers capable of solving Paraguay's pressing problems. At the
president's request, the ailing General Egusquiza attempted to form
a new cabinet, but his influence, especially with the military, had
been undermined by caballeristas. Fearing the imminence of revolt,
Aceval asked if the Brazilian minister would give him asylum. Knowing that a revolt in 1900 would throw Paraguay into anarchy, Aceval
persuaded the ministers to stay on, although Decoud and Urdapilleta
insisted on resigning after a few weeks. Aceval called Congress into
special session to deal with the plague and other problems, all of
which proved to be beyond the abilities of the legislators to solve.[11]

The delayed cabinet crisis came on March 12 when Decoud
resigned. Turning to the Cívicos for support, Aceval persuaded Fabio
Queirolo to accept the foreign affairs portfolio and brought in José
Tomás Legal to take over the ministry of justice.[12] These two men
represented a new generation, men who had few political enemies.
Legal, who was Decoud's son-in-law, had been a civil judge, and
Queirolo was a "cattle rancher who rarely appeared in Asunción.
Both enjoy well merited favor in society," the Brazilian minister
observed, "and are of impeccable honesty—which is a great deal in
this country."[13] This was the occasion that caused the minister to
observe that Decoud had been the one indispensable man in
Paraguayan government. The old warrior was weary and anxious to
retire from public life, from service to a country to which he had
contributed so much and from which he had received so little. However, he was not yet through.

The cabinet crisis was especially serious because of the great
difficulty in finding men capable of administering government posts.
Aceval had brought in Queirolo and Legal in order to have opposition
members in the government, a gesture that did not prevent irrecon-
cilable políticos from accusing him of being a tool of the generals who

had ruled the country for thirty years. Urdapilleta, the respected minister of hacienda, resigned late in June to protest a loan of 500,000 pesos to rescue the owners of a failing sugar mill. Aceval replaced him with an old convencional, Francisco Campos. He, too, had that quality so rare among Paraguay's politicians: he was honest. Beyond that he had little to recommend him.[14] By October 1900 Aceval's policy of conciliation appeared to be working so well that General Egusquiza ventured a trip to Buenos Aires to confer with Brazil's President Manoel de Campos Salles.

Election of 1901

Factional political strife intensified as the election of 1901 approached. No great foresight was needed to see that the three generals had lost much of their political clout, that the younger generation, the generation of the nineties, would no longer be denied the perquisites of political and economic power. These, indeed, were small. Colorados had sold the public domain and in the process had not neglected their own financial welfare. Still, there were young men in both parties who had great hopes for Paraguay's future and an equally great desire to play prominent roles in directing it. One of their efforts resulted in creation of the Unión Patriótica in 1900 which attempted to arouse a sense of patriotism among the people, to lift them out of their characteristic lethargy and indifference.[15]

The congressional election promised to be tumultuous. Liberals generally had boycotted previous elections to protest Colorado corruption and violence. Although Egusquiza's policy of conciliation had won over the Cívico faction with the promise of a few seats in Congress in return for its cooperation, the Radicals would have none of these crumbs and prepared for battle at the polls on February 24, 1901.[16] Despite frenetic journalistic activity and fears of an armed revolt, the election proceeded as planned by Colorados, with only one Radical winning a seat in Congress. As egusquicismo gathered strength, caballerismo continued to lose prestige. Cívicos correctly charged that the Colorados had secretly opposed Liberal candidates whom they had agreed to support. Queirolo and Legal, the Cívico cabinet members, resigned in protest.[17] The diplomatic corps had been well pleased with Queirolo, who had been trustworthy and candid in the conduct of his office. After Decoud, with whom foreign diplomats were always cautious, Queirolo was especially welcome. The rumor that Aceval might ask Decoud to return to the cabinet alarmed the Brazilian minister despite his previous praise; but Decoud went to the Senate and Juan Cancio Flecha, a graduate of the Colegio Nacional de la Asunción, became minister of foreign affairs. This appointment was a surprise and came only after more capable men had refused to help Aceval "in the arduous task of governing an ungovernable country." The political situation had deteriorated so much that Itiberê feared a revolt led by the caballeristas.[18] Far more disruptive than rumors of revolt was the popular campaign to rehabilitate the reputation of Francisco Solano López.

Apotheosis Propaganda

Leaders in this effort to deify the "martyr of Cerro Corá" were Enrique Solano López and Carlos López, natural sons of the fallen leader; Venancio López, natural son of Francisco Solano's brother Vicente; Juan Emiliano O'Leary, whose mother and other relatives had been tortured by López; Arsenio López Decoud, another nephew of the dictator; Ignacio Alberto Pane, a brilliant polemicist; and an Argentine adventurer, Martín de Goicoechea Menéndez. O'Leary made the apotheosis of Francisco Solano López a major goal in his life, devoting his considerable literary talents so successfully to this objective that long before his death the grateful Colorados had his likeness cast in bronze and mounted on a pedestal in the Plaza de los Héroes. Irrepressible and irreverent humorists immediately dubbed the vulnerable O'Leary "El Bronce." Liberals, especially the Cívicos, opposed the efforts of lopiztas to create a "cult of the tyrants"; to glorify López meant to demean his enemies, and this kept old wounds open. The lopiztas did accomplish one thing of some value in giving young Paraguayans a hero to worship at a time when their country's pantheon was singularly uninhabited.

Enrique, whose inherited claims to huge tracts of land had been denied by Brazil and Argentina, returned to Asunción in 1883 after having lived abroad with his mother, the famous Elisa Alicia Lynch. Well-educated, an excellent linguist and engaging conversationalist, he was accepted by some of Asunción's social leaders. At every opportunity he defended his father's reputation. This, indeed, was the consuming passion in his life, a dedication reinforced by memories of that lonely grave at Cerro Corá where he had helped his mother to bury his father and oldest brother. A revival of lopizmo was aided by the continued sympathy that clung to the memory of Francisco Solano López as persistently as any vine embraced its forest host. A new generation, born since 1875, was maturing, and its members knew nothing of the horrors of the Paraguayan War. Both Liberals and Colorados honored López for his fight to the death in defense of Paraguay, although many could never forgive his gross cruelty and the insatiable greed of his Irish mistress. Colorados made lopizmo synonymous with nationalism: as lopiztas, they claimed to be heirs of the virtues and heroism of the Paraguayan people. Being anti-López, therefore, was a political stance, not an unpatriotic gesture.[19] Even

Bernadino Caballero, hero par excellence of the war, decried the tyranny of López.

Those who sought the glorification of López linked their cause inseparably to the steadily growing effort to persuade new generations that López had been betrayed by his generals early in the war, by the so-called conspirators with whom Charles Ames Washburn, the American minister, supposedly was involved, and by the Paraguayan Legion, whose members fought with the Allies.[20] Many Paraguayans, especially the veterans and the postwar generation of politicians and writers, joined in the effort to reawaken a sense of patriotism among the people, to arouse a sense of pride in their nation's military performance against overwhelming odds. This movement aroused resentment against the Allies and created an ambience favorable to efforts to glorify López. The battle was a bitter one. Even before Cerro Corá, the Provisional Government on August 22, 1869, had declared López an outlaw. Writers in *La Regeneración*, organ of the Legionnaires and anti-lopiztas, villifed López; there was even a Te Deum on March 6, 1870, to celebrate his death.[21] Hatred of López spread to Santiago, Chile, where the clergy refused permission for "some souls to have a funeral for López."[22] Successive decrees, approved by men later prominent in Colorado ranks, confiscated the properties of López and Madame Lynch and reinforced the decree declaring López an outlaw. Colorado governments could have repealed these decrees, or at least could have removed the stigma from López, but they failed to do so. Certainly they had no desire to reverse the decree that "embargoed" the 22,000,000 acres claimed by Madame Lynch, some of which were sold as part of the public domain. In 1885, fifteen years after Cerro Corá, *La Democracia* and *La Verdad* excoriated López as a bloody tyrant.[23] Thereafter, Paraguayan writers became increasingly interested in the dramatic events of March 1, 1870, that left López slumped on the slippery bank of a sluggish creek while his blood stained the muddy stream. Slowly the glorifiers of López transferred his image from destroying tyrant to saintly martyr.

There were glorifiers and defenders of López long before his son began the campaign that was to end in his apotheosis in 1936, when the Febreristas on March 1, the anniversary of Cerro Corá, ordered all anti-López decrees expunged from the record and declared the marshal-president the foremost citizen of Paraguay. Padre Gerónimo Becchis had dared to praise López from his pulpit even while Brazilian troops were pursuing the hunted leader to his death. The lopizta priest, Blas Ignacio Duarte, had organized a great fiesta on the feast day of St. Francis Solano in 1871, at which there were rousing cheers for López, Padre Fidel Maíz, and General Caballero.[24] The French traveler, L. Forgues, found in 1872 that López had many admirers in Asunción, and in the same year an Argentine visitor marveled: "It is wonderful what respect many people still cherish for the name of López."[25]

Resentment against the Legionnaires who had fought with Argentina and then had become closely associated with Brazilians, accounted in part for the breakup of the coalition of López enemies and for their dispersal among the two emerging parties. Although such former Legionnaires as José Segundo Decoud and presidents González and Egusquiza remained anti-lopizta and found a political home with the Colorados, they contributed to rebuilding Paraguayan morale by glorifying war heroes. Memories of the war were still vivid in 1888 when Juan G. González, then a senator, proposed to make Humaitá a national shrine, a monument to those who had died in defense of the fatherland: "In this way future generations of youth will be shown that their fathers had defended their territory palm by palm; . . . [the country] from Itapirú to Cerro-Corá should be filled with monuments that will recall the heroism of the Paraguayan people."[26]

Honoring López as a fallen hero was compatible with the post-war rebirth of nationalism, a movement in which nearly everyone could participate. Juan Silvano Godoi, although an associate of Enrique Solano in his shadowy land claims, was no lopizta and harshly condemned partisans of oppressive Colorado political practices as morbid psychopaths. The first postwar celebration of July 14, Francisco Solano's birthday, came in 1891 when President González distributed prizes won at the Paris exposition. It was hardly a coincidence that July 14 was declared a holiday that year.[27] President Egusquiza appointed Enrique Solano as superintendent of public instruction in 1897, and Aceval continued him in office as director general of schools. While serving in this position, he seized the opportunity to carry on his campaign to glorify his father's memory. He had no difficulty in recruiting university students who were being influenced by Blas Garay, director of La Prensa, and Juan Emiliano O'Leary, who was publishing uncritical pieces praising López. Early in 1898, bookstores in the capital sold student notebooks that were embellished with the likeness of Francisco Solano, accompanied by a grossly uncritical biography of the "martyr of Cerro Corá." Enrique Solano was the author and perpetrator of this propaganda effort. López directed La Patria, popularly called La Patria Chica, a small sheet of mediocre quality. The chief of the Bureau of Information in the Department of Immigration observed: "It is lucky for Paraguay that he [López] is impecunious as well as unprincipaled [sic] otherwise he might do more damage."[28] Francisco Tapia, an Argentine who had been employed to direct the Escuela Normal de Maestros, refused to allow students to bring the notebooks to school because

López had been proscribed by the government. President Egusquiza, in his message to Congress on April 1, 1898, condemned the apotheosis effort. On the next day, during a *conferencia* (lecture) by Tapia at the Instituto Paraguayo, several young men heckled the speaker until police restored order, after which prominent young Liberals, including Teodosio González and Eusebio Ayala, escorted Tapia to his home.[29]

The campaign to glorify López continued to win adherents because it appealed to nationalistic, chauvinistic, and xenophobic sentiments, although politicians who sought support from either Argentina or Brazil were distressed by the increasingly violent attacks on the former allies. The Argentine minister, Lauro Cabral, successfully directed much of this xenophobia against Brazil. Lopiztas used every possible means to embarrass Aceval when he became president. In June 1901, when rumors were spread that Bolivian Indians were invading the north, Aceval accused "the bastard sons of the tyrant López" with trying to involve Paraguay in a war, and when a pseudonymous writer in *La Tribuna* sneered at Paraguayan military strength, *El Estudiante* objected strenuously to what a writer called calculated calumnies against Francisco Solano López and the glorious Paraguayan soldiers who had been inspired by pure patriotism to follow their great leader.[30] The coup of January 9, 1902, that overthrew Aceval caused no change in the glorification movement except possibly to encourage its leaders. Enrique Solano, angered by Brazil's brusque refusal to take seriously his land claims in Mato Grosso, frequently used the columns of *La Patria* to urge a Paraguayan invasion of Brazil's sprawling province, and even advocated annexing the area between the Bravo and Apa rivers.[31] The glorifiers intensified their efforts during the politically troubled year of 1902 when Juan Antonio Escurra was preparing to assume the presidency.

Last Coup of the Generals

Through the spring and early summer of 1901, the economic situation continued to worsen. Rapid increase in the gold premium, with a corresponding decrease in the peso's value, reflected decreased confidence in the government's ability to meet its obligations. By August, gold was at 900 and still rising. Since much of the import duty had to be paid in gold, many articles were in effect being taxed ten to fifteen times their value. Paper money advocates in Congress wanted new issues to stimulate the economy, while their opponents saw in amortization the only hope for Paraguay to emerge from its economic troubles. Francisco Campos, after struggling for thirteen months against corruption, smuggling, and administrative incompetence, gave up on August 16, 1901. To replace him as minister of hacienda

Aceval appointed Fulgencio R. Moreno (1872–1935), a brilliant young man who was then director of the Colegio Nacional.[32] Moreno, a journalist and former deputy, later won prominence as a historian and defender of Paraguay's title to the Chaco. His achievements in letters, education, and diplomacy entitle him to a palce among Paraguay's foremost intellectuals.

The coup of January 9, 1902, that removed Aceval from office was organized by Moreno and Col. Juan Antonio Escurra, the minister of war. Brazilian complicity was suspected, primarily because General Egusquiza had become increasingly friendly with Argentina and many believed that Aceval suffered from Brazilian loss of confidence in Egusquiza. The presidential question, as usual, complicated matters. Apparently both factions of Colorados agreed that Minister of Interior Guillermo de los Ríos should be the candidate. De los Ríos resigned to campaign, and Escurra wanted to name his successor as well as the minister of justice. Aceval named his own choices to the vacant posts in open defiance of the dangerous and disgruntled caballeristas and asked Escurra and Moreno to resign. General Egusquiza advised Aceval to name him as minister of war and to take over the garrisons immediately in order to forestall his enemies. Caballero acted first. On his advice, Escurra invited two prominent officers, backers of Egusquiza, to dinner—and then imprisoned his astonished guests. During the night he posted cavalry platoons and weapons at strategic points. At about six o'clock on the morning of January 9, Escurra invited Aceval to come to the cavalry barracks to talk about his resignation. The president went, escorted by a cavalry squad that gave him no choice. When Aceval refused to sign, the plotters escorted him to a waiting cell, published their manifesto, and ordered Vice-President Carvallo to call a special session of Congress to approve the coup. Egusquiza and several of his friends wisely took refuge in the Argentine legation while Guillermo de los Ríos, who refused to trust his fellow Colorados, preferred the French legation; other prominent egusquicistas prudently avoided public exposure. This scurrying for shelter left the revolutionary committee, composed of generals Caballero and Escobar, Escurra, Moreno, and Senator Eduardo Fleytas in complete control.[33]

Congress met in an extremely tense atmosphere. Escurra had alerted artillery and cavalry units to stand by for action upon a signal from General Escobar, who would leave the floor of Congress at the appropriate time. In the gallery, Caballero's rowdies greatly outnumbered the few Aceval supporters who literally braved death or physical injury to be present. Eight of the thirteen senators, including generals Caballero and Escobar, and seventeen of the twenty-six deputies were present when Carvallo called the joint session to order at 11:10 A.M. Practically everyone was armed. Knives, sword canes,

and pistols could be more persuasive than the spoken word in deciding delicate issues. Carvallo opened the session by announcing that
he had received two documents for consideration, the manifesto and
a letter, signed by the revolutionary committee, which announced
that, "animated by patriotic sentiments of national preservation,"
they had deposed Aceval, who was not fit to be president, and that
there was no disturbance of public tranquillity. The committee
pledged itself to maintain order. Then Senator Fleytas read the committee's short manifesto which charged that Aceval was a selfish
partisan whose government was weak, lacking in prestige, and disastrous for the country's credit. After a short squabble over how many
should be named, a committee of four, headed by Dr. Facundo Insfrán, pretended to study the documents while Congress recessed for
fifteen minutes. When Carvallo rang the bell to call Congress to order,
Insfrán reported that Aceval's deposition was necessary and recommended that the vice-president be placed in charge of the executive
power.

In the ensuing brief but bitter debate, Deputy Cayetano A. Carreras, a conservative Colorado, asked pointed questions. Did Aceval
resign or was he deposed? Where was the president? Had a state of
siege been declared? Defying his party leaders, Carreras reminded
them that the constitution made no provision for Congress to approve
actions such as those the revolutionary committee had taken. Answering for the committee, Fleytas revealed that Aceval was alive and
well in private accommodations at the cavalry barracks; as to the
constitutional question, he replied lamely that Aceval had to be
deposed because he had carried the country to the brink of ruin.
When Carreras continued to protest, Insfrán presented such novel
arguments that one wonders if he had any respect at all for the
constitution. He maintained that the constitution had been followed,
constitutional guarantees prevailed, the constitution had been
exalted: "A material impossibility prevents Señor Emilio Aceval
from continuing as president of the Republic of Paraguay, it is impossible; no one can deny it. . . . The opinion of the people, which is a part
of the divine power, of the will of God, public opinion, the will of the
Paraguayan people, has given legal sanction to this act of the Revolutionary Committee . . . has been calling for it as an act of mercy for
months and months."[34] This was, at least, realistic.

Dr. Insfrán could have said it better: Paraguayans had always
accepted, or at least endured, revolutions and coups as valid political
processes, and no constitutional provision could supersede the honored tradition. Another Colorado deputy, Dr. José Emilio Pérez, insisted that if Aceval was guilty as charged, he should have been
impeached according to constitutional provisions and no self-
appointed committee could usurp that power. Deputy Julián Ayala

supported Pérez against the belligerently illogical defense offered by Insfrán and Fleytas. No one mentioned the real reason for the coup, which was simply to destroy the power of egusquicistas. Senator Federico Bogarín angrily assailed the conspirators "who rise with the voice of patriotism to deceive ignorant people." The official account states laconically: "Senator Fleytas protests. The gallery also erupts in protests that drown the words of Señor Bogarín who continues speaking. The president rings the bell and then there are several shots and the premises are abandoned by the representatives."[35]

What really happened was the most disgraceful scene ever to shame a Paraguayan congress. Fleytas, offended by Bogarín's remarks, drew a pistol and started toward the speaker. Bogarín's nephew, Vicente Rivarola, rushed from the gallery and shot at Fleytas. This started a general tumult in which fists, knives, canes, and revolvers were used freely. The more athletic participants hurled chairs and other loose furniture, unconcerned whether they struck friend or foe. General Escobar managed to get to the balcony, where he waved a handkerchief to the crowd gathered outside the Cabildo. Mistaking Escobar's greeting as the pre-arranged signal, the military commander ordered artillery and small arms fire. Colonel Escurra then sent a squadron of cavalry, traditionally the presidential escort or guard, galloping across the plaza and the firing ceased.

Inside the Cabildo, Carvallo frantically rang his little bell to restore order among the screaming combatants who had wrecked the chamber. Dr. Facundo Insfrán, former vice-president, senator, founder of the School of Medicine, and a prominent member of the best social circle, lay dead on the floor. General Caballero, who had come through many battles in the Paraguayan War without a scratch, was wounded, as were senators Bogarín, Fleytas, Miguel Corvalán, and Deputy Carreras.[36]

Slowly the surviving legislators heeded Carvallo's plaintive tinkling. Congress, or what was left of it, then unanimously approved the resolution legalizing the coup and placing Carvallo "in exercise of the executive power." The old generals had won their last coup. They had destroyed the González-Egusquiza policy of accommodation with the Liberals, leaving the chagrined Cívicos no choice but to reunite with the Radical Liberals, while moderate Colorados were forced to choose between the vastly weakened Radical Colorados (caballeristas) and the Liberals. Egusquiza, Ferreira, and other prominent políticos found a warm welcome in the Argentine legation, where Aceval and his family were permitted to join them.[37]

Political effects of the 1902 events were, to use a favorite Latin-American term, of transcendental importance. All Colorado protestations of loyalty to the constitution were convincingly revealed as cynical verbiage. Liberal accusations of Colorado tyranny were substantiated beyond question. Colorado leaders had confessed their inability to govern without resort to grossly illegal use of force. And, finally, popular support for the inevitable Liberal revolt was practically guaranteed.

The Carvallo Interim

Although assured that the political squall was over, businessmen cautiously closed their metal shutters and military patrols cruised the streets to prevent crowds from gathering on January 9 and 10. Carvallo moved at once into the presidential office and appointed a fairly good cabinet to assist him. Eduardo Fleytas in interior, Dr. Manuel Domínguez in foreign affairs, José Irala in justice, Moreno in hacienda, and Escurra in war and marine apparently were a congenial team. Domínguez was a distinguished lawyer and former rector of the university. Still in his early thirties, he was an excellent representative of a brilliant group of Paraguayans who reached maturity in the eighties and nineties and who were to excel in law, journalism, and literature. Domínguez had been a founder of *El Tiempo* in 1891, contributed to many newspapers, and was an indefatigable scholar who produced significant works in history, philology, ethnography, economics, and other fields. Before his death in 1935, he was recognized as one of the continent's leading intellectuals whose work deserved a much wider audience. Perhaps his best work was *El alma de la raza (The Soul of the Race)*, published in 1918, which has become a Paraguayan classic. José Irala, born in 1865, was a prominent lawyer and political scientist, editor of *La Democracia*. These young intellectuals contrasted sharply with Escurra, who was content to allow Fleytas to dominate the cabinet.

If Carvallo really wanted the presidency, the desire does nothing to enhance his reputation for intelligence. There were constant rumors of a counterrevolt to be led by Egusquiza, who could count on Liberal support, and, the Brazilian chargé reported, "he appears to have the moral and material aid of the Argentine Republic, from which he will return in a few days." Carvallo concentrated forces in Asunción to prevent the expected coup.[38] The principal danger, however, was from Liberals who were preparing in as much secrecy as was possible, strongly supported by the Argentine minister. The premature revolt of 1891, lack of security within their ranks, and lack of cooperation had taught Liberals to prepare more carefully.

Far more important than an impending revolt was the presidential question which the deepening economic depression threatened to overshadow. Carvallo and Caballero, who had gone to Buenos Aires to escape the heat, rain, and humidity of January, had not agreed on a candidate. Reflecting desires of yerba producers, especially Escobar,

Carvallo favored increasing the duty on yerba in transit from Mato Grosso. This was a poor way to raise revenue. The country's economic situation was worse than at any time since 1869, yet Carvallo had no solution to offer in his message to Congress on April 1.[39] Cecil Gosling, the perceptive English consul, despaired for the country's future. He feared that the rival parties might bring "a number of hired assassins . . . into the towns . . . and in the event of fighting ensuing there is very little security for human life."[40]

In the midst of a gloomy autumn, Paraguayans rejoiced when Dr. Cecilio Báez returned from Mexico, where he had represented Paraguay at the Second Pan American Congress. The appearance of several thousand supporters to greet this extremely popular Liberal leader at the wharf was a warning the Colorados read correctly.[41] Báez returned to a country whose depressed economy, volatile politics, and administrative morass created an ambience in which revolutionary movements could flourish. Colorado leaders, ever vigilant and suspicious of a Liberal-Argentina combination, continued to court Brazil's support. To counter the huge and enthusiastic welcome given to Báez, they marshaled the party faithful to give Itiberê da Cunha a rousing reception when he returned from leave. Caballero, Escobar, and other prominent Colorados agreed to back Escurra and Domínguez as their candidates in the 1902 election. If the Liberals put up a candidate, Báez obviously would be their man.[42]

Following the honored political formula, Escurra and Domínguez resigned their cabinet positions to campaign, although no campaign was necessary. Liberals allowed the election of 1902 to go to the Colorados by default when their candidates resigned and Liberal voters stayed away from the polls on Sunday, August 24. Itiberê da Cunha smugly observed that Brazil was on the best of terms with the new leaders; nevertheless, he regretted that "bayonets of the army continued to prevent freedom of suffrage for Liberals and dissident Colorados." The outlook for domestic harmony was gloomy when the very bayonets upon which Escurra depended could be turned against him, and strained relations between Caballero and Escobar threatened an end to their long period of cooperation in dominating most of the administrations for nearly thirty years.[43] Among the signs that Argentina would not easily see continued Colorado dominance was the transfer of Lauro Cabral to Bolivia in September after more than seven years at his post, during which he had received two promotions.[44] His successor proved to be more than a match for Brasilio Itiberê da Cunha and President Escurra.

9

End of the First Colorado Era: Escurra and the Revolution of 1904

Although apparently successful in imposing their will on the country by overthrowing Aceval in 1902, Caballero and Escobar had in fact lost control of Paraguayan politics. Egusquiza, put into office by the Cavalcanti coup of 1894, had drifted into the Argentine orbit. Paraguay, under Decoud's influence, had denounced the provision in the commercial treaty with Brazil that provided for free trade with Mato Grosso. Trade between Mato Grosso and Paraguay suffered intolerable delays, and Brazilian producers bitterly resented the duty levied on yerba in transit through Paraguayan territory, a duty beneficial to La Industrial Paraguaya which owned more than one-half of the yerbales and was in constant competition with the Brazilian-owned Matte Larangeira. The generals, deeply involved in La Industrial, could not satisfy Brazilian demands without sacrificing their own interests. That they had no intention of doing so was seen by Carvallo's maintenance of the Mato Grosso policy.

The drift toward Argentina was the natural result of historical influences reinforced by increasingly pervasive Anglo-Argentine domination of Paraguay's economy. Brazil had no enterprises in Paraguay comparable to Carlos Casado, Ltd., the Anglo-Argentine dominated railway and tramways, the Anglo-Paraguay Land Company, shipping, and other enterprises controlled from Buenos Aires or London through *porteño* houses. By the time Julio Roca was elected for his second term as president in 1898, Argentina was more powerful, more prosperous, than at any time in its history, and its foreign policy reflected this strength. Probably, too, Brazil was still internally weakened as a result of the turmoil that followed Dom Pedro's abdication in 1889.

120

Launching the Escurra Regime

Juan Antonio Escurra, the most incompetent of all Colorado presidents, had little comprehension of Paraguay's position between Brazil and Argentina, nor did he display any inclination to be enlightened. His vice-president, Manual Domínguez, was a brilliant young man whose good advice Escurra repeatedly ignored. In his short inaugural address, Escurra called for cooperation and conciliation of Paraguayans united for the common welfare. He set laudable goals, most of which were unattainable in one administration: he would improve finances, decrease inflation, reorganize the revenue system, and strengthen the Banco Agrícola; he would develop natural resources, promote commerce and agriculture, foster industry, canalize the rivers, and settle the railway question; he would improve sanitary conditions, encourage immigration, repratriate Paraguayans living abroad, and promote education. And, of course, he would settle the Chaco dispute with Bolivia.[1] To help in this ambitious program Escurra appointed a fairly good cabinet. Eduardo Fleytas and Fulgencio R. Moreno, companions in the 1902 coup, headed interior and hacienda, respectively. Pedro Peña, then minister to Brazil, was recalled to take over foreign affairs. Cayetano A. Carreras drew justice, worship, and public instruction. Antonio Cáceres rounded out the cabinet as minister of war and marine.[2]

Escurra was entirely the product of a military career that had given him little opportunity to develop any latent intellectual powers he may have had. Born on May 6, 1859, in Caraguatá, he was conscripted on June 16, 1879. A competent, obedient soldier, he rose steadily through the ranks to become a colonel and then cavalry commander, then minister of war and marine in Acevel's cabinet. The new president was a handsome man with thick, dark wavy hair parted in the middle, and clean shaven except for the heavy mustache that swept in well-kept curves to the lobes of his large ears.[3] Mustaches were so common that rarely did a public figure tolerate facial nudity. They came in all sizes. Fleytas and Escurra probably surpassed their contemporaries in the size and length of these adornments. Guillermo de los Ríos curled the ends of his mustache; others preferred to let them droop sadly. Cayetano Carreras, Egusquiza, Caballero, Escobar, Fabio Queirolo, Marcos Morínigo, and many other public men sported beards as well.[4]

Tall and slender, Escurra made a dapper appearance. Godoi described him as a taciturn, cynical man, suspicious of everyone. Foreign observers were even less complimentary. The British consul held a low opinion of Escurra, "a more ignorant type than his predecessors, and . . . his only apparent qualification for his office is that he has the sympathies and loyalty of the Army." The American vice-consul observed: "It is a fact that the President, Colonel Escurra, scarcely knows how to read & to write, & even understands spanish not without difficulty, his mother tongue is Guaraní."[5] More significant is the report of the Brazilian minister:

> Colonel Escurra . . . is truly a political nullity, being no more than a man of the barracks, which in this country is to say a person with neither learning nor education, since the military career is still considered despicable in Paraguay, because the government is obliged to take anyone it can seize in order to organize its army. Despite his supine ignorance, to the point of scarcely knowing Spanish beyond the bare essentials for the prime needs of living, Colonel Escurra showed considerable prudence and character in the three and a half years that he administered the War ministry, in which more than once he performed valuable services for this legation, of which he was always very considerate.[6]

Escurra won the Brazilian's support by preventing an increase in the duty on yerba and by supporting freedom of emigration for those who wanted to go to Brazilian territory to work in the yerbales, on ranches, and in lumbering. Escurra, although a compromise candidate reluctantly agreed to by Caballero and Escobar, probably would continue to favor Brazil, although there was danger that he would be taken over by the glorifiers of Marshal López, a group whose activities automatically made them anti-Brazilian. *La Patria*, journalistic voice of Enrique Solano López, frequently flattered Escurra. Dr. Cecilio Báez, who led Liberal opposition to the lopiztas, actively promoted a meeting of women in the cathedral and masses in all the churches on December 16, 1902, to honor the memory of those killed by the dictators and in the Paraguayan War. Two cabinet members, probably Moreno and Fleytas, were confirmed lopiztas and kept Escurra from supporting the protest. Cayetano Carreras, whose father had been executed by López, hated the lopiztas with understandable fervor. Thus the apotheosis issue caused dissension in the cabinet at a time when more serious matters demanded unified support.[7]

Perhaps the glorifiers of López, especially such young pyromaniacs as O'Leary, seized upon the issue as a means of embarrassing the old Colorados. If so, they succeeded admirably for a time. The alarmed Brazilian minister concluded that the overthrow of Aceval had been a mistake, "considering that Colonel Escurra is very unqualified for the presidency of the Republic," and some feared that he would give official sanction to the "vicious propaganda of the sons of the tyrant López, whose audacity increases daily." *La Patria* bitterly condemned the Brazilian minister for having attended the memorial services on December 16. In mid March, Escurra withdrew government subsidies, and the paper ceased publication. The Brazilian minister could observe, a bit smugly: "Once more the Brazilian policy triumphs in this country, in spite of the criminal complicity of certain turncoat Brazilians in the execrable campaign of our enemies."[8]

One Continuing Crisis

Men who were wise in Paraguayan politics knew that the old generals could not continue to dominate the government. Some thought that instead of the generals having chosen him, Escurra probably chose the generals. The ease with which he had conducted the coup warned the quarreling Liberals that they had to unite, especially since the Colorados appeared to be stronger than ever.[9] Because of this deceptive unity among Colorados, Cívicos drifted toward cooperation with the Radical Liberals.

Colorados suffered a serious blow to their fragile harmony because of the arrest of Alejandrino Escobar and Albino Jara, sons of very prominent Colorados, who were charged with plotting rebellion against Escurra. General Escobar made a well-publicized trip to Concepción, where Albino's father, Col. Zacarías Jara, was the military commander and where workers of La Industrial Paraguaya might be enlisted against the government. If Escurra expected to give Alejandrino and Albino the same brutal treatment that other prisoners suffered, Escobar's journey warned him that he could not afford to antagonize such powerful Colorados as General Escobar and Colonel Jara.[10]

Although there were some signs of economic improvement in 1903, the situation was so dismal that complete stagnation appeared to be inevitable. As the gold premium increased, automatically reflecting the peso's decline, Paraguay could not borrow, its products could not compete in world markets, and Congress rejected plans to increase revenues by monopolizing certain products. Refusal to support Moreno, the minister of hacienda, precipitated another of the dreary succession of cabinet crises. Because of the many attacks on Moreno's financial program, Escurra replaced him with Antonio Sosa and made other changes favorable to Brazil. Antolín Irala, the new minister of foreign affairs, had a Brazilian wife, and the minister of justice, Francisco Chaves, was the son of a Portuguese. Sosa proposed drastic measures to end the financial crisis. He asked Congress to increase paper money from $f14,089,000 to $f30,000,000, to raise customs duties and to impose new ones, to expropriate one-third of the hides exported, to increase the capital of the Banco Agrícola, and to begin an ambitious public works program. Congress not only approved these measures but also increased the paper money limit to $f35,000,000 and authorized expropriation of one-half the exported hides. Partly in response to these desperate devices, the gold premium dropped 200 points in three months, causing some to believe that businessmen might have more confidence in the government.[11]

Dissatisfaction with the Escurra regime was increasing, especially within the business community, which was being alienated by governmental tinkering in economic affairs. Discounting the inevitable estrangement caused by partisan politics and disappointed office seekers, there remained a large bloc of people who would be potential supporters of the revolt that was being prepared carefully in Buenos Aires and Asunción by Liberals who merely elaborated on the plan that was so poorly executed in 1891.

Despite constant and often virulent attacks in opposition papers, Escurra permitted a surprising degree of freedom of the press. Chief of Police Francisco Miranda and Interior Minister Eduardo Fleytas could have closed such critics as *La Bastilla*, *El Grito del Pueblo*, and *El Triunfo* on easily substantiated charges of libel. The outraged Fleytas did close *El Grito del Pueblo* in June 1904 when it had gone far beyond the limits of reasonable restraint expected from any newspaper. Nearly every member and every act of the administration met with journalistic condemnation. *La Bastilla* accused Miranda of gross incompetence:

> this *gentleman* seems not to have a drop of blood in his veins nor any sign of shame for not resigning from a position for which on all counts he is unqualified. First, because of his supine ignorance and, second, because of the barbaric instincts that control him. . . . We repeat, and shall repeat to the point of boredom, that Francisco Miranda should give up his position. The unsettled forests or penal colonies are for highwaymen, cattle thieves, and gauchos, but [one of them] should not—a thousand times not—hold a public post.[12]

This tabloid, which published clever and often spiteful cartoons, charged that graft prevailed throughout the administration, that smuggling and bribery were common. Life and property enjoyed no security in Asunción, where ruffians committed crimes in full daylight close to the police headquarters while Fleytas, who had appointed Miranda, ignored the scandal. "This is simply insufferable," *La Bastilla* complained, "and for the honor of Asunción it must stop."[13] *La Bastilla*'s credibility suffered from overkill, and the propaganda campaign directed by Cecilio Báez and other Liberals probably had a much greater influence in recruiting men of substance for the opposition.

Leaders of the Opposition

Politics and economics are always so closely intertwined that neither area can be considered seriously without reference to the other. True, some leaders of the revolt of 1904 apparently did not have large economic interests at stake. General Ferreira himself, who had practiced law for so long in Buenos Aires, probably owned more property in Argentina than in Paraguay. Dr. Cecilio Báez, who providentially accepted a diplomatic appointment to Washington before the shooting started, was a land speculator among his other activities. Guillermo de los Ríos and his brother, staunch egusquicistas, were bankers and investors in various enterprises. Important directors of La Industrial Paraguaya, which owned about one-half of Paraguay's yerbales, were on the side of the rebels. That some of these businessmen were Colorados mattered not at all, especially in their continuing rivalry with Matte Larangeira.

Among the major Paraguayan financiers of the revolt of 1904 were such rich bankers as Guillermo de los Ríos, Antonio Plate, Juan Bautista Gaona, Rodney B. Croskey, and Pedro Jorba, all of whom contributed significantly to the economic rebirth of the Paraguayan republic. When the Banco de la República was organized in 1908, several of the 1904 rebels were among its directors. Pedro Marcelino Jorba was president, and it was the Jorba firm, directed by Pedro Rius and Marcelino Jorba, whose monopoly on hide exports had caused so much furor before the 1904 revolution. Prominent, too, were Emilio Aceval, Higinio Arbo, Jorge N. Casaccia, Justin Berthet, and other business and professional leaders. Some of these men tried as early as 1901 to help the Banco Francés del Río de la Plata establish a branch in Asunción. The French bank was closely connected with the Banco Paraguayo and then with the Banco de la República.[14] Gaona, Plate, Croskey, and Casaccia were directors of La Industrial Paraguaya. The major sawmill at Concepción was owned by Guggiari, Gaona y Cía. This Gaona was the son of Juan Bautista. Many of these prominent enterprisers were so closely connected by interfamily marriages that their contemporaries had to be discreet in criticizing any of them politically.

Politics and economics were facets of the same game, but that did not mean complete harmony within the larger family. Sons of Caballero, Escobar, and Jara opposed the oppressive Colorado regime established by their fathers; cousins, uncles, nephews, nieces, and other relatives often found themselves in opposing political groups. Young politicians, who had come to maturity after 1880, had to be reckoned with in both parties. Among the younger generation, sometimes called the "young intellectuals," were Modesto and José Patricio Guggiari, whose family roots were in Villa Rica, and Dr. Gualberto Cardús Huerta and Adolfo Riquelme, all of whom were to play prominent roles in Paraguay. Eduardo Schaerer, known more as a wealthy businessman than as an intellectual, possessed determination as well as wealth. It was he who, as a Radical Liberal, financed *El Diario*, which began publication on June 1, 1904, with the experienced Riquelme as editor.

Benigno Ferreira was the only Liberal with both the military and political stature to attract a strong following and at the same time to win and keep the confidence of the revolution's backers in Buenos Aires. A Colorado critic calls this elder statesman "the traitor of 65, the despot of 73," and accuses him of having had the boxes of gold from the London loans of 1871–1872 removed from the Brazilian *Princesa* to his home and that of President Salvador Jovellanos. After his defeat in the revolt of 1873–1874, Ferreira had practiced law with Wenceslao Escalante in Buenos Aires and was closely associated with the powerful Soler family. (He has also been accused of having some shady deal with Henry White, local manager of the Paraguay Central Railway. White is supposed to have given the Solers a small press on which they printed *El Cívico*. Indeed, this critic draws the possibly simplistic conclusion that one of the motives of the 1904 revolt was to settle the railway dispute in accordance with the company's desires.[15] This charge, of course, implies that Great Britain somehow was back of the 1904 revolt, an implication that rests upon extremely shaky foundations and very inconclusive evidence.)

More important in actually planning the revolt were Manuel Duarte and Adolfo R. Soler. As Ferreira's secretary, Soler looked after details and maintained close relations with fellow plotters within the Escurra administration. Soler, without the academic credentials of Manuel Gondra, was far more practical than his colleague who gave his name to the Gondra Treaty of 1923. Gondra was a teacher of the humanities, one of Paraguay's leading intellectuals, and a supposedly gentle soul whose love for books is immortalized in the famous Gondra Collection at the University of Texas. It was indeed strange to find Gondra fighting beside Duarte in the revolution. His presence among the rebels must be noted, but this prominent scholar-politician did not play a leading role in the revolt.[16]

Launching the Revolt of 1904

Architects of the 1904 revolution merely refined the plans prepared for previous revolts by the Paraguayan Committee in Buenos Aires, of which Ferreira and Godoi were prominent members. Before making any military move, they mounted a well-integrated journalistic campaign against Escurra, temporarily healed the Liberal schism, enlisted support among the military, gathered supplies, and obtained enthusiastic cooperation from the Argentine government.[17] They formed two committees in 1903 to direct strategy and tactics. The Asunción committee, headed by General Ferreira, included Cecilio

Báez, Dr. Emilio González Navaro, Emilio Aceval, and the financiers Ríos, Campos, and Gaona. Three very capable young men, Manuel J. Duarte, Domingo García Torres, and Elías García, headed the Buenos Aires committee. Duarte, educated at the Argentine Escuela Naval, was a very capable officer who enlisted men, acquired matériel, and took charge of the munitions bought in Europe by Guillermo de los Ríos.[18]

President Escurra appeared to know little if anything of these extensive preparations; at least, he did nothing to prepare countermeasures. Unwittingly he cooperated with the rebels by providing them with a ship. Needing a vessel to transport Paraguayan products, Escurra sent Enrique Soler to buy the *Sajonia* in Buenos Aires, and a Liberal, Captian Ildefonso Benegas, to sail her to Asunción. After Soler had bought the *Sajonia*, Benegas promptly turned it over to Duarte. On August 4, Duarte sailed this *buque fantasma* (phantom ship) to La Plata, where he loaded his supplies and some three hundred recruits; then, with continuing connivance of Argentine authorities, he sailed into the Río de la Plata.[19]

A message from the Paraguayan consul in Buenos Aires on August 8 shocked President Escurra into declaring a state of siege and ordering Captain Eugenio Garay to intercept the *Sajonia* with 150 infantry aboard the merchant steamer *Villa Rica*. Caballero and Escobar came to the aid of the party with a manifesto that condemned the Liberals and insisted ironically that disputes be settled within the framework of the constitution and the laws.[20] Those generals who had led the rebellion of 1873–1874, who had deposed three presidents, now had the gall to invoke the sacred constitution, a document they were somewhat late in discovering. Ignoring this hypocritical blast, Liberals fled from the capital to rendezvous at Villeta, Pilar, and the mouth of the Río Tebicuary where they would arm themselves with weapons brought by a small vessel from Buenos Aires. Duarte struck swiftly. On August 10 he anchored off Humaitá, sent a raiding party ashore that captured the village with surprising ease, and sailed on to Villa Pilar, which was to become the rebels' civil headquarters. Off this landing the *Sajonia* and the *Villa Rica* had their brief encounter in which the *Sajonia* was the easy victor. The severely wounded Garay surrendered after losing twenty-eight men killed and many wounded. Eduardo Fleytas, the cabinet minister who had accompanied the expedition, sought to escape by jumping overboard, defying the voracious piranha. Rebels interrupted his swim to the Argentine shore by fishing him out of the muddy river like a floundering *surubí*. Duarte delivered the wounded to Pilar and moved north to establish his military headquarters at Villeta.[21] Then he sailed to Bouvier, a small village on the Argentine side a few miles south of Asunción, picked up General Ferreira and other Liberals, and returned to Villeta. Liberal leaders then organized a skeleton government with Ferreira as president.[22]

Rumors that the rebels were coming kept the capital in turmoil in mid August. Many prominent rebel sympathizers sought asylum in foreign legations and consulates, while others continued to join one of the detachments that were gathering at Villeta. Cecil Gosling, the British consul, reported on August 14 that everyone was "in a deuce of a funk, thinking the time of López had returned." A rebel patrol entered Asunción that night, fired a rocket signal, and retired. Escurra sent out two confused patrols which managed to fight each other until eight were dead and fifteen wounded. At about 1:00 A.M. on August 16, the *Libertad* and the *Constitución*, formerly the *Sajonia* and the *Villa Rica*, accompanied by two smaller vessels, entered the bay of Asunción. Ferreira sent a note to Itiberê da Cunha, dean of the diplomatic corps, threatening to bombard the city if Escurra refused to surrender. Escurra was willing to negotiate but would not submit to scurrilous treatment. During the exchange of notes between Itiberê and Ferreira, government forces foolishly tried to slip up on the *Libertad*. There was a brief exchange of gunfire and some shells landed in the city. After more notes, Ferreira agreed not to bombard the city unless government batteries fired on his little fleet. Augmented by a fifth vessel, the *Pollux*, which was seized when it entered the roadstead, Ferreira set sail.[23]

Just before the rebel fleet entered the bay, Ferreira released the Liberal manifesto of August 15. Compared with criticisms previously published in the press, this manifesto, written by Manuel Benítez, was relatively mild. Benítez contented himself with stating generalized charges rather than presenting a bill of particulars against the regime. Basic as a cause of the revolution was the profound despair and distrust throughout Paraguay: "A powerful, unanimous cry of protest against the ruling government is raised from one end of the country to the other," the revolutionary committee proclaimed. Public officials, unprepared for their offices, devoid of private and public honor, had lost public confidence; "countless thefts, unlimited corruption, immeasurable rapacity, so characterize government leadership as to endanger the country and cover it with a shame that must be ended." Bad as they had been, no previous Colorado regime had sunk to the depths reached by Escurra, never had there been so little respect for law, so little concern for individual rights and personal dignity. Escurra, the rebels maintained, was an incompetent, uneducated oaf who degraded the presidency, the fruit of a half century of military dictatorship, subverted institutions, allowed unrestrained thievery and farcical elections by government of cowardly tyrants. Paraguay's government, including Congress, was a collection of buffoons bought in the market place. The courts

and the president were unutterably corrupt, while a syndicate of
cynical, unpatriotic exploiters ruled the country. Upon Juan Antonio
Escurra and his gang would rest full responsibility for all damages
and all bloodshed that might result.[24]

During the exchange of notes on August 16, Escurra had agreed to
major concessions, including his own resignation. When these overtures had been refused, the president issued a spirited manifesto to
defend his regime. Reminding his enemies that all parties were represented in the government, he declared that "the country is the
common home and no party has the right to disturb the peace of the
citizens because they should discuss their quarrels peacefully within
the Constitution and the Law." Escurra scornfully noted that there
wasn't a single name among the rebels that reflected Paraguay's past
glories. Recounting his government's achievements, Escurra could
point to the statistical office, an improved labor law, extension of the
telegraph, new immigration laws, payment of the floating debt, improvement in rural government, increased activity by the Banco
Agrícola, negotiations for modern arms, and other actions. Escurra
noted that he had offered to resign in favor of Dr. Emeterio González
or Gerónimo Pereira Cazal. Rebels could have the ministries of justice and foreign affairs, while the Chamber of Commerce could select
the minister of hacienda. He offered other possible combinations:
Francisco Chaves, Carlos R. Santos, or José Irala as president, and
two cabinet positions to the rebels. He would recognize the military
ranks awarded by them, purchase their arms, pay their expenses, and
grant a general amnesty. But the rebels also demanded that Escurra
disband the army and dissolve Congress. Confident of victory, Escurra vowed to fight on.[25]

Despite disagreement between Escurra and Ferreira on terms for
ending the revolution, the four-man diplomatic corps, led by Itiberê
da Cunha and his Argentine colleague, Alejandro Guesalaga, boarded
the *Libertad* and sailed to Villeta on August 17. Noting how far Escurra was willing to go, one need not wonder that Ferreira insisted
upon harsh terms. He would never accept any settlement that left
Colorados in control of the key ministries of war and marine and
interior. Another rebel manifesto attacked the regime at the end of
August. In addition to the general accusations, this manifesto
charged that Escurra and his officers were using the government to
enrich themselves while neglecting customs reform, redemption of
the foreign debt, development of the economy, canalization of the
rivers, improvement of education, creation of a health service, settlement of the railway dispute, and organization of a modern army.
Vice-President Domínguez repeated these charges in a manifesto
circulated secretly before he himself deserted to the rebels. Besides
repeating accusations in other manifestos, Domínguez indicted Es-

curra and his favorites for brazen grafting in buying supplies for the army.[26] The score in the this battle of manifestos was about even.

The revolt dragged on for several weeks while Ferreira had to content himself with capturing river towns, interfering with neutral shipping, and occasionally risking a thrust toward Asunción, which Escurra held with some ten thousand troops. Ferreira and Duarte had no difficulty in capturing Villa Hayes, or, rather, in accepting its surrender, since the garrison promptly joined the rebels. More important was control of the remote center of Concepción where there was considerable discontent with Escurra's government. Ferreira sent Comandante Elías Ayala on the *Constitución*, with Captain Albino Jara leading a land expedition of 100 men, to capture the northern city. Ayala was supposed to reach Concepción ahead of Jara. Colonel Zacarías Jara, father of Albino, commanding government troops in the north, moved south from Bahía Negra to Concepción and was there to greet the rebels. With the government forces were the minster of war and several prominent officers. The two Jaras conferred and avoided a conflict when Colonel Jara agreed to go back to Bahía Negra to protect the frontier. Ayala, joined by Captain Patricio Alejandrino Escobar, sailed back to Villa Hayes, which became headquarters for his Army of the North.[27]

Rebel control of the river caused Escurra untold damage and could have involved Brazil directly in the conflict had officials at Itamaraty been sufficiently interested in the revolt to risk a direct confrontation with Argentina. Duarte became so arrogant that he stopped and searched the Argentine *La Golondrina*, an act that caused so much annoyance in Buenos Aires that soon a flotilla of four gunboats began to patrol the river. Guesalaga ordered the naval commander to exercise great restraint, obviously unwilling to risk the chance that Escurra might receive military supplies.[28]

Ferreira's war of attrition fatally weakened Escurra's ability to resist, encouraged desertions from the army, and caused Liberals to flee from Asunción at every opportunity. As Escurra's government teetered on the verge of collapse, the diplomatic corps intensified conciliation efforts. The loss of so many towns, disaffection among government troops, Argentine supply of arms to the rebels, inability to get supplies past rebel ships, Brazil's refusal to send aid, and rising discontent in the country made eventual surrender inevitable. Ferreira and his committee practically ignored Escurra in the protracted negotiations and directed their proposals primarily to generals Caballero and Escobar, to whom Escurra was of no importance once possession of their own properties had been guaranteed by the rebels. Ferreira protested that the Liberals were motivated by the highest ideals and were fighting only to eliminate corrupt men and corrupting forces "that exhausted the nation's wealth, suppressed suffrage, and mocked the democratic rights of the people."[29] The dreary negotiations, occasionally punctuated by military action, could have been ended quickly had Guesalaga cooperated with Itiberê da Cunha. Instead, the Argentine waited until Escurra's troubles would force him to accept Ferreira's harshest terms.[30]

The October stalemate, Itiberê reported, intensified misery everywhere: "The country is deserted and abandoned, commerce and industry are paralyzed; the time for planting has passed and the cattle breeding ranches have been pillaged. Considering this sad prospect, whichever of the parties wins the victory will win ruin and desolation as trophies." The government left the door open for negotiations, but Ferreira would not agree to any terms that left the Colorados with political or military power. As Itiberê observed accurately, Escurra would be easier to deal with once Escobar had resigned from the cabinet. Government forces had been inactive simply because they lacked supplies needed for an offensive, although the government had literally begged Brazil to sell such supplies or at least to provide armed escort for arms that might be obtained in Montevideo or Buenos Aires. Lacking specific instructions form Rio de Janeiro, Itiberê had not attempted to force rebel observance of neutral rights and had refrained from lodging a forceful protest when Argentine gunboats had anchored beside the Brazilian *Tiradentes* in order to interfere with its actions. The Brazilian minister ended his long report with a well-founded warning: "There is no doubt, then, that the revolutionaries and their Argentine allies are determined to seek a pretext for an international conflict, and the old rivalry of Argentina, so proud today of her rapid progress and of her powerful navy, are facts that should not escape the perception and vigilance of the Federal Government."[31]

This long, revealing despatch from Itiberê da Cunha testifies to the great progress Argentina had made since Cavalcanti had brazenly manipulated Paraguayan politics in 1894. Rio Branco obviously had no intention whatever of antagonizing Argentina, ample proof that Brazil had abdicated its former powerful position in Paraguay. When Escurra again asked for a Brazilian convoy to bring arms to Asunción, Itiberê refused without bothering to ask his government.[32]

Paraguay's situation was especially gloomy in mid November. The disruption of normal economic processes caused a general increase in misery as living standards, already abysmally low, declined further. Cries for peace came from all sides. In Buenos Aires, a delegation was being organized to promote a settlement that seemed to elude the best efforts of Paraguay's diplomatic corps. Guesalaga, ordered by his government to cooperate in efforts to bring about peace, replied that he would do so gladly if one of the parties would take the initiative. After a long conference with Escurra on November

16, and then with the minister of foreign affairs, Guesalaga had to admit failure. Escurra continued to hope for arms although the military situation worsened daily. The small rebel armies at Villa Hayes and Villeta could not be dislodged by Escurra's dispirited troops and moved unhindered by river and virtually so by land. There was one bright spot. On November 8, Itiberê da Cunha had received authority to convoy Brazilian merchantmen and had brusquely warned Ferreira to stop his river piracy. Ferreira agreed gracefully. Refusing to trust him, Itiberê ordered convoys for every Brazilian vessel sailing from Corrientes or Concepción.[33]

Escurra's position was hopeless by the end of November. Argentina refused to allow any arms to reach Asunción; the rebels attacked and captured Encarnación, through which some supplies had been reaching the government. Guesalaga, following orders, appeared to be more cordial toward his Brazilian colleague, who presumed that the government of President Manuel Quintana had decided not to risk antagonizing Brazil beyond the present strained relations. One may also surmise that Quintana was aware of Hipólito Irigoyen's plans for revolution in Argentina and wanted to avoid international complications. Itiberê da Cunha entertained a hearty dislike for Guesalaga, whom he held responsible for the persistent rumors that Brazil was aiding Escurra. By means of captured letters, Guesalaga was able to prove that Paraguayans had been spreading the rumors in an effort to involve Argentina and Brazil in war. Anyway, whether through negotiation or by military means, the rebels would soon win the revolution, and Itiberê admitted "that the wise abstention and neutrality of Brazil was a decision of high political foresight, making it possible right now to guarantee to Your Excellency that the treacherous maneuvers of our rival in the Plata will not have the effect she hoped for, whereas our influence and prestige will endure, and even increase greatly when we can say that we have a true war and merchant marine."[34]

As the Brazilian minister had predicted, President Escurra initiated the conference that ended hostilities when he offered to meet Ferreira aboard ship off the mouth of the Pilcomayo on December 12. From Asunción, Escurra, two cabinet members, and the diplomatic corps sailed on the Argentine monitor, El Plata. At the Pilcomayo, Ferreira, Duarte, Adolfo Soler and an Argentine delegation came aboard for a conference presided over by Itiberê da Cunha. Escurra accepted terms essentially similar to those proposed by Ferreira in October. He agreed to resign in favor of Juan Bautista Gaona; the army was to be reorganized; "free" elections would be held without Colorado participation; the ministries of interior and justice were allotted to Colorados but without control of the capital police. After Escurra had disbanded all but two army batallions, Itiberê da Cunha would notify Ferreira who would then enter the capital. Provisions of the Pilcomayo Pact were implemented so promptly and smoothly that Ferreira was able to arrive on December 18, but postponed the ceremonial entry at the head of his troops until December 24 in order to merge the celebration with Christmas festivities.[35]

Unfortunately, the Pilcomayo Pact settled nothing conclusively. All the old party and factional rivalries continued; some, indeed, were intensified, with the result that Gaona was driven from office in less than a year.[36] If domestic results of the revolution were relatively unimportant, the outcome externally was vastly different. Argentina had sponsored the revolt and Brazil had done nothing to perpetuate its own influence. Paraguay, swept back into the Argentine orbit, would remain an Argentine satellite for many decades. Brazil's great foreign minister, Barão do Rio Branco, much more concerned with settling Brazil's many boundary disputes, no longer feared that Argentina entertained serious ambitions to reconstitute the old Viceroyalty of La Plata.

10

Sparring with Old Enemies

Paraguay's postwar relations with Brazil and Argentina were controlled by conditions over which the emasculated nation could exercise little influence. During the postwar decade, Brazil had prevented Argentina from expanding northward to Bahía Negra, thus nullifying a provision of the treaty of the Triple Alliance. Paraguay's treaties of 1872 with Brazil and 1876 with Argentina reestablished peaceful relations, permitting Paraguay to pursue its independent career, lurching from one revolution to another while Brazil and Argentina continued their rivalry for Platine influence. In this rivalry for domination of what has come to be called "the southern cone," and in the Misiones boundary dispute, Paraguay had to be neutral. In the frustrating quest for cancellation of the ridiculously bloated war debts, Paraguay could exert almost no pressure on either creditor. Even when turmoil in Mato Grosso seemingly offered an opportunity to embarrass Brazil by aiding the outlaws, Paraguay was far too weak to embark on such a dangerous venture. Colorado leaders could derive some satisfaction from renegotiating the postwar treaties, from Decoud's success in blocking the old Hopkins claim,[1] and from gradually reestablishing diplomatic relations with other countries and participating in international expositions and multilateral treaties concerning noncontroversial matters. These actions restored Paraguay as a member of the family of nations.

Argentine-Brazilian Rivalry

In the resumed Argentine-Brazilian rivalry for control of Paraguay, in which Argentina held the long-run advantage, Brazil's larger occupation force, plus reinforcements readily available in Mato Grosso, gave

134

her the immediate advantage, at least until the evacuation of foreign troops in 1876. Argentina's edge came from commerce, geography, and historical heritage: a common culture, membership in the colonial Viceroyalty of Río de la Plata, and the plain fact that Buenos Aires controlled Paraguayan trade with Argentina where the country sold practically all its exports and which was the source of most of its imports. Affonso de Carvalho, the Brazilian chargé in Asunción, stated this clearly in 1886: "It is certain that this republic finds itself in complete dependence on Argentina. Buenos Aires is the only port of importation for Paraguay's trade, and that is why the commerce of Asunción is subject to all of the fluctuations in Buenos Aires."[2]

Paraguay's two presidents in the critical 1880s appeared to favor Brazil more than Argentina, although neither Caballero nor Escobar had any particular reason to be pro-Brazilian other than the fact that their most prominent political enemies were pro-Argentine. During their dictatorial regimes, Anglo-Argentine capital invested heavily in Paraguayan land, the railway, and the tramways of Asunción. Actually, Decoud represented the Paraguayan position well when he told the British minister, Edmund Monson, that the Argentine-Brazilian rivalry was the best guarantee of Paraguay's independence. The only danger was a very remote possibility that Argentina and Brazil might agree on a common course, then, Decoud exclaimed, "Ay del Paraguay!" which means, roughly, "God help Paraguay!" Monson concluded that neither country was benevolent toward Paraguay, and "both treated her with an arrogance and want of consideration which are bitterly resented" in Asunción: "The feeling that her former foes are pursuing a policy the object of which is to keep Paraguay in a state of prostration serves to perpetuate and augment the bitterness of the resentment entertained by the vanquished toward the victors." Monson could see no chance at all that Paraguay would ever join Argentina against Brazil.[3]

Argentine representatives in Asunción for the most part were not especially clever. The chargé in the late 1870s, Dr. Tristán Achaval Rodríguez, so antagonized President Bareiro that Paraguay several times intimated that he should be recalled. Fortunately, Rodríguez was elected to the Argentine Congress, and Col. Enrique B. Moreno replaced him in October 1880. Moreno stayed a few days, then returned to Buenos Aires, ostensibly to look after personal affairs; but he returned on December 2 on the armored *Constitución*, which remained at his orders. After conferring with Decoud, Moreno returned to Buenos Aires on the gunboat, and on December 15, Col. Lucio Mansilla, a favorite of Gen. Julio Roca, recently elected president of Argentina, arrived for a short visit. Mansilla, en route to Europe "on important commissions . . . one of which related to armaments, gave a weak excuse for his detour—he wanted to say goodby to friends in Asunción!" These activities greatly alarmed the very capable Brazilian chargé, José de Almeida e Vasconcellos, who put no faith in Argentine protestations of good will nor in the Hispanic peoples generally. He was positive that war between Argentina and Brazil was inevitable within a year or so and foolishly advised a preventive war: "I still say that I judge it to be a deplorable necessity for the Empire, because the sacrifices that we shall make will be smaller than those demanded by a permanent armed peace to which we shall be obligated in order to restain the bellicose Republic."[4]

The growing hostility between Brazil and Argentina over the exact location of the boundary of Argentina's Misiones province with Brazil appeared to lend credence to the chargé's fears. His successor believed that Paraguay, suffering severe financial problems, would turn to the country that gave it the most aid. Relations between Paraguay and Argentina were strengthened by the arrival of Dr. Héctor Alvarez as minister resident on a well-manned ironclad, General Roca's impending visit, the plan to complete telegraphic communications (which was done at Paso de Patria in 1883), and Decoud's attendance at the Buenos Aires Continental Exposition in 1882. It is doubtful if anyone believed the assertion in Paraguay's most prestigious newspaper that Decoud was going to Buenos Aires for a vacation. Decoud was concerned about rewriting the 1876 treaty and also proposed a commercial union of Brazil and the Platine countries,[5] a proposal that is another example of the vision of Paraguay's foremost statesman.

Tension between Argentina and Brazil over the Misiones boundary reached a climax in 1882, with far more saber rattling in Rio de Janeiro than in Buenos Aires, especially by Barão Cotegipe. General Roca did strengthen Argentina's armed forces, but at the same time he sent Nicolás Avellaneda to Rio de Janeiro on a goodwill mission. Cotegipe accused Argentina of having a protectorate over Uruguay. The British minister correctly observed that if this were true, it was because of a "community of race and origin" and not the result of intrigue.[6]

From Montevideo, Cotegipe's good friend, Paraguay's Juan José Brizuela, admitted that he did not know what his country would do in the event of an Argentine-Brazilian war. He noted that the Argentines had been especially attentive to Decoud and that Argentine diplomacy was active in Asunción while Brazil appeared to be indifferent. Later Brizuela assured Cotegipe that Paraguay would be neutral, but he was not sure about Uruguay.[7] Paraguayan neutrality really was not a serious matter except for the provisioning of Mato Grosso. Fortunately for all concerned, Argentine-Brazilian hostilities were confined to verbal exchanges and oratorical salvos.

Treaty Revision

Decoud took advantage of Argentine-Brazilian tension to press both countries for revision of postwar treaties. On March 5, 1881, Paraguay denounced the commercial treaty of 1872 and began the long, bickering process of revision, watched carefully by the Argentine minister. When the Brazilian chargé, Henrique Mamede Lins de Almeida, could gain no advantage over Decoud, he reported petulantly that the Caballero government was completely dominated by Argentina.[8] After two years of negotiations, a new treaty was signed on June 7, 1883, and finally ratified on May 28, 1884. The most significant provisions were articles 13 and 19 which provided for free trade between Paraguay and Mato Grosso, and a 50 percent reduction of duties collected by Paraguay on imports carried by Brazilian subsidized ships.[9] The new treaty was by no means a resounding diplomatic triumph for Decoud.

Paraguayans generally expected the new Argentine minister to Paraguay in 1882, Héctor Alvarez, to do something to meet their desire for treaty revision, but in frequent conferences with Decoud, Alvarez reiterated his lack of instructions to do anything and so avoided the issue. Unable to make progress in Asunción, Decoud decided to visit Buenos Aires, where he could attend the Continental Exposition and confer with Argentine officials. Alvarez had little advice for his government concerning the trade concessions Decoud wanted, except to ask: "If we were at once to concede everything that Paraguay asks, what resort would we have at hand to influence her policy toward Brazil?" Paraguayan officials, Alvarez believed, were careful not to be effusive in expressions of friendship for Argentina for fear of antagonizing Brazil: "Brazil without doubt believes firmly in the present predominance of our influence in Paraguay."[10] Since Decoud made no progress in Buenos Aires, the negotiations dragged on wearily in Asunción until January 31, 1885, when Alvarez and Decoud signed a new treaty of friendship, commerce, and navigation,[11] which changed matters very little.

The War Debts

At the end of the war, treaties with the victors bound Paraguay to pay all their war costs plus damage claims of private citizens. These terms were so ridiculous that one can only wonder that intelligent men would have insised upon including such an absurdity in the treaties. The reason was a requirement of the Triple Alliance treaty of May 1, 1865: "The Allies will demand from this Government the payment of the expenses of the war which they have been forced to carry on, and also the payment of damages caused to public and

private property, and to the persons of their citizens."[12] Just how
much Brazil and Argentina claimed was never determined with any
degree of accuracy. Estimates of the debt with interest have gone as
high as £300,000,000. The total is unimportant because Paraguay
never would have paid the war costs of the three allies. There was
more support in Argentina for cancellation than in Brazil, which was
typical of the postwar sentiment in the two countries, and reveals a
basic weakness of Brazil in postwar relations with Paraguay. Each of
the former allies feared that the other would consider cancellation as
an attempt to gain influence in Paraguay. After Uruguay took the first
step by cancelling the war debt, British envoys found that each of the
other allies was willing if the other would make the first move.[13] The
matter of private claims was something else entirely and was left to
mixed commissions to determine.

The Paraguayan-Argentine Mixed Commission began its work on
April 27, 1877. Officially it was the Comisión Mixta Internacional de
Reclamas Argentina-Paraguaya. After 358 sessions extending to
November 12, 1883, the commission had granted 2,808 claims total-
ing $f10,126,133.59 and thrown out claims for more than
$f2,400,000.[14] Paraguay dutifully began to deliver the *polizas*, or in-
demnification bonds, to claimants in the same year.

Brazilians made a much greater fuss over claims than did Argentina. The Paraguayan-Brazilian Mixed Claims Commission began its
work on December 16, 1872. Paraguayans deliberately sabotaged its
efforts through frequent changes in personnel and so many absences
from scheduled meetings that often several months elapsed between
sessions. When José de Almeida e Vasconcellos became Brazilian
chargé in August 1877, only 606 claims had been adjudicated. In
numerous despatches, the Brazilian chargé reported the progress of
the commission, always complaining about its too leisurely pace.
Finally, on April 21, 1881, the Brazilian government gave up and
ordered the commission to close its books. By that time, $10,458,614
had been awarded to several hundred claimants.[15] The totals
awarded to Argentine and Brazilian claimants were almost too close
to be a coincidence.

Paraguay adopted a policy of delaying delivery of the Brazilian
polizas as long as possible. Carlos Saguier advised President Gill to
"work ceaselessly with the patriotic purpose of obtaining isolated
concessions from Argentina and Brazil, which would then arouse the
pride and nobility of the other, and thus little by little we shall be
placing ourselves in a condition of being free from paying war indemnities."[16] This, indeed, is what happened, with full approval of
the Argentine government, which advised Gill to delay delivery of the
polizas since Brazil would immediately demand payment with interest. Brazil, obviously, was playing on its favored position. Facundo

Machaín, Paraguay's minister of foreign affairs in 1875, resigned
rather than deliver the polizas to Brazil.[17] Paraguayan officials frequently protested that payment of the awards was an impossibility
that everyone recognized. When Juan Antonio Jara made this point,
Vasconcellos replied sympathetically but insisted firmly that
Paraguay would be responsible for whatever consequences might
follow refusal to deliver the polizas. He admitted that Paraguay could
not pay at once, but the claimants could wait and if Jara refused to
deliver the polizas, Vasconcellos would give each claimant a certified
copy of the award. Jara replied that he would deliver the 1,134 polizas
with the understanding that they could not be paid. Still he dribbled
them out in batches over a full year, completing delivery in July
1880.[18]

Paraguay made good use of the Argentine-Brazilian rivalry in her
efforts to have the war debts canceled. During the war, when discussing possible peace terms, Argentina's foreign minister assured President Bartolomé Mitre that although the Triple Alliance treaty might
require Paraguay to pay war costs, the Allies should give up the idea
because of Paraguayan losses and the country's obvious inability to
pay. Brazil and Argentina, he was confident, would not try to collect,
but he was doubtful about Uruguay.[19] After the war, Uruguay showed
far more statesmanship than either of the other allies in dealing with
Paraguay, partly because she had little to lose. While Argentina and
Brazil kept up the silly pretense that Paraguay must pay the entire
cost of the war, plus private claims, Decoud went to Montevideo to
negotiate with Uruguay's foreign minister, Enrique Kubly. Within a
few weeks they signed the treaty of April 20, 1883, by which Uruguay
renounced all its claims for war damages. In article 2, Paraguay
acknowledged a debt of $3,696,000 to Uruguay, and in article 3
Uruguay renounced the debt but not the personal damages that
Uruguayans might claim. Such claims had to be presented within
eighteen months. However, no Uruguayan ever presented a claim for
damages. Two years later, the Uruguayan gunboat *General Artigas*
brought a delegation headed by the minister of war, Gen. Máximo
Tajes, to return trophies captured by Uruguay during the war. A
grateful government changed the name of Plaza San Francisco to
Plaza Uruguay, Congress conferred honorary citizenship on all members of the commission and made President Máximo Santos of
Uruguay an honorary general in the Paraguayan army. Each country
raised its diplomatic representative to the rank of minister resident.[20]
Paraguay and Uruguay had no more diplomatic problems during the
Colorado era.

Before giving Uruguay too much credit for its magnanimous
renunciation of war damages, one should remember that Brazil had
subsidized Uruguay's war effort with 600,000$000 contos. When the

Brazilian treasury threatened to end the subsidy, Uruguay's leaders were greatly distressed and again expressed their desire to withdraw from a conflict to which they had contributed all they could. To keep Uruguay in the war, Brazil continued the subsidy to the end of April 1868, making four more payments of 120,000 patacones monthly.[21] Uruguay's contribution to the allied victory had been very slight and its losses, both financial and in troops, were insignificant.

Paraguayan and other writers never tired of reminding the creditors that they had declared war against López, not against the Paraguayan people, and that Argentina's Mariano Varela had stated the doctrine that victory did not confer any rights over the integrity of the conquered—yet collection of the war debts could be accomplished only by "mutilation and extortion." Argentine statesmen constantly championed cancellation, knowing that they were embarrassing Brazil, but they stopped short of actual cancellation themselves. This attitude won Paraguayan support and good will, especially since it was believed that the Buenos Aires press was unanimous in favor of cancellation, as were the Argentine people. In view of Paraguay's poverty, miniscule government income, and shattered economy, the pretense of claiming a war indemnity was absurd, but until the debt was canceled, it would cast a shadow over the country's credit. When César Gondra introduced a bill in the Paraguayan Senate asking both creditors to cancel the debt, the Brazilian minister reported that Gondra was revealing the Machiavellian hand of Argentina.[22]

Paraguayans needed no prompting from Argentina. Immediately after his inauguration on November 25, 1882, President Caballero had expressed a desire for closer relations with the Empire and baldly stated that Brazil should help his country. Such a request deserved attention because Caballero recognized in Brazil the only country that could help and protect Paraguay disinterestedly. Argentina in 1886 was willing to renounce the debt, but since Paraguay's debt to Brazil was so much larger, the Argentine minister of foreign affairs insisted that Brazil should make the first move. Decoud relayed this information to Brazil's chargé, who could do nothing other than refer it to his superiors.[23]

Paraguay continued the drive for cancellation, despite the fact that neither Brazil nor Argentina asked for payment. A report from Rio de Janeiro that a group there was asking for cancellation and return of war trophies aroused great enthusiasm in Paraguay. The editorials, demonstrations, and resolutions that appeared in Asunción as a result of this rumor caused the Brazilian minister to surmise that they were inspired by President Julio Roca. On March 19, 1899, a very warm and muggy day, there was a huge demonstration in the Plaza de la Independencia, where major political figures joined a multitude of common folk, estimated at five thousand, to hear speeches and bands, after which large numbers of enthusiastic demonstrators paraded to the Argentine, Brazilian, and Uruguayan legations.[24] This would have been a good time for Brazil to cancel the debts as a gesture of goodwill, especially to counter the anti-Brazilian lopizta propaganda, but the opportunity passed. Dr. Eben Flagg, the American vice-consul, advanced a plausible theory to explain the refusal of Brazil and Argentina to change their policy: "If at anytime either of these powerful neighbors would encroach upon Paraguayan territory, or attempt to assume a protectorate over her it would make them responsible for the enormous debt and thus the very *existence* of the debt, even though the Paraguayans could never pay it, served as a means of securing to Paraguay her independence."[25]

Existence of the war debt was poorly known to diplomats of many countries. As the years passed, there were occasional flurries of cancellation agitation which focused attention on these relics of the Paraguayan War. Paraguay continued to ignore the debts as an obligation, and their existence ceased to have any effect on Paraguay's credit. The Argentine Congress officially canceled the debt on August 11, 1942, and Brazil followed suit in 1943,[26] thus ending a controversy that never should have occurred.

Concepción and the Mato Grosso Frontier

Concepción, capital of the department of the same name, is a river port about five miles north of the Río Ypané, a navigable stream much used by yerbateros to float chatas loaded with bales of yerba. For the huge area to the northeast and for southern Mato Grosso, hunting ground of the fierce jaguar, refuge for nomadic Indians, and haven for rustlers, smugglers, and assorted outlaws, Concepción was the metropolis, the most important settlement in northern Paraguay. It was stil a frontier community at the end of the nineteenth century.

Mato Grosso is a huge wilderness covering 475,000 square miles, with a population of about 1 million and growing rapidly. In the eighteenth century, Mato Grosso and its capital Cuiabá were as wild or wilder than any frontier in the Americas. Vera Kelsey exaggerated very little in her graphic description of *bandeirantes*, gold hunters, assassins, and thoroughly bad men who sought fortune or refuge in that remote area. Seventeenth-century bandeirantes discovered placer gold in large quantities, and some of them found prospecting to be much more profitable than efforts to enslave the wild Indians who roamed the area.[27] So many bandeirantes visited or settled in the Cuiabá-Corumbá-Coimbra areas, far west of the ineffective Demarcation Line of 1494, that Spain's claim to the territory was completely nullified. What Spain might have done, and eventually Paraguay, had

the conquistadores expended their efforts north of the Rio Apa, will
forever remain one of the great "ifs" of the area's history. The fact
remains that Brazilians did move west and northwest from São Paulo
and other centers to claim some of the richest land east of the Andes,
while Spaniards from Paraguay dissipated their energy in futile
expeditions to the realm of El Rey Blanco, the fabled White King of

Map 3. The Upper Paraguay and Mato Grosso

Peru. Fabulous as are the stories of gold in Brazil, the auriferous area of Mato Grosso covers but a small fraction of its vast territory. The forest and agricultural lands of the province far exceed in value the minerals thus far discovered and exploited.

Mato Grosso was not neglected by explorers of the nineteenth century. One of them was the French geologist Dr. Emanuel de Bourgade la Dardye, who found much of interest during his expedition of 1887–1889 in the southern part of the territory. Bourgade was interested primarily in Paraguay and penetrated into Mato Grosso to examine affluents of the Río Paraguay. On his authoritative map of 1889 he showed only two *fazendas* (ranches) on the Brazilian side of the river in the space between Bahía Negra south to the Apa, a distance of 192 miles. Winding down from the north, the Río Paraguay turns southeastward at Corumbá, then bends leisurely southwestward for about one hundred miles before wriggling southward hundreds of miles to its junction with the Paraná above Corrientes. At its southward turn, the Río Negro, a short tributary some fifty miles long that rises in the vast marshes of the upper Paraguay, joins the main stream. Just south of this junction, on the Chaco side, is the small landing of Puerto Caballo, and eight kilometers straight south overland is Bahía Negra, about sixteen kilometers by river from Puerto Caballo. This area was very important in determining the present boundaries of Brazil, Bolivia, and Paraguay. To the east lie the great pastures that extend to Campo Grande and which, if properly exploited, might have made colonial Paraguay or colonial Brazil the great rival of Argentina in the production of cattle. Bahía Negra, also called Chamococo by the Indians and Puerto Pacheco by the Bolivians, was surrounded by high land fit for cultivation. On the Brazilian side a Colonel Malheiros had established a large fazenda that produced fine cattle. Malheiros also cultivated land on the Chaco side[28] and owned at least one river vessel that made regular trips to Asunción.

The Rio Apa, whose origins in the Amambay foothills was disputed until the Brazilian-Paraguayan Boundary Commission agreed on its source in 1878, is of no importance to commerce. One of its mouths at the confluence with the Paraguay is closed by a sandbar much of the year, and the other is navigable for only a very short distance. Easily crossed, the Apa was no barrier to raids from either side and merely marked one of the wildest frontiers in South America.

The decision of the Boundary Commission left a huge Indian-infested area between the rivers Branco and Apa to Brazil. A few daring frontiersmen exploited the rich agricultural and forest resources of the region, despite the hostility of at least three groups of Indians—the Chamococos, Angaites, and Sanapanas—who raided

across the Paraguay. Most warlike were the Chamococos, who undoubtedly were responsible for the deaths of scores of *mineros* (yerba
workers), explorers, missionaries, and herders from various fazendas.
There were large stands of yerba that beckoned yerbateros from
Concepción province, and the fazendas along the left bank of the
Paraguay in Mato Grosso were as exposed to Indian raids as were any
ranches in Mexico's far northern provinces of Arizona and New
Mexico, or Argentina's southern Pampas. These fazendas produced
fine cattle, for the land was covered with rich grass that provided
expansive pastures in areas not subject to flooding.

Dangerous and annoying though they were, Indian raids were
not the only complaints of Brazilian and Paraguayan residents in
Mato Grosso and northern Paraguay. Most of the itinerant workers on
Brazilian fazendas were Paraguayans, and tales of their mistreatment found ready publication in columns of *El Municipio*, Concepción's influential paper, but *El Municipio*'s editor rarely concerned
himself with inhuman conditions under which mineros worked in the
yerbales of Matte Larangeira and other Brazilian and Paraguayan
companies.[29] Another complaint was cattle rustling. Merchants in
Concepción, especially Carlos and Brasilio Quevedo, provided an
open market for cattle. On one occasion in 1897, they had bought
5,000 head from Captain João Cayetano Teixeira Muzzi for the considerable sum of 100 contos (nearly $25,000). With only ten men,
Carlos Quevedo went north to drive the herd to Concepción. The trail
boss had driven one-fifth of the herd a short distance when an armed
band, led by a government official, stopped the drive. Muzzi had been
fined 30 contos for his role in a recent revolt in Minas Gerais and the
cattle were held as security. A Brazilian investigation showed that
Muzzi was a notorious rustler whose activities had helped to keep
southern Mato Grosso in turmoil in the early 1890s, especially in the
area of Nioao village, which lay some one hundred miles north of the
northeastern "corner" of Paraguay. Muzzi and Quevedo appeared to
be business partners, with Muzzi the rustler boss and Quevedo the
fence.[30]

Occasions such as the Quevedo-Muzzi brouhaha were less frequent than the many complaints of maltreatment received by the
Paraguayan consul general, Mariano Galeano, at Corumbá. This was
an important post, because Mato Grosso had been in near anarchy
and outright rebellion for many years. Despite these unsettled conditions, many Paraguayans sought employment on the fazendas and
yerbales operated by Brazilians, such as the Companhia Cibils and
Matte Larangeira. Investigation of the complaints generally proved
them to be groundless, at least in the opinion of the investigators.
Merchants and ships' captains had good reason to complain about
their treatment by Brazilian authorities who did nothing to expedite

trade with Paraguay, a trade that increased substantially in the 1890s and overwhelmed Mato Grosso's facilities. Haughty pilots boarded Paraguayan vessels, demanded special treatment, and when they finally reached Corumbá, often made the vessels wait for hours before being allowed to dock.[31]

Corumbá, Coimbra, and Cuiabá (or Cuyabá) were by no means the most attractive towns in Brazil in the 1890s; however, various foreigners, many of them missionaries, other adventurers and gold hunters, survived the perils incident upon reaching these outposts of the bandeirantes. A notorious affair in 1899 was the Williamson expedition from Cuyabá. James [?] Williamson and an Englishman identified only as Foster obviously had gone up the Paraguay from Asunción to Cuyabá for the purpose of exploring southward. John W. Price, an American missionary in Cuyabá, Mr. E. Kirk, who had a land grant in Mato Grosso, Foster and another adventurer joined Williamson. The whole party was murdered by Indians. The American consul concluded: "The general impressions are that he who ventures into that vast forest or wilderness, unless well prepared, takes his life in his own hands, either by fever, starvation, losing himself or by murder."[32]

Raids by hostile Indians on both sides of the upper Paraguay continued into the 1900s, encouraged by ineffective expeditions sent to rescue women and children who were held captive. Among many such incidents, one may note the foray of Caduveos Indians who, fancying the cattle available on the Malheiros fazenda, raided the herd and killed the small force that pursued them. Colonel Malheiros, unable to obtain protection in Mato Grosso, sought help from the Paraguayan garrison at Olimpo and even carried his complaint to the Brazilian minister in Asunción.[33]

Maintenance of order in southern Mato Grosso was a task handled poorly from Rio de Janeiro. Cuyabá, Coimbra, Corumbá, and smaller settlements harbored an unruly lot of adventurers who made revolution chronic in Mato Grosso in the 1890s. In May 1892, rebel forces attacked the government garrison in Cuyabá and nearly succeeded in capturing the city. Both loyal and rebel vessels prowled the Paraguay, and sympathetic Paraguayans were accused of providing supplies for the rebels.[34] Another conflict broke out on September 27, 1901, with rebels using Paraguay's Fuerte Olimpo as a base. Again there were complications. Jean Baptiste Vierci, head of the Casa Vierci y Hermanos, was the father-in-law of Guillermo de los Ríos, financier and Paraguay's minister of interior. Vierci owned three ships, the *Pollux*, the *Posada*, and the *Leda*, that were prominent in the Mato Grosso trade. The firm, notorious as smugglers and buyers of stolen cattle, had a store in Corumbá. Senator Federico Bogarín, a prominent leader of the Paraguayan Congress, had an estancia on the northern frontier and was an associate of Juan Ferreira Mascarenhas, who was suspected of being involved in directing stolen cattle to Bogarín's estancia. Sales of stolen cattle in Paraguay provided funds for the rebels and became so flagrant that Mato Grosso ports were closed for several weeks. The so-called rebellion was essentially an outbreak of lawlessness during which cattle rustling threatened to destroy the fazendas.[35] The Mato Grosso rebellion ended quickly when two stern caudilhos from Rio Grande do Sul were brought in to direct government operations. Presidents Aceval and Escurra had both failed to prevent violations of the Mato Grosso frontier, a task in which they had no cooperation from Rio de Janeiro.

11

Colorados and the Chaco Boreal

The dispute with Bolivia over ownership of the Chaco Boreal was the most serious diplomatic issue that the Colorados faced during their first long tenure. It involved not only Paraguay and Bolivia, but Brazil and Argentina as well. The northern Argentine-Bolivian boundary had not been defined. Both countries claimed the Tarija area. Bolivia, Paraguay, and Brazil also had an undefined boundary in the Bahía Negra region on the upper Paraguay. Any bilateral negotiations here had to consider the third party. If Brazil favored Paraguay, then Bolivia could be expected to take a more recalcitrant stand over Brazilian infiltration into the Acre, a vast rubber-rich region over which Bolivia exercised only nominal control. Bolivia's disputes with Brazil and Argentina would not have concerned Paraguay, except near Bahía Negra, had it not been for the lurking possibility that the long controversy might lead to war, as indeed it did in 1932 after four years of minor clashes. Both countries would be vitally concerned about their neighbors' attitudes. The Empire and its successor republic had a significant stake in maintaining peace between the Chaco rivals and therefore applauded efforts to settle the dispute by direct negotiation.

The Disputed Chaco

The Chaco Boreal is a vast area of many millions of acres bounded on the south by the marshy Río Pilcomayo and on the east by the Río Paraguay. Most of the area is relatively low and flat. The plain rises to the northwest where the Chaco disappears in Bolivia's eastern highlands which, together with the Río Parapití, and the Bañados (swamps) de Izozog, form a fair natural boundary (see map 4). The northeastern geographical boundary is marked by two low sierras and the Río Otuquis. Although geographers can quibble over this description of natural boundaries, these limits are as accurate as any claimed by the disputants, who had no irrefutable authority to support their claims, and geographical knowledge of the area was so poor that location of the principal streams in a fluvial complex, or of a boundary stream named in old documents, was rarely indisputable. Even definition of the Río Pilcomayo was so difficult that Paraguay and Argentina had a fairly friendly argument over which of several sluggish streams was the principal channel. In the central part of its course, the Pilcomayo is a huge swamp with various currents that eventually combine to form an identifiable river.

Map 4. Colorado Boundary Treaties and Chaco Land Classification

   The failure of Spain to define colonial boundaries accurately gave rise to scores of boundary disputes after the colonies became independent countries. In relation to the Chaco, the major disputants were Argentina, Bolivia, and Paraguay. Bolivia's claims on its southern border conflicted with Argentina's claims on its northwest. This Argentine-Bolivian dispute had little concern forParaguay after the Machaín-Irigoyen treaty of 1876 had recognized the Chaco Central as Argentine territory. After occupying Tarija in 1826, Bolivia attempted further expansion taking advantage of Argentine turmoil. Bolivia had also advanced claims to the northern Chaco Boreal. When Paraguay and Argentina signed the Varela-Derqui treaty of July 15, 1852— which Argentina rejected—Bolivia's chargé in Buenos Aires, Juan de la Benavente, had protested that the treaty ignored Bolivia's perfect title to the Río Paraguay between 20° and 22° S. This "Benavente protest" was to be cited frequently by Bolivia in the future.[1]

   During the Paraguayan War, Argentina's foreign minister, Rufino de Elizalde, and Bolivia's envoy, Quintín Quevedo, signed a treaty on July 9, 1868, in which the two countries vowed that their Chaco dispute would be settled peaceably. This treaty also referred to the matter of Bahía Negra, since the Triple Alliance treaty of May 1, 1865, defined Argentina's territory as reaching to that distant port on the Río Paraguay. In 1869, Mariano Varela and Quevedo signed a protocol that promised a Bolivian-Argentine treaty of limits after the Paraguayan War ended.[2] To protect various religious missions in the upper reaches of the Pilcomayo basin, Bolivia began to establish military outposts in 1871. Beginning in 1872, Argentina vigorously rejected Bolivian claims and reestablished her control over the disputed area.[3] During the postwar negotiations in 1872, Bolivia zealously advanced her claims by sending Mariano Reyes Cardona to Buenos Aires. When Dr. Carlos Tejedor refused to consider Cardona's arguments, the Bolivian went to Rio de Janeiro, where the Brazilian minister of foreign affairs dismissed his protest with the brusque comment that "the bank of the Paraguay River is of no importance to Bolivia."[4] In complaining about this cavalier treatment, Bolivia's minister of foreign affairs, José M. del Carpio, reminded the Argentines of the 1860 negotiations, and when Paraguay and Argentina signed the Machaín-Irigoyen treaty in 1876, he complained that the two countries "had assigned all of the Bolivian Chaco, despite being separated from it by the national boundaries of the rivers Paraguay and Bermejo." So far as the still unannounced Hayes Award was concerned, it could not affect Bolivia's title. Dr. Carpio stated Bolivia's claims so well that the scores of volumes written later failed to improve upon his presentation. Penetrating to the heart of the matter, Carpio stated:

In the first place, there is no need, either historically or geographically, [for Bolivia] to bury herself in the obscure labyrinth of annals from remote centuries, dusting off and turning over archives like the Argentine Government and its patient bibliophiles and writers have done, in order to discover who were the first Chaco explorers, the first ones who, obtaining authorization from the kings of Spain, penetrated into that desert for the purpose of conquering, civilizing, or settling it, and whether their efforts did or did not have any effects, since this is a task as tiresome as it is superfluous and irrelevant, because the only data that can come from this material are the geographic demarcations established by the Spanish metropolis for its American colonies . . . following the time-honored divisions and subdivisions of the Royal Audiencia.

In Bolivia's case, the Audiencia of Charcas had jurisdiction over all the Chacos and Bolivia inherited that jurisdiction under the principle of *uti possidetis,* that a colony retains its territory when it gains independence. After giving the Argentine president a good lesson in history, Carpio summarized the case: "En una palabra, el derecho de la fuerza opone la fuerza del derecho" (In a word, the law of force contradicts the force of law).[5]

Carpio's title recital was essentially the same that all Bolivians used in disputing ownership of the Chaco Boreal. Just as vigorously, Paraguayan scholars defended their country's claims. Investigators combed the Spanish archives for documents, and such writers as Alejandro Audibert, Blas Garay, Eusebio Ayala, Cecilio Báez, and Fulgencio R. Moreno wrote learned treatises on the question.[6] So many candidates for the Doctor of Jurisprudence degree wrote to defend Paraguay's Chaco title that they are still called "Doctores en Chaco."

Basically, Paraguay's claims rested on discovery, exploration, and settlement (on the right bank of the Río Paraguay), and on the principle of *uti possidetis.* The very observant British diplomat, Arthur Vansittart, wrote in 1882: "The Gran Chaco on the west of Paraguay as far as Bolivia has from time immemorial been acknowledged as pertaining to the jurisdiction of Paraguay, from the River Pilcomayo on the south to Bahía Negra on the north . . . but this immense territory, twice as large as Paraguay proper, is only known to unsubdued Indians."[7] Just how far was "as far as Bolivia"? Begging the question like this certainly did not solve the problem of ownership, a matter to which all Colorado presidents gave their attention.

The Bravo Concession and the Decoud-Quijarro Treaty, 1879

The first postwar Chaco treaty between Bolivia and Paraguay was signed in 1879. Ratification of this pact would have helped to pave the way for realizing the ambitious plans of Francisco Javier Bravo, whose concession of August 1879 was the first to contemplate extensive Chaco development. As a young man, Bravo had spent several years in southern Brazil agitating against the Argentine dictator Manuel de Rosas and his Uruguayan puppet, Manuel Oribe. Bravo was Gen. Fructuoso Rivera's secretary in 1846 and 1847, then served as a sutler for Brazil during the war against Oribe and Rosas. Bravo added to his fortune as a sutler for Brazil during the Paraguayan War. Like many others who became intimately acquainted with Paraguay during the allied occupation, Bravo developed a plan to promote his own interests through a grandiose project. He approached President Bareiro in 1879 with a proposal for building a railway across the northern Chaco to link Bolivia's Santa Cruz with a port to be built on the Paraguay River. The scheme called for towns along the railway, European immigrants, and enterprises to provide traffic for the railway and to exploit supposedly great salt beds, large areas of bromelia that could be used in paper production, cinchona, indigo, "auriferous soils [and] land extraordinarily fertile for the cultivation of cotton and tobacco."[8]

President Bareiro, in recommending that Congress grant Bravo a concession "of that part of the national territory of the Chaco included between the north and west frontier, and the parallel that runs twenty leagues south of Bahía Negra, that is, one degree, for the purpose of building railways and to colonize this territory,"[9] emphasized two points: replacing the wild hordes of Indians with civilized communities and opening an overland route to Bolivia. The result would be a tremendous increase in wealth for Paraguay and the cementing of friendly relations with Bolivia. The concession, granted by Congress on August 5, 1879, made the Bravo enterprise practically sovereign in a region of more than 10 million acres. The power to levy import duties of 25 percent and export duties of 2 percent, with an additional 1 percent on both for public works, aroused opposition of the Brazilians, who insisted that any goods bound for Mato Grosso must be free of duty, as provided by the Cotegipe-Loizaga treaty of 1872. When the Brazilian chargé formally protested against the customs provisions, Decoud reassured him that Paraguay would honor its treaties, an assurance greeted with skepticism by Brazil's foreign minister, who replied that since Paraguay had failed to deliver the polizas, Decoud's assurance could not be accepted without reservation.[10]

One of the many rumors that soon circulated about the Chaco enterprise was that Bravo was backed by a strong banking house in London. Bravo spent some $60,000 of his own fortune to sent out two exploring expeditions. One, commanded by an engineer, followed the well-known trail from Fuerte Olimpo to Santa Cruz de la Sierra which had been used in colonial times by all who had legal business with the Audiencia of Charcas and by Bolivian Indians who brought trinkets and bags of medicinal herbs to Asunción. This trail went by way of the Salinas de San José, about 240 miles due northwest of Olimpo, and then northwest for another 140 miles to Santa Cruz. The first group reached Salinas de San José without difficulty and waited in vain for the second group, which became lost and perished on the way.[11]

Undismayed by this costly failure, Bravo enlisted the aid of a Frenchman, Gabino Monguillot. They formed a corporation optimistically capitalized at £600,000 and went to England to obtain funds. Returning from London in May 1880, Bravo and Monguillot informed the press that they had a contract that assured them of £600,000 to start, and £2,000,000 more to complete, the grand scheme that called for construction of the railway, purchase of steamers, erection of customs houses and railway stations, and many more projects, which would cost 30,000,000 gold pesos and require seven years to complete. The Empresa Bravo-Monguillot expected to be self-sustaining within three years after spending £2,000,000 and able to earn all the funds needed to comlete the plans. But none of this could happen until Bolivia gave its approval and granted the necessary concessions. With visions of wealth and supreme confidence in his project, Bravo sought Bolivia's sanction.[12] Before granting the concession, Bolivia wanted a boundary treaty with Paraguay. Many years later Bravo claimed credit for having triggered the events that caused Bolivia to send Dr. Antonio Quijarro to Paraguay to negotiate the treaty.

When the Bolivian envoy arrived in Asunción, he found the Paraguayans receptive and conciliatory. At his reception on September 25, 1879, Quijarro referred to the serious turn of events in the War of the Pacific as marking the time for Bolivia "to establish a new era in its relations with the Plata republics by opening expeditious means of communication." He assured President Bareiro that Bolivia would conscientiously cultivate good relations with Paraguay. Bareiro replied that Paraguay had always been interested in closer ties with Bolivia, and, despite the desert barrier to commercial exchange, anticipated eagerly the time when the two countries would be more closely united.[13] These diplomatic niceties were by no means a mere formality. In very smooth negotiations neither country presented a lengthy, documented defense of its Chaco claims.

In a surprisingly generous mood, Decoud agreed to a boundary which, starting at the mouth of the Apa River, ran due west to the Pilcomayo (see map 4).[14] By this agreement Decoud would have surrendered at least one-half of the Chaco that Paraguay eventually came to own. No wonder that the Colorado leaders decided to keep the treaty terms secret until Congress could convene! The reason for this generosity was, as President Bareiro explained to the Brazilian chargé, a desire to avoid quarrels over the Chaco and not to risk an arbitral decision. Bareiro and Decoud, obviously, had little faith in Paraguay's ability to prove title to the Chaco as far north as Bahía Negra. Brazil's foreign minister was immensely pleased that Bolivia had come out so well and hoped that both countries would quickly approve the treaty.[15]

The Decoud giveaway met with severe criticism in Paraguay, especially from Liberals. Editorial opinion unanimously condemned the treaty, and Congress rejected it.[16] The Bolivian Congress gave its approval on August 3, 1881, provided Paraguay would grant one or two ports on the Pilcomayo. In an effort to obtain Paraguayan approval, Bolivia sent Eugenio Caballero to treat with Decoud. By this time Bernardino Caballero was president and was far less inclined than Bareiro to be generous in dealing with Bolivia. All that the Bolivian envoy could achieve was a protocol which provided that proposed modifications in the Decoud-Quijarro treaty could be made indefinitely. Bolivia might have gained a more favorable reception for the treaty without the proviso for ports on the Pilcomayo—which were impossible, anyway—but its congress was adamant. Dr. Quijarro had hoped that a road could be opened from Santa Cruz to Paraguay, but by 1885 he was more interested in a railway to Corumbá.[17]

The Suárez Arana Concession and the Aceval-Tamayo Treaty, 1887

The second pact between Bolivia and Paraguay was also preceded by an unsuccessful attempt to gain economic development of the Chaco. Miguel Suárez Arana, a Bolivian who was "the owner and sole manager of the Empresa Nacional de Bolivia," asked Paraguay in 1884 for a concession to explore the Paraguay River in order to establish a port from which a railway and road would cross the Chaco and connect with Sucre. The Paraguayan government, in granting its permission, carefully reserved all its territorial rights. The Bolivian set his enterprise in motion on June 16, 1885, when he sent five small ships and two large barges upriver from Rosario, a port about one hundred kilometers north of Asunción, to Bahía Negra, a voyage of well over five hundred fifty kilometers up the winding Paraguay. The *Bolivia*, largest of the supply ships, was expected to be in regular service.[18]

At Bahía Negra, Suárez Arana built a port which he called Pacheco. (Because Chamococo Indians occupied the Chaco opposite Bahía Negra, the small bay and port often were called Chamococo.) The new port was south of the line that marked Paraguay's northernmost claim. The region was so swampy that persons who knew the area well believed that the work of several months would be completely wasted unless enormous sums were spent. Suárez Arana definitely had established his port on land claimed by Paraguay, although it was at least eighty leagues north of the Decoud-Quijarro line. At first the Paraguayan press expected great things from the Puerto Pacheco development. *La Democracia* advised Bolivia to subsidize a line of steamers to run from Pacheco to Europe, and *El Orden* was almost lyrical in recounting Bolivia's great natural wealth that could find an outlet through Pacheco.[19]

Suárez Arana lacked the resources necessary to complete his plans. On the verge of bankruptcy, he appealed to the Bolivian government to take over the concession and reimburse him for his expenditures. The Bolivian congress approved and sent its minister resident in Buenos Aires, Santiago Vaca Guzmán, to Asunción to make arrangements with the concessionaire. Difficulties arose in negotiations with Suárez Arana, but Guzmán made a trip to Puerto Pacheco in November 1886 to inspect the work in progress. At this point, Brazil's consul in Asunción warned his government that the project would threaten the prosperity of Corumbá by usurping its role as a trading center. Moreover, he advised encouraging discontented European immigrants in Asunción to settle in Mato Grosso. If Puerto Pacheco should be successful, Brazil would have to consider establishing a rival settlement on the opposite bank. The Suárez Arana project might also be a threat to the Argentine railway being built toward Bolivia, since it would be a transportation route that would carry both Bolivian and Brazilian products to the Argentine port of Rosario. Even the Madeira-Mamoré railway, being built by Brazil around falls on the Mamoré to give access to the rubber-rich Acre territory, would affect Mato Grosso, then isolated and remote from other parts of Brazil. The interests of Mato Grosso had to be considered, the consul insisted.[20]

After the Bolivian government had nationalized the Suárez Arana enterprise, it sent detachments of troops to Puerto Pacheco and raised the Bolivian flag. To forestall any further argument with Paraguay, Bolivia sent Dr. Isaac Tamayo as its minister to revive the Decoud-Quijarro pact or, failing in that, to sign a new treaty. Tamayo was also authorized to indemnify Suárez Arana. Reports circulated that Bolivia would give up the plan to build a vehicular road and instead concentrate on a railway. Tamayo, according to rumor, stopped over at Rosario de Santa Fé in Argentina to discuss railway plans with Carlos Casado del Alisal, a major railway builder and colonizer who had also invested heavily in Chaco land and in Paraguay's soon-to-be-opened Banco de Comercio.[21]

Tamayo's cordial welcome on May 20, 1886, led him to believe that his mission would be successful, but opposition was increasing in Congress and in the press to Bolivian acts of sovereignty at Puerto Pacheco. Bolivia treated the area as her territory, as though the Decoud-Quijarro treaty had been ratified. To guard Paraguay's interests, President Caballero decided to reestablish a guard at Fuerte Olimpo on the Chaco side about midway between the mouth of the Apa and Bahía Negra. Olimpo, of course, was also in the area that would have been Bolivian under the Decoud-Quijarro treaty. Although Tamayo protested against the proposal, the garrison was reestablished on August 10, 1886. Brazil, having its own boundary dispute with Bolivia, hoped that the Chaco boundary would be settled peacefully. Avoiding direct intervention, the Empire exerted discreet pressure on Paraguay to sign a treaty with Tamayo.[22] Considering the complexity of the Chaco dispute, negotiations between Tamayo and Dr. Benjamín Aceval proceeded smoothly. The treaty which they signed on February 16, 1887, was even more favorable to Bolivia than the treaty of 1879. Again eschewing any presentation of claims and counterclaims, the negotiators divided the Chaco into three sections. The first, from the mouth of the Pilcomayo north to the mouth of the Apa, then west to 63° west of Paris, and south to the Pilcomayo, would be indisputably Paraguayan territory. The second area, to be arbitrated by King Leopold of Belgium, was the region from the mouth of the Apa to one league north of Olimpo, then west to 63° west of Paris, and south to the Apa parallel. The third area was the rest of the Chaco, recognized as Bolivian territory. By this very unusual treaty, Paraguay would have surrendered claim to all but 124,000 of the Chaco's estimated 340,000 square kilometers, assuming an arbitral decision favorable to Paraguay. Again the Colorados had proposed an outrageous giveaway of Paraguayan territory. Although President Escobar strongly defended the treaty, the Paraguayan Congress rejected it overwhelmingly.[23]

The Paraguayan congress persistently refused to approve ratification, although the time limit was extended to November 1888. Part of the reason was the lucrative land sales that Paraguay was making in the disputed area. Bolivia sent more armed detachments into the Chaco, reinforced Puerto Pacheco, and rejected Paraguayan efforts to exercise jurisdiction over the colony. Preparing to counter these moves, Paraguay on January 13, 1888, divided control of the Chaco between officials at Villa Hayes and Fuerte Olimpo, the latter's jurisdiction to extend to Bahía Negra. The Bolivian chargé, Claudio Pinilla, demanded an explanation.[24] Decoud replied soothingly that Paraguay was merely tightening security measures against Indian raids in the area and relations between the two countries should not be affected. Then Paraguay sent an expedition of seventy-five well-armed men to reenforce the small detachment at Olimpo and re-

jected Pinilla's protest with the assertion that Paraguay had maintained sovereignty over the area "since time immemorial," a phrase
that became a favorite with the "doctores en Chaco." Pinilla rebuked
Decoud, stating that Bolivia would not recognize Paraguay's acts as
an exercise of "legitimate" sovereignty—as though there could be
any other kind—but Decoud, awaiting the arrival of Santiago Vaca
Guzmán as Bolivia's minister, reiterated that occupation of Fuerte
Olimpo, which the Bolivians always called Fuerte Borbón, was a
legitimate exercise of Paraguayan sovereignty and no appeal could be
made to an unratified treaty. "The truth is irrefutable," Decoud
wrote, apparently assuming that the truth had been determined.[25]
Juan Crisóstomo Centurión, an old and faithful lopizta, replaced
Decoud as minister of foreign affairs on September 28, 1888. When
Pinilla learned that Paraguay had seized four Bolivians at Puerto
Pacheco, he sent a strong protest to Centurión, who defended the
action, denying that Bolivia had ever held title to Pacheco. Pinilla
immediately broke off diplomatic relations after he had restated his
country's case and Centurión had replied with a long, closely
reasoned defense.[26]

Pinilla had reason to be disturbed. The Paraguayans had brought
Bolivia's "governor" at Pacheco and the secretary of the Bolivian
legation as prisoners to Asunción. The arrest of "Governor" Enrique
Moscoso was evidence that Decoud had not been bluffing when he
informed Brazil's chargé in April that Paraguay would "send military
detachments to occupy the Chaco as far as Bahía Negra, and land
forces in Puerto Pacheco with orders to arrest every person who
claimed to be a Bolivian authority."[27]

These events aroused some fears in Argentina that the two countries might go to war over a "desert" that neither could exploit.[28]
However, Pinilla was not threatening a war, nor was Paraguay ready
for a conflict. Carvalho reported that there would be no war, "since
the immense distance that separates Paraguay from Bolivia, appears
to make an armed invasion out of the question for either country."[29]
The Paraguayan press was conciliatory, especially *El Paraguayo*,
which referred to Pinilla as a perfect gentleman, "a distinguished
diplomat, modest and prudent," who won friends for his country.
Centurión, although defending Paraguay's course, was annoyed by
the arrests at Pacheco and was not impressed by the excuse that
Bolivia was trying to stir up the savage Chamococos, who were a
constant menace.[30]

Worried about a possible Bolivian-Paraguayan war, Brazilian
officials reenforced Corumbá and other points in order to be certain
that Brazil's neutrality would be respected. Field Marshal Manoel
Deodoro da Fonseca, military commander of Mato Grosso, en route to
Corumbá with troops, put in at Asunción where he waited for the

president of Mato Grosso to join him for a conference with President Escobar in January 1889.[31] Brazil and Argentina offered their good offices to smooth Paraguayan-Bolivian relations. Bolivia made the first moves by approving the Aceval-Tamayo treaty on November 23, 1888, and by sending Pinilla as minister plenipotentiary on special mission to exchange ratifications. However, the Bolivian ratification had come after the time limit had expired, so Paraguay had a good excuse for refusing favorable consideration of the unpopular treaty. Nevertheless, Pinilla waited for a month in the sweltering summer before blasting the Paraguayans in a scorching letter which *La Razón* published on January 6, 1889. In this undiplomatic outburst, Pinilla claimed for Bolivia the entire Chaco from Bahía Negra to the mouth of the Pilcomayo.[32] Bolivian firebrands continued to advance this extreme claim for more than four decades.

The Chaco dispute had taken an ugly turn. Francis Pakenham, the British minister in Buenos Aires, noted that Pinilla's "manifesto" of January 6 seemed to be directed against holders of Chaco land-warrants issued by the Paraguayan government.[33] Despite all the diplomatic posturing and frontier provocations in the Bahía Negra area, Pakenham was not worried: "The Bolivian frontier question is not one likely to reach an acute stage for many years to come, and I have no doubt that before it does mutual concessions will be made, resulting in an advantage to both sides. It is probable that both countries know well the real limits of each other's demands, and that in arrangements with foreigners the Paraguayan Government will be careful to keep within the bounds of their probable future frontier."[34]

A few months after Pinilla had gone home, the Bolivian government granted a concession to Dr. Antonio Quijarro, representing Perry, Cutbill, de Lungo y Cía., for a railway from Puerto Pacheco to Santa Cruz. In commenting on this renewal of the railway project, Pedro Pablo Barba, a Bolivian who edited *El Independiente* in Asunción, observed that a railway would be a great boon to both countries by creating new markets and outlets for goods. Barba also insisted that Paraguay's occupation of Pacheco did not confer title to the area. Other Paraguayan papers, much more independent than *El Independiente*, favored new efforts to end the dispute. Whether inspired by Bolivia or the result of honest opinions of various editors, conciliatory editorials apparently encouraged Bolivia to appoint another envoy. Dr. Mariano Baptista, with Claudio Pinilla as secretary, received the dubious honor of fencing with the Paraguayans.[35]

With settlement of the Chaco proceeding rapidly, at least along the river, Paraguay was in no hurry to treat with Baptista. Although a Bolivian vice-president, Baptista could not get a single conference to discuss limits. While he was waiting, the press again urged negotiation. *La República*, in asserting that the whole country wanted a peaceful solution, advised that concessions had to be made. *La Demo-cracia* published contributions from Teodoro Chacón, the Bolivian consul, who wrote a series of articles defending Bolivia's position and asking why Baptista had been kept cooling his heels for two months. Discouraged by Paraguayan indifference, Baptista left Asunción in October after delivering a memorandum to the foreign office. President González, in his annual message of April 1, 1892, informed Congress that his government was assembling documents to prove Paraguay's title to all the Chaco northwest to the Río Parapití, a work necessary in view of the extension of Bolivia's claims from the line claimed by Benavente in 1852 to include the Chaco all the way to the gates of Asunción.[36]

Failure of the Third Chaco Treaty—Benítez-Ichazo, 1894

In response to Uruguay's good offices, Bolivia made another effort to settle the dispute in 1894. Dr. Telmo Ichazo, a very capable Bolivian diplomat, arrived at Asunción in the midst of the Cavalcanti coup of June 9, 1894, which overthrew President González. This political turmoil caused Ichazo's reception to be postponed until July 20, after which he began discussions with Gregorio Benítez, Paraguay's new minister of foreign affairs. The result was the Benítez-Ichazo treaty of November 23, 1894, by which Paraguay again would have surrendered a large part of its Chaco claim. Starting three leagues north of Fuerte Olimpo, the line agreed upon ran southwest to the Pilcomayo at 61°21" west of Greenwich (see map 4). This entirely arbitrary line satisfied no one. President Egusquiza sent the treaty to Congress on July 28, 1895, with a recommendation that it be approved; but Congress appointed a commission to study the document. The Bolivian president refused to send the treaty to his congress.[37]

The Benítez-Ichazo treaty raised some interesting questions. Were its terms dictated by Brazil? Had land speculators brought pressure to bear on the negotiators? Was Argentina involved in any way? The angered and bewildered editor of *El Pueblo*, as well as other journalists, charged that the Colorados had allowed Paraguay to become a Brazilian protectorate: "They are proud to be under the protection of Brazil." Gomes Pereira, the Brazilian chargé, replied heatedly in a letter promptly published by *El Pueblo*. Noting that the zone between Fuerte Olimpo and Bahía Negra had been withheld from sale, *El Centinela* reported that speculators were seeking concessions. President González had commissioned a serious study of Paraguay's title, and, despite corruption in his administration, he did respect the nation's sovereignty.[38] Gomes Pereira saw the Argentine influence at work. To keep Bolivia from direct outlets to the Río de la

Plata, Argentina had agreed to build a railway to Bolivia. Moreover, he continued:

> since Argentina has a party—the Liberal party—in this republic, it is precisely this party whose objectives are compatible with the policy of José Segundo Decoud, who was overthrown by the revolution of June 9. [Argentina] may easily succeed in the disruptive task of creating obstacles to the ratification of that treaty [Benítez-Ichazo], especially because the party organ, the newspaper "El Diario," is now directed by Dr. Alejandro Audibert, a man of moderate education but of bad character, always disturbed by a restless ambition, and who, personifying everything that creates bad feeling toward Brazil and sympathy for Argentina, plays a very special role in this question of limits, being the author of a book entitled "Los límites de la antigua provincia del Paraguay," and therefore the only person competent to represent the interests of this republic in that question, and for that reason he has for years written against every proposed settlement of that dispute.[39]

President Egusquiza, in urging a settlement with Bolivia, insisted on the need "to harmonize the rights of Paraguay with economic interests and the cause of American fraternity."[40] Bolivia's rulers, still optimistic, in 1896 sent Dr. Rodolfo Galvarro as the minister to Asunción. Galvarro failed to gauge accurately Liberal opposition to the treaty and sought support from Egusquiza, Caballero, and Escobar. *El Pueblo*, tireless in its opposition, insisted that Paraguay would surrender 7,000 square leagues of the Chaco if the Benítez-Ichazo treaty were ratified. Confronted by a rising tide of Liberal-sponsored criticisms, the Colorados retreated. Stalling as usual, the Congress in November commissioned Benjamín Aceval and Cecilio Báez to make a study of Paraguay's title and decided to postpone further treaty negotiations until 1897, so Bolivia recalled Dr. Galvarro.[41]

Conflicting Concessions and Hardening Attitudes

Suárez Arana's concession had been nullified effectively by Paraguay's occupation of Puerto Pacheco. Still pending was the old concession to Francisco Javier Bravo, who deluded himself for several years with the fantasy that he could carry out his grand scheme. Another ambitious enterpriser, E. F. Swan, representing the American Development Company, obtained a concession from Bolivia early in 1897 to build a railway and telegraph and telephone lines from the Paraguay River to Santa Cruz. Having no diplomatic representative in La Paz, Paraguayans were surprised when the press reported this concession. José Segundo Decoud, again Paraguay's foreign minister, immediately protested to Bolivia's Consul Chacón, while the minister of war sent reenforcements to Fuerte Olimpo and Puerto Pacheco.

Many young Paraguayans volunteered for military duty, and Congress in secret session on July 12 authorized calling out the national guard. Surprisingly, the Brazilian minister reported that there was no war fever in Asunción,[42] but the dispute had become increasingly serious, with the two countries rapidly assuming positions that would be difficult to modify.

Decoud and his Bolivian counterpart exchanged several notes during the rest of 1897. When pressed for an exact definition of lands to be granted to the American Development Company, the Bolivian deftly avoided the issue, except to state that 3,000 square leagues were in the Chaco along the Paraguay River, and 2,000 were in the Santa Cruz and Beni areas. When queried by the American consul, Chacón provided a summary of the dispute which insisted that Bolivia's title was clear and that it was absurd for Paraguay to claim as far as the Parapití River. Chacón ridiculed the outcry in *La Democracia* against the grant as pointless, jingoistic propaganda; his own country was calmly waiting for approval of the Benítez-Ichazo treaty which would benefit both countries. Because of the desert that separated them, Paraguay and Bolivia could not go to war and, ultimately, the dispute would have to be arbitrated.[43] Chacón was a poor prophet.

The Decoud-Gómez diplomatic encounter was characteristic of all such episodes: each side asserted its claim to the Chaco, neither would concede anything, and every act by either claimant in the Chaco was certain to draw a vigorous protest from the other. The Brazilian minister to Paraguay, who had also been stationed in Bolivia, assessed the situation accurately: despite Bolivia's conciliatory replies to Decoud's protests, Paraguay reenforced its frontier garrisons, repaired the forts at Bahía Negra (Pacheco) and Fuerte Olimpo, and encouraged Catholic and Protestant missionary efforts to convert the Chaco Indians and to create agricultural colonies, "some under the direction of the Silesian order, and others under military control, all of which tend to strengthen Paraguay's rights in that disputed territory." He noted the virulent, insulting language in Bolivia's official press which charged that it was useless to negotiate with a country that resorted to such means as Paraguay was using to usurp Bolivian territory. Not content with diatribes, Bolivian journalists favored preparations to attack the Paraguayans in the same way that the savage Tobas were attacked when they raided Bolivian border towns. So, Itiberê da Cunha concluded, the Chaco dispute daily became more serious, especially since Bolivia planned to send a large military expedition to Puerto Suárez, on the Paraguay about twenty kilometers west of Corumbá, ostensibly to explore adjacent areas but in reality to seize Puerto Pacheco. The Paraguayan press had responded to this news with bellicose invective, boasting wildly that Paraguay could easily field ten thousand perfectly armed men![44]

Continuing his long report, Itiberê noted that Paraguay, preoccupied with defense of its Chaco frontier, had prepared its northern forts to withstand a ninety-day siege, by which time they could be reprovisioned by river craft. A telegraph line had been completed between Olimpo and Bahía Negra, and the line from Asunción had reached Concepción, a short distance from Mato Grosso. If Brazil declined the proposal to link up with the Paraguayan line, then Paraguay would build along the Chaco side to Bahía Negra. Paraguay's preparations were the logical result of President Severo Alonso's declaration at a banquet in La Paz in 1894, when he boasted while vice-president that his country would settle by force those questions that could not be decided by law. When the Chilean minister had demanded an explanation, Alonso said he was referring exclusively to Paraguay. Unfortunately, Itiberê continued, Bolivia had a very strong reason for its arrogance, a reason that Brazil could not ignore:

> Today it is well known that the aggressive attitude of the Bolivians toward this Republic is caused by the strong support that the Argentines are giving them in this dispute, which may also be inferred from the tone taken by the propaganda in the porteño press in favor of their probable future ally, although the press itself confesses ingenuously that the Argentines recognize the proverbial bad faith of Bolivian governments and should not expect to meet with anything but deceit and ingratitude, as the most important organs of the Platine press have just declared.[45]

Since matters had reached this state, the Brazilian minister could see no hope for approval of the Benítez-Ichazo treaty by either country. The Paraguayan Congress would meet on April 1, and one of its first concerns would be the treaty. The Aceval-Báez report, based on ample documentation, recommended rejection of the treaty and opposed any concession to Bolivia. Dr. Blas Garay, who had researched the Spanish archives, was coming with copies of documents that proved Paraguay's perfect title to the entire Chaco. Itiberê da Cunha concluded his assessment with the prophecy that was to be fulfilled three decades later: "If events do not change and continue in the same aggressive stance, it is much to be feared that a violent encounter will result between the Paraguayan-Bolivian frontier garrisons and result in a real war between the two neighboring republics."[46]

With events seemingly leading the two countries into war, Colorado leaders sought a peaceful solution. Although copies of the Garay documents were at hand, President Aceval in April 1899 sent Dr. César Gondra as minister to Chile, Peru, and Bolivia. The revolution that deposed the bombastic Bolivian President Alonso in December 1898 kept Bolivia in turmoil until General José M. Pando, head of the revolutionary junta, established his control. During these tumultuous months, Dr. Gondra decided not to attempt negotiations with the junta.[47]

Paraguay's government kept a close watch on the progress of Bolivia's argument with Chile and appeared to be alarmed by the bellicose tone of the Bolivian press. The role Argentina and Brazil might play in the Chilean-Bolivian dispute was an important consideration. Moreover, Brazil and Bolivia were arguing over the Acre territory, and Paraguayans feared that Brazil might support Bolivian ambition for a port on the Río Paraguay. Trusting neither Argentina nor Brazil, Paraguay's foreign minister, José Urdapilleta, toyed with the idea of asking for protection of the United States and told Dr. Ruffin that the two countries might try to absorb Bolivia and Paraguay. Urdapilleta and Ruffin had met at a New Year's Eve party, and so the two might well have been under the influence. Paraguay continued to build the telegraph line to Bahía Negra, sent troops to reenforce that distant outpost, and put Col. Juan Antonio Jara in command.[48]

Optimistic enterprisers continued to propose railway construction to link Santa Cruz with the Río Paraguay. In October 1900 Wilhelm König y Cía. proposed a line from Santa Cruz to the western margin of Laguna Gaiba on the Paraguay about one hundred fifty kilometers north of Corumbá. Antonio Quijarro, Bolivia's confidential agent to Asunción, asked the Brazilian minister in Buenos Aires, Cyro de Azevedo, to aid a Bolivian exploratory commission to be headed by the English Captain Henry Holland. Azevedo received the request coldly. Brazil had no desire to promote a port for Bolivian exports to Buenos Aires.[49]

As reported in *La Patria Paraguaya* on October 9, 1900, the König proposal was to build from Santa Cruz to Corumbá with a branch to Bahía Negra. Holland would be aided by two capable Bolivians in surveying the route. This paper did not oppose the project as long as Bolivia did not try to steal Paraguayan territory. The plan caused alarming rumors in Concepción, where reports circulated that enemy forces at Puerto Suárez were preparing to attack Bahía Negra. Captain Holland on the steamer *General Pando* sailed the 200 kilometers from Corumbá to Laguna Gaiba and reported that a port at Gaiba was a feasible terminus for a railway from Santa Cruz.[50]

By this time the Chaco dispute had taken on all the characteristics that prevailed until the outbreak of war in 1932. Each country insisted on the validity of its title, appealed to the principle of *uti possidetis*, refused to approve treaties, and strengthened military and civil control over the contiguous Chaco. Both countries granted concessions for exploitation of Chaco resources, sought support from Argentina and Brazil, and encouraged outbursts of journalistic jingoism. Itiberê recalled the "solemn declaration of ex-President Fernández Alonso at a parliamentary banquet in La Paz, where he said that Bolivia would arm itself and prepare to compel Paraguay to approve the treaties either by reason or by force, and there is no doubt that General Pando holds the same attitude."[51] Paraguay refused to negotiate with Quijarro, who had been sent on a secret mission, unless he presented his credentials; Quijarro refused to do so without first discussing the prospects for a settlement. Frustrated by this impasse and suffering from ill health, Bolivia's not-so-secret envoy returned to the slightly better climate of Buenos Aires.[52]

In the midst of a resurgence of Paraguayan military spirit, a few conciliatory voices were heard. They condemned the warmongers for ignoring difficulties already being faced by a bankrupt government and discounted such wild rumors as that which asserted President McKinley's plan to establish an American colony in the Chaco. Itiberê da Cunha sensed a grave weakness in the country "and certain serious signs that presage the approach of a storm, whose imminent danger will not be easy to avoid."[53]

Annual reports of Paraguay's ministers of foreign affairs reported on each year's wrangling with Bolivia. The *Memoria* of 1903, for example, referred to Bolivia's note of March 27, 1902, and Paraguay's renewed defense of its title. Bolivia had awarded a concession to an enterprise identified only as L'Africaine to build a port at Pacheco and a railway to Santa Cruz and Sucre. Bolivia's consul asked permission for this company to import supplies free of duty. Paraguay gave a guarded consent, provided that the construction occurred in an area not claimed by Paraguay, and appointed an engineer to be present to protect Paraguay's sovereignty.[54] Bravo also refused to leave the scene. Early in 1902 he sought a renewal of his concession to the Compañía del Distrito Oriental de Bolivia, and thought he would succeed. But his plans again crumbled in confusion and Bolivia instead granted the Acre to a North American syndicate with rights that conflicted with Bravo's claims. Brazil in turn bought the syndicate's concession for £100,000 and obtained Acre from Bolivia by the Treaty of Petropolis on November 17, 1903. Acre is far removed from Paraguay, but the treaty defined the Brazilian-Bolivian boundary as starting at Bahía Negra in the Chaco. Paraguay, of course, protested, having reached a point that prevented any government from ceding territory or submitting to arbitration, a stance that pained Brazil's Barão Rio Branco, who was trying to put a peaceful end to boundary disputes, invariably to Brazil's advantage. Some Paraguayans, in the midst of the revolt that ended Colorado rule in 1904, even entertained the absurd dream of extending their claim northward to the Jauru

River. These dreamers belonged to the Liberal party, which was then receiving aid from Argentina.[55]

The first Colorado era ended with Paraguay's claim to the Chaco uncompromised, although Colorado leaders had given Bolivia magnificent opportunities to gain a large part of the region. Bolivian recalcitrance and the opposition of Paraguayan Liberals had saved Paraguay from what could have been disastrous Colorado diplomacy.

Part III

THE ECONOMIC WAY

Paraguay's survival after the War of the Triple Alliance depended upon economic rehabilitation, a fact seen clearly by such young Liberals as José Segundo Decoud:

> The future of Paraguay continues to be a serious problem, whose solution has not yet been studied in its vast and multiple interrelationships with the detail that it merits. Efforts made have been fruitless, the remedies inapplicable to the illness, and the palliatives have served only to prolong the long decline and prostration in which a disastrous war, without parallel in the pages of modern history, has left us.
>
> The truth is that our progress is indefinitely delayed and the intellectual and moral improvement of the people become more difficult every day. Production is relatively precarious, the State's revenues are exiguous, immigration does not flow to our shores, and our population remains stationary. Meanwhile, commerce does not progress, industries do not develop, the circulating medium is very scarce, interest on money high, and consumers' goods exorbitantly expensive.

José Segundo Decoud
Cuestiones políticas y económicas, p. 3

12

The National Patrimony

Ruling Colorados faced a dilemma as old as nation states: what should be done with the land? Public ownership of the land had been promoted by creation of numerous state estancias under Francia and the Lópezes; after the Paraguayan War, these estancias, plus the confiscated estates of the López family, formed the nucleus of the public domain in eastern Paraguay. The extent of government holdings was unknown. There had never been a survey, and landownership often was determined by the ability of a claimant to command the force necessary to expel intruders and to defy government officials. Private ownership was difficult to prove because most of the documents had been lost or destroyed during the war; however, the loss of documentary proof of ownership affected relatively few people, and the universal practice of squatting on a piece of land and planting a few subsistence crops greatly reduced the importance of holding a legal title.

The question of "landless masses" was not a serious political issue in a country where the masses had never had a spokesman. Colorados were not in the least concerned about the consequences of creating a landed oligarchy, but they were concerned about adopting a land policy that would result in long-range benefits to the nation. Before Caballero seized power in 1880, Paraguay's public lands had been used as collateral for foreign loans and as a source of revenue from sales and rentals. To promote Paraguay's economic health, Colorados realized that the country's credit must be restored, deficits had to end, private enterprise through foreign investment must be promoted, and the immigration of European farmers must be encouraged. To realize these goals, two major programs were to be undertaken concurrently, and both involved disposal of the public domain. Congress must authorize the sale of public lands and yerbales, and a settlement must be negotiated with the English bond-holders.

The Public Domain

Paraguay began its uncertain course as an independent republic in 1811 with a confused land situation inherited from the colonial period. Despite various laws and decrees to restrict the formation of large estates, the best lands of eastern Paraguay were held by *encomenderos* (large colonial landholders). Most of the land was very sparsely settled, a disproportionately large number of people being concentrated in and around Asunción, forming the core of what has been called "nuclear Paraguay." Expulsion of the Jesuits in 1767 was followed by seizure of mission lands. Other lands came to the state through confiscation or through inability of occupants to prove title, as required by a decree in September 1825. From these confiscated lands came the many "estancias de la República" that produced large quantities of livestock. Under Carlos Antonio López (1840–1862), changes were made in the land policy that allowed occupants to buy up to four leagues of land, about twenty-nine square miles, at two-thirds of its evaluation after having occupied it for eight years in each of which a tax of 5 percent of the land's valuation had been paid. Obviously it was the hacendado, not the campesino squatter, who acquired land under this policy.[1] A decree of January 2, 1846, reserved for the state all the yerbales and the best forests. Another decree, on October 7, 1848, confiscated the lands owned by mestizos, Indians, and a score of towns. This decree, Carlos Pastore writes, "completed the possession by the State of all the principal sources of wealth of the country, it facilitated a definite and complete mercantile policy and marks a date that closes one epoch and that gives rise to a new one in the history of the struggle for the holding of land in Paraguay between the European conquerors and their successors on one hand, and the Guaraníes and their descendants on the other."[2] The result of these López policies was that by 1849, "almost all of the territorial area of the Eastern Region belonged to the state, and three hundred thousand head of cattle and horses were gathered on sixty-four great estancias and in various smaller places called 'La Patria.' "[3]

The national patrimony provided the government with so much wealth and rental income that taxes were practically unknown. Francisco Solano López was engaged in the Paraguayan War so soon after becoming dictator in 1862 that he had no chance to make drastic changes in prevailing land policies. A subservient Congress did authorize López in 1865 to pledge rentals and proceeds from yerba sales to guarantee interest and principal of a loan of 2,500,000 pesos fuertes,[4] but the loan could not be negotiated. This act was significant as the first attempt to use the national patrimony as collateral.

When the second Paraguayan republic began its tempestuous career with adoption of the constitution of 1870, Francisco Wisner de Morgenstern estimated the country's area as being 16,590 square leagues.[5] Wisner divided this area among 840 leagues of yerbales, 7,200 leagues of pasture lands (campos), and 8,550 leagues of forests. Only 261 leagues of the total were in private ownership, leaving 16,329 as public domain. Wisner must have included some of the Chaco, since the area east of the Río Paraguay could not possibly have been stretched to more than 16,000 leagues. Carlos Pastore, the principal authority on Paraguay's land system and problems, accepts Wisner's estimate.[6]

Titles and Sales, 1870–1883

Loss of archives and destruction of records during the Paraguayan War left land titles in utter chaos. Laws of April and May 1871 required the registration of all titles acquired at any time.[7] An act of May 25, 1872, allowed squatters to gain title to lots in common lands (ejidos) that traditionally belonged to towns. Much of the land passed fraudulently into private ownership as a result. Then an act of 1873 provided that proprietors—a term so loosely interpreted that squatters were included—who had lost titles during the war could establish their rights on the testimony of witnesses before local justces of the peace and so obtain títulos supletorios (supplemental or substitute titles). This act caused much litigation. Teodosio González cites one case in which Doña Cipriana Recalde de Sosa sold a ranch. When the buyer was absent, Doña Cipriana's sons filed for a supplemental title on the ranch and the legitimate owner had to go through nine years of litigation to recover his property.[8] Another law in January 1875 created the Public Land Office (Oficina de Tierras Públicas) within the Junta de Crédito Público (Public Credit Office). Those who claimed to be landowners were required to show copies of their titles to this office, under penalty of being considered squatters.

The era of land sales began in November 1875 when Congress authorized the sale of land at public auction to raise $f6,000,000, one-half of which had to be paid in gold or silver. This law resulted in dispossession of many small farmers who had neither the precious metal nor public debt certificates with which to pay for the land they occupied. An act of December 15, 1876, set the price for public land at $f15,000 per league, payable in coupons of the internal debt. Since these coupons were selling at about one-third of their face value in 1882, in that year one could obtain a league of public land for about

$5,000 in gold or silver, or about $1.08 per acre. The next significant act was adoption of the Argentine Civil Code, effective January 1, 1877, which contained a provision by which squatters who had been left undisturbed for fifteen or thirty years, depending upon the presence or absence of the owner, could obtain clear title to the land.[9] Probably very few squatters knew anything about this provision.

Paraguay resumed limited sales of public domain in 1883 in order to raise $f300,000. The act of September 24 divided land in eastern Paraguay into three classes. Class I included lands in the most populous *partidos* or districts, and were priced at $f1500 per league. Forest lands and yerbales were placed in Class II for sale at $f1000 per league, and the poorest lands were priced at $f800 per league in Class III. Dr. Pastore severely criticises this act for making possible the creation of huge latifundia, dispossession of squatters, and alienation of the public domain for the benefit of foreign capitalists and the native upper class.[10]

Disposal of the Public Domain, 1885-1900

Although the act of 1883 was a serious blow to the small farmer, the laws of 1885 were catastrophic. The government's financial situation was so critical as a result of the economic crisis that surfaced in January 1883 that once more Caballero and his advisers, primarily José Segundo Decoud, resorted to sale of the public domain for relief. Two acts were to result in alienation of much of the public domain not already for sale under the 1883 law. The first, on May 28, provided for sale of yerbales at public auction, at upset or minimal prices of $1.50, $1.25, and $1.00 per *cuadra* (1.854 acres), depending upon distance from a navigable stream. Thus yerbales were priced at from $2,500 to $3,750 per league.[11] On July 11, 1885, Congress passed the most important land law in Paraguayan history. This act authorized the sale of all public lands, divided into five classes. Nearly all Class I and II lands, priced at $1,200 and $800 per league were in eastern Paraguay. Chaco lands were in Class III, IV, or V (see map no. 4) and sold for $300, $200, and $100 per league. Payment was to be made in legal tender or in public bonds, one-fourth down and the balance in three annual installments.[12] In a vain attempt to encourage colonization, the law reduced the price of Chaco land by 50 percent if the purchaser would introduce twenty-five European families of three members each for every ten leagues within the payment period. Squatters on public land had one year in which to obtain titles, after which they would pay rent of 25¢ per cuadra.[13] Theoretically, no one could buy more than one-half league of cultivated land, an area well beyond the resources of Paraguayan farmers.

Passage of the acts authorizing sale of the yerbales and the rest of the public domain resulted in an increase in the value of Paraguayan lands on the open market. The grazing lands, or campos, in south-western Paraguay could be had for a small fraction of the cost of Argentine land, even in neighboring Corrientes. Argentine ranchers, therefore, hastened to take advantage of the Paraguayan bargains. In the frantic rush, officials, legislators and politicians generally gathered like buzzards to grab the land for resale at fantastic profits; "Modest public employees with monthly salaries not exceeding 60 pesos paper, acquired tens and hundreds of leagues of the best lands and yerbales, paid the first installment with money borrowed from the Banco Nacional and resold their rights to foreign speculators."[14] An Argentine visitor in 1887 observed that "properties that were offered in 1886 at 1000$ per league are now changing hands at 3,000$ and new estancias are being established in the south and northeast. To judge by the crowds that land by every steamer at Asunción, by the number of banks that are being started, by the growing traffic of railways and tramways, there can be little doubt that Paraguay is going ahead at last."[15] More to the point was a cartoon in El Látigo that showed Paraguay as a nude seated at a table, one elbow on a map of eastern Paraguay, her hands covering her face. The caption read: "The poor Patria, outraged and dishonored, weeps to see her principal lands sold and divided by her evil sons!"[16] During the first three full years after passage of the 1885 act, the total sales reached a value of $f5,529,642, more than one-half of the total for the years 1886–1900. Thereafter, sales fell off drastically. The value of land sales fell from $f703,206 in 1889 to about $f5,137 in 1900. Receipts from yerbales sales held up much better, fluctuating from $f786,292 in 1886 to a low of $f37,071 in 1895, but recovering to $f275,602 in 1900 (see table 3).

By the end of the century, more than 7,035 leagues of land had been sold in the Chaco to seventy-nine persons or companies for $f906,324.40, an average of $f128.83 per league, or less than three cents an acre.[17] The Argentine enterpriser, Carlos Casado, obtained more than 3,000 leagues (13,995,000 acres) in the Chaco and in eastern Paraguay; Domingo Barthe, a Frenchman who had come to Paraguay in 1871, emerged with over 1,250,000 acres of forests and yerbales in the Alto Paraná. At the end of the land orgy, the public domain in the Chaco had shrunk to 1,101 leagues and had all but disappeared in eastern Paraguay,[18] where sales of farm lands, pastures, forests, and yerbales totaled 8,904 leagues. Eleven buyers obtained 3,183 leagues, or an average of about 1,340,000 acres each. In all Paraguay, including the Chaco, 15,965 leagues, or nearly 74,000,000 acres, were sold for approximately $10,000,000 in cash and promissory notes. If Wisner's estimate of 16,329 leagues of public domain was accurate, 304 leagues remained.

Colorado land sales did result in greatly increased revenues for

Table 3

Receipts from Sales of Public Lands and Yerbales, 1885–1900
(in pesos fuertes, 1 peso nominally equal to $1.00 U.S.)

	Public Lands	Yerbales	Total
1885	549,510	60,000 ?	609,510
1886	1,268,795	786,292	2,055,087
1887	1,179,941	506,312	1,686,253
1888	1,393,147	395,155	1,788,302
1889	703,206	112,097	815,303
1890	84,740	240,133	324,873
1891	73,346	102,263	175,969
1892	64,000	300,355	364,355
1893	41,475	897,156	938,631
1894	37,871	459,979	497,850
1895	82,589	37,071	119,660
1896	22,351	466,058	488,409
1897	25,165	285,724	310,889
1898	9,643	104,045	113,688
1899	9,398	104,048	113,446
1900	5,137	275,602	280,739
Totals	5,550,314	5,132,650	10,682,964

Sources: *Memorias* of ministers of interior and hacienda, presidential messages, newspapers, and consular reports. Statistics given in *Memorias* and presidential messages often could not be reconciled. Figures for 1892, 1895, and 1900 are especially suspect. Official reports often do not distinguish between cash received and value of lands sold. Buyers were required to pay 25 percent in cash and the balance in three equal installments.

the treasury and in the creation of such huge enterprises as Carlos Casado, Ltd., which built a port some twenty kilometers south of the Apa, penetrated the Chaco with narrow gauge railways, established huge cattle ranches, built a large steam sawmill and plants to extract tannin from quebracho bark, and became the principal supplier of railway sleepers and lumber for the Argentine market.[19] The Casado enterprise undoubtedly added considerable strength to Paraguay's claim to the Chaco and brought economic benefits to the country. The individual farmer never could have attempted such development. In eastern Paraguay, speculators bought huge tracts of land and the astronomical rise in prices effectively kept the small farmer out of the market. Creation of these large holdings displaced squatters, drove up rents, restricted immigration, and even resulted in illegal acquisition of common lands belonging to towns, several of which were completely surrounded by private holdings. The chief beneficiaries were speculators and such huge enterprises as La Industrial Paraguaya, the Anglo-Paraguay Land Company, Domingo Barthe, and Carlos Casado. Small farmers and agricultural laborers were condemned to being landless *peones* who often had to emigrate to find employment.[20] President Escobar made a feeble effort to alleviate the bad effects of land sales by sponsoring a *ley de hogar*, or homestead act, to give sixteen cuadras (about twenty-eight acres) to each occupant of public lands. Immigrant farmers would receive the same privilege. Escobar told the Congress that "it is an American maxim, inspired by republican sentiment, that the public lands belong to the people as a sacred trust for their own benefit, and should be allotted in limited parcels, free of cost, to settlers who are not landowners."[21] This hollow, hypocritical oratory did nothing for the dispossessed campesino.

In 1871, a perceptive member of the Chamber of Deputies, Jacinto Chilavert, asked the government to expropriate lands "which undoubtedly it has alienated to private persons, without considering that there were a large number of settlers who were injured by that sale." Moreover, he charged, the government had sold all the public domain without considering the needs of colonization, and had even sold lands excluded by law from sale.[22] In defense of the government policy, it should be noted that buyers were expected to colonize their lands. Instead, the American vice-consul observed in 1895, "the speculator is doing so much to prevent the settlement of the land as though he were an enemy to the progress of the country, for he manages to keep at least one step in advance of the immigrant so that if the land is not actually monopolized, it is relatively so." Large holdings forced ruinous increases in rent, and banks contributed to the speculative orgy by loaning far too much on the land. "The same thing had happened before in the Argentine, but Paraguay in the fever of excitement, did not heed the warning."[23] Nor did buyers concern themselves with the wisp of a cloud that drifted in from the past to throw a light shadow over many titles.

The Lands of Madame Lynch

A very controversial land claim, but one with little merit, was maintained by Enrique Solano López for many years. This notorious case had its origin in the supposed sale of huge areas by Francisco Solano López to his mistress, Elisa Alicia Lynch, between 1865 and 1870: 437,500 hectares (1,089,375 acres) of public lands in the Chaco Central between the Pilcomayo and Bermejo rivers; 33,175 square kilometers (8,197,542 acres) north of the Rio Apa; and 3,105 square leagues (14,382,360 acres) in northwestern Paraguay between the rivers Jejuí and Apa—a total of 23,669,277 acres. In addition, Madame Lynch claimed numerous parcels of land and houses in Asunción and other towns.[24]

Paraguay's postwar governments enacted a series of measures to regain properties claimed by Madame Lynch and survivors of the López clan. A decree of March 19, 1870, placed all their property under government control, leaving very little chance that any of it would be returned to them. Madame Lynch was not going to give up without a fight, as she demonstrated in the courts of Edinburgh where she attempted to recover a large sum from Dr. William Stewart.[25] When she reached Bordeaux late in 1870, Madame Lynch made what must have been a dramatic call on her long estranged husband, Dr. Javier Quatrefages, who was then chief medical officer at the military hospital. On December 7, 1870, Dr. Quatrefages signed a statement asserting that in Paris on October 19, 1854, he had granted Elisa complete power over all her property and had surrendered any claim he might have as a result of their marriage. In Buenos Aires briefly and then in Asunción, Madame Lynch sought validation of her fantastic real estate claims. Back in London in 1879, she gave her son Enrique power of attorney to deal with the governments of Uruguay, Argentina, Paraguay, and Brazil.[26]

Enrique Solano López in Buenos Aires had made the acquaintance of prominent Paraguayan exiles, few of whom had any reason to look with favor on anyone bearing the López name. These exiles were united loosely in the Paraguayan Committee, of which Jaime Sosa Escalada, Benigno Ferreira, and Juan Silvano Godoi were prominent members. This committee suffered severe reverses from defeat of the Godoi revolt in 1879 and was receptive to a scheme to replenish its finances. On June 5, 1881, the Committee met in extraordinary sessions with Dr. Ferreira in the chair, and as a result of its deliberations, named Godoi as its envoy to Europe to negotiate a loan which would be guaranteed by "one of the great properties of Sr. Don Enrique Solano López . . . who accompanies him on his voyage to Europe in the role of secretary of this committee."[27]

Accompanied by the brothers Carlos and Enrique, and with a passport issued by the Paraguayan consul in Buenos Aires, Godoi sailed for Southampton on July 11, 1881, aboard Lamport and Holt's *Maskelyne*. Pleading political reasons, Godoi asked that his name be kept off the passenger list. The purpose of this voyage, the British minister reported, "is to dispose of 90 square leagues of land in the San Pedro Government [department] of Paraguay of which land he obtained the title deeds by abusing the weakness of a certain widow Varela." Egerton advised the Foreign Office to alert the police so that unwary purchasers might not be lured into buying from Godoi, whose right to sell was questionable.[28]

The scheme presented by Godoi was imaginative, brazen, and calculated to separate fools from their money. In order to increase the value of Paraguayan bonds in the London market and to restore Paraguay's credit, Godoi proposed to float a loan advantageous to all parties. One-third of the proceeds would go to the committee; the bankers would use one-third to buy Paraguayan bonds, and

> the last one-third will be invested in agreement with Sr. Godoi in the unearthing of a large sum hidden by the Marshal President Francisco Solano López during the War of the Triple Alliance. Sr. Godoi now has possession of the maps, explanations, and other data. Having achieved recovery of the money, that amounts to the sum of three million pounds or more, the rest of the bonds in circulation will be retired, in agreement with the bondholders . . .
>
> The Brazilian lands pledged for the transaction consist of yerbales for the most part—and of lands of the highest quality because of the riches they possess, the natural resources that they contain, the forests of precious woods that include all varieties known in America. There also exist in this property broad stands of rubber, indigo, quantities of marble of different colors—mines of copper and gold.[29]

Godoi interested unnamed brokers in the scheme—buried treasure, gold mines, forests abounding in precious woods, and other figments of a very fertile imagination that would have done credit to the slickest con man who ever made a pitch. After being satisfied with Godoi's identity, the brokers agreed to a loan of £200,000, one-third in cash; but they wanted a delay of three months, obviously to check on the security offered. Godoi then turned to another group and apparently had matters well arranged when Enrique and Carlos talked too freely. Then the English merchants "les dió con la puerta en las narices" (shut the door in their faces), as Godoi reported. The door indeed was slammed on their dreams of wealth, so Godoi left the talkative boys to their own devices while he sought to make a deal in Paris, Hamburg, or Brussels. None of these efforts resulted in finding investors lured by the prospect of unearthing phantom treasure.[30]

After his return to South America, Enrique went to Asunción in an effort to obtain aid from President Caballero, another of his mother's old friends. Caballero promised to do everything he could to help release the Lynch lands from the 1870 decree, but warned that only the courts could lift the "embargo." Enrique received similar empty promises of help from Escobar and Decoud, empty because he had returned too soon to the capital where resentment against Madame Lynch and Marshal López was deep seated. Héctor Francisco Decoud admitted that Enrique was a "complete gentleman— but is not suited for Paraguay, given present conditions. He will never be able to live here in the manner that he dreams of and desires." Moreover, he was too fond of wine and talked too much.[31]

During her last stay in Buenos Aires in 1885, Madame Lynch

sought vainly to obtain Argentine recognition of her claim to land in Formosa. Failing in her efforts, on February 3, 1885, she ceded to Enrique all her immense land claims. In order to realize something from the vast property of 3,105 leagues in Paraguay, Enrique attempted to legalize its status. He sent an agent to Asunción who, on May 13, 1885, obtained from the registrar of mortgages a certificate to the effect that there were no liens or claims against any property belonging to Elisa Lynch. The registrar neglected to determine if any real estate had been registered in her name! Armed with this meaningless certificate, Enrique sold most of the property to a group of Argentine speculators led by Francisco Cordero. The deal was made on May 26, 1885, for 250,000 Argentine pesos. When the buyers sought to obtain title to the property, they raised a storm of protest in Asunción. The Cordero syndicate filed suit in Paraguay to obtain validation of its claims and enlisted the aid of the Argentine government in an effort to influence the Paraguayans.[32]

Excitement in Paraguay over the López-Cordero claims, aroused by articles in *La Nación* and *El Paraguayo*, reached a climax at the end of 1887. The irresponsible, satirical paper *El Látigo* charged that Caballero and Decoud had offered to validate the claims for one-half the area, but López had refused to surrender more than one-third. Col. Juan A. Meza, minister of interior, turned for legal advice to Dr. Ramón Zubizarreta, dean of the Law School, who declared that there really was no problem since under a law of 1871, all claimants of real property were required to register their titles, something that neither Madame Lynch nor her son had ever done. Therefore, the López-Cordero claim was without merit. Nevertheless, the Cordero syndicate, with support from the Argentine government, continued to press its claim.[33] The Supreme Court heard the case in March 1888, and the three judges concurred with Zubizarreta's opinion. This decision relieved Escobar's government, which was engaged in selling huge areas of the lands claimed by López and Cordero. Still Enrique persisted in his quixotic quest. On December 26, 1888, he sold 300 square leagues on the Aquidabán to Cordero, Godoi, and Juan Antonio Arjerich, for 135,000 pesos, the title to be delivered within fifteen days.[34] Of course, Enrique had no title to deliver.

The outcome of the claims in Argentina was somewhat different. López, acting with full authority from his mother, presented his Chaco claim to the Argentine government in April 1883, arguing that the purchase was valid and that Argentina, in 1876, had agreed to respect property rights in the Chaco Central. This claim was rejected. Then the Argentine Congress on October 27, 1884, enacted a law that recognized titles granted by provinces, so López again filed a petition with the attorney general. In May 1888 an unwary official registered the land in the López name. Following this victory, Enrique was able to sell off his Chaco lands, but in 1896 another administration declared that the registration was null and void. The Argentine Supreme Court in subsequent litigation upheld this decision in 1911, and in 1920 all lands that had been claimed by Madame Lynch were declared public domain. Nevertheless, many who had bought from López and Cordero were able to keep their property under the rule that thirty years of peaceful possession conveyed good title.[35]

Settlement with the Council of Foreign Bondholders

Buyers of Paraguay's 1871 and 1872 bonds persistently insisted upon payment. Their spokesman was the prestigious Council of Foreign Bondholders, which was ably directed by the noted financier Edward P. Bouverie. In an effort to settle the debt, Cándido Bareiro had signed an agreement with the council in 1875, the terms of which included sale of the railway, creation of a bank, and trading part of the public domain for some of the bonds.[36] Brazilian opposition killed this agreement, and Paraguay continued to default on scheduled payments of interest and principal. President Caballero in 1885 had little difficulty in persuading Congress to authorize sale of the public domain to raise revenues, and, of course, he was aware that the public lands had been pledged as security for the loans of 1871 and 1872. Sales of these lands could not proceed until an agreement had been reached with the bondholders. To remove this obstacle, Caballero sent Decoud to London to negotiate with Bouverie.

After protracted discussions, Decoud and Bouverie signed an agreement on December 4, 1885. The principal provision of this agreement was the exchange of 500 leagues of public domain for the unpaid interest of £1,500,000, thus valuing the land at £3,000 per league, which was considerably more than the prices set by the laws of 1885. Each matured coupon for £100 entitled the holder to a warrant for 830,000 varas (145 acres). The corporate result of this agreement was formation of the Anglo-Paraguay Land Company, which exchanged two shares of stock for each warrant. By July 1890 the company had exchanged 276,380 shares worth £1,381,900 at par for 138,190 warrants.[37] The Anglo-Paraguay Land Company made the most of its opportunity. To select the 500 leagues, Bouverie wisely named Henry Valpy, whose extensive knowledge of Paraguay had been gained during several years as an engineer and railway builder for the López dictatorships. Valpy visited Asunción in May 1887, conferred with officials who agreed to suspend land sales for the rest of the year, then returned briefly to London. Back in Paraguay in January 1888 Valpy spent several weeks inspecting available land before designating 500 leagues and the island of Yacyretá. In his report to the company, Valpy described lands rich in timber and yerbales, fertile agricultural areas, and luxuriant pastures. Yacyretá, with an area of perhaps 25 leagues, would support up to 10,000 cattle and had valuable quarries and orange groves. Proceeding with Paraguayan promptness to survey the lands, the government completed allocation and cession to the company on October 27, 1895.[38] This settlement with the English bondholders, together with public sales, effectively disposed of Paraguay's public domain without solving the country's financial problems. Paraguay, at tremendous cost, had reduced its public debt by $3,000,000 gold and had promoted the creation of another foreign enterprise.

13

Foundations of a Capitalist State

A major feature of the Colorado era, so obvious in retrospect, is the fact that Paraguay was going through an economic revolution. The great dictators had created a rudimentary socialist state in Paraguay. Francia had brought about a social revolution by nearly destroying the upper classes, he had established great state-owned estancias, he controlled all foreign trade, and he made the people work. Carlos Antonio López relaxed the severity of Francia's rule without seriously changing its nature. Properly called "The Builder," the first López brought in foreign technicians who established modern industries, built a railway, an iron foundry, a shipyard, the defenses of Humaitá, a telegraph line, and imposing buildings. López devoted much attention to improving agriculture and animal husbandry and took the first tentative step toward establishing a foreign agricultural colony. Paraguay's defeat in the War of the Triple Alliance ended the republic created by Francia and Carlos Antonio López. Upon its ruins a new economic order would rise. And its model would be British and United States capitalism. Private enterprise, government favors to capitalists, sale of public lands and the railway, promotion of immigration, protective tariffs, development of communications and transportation—these and compatible measures created the shadow of a capitalist state, and its creation was a revolution, a break with the past as significant as the revolution wrought by Francia and López. However, the new capitalism rested upon an infrastructure entirely inadequate to maintain a viable economy.

Postwar Recovery

Foreign visitors and Colorado officials often saw Paraguay's economy in a much more favorable light than it appeared to residents. The

179

British minister, Sir George Petre, and his second secretary, Arthur G. Vansittart, visited Paraguay in 1882. Petre was not very enthusiastic but did report that some recovery had occurred. Although there were no published "official statistics of any kind," he left Vansittart to prepare a lengthy report.[1] After six months in the country, Vansittart could see a fine future with peace, increasing prosperity, "and with enlightened and liberal statesmen (such as the present Government) to promote the welfare of the people, in encouraging foreigners to come out . . . by settling pending claims, by showing themselves to be in earnest . . . Paraguay has every reason to hope that she will regain her former prosperity and rank among the great South American Republics."[2] President Caballero reflected this optimism in his message to Congress in 1883. Although his references to Colorado observance of constitutional rights was sheer nonsense, his faith in the future and his warm invitation to immigrants "to come to inhabit this new land of promise," were sincere. Caballero's message reads much like Decoud's report of 1884 that noted the maintenance of governmental stability and "the noble efforts of this people in their laborious and unwavering task of reconstruction."[3]

Casual diplomatic visitors continued their favorable reports through the 1880s. Judge John E. Bacon, American minister to Paraguay and Uruguay, found superlatives in order. Paraguay in 1885 was in "a more flourishing condition than at any time since the disastrous war with the Allies, with every reasonable prospect of a large increasing trade in cotton, tobacco, rice, coffee, sugar, fruits, cattle, hides & the cereals generally. As is stated in one of the leading journals of Buenos Ayres 'her lands are the most fertile upon earth & her climate sunny & salubrious beyond expression.' " After a year's absence, Francis Pakenham, the British minister, in 1890 found "great improvement . . . in the condition of the city of Asunción."[4]

Undoubtedly there had been considerable economic recovery by the mid 1880s. Still, a Paraguayan editor correctly found fault with administrations for being too much concerned with staying in office and for not taking positive development measures. If the country prospers, he wrote, "the government will soon live in abundance." The country needed permissive and generous laws, not long-run concessions, to attract foreign investment.[5] At the end of his administration in 1890, President Escobar could have pointed to many signs of economic development: Asunción had some paved streets, more tramways, limited telephone service, functioning banks, and a trickle of immigration; both foreign and domestic trade had increased; economic depressions had been overcome; and many estancias were flourishing. President Egusquiza predicted that "Paraguay will become great and strong. [We have seen] the reorganization of a nation that rebuilds itself on its ruins, courageously recovering from its past wounds that nevertheless leave a deep mark on its history." His successor, President Emilio Aceval, realistically informed Congress that, despite improvement in agriculture, Paraguay lacked almost everything—roads, commerce, industry, dedication to hard work, and capital to support enterprisers. He was more optimistc a year later, asserting that Paraguay had accomplished "the miracle of its resurrection" in three decades of reconstruction. "In the midst of its own debris and ruins the breath of liberty has reappeared with the clear vision of its destinies."[6] The facts, however, belied this brave optimism. What appeared to be a general recovery was primarily the result of corporate activity, and that was confined primarily to the railway, navigation, exploitation of forest products, and cattle raising.

Except for the restrictions and requirements in concessions granted by Congress, business in general was free from hampering regulations. Even the moderate export taxes on yerba, tobacco, and hides were far from burdensome. Both import and export duties were easily avoided by bribery and notoriously widespread smuggling. Except for the annoying license fees, an insignificant inheritance tax, and, in the late 1890s, a small land tax, there was no tax burden. Even the land tax, the *contribución directa*, was not levied until there was no more public domain to sell.

Paraguay lacked the capital and credit needed to finance economic development. There were a few wealthy hacendados and owners of yerbales who performed informal private banking functions. After several false starts, fairly adequate banking institutions were in operation at the end of the Colorado era. Capital for the major projects came from foreign investors who were prominent in Paraguayan business circles and controlled the largest of the country's 841 commercial houses, which represented an investment of only $f2,751,119 in 1885. The leading investors were Italians, Spaniards, and French. English investment, which had not yet become significant in 1885, was dominant five years later when the total was estimated at nearly £9,000,000,[7] and represented broad interests, as one diplomat reported: "The steamers navigating the rivers are British, the railway is British, and so are the tramways, moreover most of the banking capital of the country is British and a considerable portion of the public lands has now become the property of the British bondholders."[8] In addition to the Paraguay Central Railway, capitalized at $2,100,000 gold, the Anglo-Paraguay Land Company, with $620,000, headed the list of corporations. Paraguayans, of course, participated heavily in La Industrial Paraguaya and the Banco Mercantil, each capitalized at $500,000 gold.[9]

Opportunities for capital investment were numerous in Paraguay, as consuls often reminded their governments. John N. Ruffin, the last American consul during the Colorado era, made many recommendations and spent a considerable amount of time in the United States visiting Philadelphia, Cincinnati, Chicago, and other cities where his speeches to chambers of commerce often were reported at length. These efforts were appreciated in Asunción where editors uniformly praised Ruffin for his interest,[10] although they resulted in very little American investment.

Poor trade conditions and dependence upon Argentine markets added to the uncertainty of Paraguay's economy. Freight charges were so high that imports were priced beyond the reach of all but the wealthy few. The accumulation of unsold goods in commercial houses immobilized native venture capital and seriously affected customs revenues by reducing the volume of imports. Cash was in such short supply that merchants who provided goods for the interior received most of their payment in produce, much of which would have to be exported to Argentina where numerous shipments arrived in unmarketable condition. This barter economy promoted fraud as merchants attempted to recoup losses by the self-defeating practice of exporting inferior products.[11]

The Enterprisers

Congress exercised minimal control over business enterprises unless special favors were involved. Merchants, vendors, and professionals could set up shop after paying a license fee, but more ambitious enterprisers had to petition Congress for concessions. On occasion, special considerations justified this time-consuming hindrance to private enterprise, as when customs duties were reduced or suspended to encourage an industry, a monopoly was granted, public property was involved, government investment or attributes of government—such as emission of paper money—were solicited, or treaty obligations were affected. On the whole, Congress was very liberal in granting concessions.[12]

Congress granted numerous privileged concessions in the pre-Caballero period. One of the earliest, in September 1871, went to Ricardo Antônio Mendes Gonçalves, to start a soap and candle factory, with importation of machinery free of duty. Mariano Zamborini in 1872 obtained exclusive right for five years to such cigar brand names as Napoleones, Bismark, Pedro II, General Mitre, Caazapá, Triple Alianza, Conde d'Eu, and others. Also in 1872, Juan Junques obtained a five-year monopoly on manufacturing ice. Other concessions went to producers of wine, beer, carriages, and refined sugar. Cayetano Ituruburu y Cía. in 1876 obtained a concession to grow rubber trees on four leagues of public land in the Concepción area. The company was to plant 4,000 trees in four years. Edward Augustus

Hopkins, of prewar fame, was granted permission in 1878 to start an industrial-agricultural establishment at Puerto Olivares, about seventy-five kilometers upriver from Asunción, with a ten-year exemption from taxes and a waiver of customs duties on materials imported for the enterprise. Gregorio Torres in 1878 received a grant to start a steam factory to extract peanut and other oils. Many of these and other concessions failed to produce thriving enterprises, but they do show that there were men with imagination. Some succeeded, like the partnership that opened a soap factory in the Recoleta district in 1882. Using modern machinery and native raw materials, forty workers produced enough soap to supply the entire country.[13] Small enterprisers of this kind slowly caused the economy to improve so much that large investors were attracted to banking, ranching, shipping, lumbering, and milling.

Asunción grew slowly as a business center, preserving a position it had held in the country for more than four centuries. In 1901, there were 160 commercial and industrial establishments in the city, many of whose owners and managers belonged to the Chamber of Commerce which was organized in 1897 as the Centro Comercial del Paraguay. This group sponsored various projects and through its thirteen special committees not only made recommendations to Congress but also adopted measures to promote all aspects of Paraguay's economy, all, that is, except the welfare of labor.[14]

Labor and Wages

Low wages and poor working conditions, which meant virtual enslavement in the yerbales, were so common that one should discount the constant complaint that Paraguayan men were lazy. Even the intellectuals, who had the Spanish grandee's aversion to calloused or blistered hands, joined the chorus of condemnation and insisted that the only hope for a good supply of labor was for a larger population, especially foreigners. Criticisms of the Paraguayan worker had some basis in fact, but they ignored the abysmally low wages, the contempt with which the poor were treated, chronic hookworm and other debilitating diseases. Conditions were especially bad in the yerbales which produced Paraguay's principal crop and major source of foreign exchange for many years. A decree signed by President Salvador Jovellanos on January 1, 1871, made the yerba worker a virtual wage slave. He could not quit without his employer's written consent; violators could be returned to the employer and made to pay costs involved in their apprehension; every worker and employer had to have a written contract, setting forth the duration and all conditions of labor: wages, hours, and supplies to be advanced. All authorities were required to support efforts to apprehend fugitive contract workers. The laborer could not change his patrón without permission and then only if he was out of debt. Peones could file complaints with local justices of the peace, a privilege that only rarely led to decisions in their favor.[15]

Many Paraguayans, belying the canard of their habitual laziness, sought work in Brazilian yerbales. From Mato Grosso came evidence that workers were held in virtual slavery in the Corumbá area,[16] where conditions of employment were practically identical with those in Paraguay. The Brazilian chargé in Asunción blamed the law, not the employers, while admitting that many peones had to be forced to work. Formerly,

> proprietors struggled with the greatest difficulties. Because of the remote places where the yerbales are located, only the worst people would go, deserters and fugitives from the police who went with the intention of continuing their thieving and nomadic life. Today that service is perfectly organized and I am told that there are no abuses. The indolence of the workers is what keeps them subject to the patrones. Hardly eight months of the year are required to work the yerbales; the peons could use the other four months to pay off their debts, but they prefer to spend that time drawing on their future labor.[17]

Unfortunately, this unsympathetic indictment of the minero was characteristic of employer attitudes: the worker and the worker alone was responsible for his condition. It is a relief to find the secretary of Asunción's Chamber of Commerce much more perceptive:

> In the vast dominions of La Industrial Paraguaya lives a real city of peones and their families. There is nothing as interesting as the study of the life that those four thousand peones, more or less, live in the midst of the yerbales, a great distance from the closest towns. No day laborer in the world would be able to survive that life of labor, of privations, and of dangers to which the yerbatero is condemned; only the Paraguayan peón can resist the rigors of that almost superhuman labor. Much before dawn, when the yerbal is still dark, the yerbatero is already up, with machete in hand, gulping his frugal breakfast in order to begin the day's work at once. He sleeps at the foot of the trees where he works, sometimes stretched out on a hammock slung between two branches, sometimes huddled on the ground on the mulch. And his sleep is always light because the yerbatero knows that in the depths of the forest a hundred perils lurk: he senses the almost imperceptible noise that the animals that live in the yerbal make as they walk on the leaves or trunks. At times, when the fatigue of more than ordinary work keeps him asleep, some viper comes to sting him and then the peón, heroic in suffering, calmly cuts from his body the flesh poisoned by the reptile's teeth. They live by the hundreds in the yerbales, under the orders of a number of foremen. They rarely fight despite being armed constantly. The community of that life of danger and labor creates among them ties like those of a family and they esteem one another, they care for and mutually aid one another.[18]

Wages throughout the world were entirely inadequate to permit a decent standard of living, but in semitropical and tropical countries they were probably the lowest. Dr. Edward Kemmerich, director of a meat processing plant, wrote in 1901 that "wages in Paraguay are extremely low. We pay at present for a good laborer only $5 gold per month or 15 cents per day, including board." And the board was cheap "because the country produces very good and cheap meat, mandioca, yams, oranges (the latter an enormous quantity of the best quality), tobacco (100 cigars for a few cents), Indian corn, bananas and many other fruits."[19] (The cigars referred to were stubby things about three inches long which women rolled rapidly, generally using their own saliva to moisten the leaves.) In the same year one of the first expressions of concern for workers appeared in a newspaper that called for protective laws. To escape degrading exploitation, young men emigrated by the thousands to Argentine and Brazilian establishments, "lured by the deceitful legend of the workshops and yerbales, because they lacked their own land to work and even did not know . . . the attractions of an established home and because daily employment is not sufficiently remunerative to attract them." As late as 1901, domestic workers in Asunción received from $2.50 to $5.00 gold per month, equal to 225 to 450 paper pesos, while wages of the ordinary day laborer were 45¢ per day, triple the rate in rural areas.[20]

Transportation and Communication

Shallow, sluggish rivers, intermittent streams, cart tracks, trails, and one short, dilapidated railroad comprised Paraguay's interior transportation system in 1880. The Río Paraguay was generally navigable along the entire western edge of eastern Paraguay and to the far northern cities of Brazil's Mato Grosso. The Paraná, navigable on the south and southeast, turned southward at its junction with the Paraguay and gave access to the important Argentine ports of Rosario, Sante Fe, and Buenos Aires. At the end of the Colorado era, there were a few bridges over interior streams, the railway had been extended beyond Villa Rica, and a few kilometers of narrow gauge railway penetrated into the Chaco from Puerto Casado. Many of the interior rivers, especially on the east, were broken by rapids as they descended to the Paraná or were too shallow for navigation for all but the raftlike chatas.

The Paraguay, truly a great river, was fickle and dangerous. Varying depths of water, shifting sandbars, ill-defined banks, powerful and erratic currents, challenged the skills of river pilots. Sandbars also formed in the Río de la Plata and at times were a serious threat to navigation. Most of the river ports were merely stopping places, landings where river craft anchored precariously offshore while workers used moveable platforms, boats, and rafts to handle passengers and cargo. Only Asunción, favored with a quiet island-protected bay, had a port where ships could anchor or lie alongside an inadequate wharf. Asunción, Concepción, Pilar, and Encarnación had customs houses.[21]

Colorado governments did very little to improve land transportation. Obsessed by the railway, they generally ignored the more important problem of building roads and bridges. What Vansittart reported in 1882 was still true two decades later: "Paraguay has very imperfect cart roads."[22] What passed as roads were little better than bullock tracks, deep in sand in dry weather, quagmires in wet, a constant challenge to teams of oxen dragging two-wheeled bullock carts under the guiding whip of a barefooted driver.[23] Not until 1887 did Congress create a highway department, an agency inadequately financed even after 1900 when the Banco Agrícola had charge of bridges and roads. When the Liberals took over in 1904, the few roads still had their old deep ruts, "their holes and ravines. They were the same colorful roads that the conquerors followed, like the route from Ajos and Yhú to Curuguaty, built by Melo de Portugal [governor from 1778 to 1785], or those opened by the consuls Mariano Roque Alonso and Carlos Antonio López, like the trail from Caaguazú to Villarrica and the road parallel to the Paraná."[24]

These primitive conditions gave added importance to the Paraguay and Paraná rivers, where the flags of many nations flew from a wide variety of vessels (see tables 4 and 5). River steamers

Table 4

Ships Calling at Asunción, 1879–1881

	1879		1880		1881	
Nationality	No.	Tonnage	No.	Tonnage	No.	Tonnage
Argentina	144	15,269	160	18,743	172	20,265
Brazil	27	5,903	54	9,209	58	12,123
England	10	1,171	4	684	1	(gunboat)
France	1	(gunboat)				
Italy	1	40	1	40		
Paraguay	13	531	9	430	14	538
Spain			1	198	2	396
Uruguay	10	623	12	808	17	1,537

Source: Vansittart, *Report*, p. 136.

Table 5

Steamers and Sailing Vessels Calling at Asunción, 1886–1890

	Number		Tonnage	
	In	*Out*	*In*	*Out*
1886	3,784	3,748	106,741	95,676
1887	3,315	3,846	133,607	134,807
1888	4,232	4,227	181,054	181,167
1889	3,298	3,363	183,724	173,271
1890	2,950	2,945	177,692	167,159

Sources: DCR No. 1006, *Paraguay 1891*, p. 24; MI, *Memoria, 1890*, p. 68; Bourgade, *Paraguay*, p. 131.

making the Buenos Aires–Asunción run were very small, averaging between 174 and 300 tons, drawing about six feet. The round trip required fifteen days, allowing six to seven days upstream, two or three days in port, and five days for the return. A Brazilian line ran the 1,700 miles from Montevideo to Corumbá, where a smaller vessel carried goods and passengers another 600 miles to Cuyabá. Until shipping increased, it was "quite a favor to get cargo shipped at all."[25] Before the Platense Company bought out its rivals, the traveler enjoyed luxurious river vessels: "constructed especially to accommodate passengers, they have stately saloons, elaborately carved and furnished with costly tapestries; they are lighted by electricity, and made gay with the choicest flowers, and they are in every respect equal in their appliances and comfort to the best hotels in Europe."[26]

The number of vessels running regularly on the Paraguay, and the service they provided, had improved markedly by 1885. Three shipping lines monopolized the major traffic. Lloyd Brasileiro ran the *Rapido* and the *Rio Apa* monthly to Mato Grosso ports, calling at Pilar, Asunción, and Concepción. Lloyd Argentino had from nine to twelve boats in service between Montevideo and the Alto Paraguay. Among the best were the *Rio Paraná*, the *Uruguay,* the *Cisne,* the *Taragui,* and the *Mensajeria Argentina.* One private line ran three boats between Corumbá and Asunción. Paraguayans had two steam launches and a number of chatas in service.[27] The chata was an important part of river transport. Cheap to build, it was essentially an eighteen-foot barge that tapered at the ends. A forty-eight pounder could be mounted on a brass swivel in a foot-deep circular depression in the center. Chatas used for commercial purposes on the Jejuy and Tebicuari rarely mounted guns, although Indian attacks on the upper

Paraguay made defense necessary until the end of the century. Altogether, in 1885 it is estimated that there were 875 boats on the rivers, of which 315 were Argentine and 19 Brazilian.[28]

River navigation was absolutely vital to the economic life of Corumbá, Coimbra, and Cuyabá in Mato Grosso, and ships serving these ports added much to Paraguay's economy.[29] The four vessels serving Mato Grosso from Montevideo in 1890 were joined by seven from Asunción in 1901 (see table 6).

The British La Platense Flotilla Company greatly expanded its service in 1886 and served all ports in Paraguay to Concepción until poor management and stiff competition forced it into liquidation in 1892. By 1896 only two lines were making the Buenos Aires–Asunción run with one weekly steamer each. Lloyd Brasileiro, bankrupt in 1900, continued to run from Montevideo to Corumbá, calling at Asunción and Buenos Aires. Argentina dominated river traffic throughout the Colorado era, maintaining an effective monopoly of Paraguay's carrying trade to foreign ports. Paraguayans, of course, had an overwhelming advantage in the coastal trade. By the end of the century, Nicolás Mihanovich, consul-general of Austria-Hungary in Buenos Aires, monopolized the river traffic. With headquarters in London and with British capital backing the enterprise, the company was incorporated in 1909 as the Compañía Argentina de Navegación Nicolás Mihanovich, Ltd. Capitalized at £2,692,468, the company

Table 6

Vessels Serving Mato Grosso, 1901

Name	Type	Tonnage	Home Port	Mato Grosso Terminus
Rapido	Steamer	270.0	Montevideo	Corumbá
San Antonio	Steamer	167.0	Montevideo	Corumbá
Salto	Steamer	174.0	Asunción	Porto Murtinho
San Francisco	Patacho	170.0	Montevideo	Porto Murtinho
Pollux	Steamer	57.0	Asunción	Corumbá
Quequay	Chata	37.0	Asunción	Corumbá
San José	Chata	15.5	Asunción	Corumbá
Leda	Steamer	148.0	Asunción	Corumbá
Filomena	Steamer	50.0	Montevideo	Corumbá
Ilex	Steamer	20.0	Asunción	Corumbá
Cochipó	Steamer	22.0	Asunción	Corumbá

Source: Eduardo Fasciotti to Domingos Magalhaes, Sec. 4ª No. 10, Asunción, April 10, 1901, RCBA-Or 238/3/12.

soon had 263 vessels in service calling at ports from Tierra del Fuego to the Alto Paraguay.[30]

American capitalists showed little interest in the river trade. Consul Ruffin at the end of 1902 recommended a fleet of barges drawing from three to five feet that could take shipments from Mato Grosso to downriver ports and bring back American merchandise warehoused in Buenos Aires, and at rates that would undercut the high charges of Mihanovich. It cost about 30 percent more to ship some goods from Asunción to Buenos Aires than from Buenos Aires to New York.[31] Like so many of his other practical suggestions, Ruffin's barge proposal was ignored. The Argentine monopoly permitted continued exorbitant rates which were a major handicap to Paraguay's economic development. Even completion of the railway to Encarnación would have provided little relief since the road would connect by ferry with an Argentine line at Posadas.

Railways—Real and Planned

Carlos Antonio López had the foresight to realize Paraguay's need for rail transportation. The result was the construction of the railway from Asunción to Paraguarí, a distance of seventy-two kilometers, which began service in 1861.[32] Neglect and deliberate destruction during the war left the railway in very poor condition. The Brazilians made some improvements for which Paraguay gave its notes when the government took over the railway in 1871. The Brazilian foreign office instructed its Paraguayan representatives to "give constant attention to the payment of these notes, which today with unpaid interest amount to $103,658.18 hard dollars, in case the Paraguayan government should contract any loan, or make any transaction concerning the railway."[33] Brazilian consuls and diplomats faithfully followed the admonition. Paraguay, of course, could not pay the notes as they came due. When Travassos, Patri y Cía. bought the railway in 1877, Brazil accepted the buyers' notes for the debt due.[34]

João de Freitas Travassos lacked the financial finesse of his partners. He submitted padded expense accounts, failed to deliver $f55,000 in shares to the general manager, and fell behind in paying his salary. These derelictions would be worthy of little notice had they not caused a bad rift in the very important Brazilian community upon which rested much of Paraguay's prospects for prosperity, as well as support against Argentine political machinations. The dispute went to the Brazilian consul, who, after carefully studying the manager's accounts, concluded that although Travassos was less than honest, a scandal must be avoided. Travassos withdrew from the company in March 1885, and Ricardo Antônio Mendes Gonçalves replaced him as a principal partner. Mendes, Patri y Cía. sold the railway back to the government in January 1886, but continued to manage it and became contractors to extend the rails to Villa Rica, some 74 kilometers beyond Paraguarí, at a contract price of about $18,200 gold per kilometer.[35] Unable to make payments due on this contract, the government, using the services of Dr. William Stewart, sold the railway to British capitalists who organized the Paraguay Central Railway Company, Ltd., on February 5, 1889, and paid Paraguay £210,000 and 21,000 shares of preference stock. The government obligated itself to guarantee a return of 6 percent annually on the cost of the line, and would receive 35 percent of the gross income if the company's revenues permitted. Perry, Cutbill de Lungo & Co. was given a five-year contract to complete the 217 kilometers from Villa Rica to Encarnación.[36]

For a while it appeared that the railway enterprise would prosper. Patri delivered the complete line to Villa Rica on December 25, 1889, and Perry, Cutbill, de Lungo built another 100 kilometers of shoddy railway that stopped abruptly near the Río Pirapó in a cattle pasture 117 kilometers short of Encarnación, then declared bankruptcy after the government defaulted on the guarantee in 1891. There ensued several years of acrimonious charges and counter-charges, investigations, heated debate, and abortive agreements that finally ended in 1907, three years into the Liberal era.[37] Four years later the railway was completed to Encarnación. Poor as it was, the service provided by the Paraguay Central was an important factor in Paraguayan economic recovery from the War of the Triple Alliance.

Argentine and Brazilian leaders were well aware of the strategic and economic importance of a Paraguayan railway system and its foreign connections. Completion of the Paraguay Central to Encarnación would provide an alternative to river traffic, but it too would lead to Buenos Aires. Should a railway be built across the Chaco, connecting Bolivia with the Paraguay River, much of that country's trade would also be funneled through Argentine ports. At stake, too, was Brazilian development of its vast hinterland, especially Mato Grosso, whose remote cities depended upon the Río Paraguay. Brazil desperately needed one or more overland routes, one to tap the Paraguayan market and another to penetrate the wilds of Mato Grosso. These routes would relieve Mato Grosso from dependence upon a river traffic monopolized by Argentina, weaken Argentina's hold on Paraguay, and facilitate the movement of Brazilian troops in the event of civil or international war. These considerations add significance to the contest for railway concessions between 1885 and 1891.

Edward Augustus Hopkins held stubbornly to his dream of becoming successful in Paraguayan enterprises. While the American minister, Judge John E. Bacon, was pressing for payment of the old Hopkins claim, Hopkins himself became involved in a trans-Chaco railway scheme. After giving up his sawmill at Villa Hayes, he conceived the idea of completing the railway from Villa Rica to Encarnación where it would connect with Posadas. Then he would carry the railway to Villa Hayes, either by bridge or tunnel, and build across the Chaco to Bolivia. This was the proposal that General Thomas Ogden Osborne, a former American minister to Argentina, presented to President Escobar on August 28, 1886. Escobar welcomed the idea and recommended it to Congress,[38] but Osborne and Hopkins had to be satisfied with the Chaco concession. Hopkins and not Osborne was the real mover behind the proposed Chaco railway, which he called his "life-long plan of a Railway across the Chaco from Asunción to Bolivia. . . . I was obliged to take it [the concession] out in his [Osborne's] name on account of my yet unsettled claims against Paraguay."[39]

After much debate, Congress finally awarded the Osborne concession in September 1887. This law granted the company the right of way and alternate lots ten kilometers wide and twenty kilometers deep, on each side of the railway for each fifty kilometers of completed line from Asunción to Puerto Magariños on the Pilcomayo. Since Magariños was located at about 61°40' W., it is interesting to note that Paraguayans would call this proposed line the Ferro-Carril á Bolivia, a tacit admission that Paraguay's claim to the Chaco did not extend beyond that point. Since the project called for at least $20 million in capital, considerable skepticism was justified, especially in view of Hopkins' reputation.[40] The railway never materialized, and there is still no bridge across the Paraguay nor a tunnel under it. Proposals for a railway connection between Paraguay and Brazil were equally unsuccessful.

The first postwar interest in linking Brazil and Paraguay by rail came in 1872, when an English expedition was scheduled to leave Asunción in September to explore a route for a line from the mouth of the Apa across southern Mato Grosso, then southward to Rio Grande do Sul. Four years later Brazil's great financier, the Viscount Mauá, had a survey made for a 1,000-mile line from Curitiba to Bolivia, but this, too, came to nothing.[41] There were other proposals for railroads to serve remote areas of Paraguay, the boldest of which came from the French explorer-geographer, Emanuel de Bourgade la Dardye, who explored a route across Paraguay in 1887 for the proposed 800-mile Transcontinental Railway from Asunción to Santos. Associated with him were Leonce de Modave and Manuel Obert, who had the support of French capitalists. The line would run from Asunción to Igatimí via San Estanislao and then "to the northeast boundary where the Sierra Mbaracayu joins the Sierra Amambay, . . . would cross Brazil somewhere near lat. 24°, and have its terminus at Santos, the chief port of the province of San Paulo."[42] Paraguay granted the concession to Modave on June 5, 1889, on condition that he deposit $20,000 in gold as earnest money. When the Modave concession lapsed, Obert sought a concession for the same project, with the addition of a line that would run southeast from Igatimí to Tacurupucú on the Paraná. This proposal aroused strong opposition from the pro-Argentine press; nevertheless, Congress granted the concession on August 27, 1891.[43] This transcontinental line never left the drawing board. Other forms of communication enjoyed greater success.

Mails, Telegraph, and Telephone

All the postwar governments sought to end Paraguay's isolation from other countries and to bring all parts of the country into closer communication with Asunción. Among the many achievements of the Provisional Government was organization of the postal service in 1869. Although a satisfactory statistical summary cannot be made for the 1870s, one can safely assume an increasing exchange of letters and printed matter from year to year. The Asunción post office handled some forty-eight thousand letters in 1880 and over sixty-three thousand in 1881. During the same years, newspapers and other printed matter handled at Asunción increased from about thirty-three thousand to fifty-one thousand pieces. Most of this exchange was with Buenos Aires.[44] Interior towns along the railway were served fairly well, a service that increased as the railway moved slowly toward completion at Encarnación. The Escobar administration extended interior mail service by coach and riders until in 1889 the president could report that distant towns, formerly deprived of communication with the capital, were being reached by mail service "that carries to them culture and civilization with the circulation of books and other printed matter, which also improves the movement of commerce throughout the country."[45] By 1890, the number of pieces handled at the Asunción post office had passed the million mark and increased rapidly through the 1890s.

Telegraphic service also showed a significant gain under the Colorados. Richard von Fischer-Treuenfeld and Hans Fischer built the first telegraph line in 1864–1865 from Asunción to Humaitá. The first section to Villeta opened on October 16, 1864, with telegraphers trained by Fischer-Treuenfeld. This line was destroyed during the war. President Caballero had it rebuilt to Paso de Patria and on April 18, 1884, the line connected with the Argentine telegraph built north from Corrientes. However, the 'connection' for five years was a fat telegrapher who carried messages by canoe from Paso de Patria across the Río Paraná. Finally, in September 1893, a cable under the

Paraná connected the lines, and Paraguay at last was tied in with the worldwide communications network.[46]

Paraguay's first telephone service also began under General Caballero. Congress granted the concession in July 1884 to Rodney Croskey and two associates whose company began service in Asunción on January 1, 1885.[47] This new means of communication, installed in Paraguay so soon after its invention, was so limited that it had very little effect on business or social intercourse during the Colorado era. Even as late as 1928, telephone service in the capital was so uncertain that messengers were still indispensable.

14

Basic Industries

Paraguay's postwar industrial development was hampered severely by political turmoil, allied occupation, and the lack of stable financial institutions. These and other factors combined to discourage enterprisers who might venture to invest in the war-ravaged country. After 1885, when the Colorados attracted speculators by selling off the national domain, ranchers, lumbermen, and railroaders turned increasingly to Paraguay as a field for development. Establishment of banks also provided very necessary credit facilities. A few Paraguayans, too, had accumulated reserves to invest in exploitation of natural resources. However reprehensible Colorado political oppression may have been, there is no denying that the Colorados helped to create the atmosphere needed for economic progress.

Agriculture, animal husbandry, and exploitation of forest products were the foundations of the Paraguayan economy, and practically all the industries started in the last quarter of the nineteenth century were processing plants directly connected with this trinity. The war had destroyed animal husbandry, only a few people were left to till the soil, and the production of timber products and yerba suffered from chronic labor shortages.

Agriculture

Paraguayan agriculture suffered from uncontrollable natural handicaps. Recurring droughts, huge swarms of locusts, and occasional floods and frosts were very destructive. The 1890s were particularly bad. Nearly every year of that decade brought the locust scourge which was so serious in September 1897 that in many departments committees were appointed to supervise efforts to kill the insects. In August 1898 when locusts originating in southern Paraguay invaded nearly all the country, some seventy-three thousand people were mobilized to fight the *acridio*, and their efforts saved the crops from total destruction.[1] Locust infestations generally came during periods of drought which added to the farmers' misery by drying up small streams and so lowering the rivers that barges loaded with yerba and other products could not move. Paraguay's great agronomist, Moisés S. Bertoni, called the drought of 1895–1896 the worst in two or more decades.[2]

Other handicaps included the continued use of such primitive tools as the wooden plow *(arado yvyrá)*, the lack of roads or railways to move crops to market, wide fluctuation in prices, the lack of sufficient credit, and endless battles against weeds and insects. Paraguayan farmers lacked the incentives needed to place agriculture on a high plane in the social order. Animal husbandry was far more attractive, and the seductive promises of yerbateros lured workers from the small cultivated plots that produced little more than the bare necessities. No matter how hard the campesino worked, his labor could not yield enough to provide any luxuries for himself and his family.[3]

Without exception, postwar presidents recognized the importance of agriculture. President Escobar in 1889 reminded Congress: "As a principal source of wealth, the future prosperity and improvement of the country depend upon its development." Only agricultural prosperity could end the unfavorable balance of trade and provide firm foundations for industrial prosperity. President González could see little improvement in 1891, when many campesinos deserted the farm for more lucrative employment; nevertheless, by the end of his term he could point to considerable progress in both agriculture and animal husbandry. Presidents continued to contrast the great fertility of Paraguay's soil with the small volume of production. As President Egusquiza said in 1896, Paraguay's farms could produce a thousand times more than they were yielding, and efforts would be made to stimulate farmers to adopt better methods.[4] Unfortunately, Colorado presidents also pursued policies that favored the large enterpriser and concentration of land in the hands of speculators.

To encourage the small farmer, Congress enacted a fairly favorable law in 1876. Farmers who occupied public lands would be given 100 varas (about 808 square feet) for each 4 varas they purchased, and could buy 15 plots of like size within two years—all at 6 pesos per 100 varas payable in certificates of the internal debt. Under the same law, any farmer, native or foreign, could buy a plot of about 10 cuadras at the same price on easy terms. A comprehensive act of December 20, 1890, appropriated 200,000 pesos annually for ten years to promote agriculture and such processing industries as sugar, textile, and flour mills, distilleries, and other enterprises. Another law encouraged empresarios to establish agricultural colonies near the railway. Each colony was to have thirty families of four members each, and each family was to buy a plot of at least 25 cuadras (about 46 acres) with the option to buy another plot of equal size. The Banco Nacional would aid in financing and the government would provide free passage for immigrants.[5]

To aid in financing agricultural operations, Congress created the Banco Agrícola in 1887, and in 1894 a Council of Agriculture and Industry within the bank directed its agricultural work. Despite efforts of the bank and its council, many farmers were indifferent and few industrialists used the available credit. Under the presidency of Christian G. Heisecke, the council administered the Banco Agrícola; liquidated the Banco Nacional; built five tobacco dryers; relieved the severe effects of drought by buying corn and selling it at cost; administered the Granja Tabaclera in Villa Rica; drilled artesian wells, operated the school of agriculture, a model farm and a produce market; built roads and bridges; promoted the production of coffee and cotton; distributed seeds, and started the production of grapes to supply a wine industry near Villeta, Areguá, and other towns. One enterprise encouraged by the council was La Azucarera, which started a mill at Ibitimí (also spelled Ybytimí) in 1898 with enough capacity to supply the country's demand for sugar. Tireless in promoting new projects, Heisecke gave especial encouragement to Emilio Johannsen's Colonia Elisa at San Lorenzo de la Frontera, which became the country's prinicpal banana center; to encourage pineapple production, the Banco Agrícola distributed 100,000 plants from Pernambuco.[6]

Heisecke's dedicated labors caused the minister of interior to give a glowing report on agriculture and animal husbandry in 1899. The tobacco harvest had been excellent, the Azucarera del Tebicuary had fulfilled its promise, and estimates of crop production showed a spectacular increase over previous years.[7] Nevertheless, agricultural development affected no more than an infinitesimal part of the country's area, and there was little reason for the British consul to change his evaluation of 1896:

> Until the Paraguayan can be induced to cultivate the soil intelligently, and to raise in a less primitive manner and on a larger scale crops for which markets might be found, . . . such, for instance, as cotton, coffee, or rice, all of which grow well in Paraguay, trade is not likely to improve rapidly or foreign capital be attracted to the country. But the Paraguayan peasant is not industrious and cannot be relied upon for regular and continuous work. Owing to the climate and to the natural fertility of the soil he need labour but little to supply his very simple wants. A little maize, mandioca, tobacco, and a few oranges are sufficient for him, and if he has a surplus large enough to buy clothing and some few other necessities he is quite content. Hitherto he has had no direct taxes to pay, and, therefore, has been under no compulsion to

work. He is seldom thrifty, and he will, it is said often gamble away in an hour what it has taken him a week to earn. His wife and daughter, on the other hand, are energetic and industrious, trudging daily many miles to market to sell the produce they carry on their heads or on the back of a single donkey.[8]

The typical *chacra*, a little farm, was a patch of two to five acres of poorly cleared ground that surrounded a thatched hut. Women wielding long sweeping brooms kept the small yard and clay floor of the hut clean of debris. A nondescript dog, neglected chickens, and a few pigs roamed at will except where crude fencing protected food crops from their marauding. Agriculture suffered from the persistence of primitive production practices. There was no scientific seed selection, fertilization, or cultivation. After burning their fields, a common practice to control insects and to discourage the growth of weeds, farmers planted seeds, tubers, or shoots by hand in trenches or holes prepared by the hoe, a method little advanced over the planting stick, and all the cutting was done with the machete. Steel plows were sometimes mentioned by advocates of improved agriculture, although the campesino had neither the resources to buy them nor the animals to pull them. Only the more prosperous farmers owned oxen needed to drag the wooden plow and to pull the high-wheeled cart indispensable for hauling cash crops to market.

Crops

Mandioca and maize were Paraguay's principal food crops and were supplemented by widely grown but limited acreages of beans, potatoes, peanuts, and sugar cane (see table 7). Alfalfa produced five or more cuttings annually. Despite government efforts to promote

Table 7
Principal Crops and Cultivated Acreage, 1890
(total acreage = 22,746,278)

Crops	Acres	Crops	Acres
Maize	8,229,823	Potatoes,	
Mandioca	7,051,862	vegetables	540,894
Beans	2,574,965	Rice	371,492
Tobacco	1,980,611	Alfalfa	192,736
Sugar cane	887,796	Cotton	126,313
Peanuts	719,816	Coffee	69,970

Source: DCR No. 1006, *Paraguay 1891*, p. 20.

cotton and wheat production, neither crop had achieved much importance by the end of the century, and wheat was imported from
Argentina to supply the flour mill in Asunción. Many efforts, dating
from the Francia period, had been made to increase the cultivation of
cotton. A cotton industry had been included in the dreams of Edward
Augustus Hopkins, and Carlos Antonio López had imported seeds
from the United States for free distribution to farmers. Caballero's
government offered free land, free seeds, and exemption from military service to farmers who would grow at least 4,000 cotton plants.[9]
These efforts resulted in no significant production until the 1890s
when more than 120,000 acres were regularly planted to cotton.

Coffee trees, introduced into their missions by Jesuits, could
thrive in the rich Paraguayan soil. Trees that escaped the frequent
frosts produced a bean that yielded a satisfactory brew that was
superior, some enthusiastic aficionados believed, to the Brazilian.
Although government subsidies encouraged coffee growing, especially in agricultural colonies,[10] expansion of production was severely limited by the overwhelming preference for mate, Brazil's
tremendous advantage, and the threat of frosts.

Oranges, both bitter and sweet, grew in such great profusion that
they had only a nominal value. One thousand sweet oranges delivered to a river vessel brought $1.25 in 1881, a year in which nearly 48
million were exported, mostly to Buenos Aires. Bitter oranges had no
value, but leaves of the tree were the source of increasing amounts of
essence of petitgrain, widely used in perfumes. Banjamín Balansa
began the petitgrain industry at Yaguarón in 1876. No efforts were
made to improve the quality of sweet oranges, nor to increase the
yield of the trees that grew so profusely with no care whatever.
Experiments in the mid twentieth century proved that a dramatic
increase in the yield of leaves from the bitter orange and of fruit from
the sweet orange could be obtained by growing both species in plantations.

As common as orange peelings discarded along the streets were
the short cigars favored by Paraguayans of both sexes and all ages.
Tobacco grew well in the rich, red soil of the country, especially
around Barrero Grande, Atyra, Tobatí, and Piribebuy, and provided
the small farmer with an easily exported crop. In the early 1880s,
upward of 5,500,000 kilos were produced annually. The blue variety
(peti-hoby) predominated around Villa Rica and met domestic needs;
a yellow variety (peti-porá) was exported to Argentina, Uruguay, and
Chile. In the last years of Colorado rule, warehoused tobacco doubled
in quantity, a tribute to the work of the Oficina Revisadora de
Tabacos y Mercado de Frutas established by the Banco Agrícola.
From 2,568,836 kilos in 1900, the quantity of warehoused tobacco
increased to 5,048,265 kilos in 1904.[11]

As was true with other crops, poor quality and careless methods of handling restricted tobacco yields. A very knowledgeable traveler called the ordinary Paraguayan cigar an abomination,[12] but the small cigars were so cheap that the smoker could discard several until one was found that suited the taste. Tobacco production also suffered from lack of industrious workers; "The men seem little inclined to labor imposing this generally upon their women, and as a result the exports of the country are chiefly articles of spontaneous production such as yerba, found growing wild, oranges from old plantings, timber & &. The main if not only cultivated product for commerce being tobacco."[13] Low tobacco prices from 1893–1895 made the crop not worth growing except to meet domestic needs. In the midst of these depression years, Argentina raised the duty on Paraguayan tobacco to 50¢ gold per *arroba* (about 25 lbs.) in 1894, a move that effectively killed the export trade. Although the duty was gradually lowered to 15¢ as of January 1, 1897, both farmers and exporters suffered until an increase in prices helped to revive the trade. Still, prices were discouraging: about 30¢ per arroba for the poorest grade and $1.25 for the best in 1897.[14]

This experience with the Argentine tariff proved to be the salvation of Paraguay's tobacco industry since it led the Banco Agrícola to intensify its efforts to improve the product in order to find European markets. The advice of Cuban experts and the construction of several drying sheds resulted in such dramatic improvement that Paraguayan tobacco found ready acceptance in Hamburg, Bremen, and Amsterdam. Prejudice against Paraguayan tobacco gradually disappeared and by 1919 it was the most important of all Paraguayan exports.[15]

Paraguayan agriculture could have been much more diverse, but little progress was made until the Servicio Técnico Interamericano de Cooperación Agrícola (STICA) brought aid from the United States in 1944. Lack of capital and indifference to diversification could have been overcome, in spite of the handicap of competition from neighboring countries.

Animal Husbandry

Paraguayans much preferred animal husbandry to farming. Tilling the soil with primitive instruments was generally regarded as woman's work, whereas to own a horse was a status symbol, superior to being compelled to ride a burro. The Paraguayan cowboy was never as celebrated as the Argentine gaucho or the Chilean huaso, nor was there a José Fernández to create an idyll like *Martín Fierro*, a classic that immortalized the Argentine gauchos. Still, the hacienda, with its broad pastures and freely roaming herds, was much preferred to the farmer's patches of mandioca and maize, his chickens, pigs, and goats.

The Paraguayan War destroyed the thriving cattle industry that had been nurtured by Francia and the first López. During the postwar decade, cattle had been imported from the Argentine provinces of Corrientes and Entre Ríos, and from Mato Grosso. Under an act of 1880, public land other than the municipal ejidos could be rented for periods of two to five years, with the option of purchase or renewal of the lease. Annual rentals were ridiculously low: sixty pesos fuertes for a league of first class land, and fifty pesos for second class. Foreigners, mostly Argentines and Italians, dominated the industry during the Colorado era until the French La Fonciére and similar enterprises developed cattle raising on a large scale toward the end of the century. In the early 1880s, Luís Patri had more than seven thousand head of cattle grazing south of Asunción. Several foreigners owned herds of fifteen hundred or more and many farmers had from twenty to three hundred head.[16]

The German poet and writer Dr. Ernst Mevert bought Dr. William Stewart's beautiful hacienda near Ybytimí. Described as "the only bit of good estancia land on the road from Asunción to Villa Rica," this property supported several thousand cows in sleek condition."[17] A league of good land could easily support 2,000 cattle. By the mid 1880s, Paraguay was once more self-sufficient in cattle, although blooded stock needed to be imported to upgrade the herds. Government figures, always suspect, reported 500,000 horned cattle in 1884, and more than 700,000 in 1886. By the end of 1902, the number exceeded 2,700,000 and the numbers of other animals had increased spectacularly (see table 8).

Growers of livestock had to contend with several diseases. Although the British consul reported healthful conditions in 1898, such pests as ticks, flies, snakes, and jaguars took their toil. Aftosa (hoof and mouth disease) appeared in nearly all departments in 1900, a year in which the government launched a campaign against cattle rustlers. Horses and mules were subject to what Dr. Stewart diagnosed as *mal de cadera*, which resembled India's kumree. This disease attacked animals that grazed in swampy ground, causing a weakness in the haunches, and generally ended fatally after a few months.[18]

Several companies were organized for agricultural operations in the Colorado era, some of which concentrated on animal husbandry, others on crop production, and some produced both livestock and crops while exploiting yerbales and timber resources. The huge increases in cattle and horses resulted from their operations. Some concessionaires failed, as did Dr. Adolfo Doering and Dr. Luís Hasperath, a partnership that planned a model sugar plantation, coffee and cotton plantations, cattle estancias, and other enterprises. Also in

Table 8

Estimates of Livestock in Paraguay, 1877–1902

	Cattle	Horses	Mules	Sheep	Asses	Hogs	Goats
1877	209,525	21,140	1,299	6,668	1,500	3,026	?
1886	729,796	62,386	1,925	32,351	2,239	12,250	11,102
1887	912,245	88,106	2,763	42,490	2,463	13,375	15,542
1888	1,000,000	100,000	3,000	50,000	2,500	?	?
1890	861,954	99,693	2,433	62,920	2,188	10,788	14,656
1900	2,283,000	182,719	3,453	214,020	4,035	23,850	32,255
1902	2,743,665	217,882	8,983	222,286	5,227	87,491	49,599

Source: Freire Esteves, *El Paraguay constitucional*, p. 173; ME, *Memoria 1888*, pp. 55–59; DCR No. 1006, *Paraguay 1890*, p. 18; Schurz, *Paraguay*, p. 64. The figures for 1888 obviously are outright guesses, and those for 1900 probably are considerably too high.

1899, the Estancia Guaviyu Company, Ltd., registered in London, was capitalized at £60,000 for the purpose of acquiring and operating lands in the Plata area but apparently never operated in Paraguay. During the late 1880s, Argentines and Paraguayans organized a company that held some 280 leagues of pastures, forests, and yerbales in northern Paraguay. When the company was being liquidated in 1902, the Société Fonciére du Paraguay acquired its assets, which included more than 50,000 cattle. La Fonciére, organized in 1898, had huge holdings by 1919. Its 248 leagues east of the Paraguay River between the Aquidabán and Apa rivers were divided into twenty estancias which employed 200 men to look after 150,000 cattle.[19]

The great increase in foreign investment during the Liberal era after 1904 brought such important enterprises as Liebig and International Products Company to Paraguay. These and other large scale operators wrought tremendous improvements in animal husbandry, provided employment for many workers, increased trade, and, inevitably, added to government income.

Exploitation of Forests

A bewildering variety of trees in Paraguay's magnificent forests could be exploited commercially. There were at least seventy varieties suitable for industrial use; sixty-nine trees and shrubs with medicinal properties; forty-three useful in ornamental planting; four that produced tannin and extremely hard wood; fifteen trees, shrubs, and plants that yielded dyes; eight from which fibrous materials were obtained; and thirty-eight wild fruit-bearing trees. Overwhelmed by the green masses of forests that mantled the country, a British minis-

ter exclaimed: "The wealth of the timber is immense, all the hills—
and the whole country is hilly—being covered with splendid trees,
and all the marshy shores of the Paraguay are a vast forest."[20]

The forests provided an inexhaustible source for railway sleepers, beams, posts, pilings, and planks. Bark of the *curupay* and *quebracho colorado* yielded tannin, while their dense reddish wood defied oxidation and insect pests. Quebracho, which grew primarily in
the Chaco near the Paraguay River, was harder, heavier, and more
durable than curupay. The several varieties of *urungay-mí* had qualities similar to quebracho but were less plentiful. An excellent, relatively light hardwood with a beautiful grain was the *peterevi*, much
used in furniture. Several varieties of *lapacho* added color to the
landscape with their gorgeous blossoms and were excellent for railway sleepers, timbers for ships and boats, and spokes for wheels. The
lapacho crespo, with its curled grain, was made into beautiful heavy
furniture. Several kinds of cedars that grew in the south, southeast,
and Alto Paraná, had a soft wood much in demand for furniture,
doors, shutters, and boxes. Plentiful, cheap, and easy to work,
Paraguayan cedar was used in Europe to make cigar boxes. Indians
made canoes from the *timbó* that thrust its branches to great heights
as it reached for the sky above vine-matted forests. Much like the
timbó was the *samahú*, which grew to a height of more than seventy
feet and yielded vegetable silk. Natives used it to some extent in
making ponchos, but, a British consul observed, "the cost of extract-
ing the down and the utter indifference of natives to work, together
with absence of roads in the interior of the country renders it difficult
to obtain large quantities regularly." The samahú also had a "strong
fibrous substance . . . beneath the bark, which is used by the natives
for various purposes." The silky fibers from seed pods were the
"down" referred to by the consul and could be used like kapok for
stuffing pillows.[21]

Several companies were formed to include sawmills among their
enterprises. Small mills were numerous, and their owners showed a
fine disregard for government-owned timber. Among the topics discussed by President Caballero, José Segundo Decoud, and other notables who met at Dr. Stewart's home in July 1883 to welcome the
British chargé, was the thriving trade in timber stolen from government lands. President Caballero, aware of the problem, acknowledged that the government was losing heavily from lack of regula-
tion. With commendable speed, only eighteen months after Stewart's
party, Congress enacted legislation to prevent exports of timber
products without payment of fees and to limit the size of areas that
could be cleared for agricultural towns and fields. Far more important for the control of forest exploitation was the formation of well-

financed enterprises to which the government sold huge areas at absurdly low prices. The companies would, at least, attempt to prevent thefts from their property. Carlos Casado, Ltd., was the first company formed in the Colorado era to exploit timber resources on a large scale. Others followed in due course, but as late as 1941 Paraguayan mills were using such primitive production methods that Brazilian, Chilean, and American lumber was often cheaper than the Paraguayan product in Platine markets.[22]

Several efforts were made to establish a rubber industry, but all of them failed. Probably the first enterpriser to make the effort was Cayetano Ituruburu who obtained a concession in 1876 to start a plantation at Tacuatí Loma in Concepción department. Required to plant 4,000 *cautchú* trees within four years, Ituruburu gave up the effort.[23] There were also expeditions into Mato Grosso to search for rubber trees. One left Asunción in 1887 with two British subjects in the party. No word as to its progress or fate reached Asunción until December 1889, when the British consul received "trustworthy information to the effect that the whole party had met its death in the northern region [Mato Grosso] of Brazil at the hands of the Mivas tribe of Indians." When a second expedition, organized by a French company under command of a Bolivian, set out in July 1900 to search for rubber, two Englishmen again were among the explorers.[24]

A man who deserves to be rescued from obscurity is William Kiehl, born at Hall in Yorkshire to Dutch parents. Educated in Holland, he spent three years in the Congo Free State and in 1899 was an attaché to the ephemeral Transvaal Republic's legation at The Hague. Kiehl resigned by request when he outraged his government by providing information to Henry Howard, British minister to The Hague. What led him to Paraguay we do not know, but by mid 1901 he was "engaged in Rubber Planting in a district called Horqueta" where he constructed buildings and planted 5,000 small rubber trees. Kiehl was unable to establish cordial relations with the natives, who burned his plantation and threatened his life. When Consul Gosling protested vigorously to the Escurra government, Kiehl's treatment but not his fortune improved.[25]

Foremost among Paraguay's scientists was Dr. Moisés Bertoni, the Swiss-born director of the School of Agriculture. Bertoni was tireless in investigating Paraguay's flora. Guaraní folklore, which is rich in tales of medicinal herbs, also attracted his attention and, when he discovered something of interest, shared his knowledge by publishing scientific papers. One of his discoveries was the small shrub called *caa-ehe*, whose leaves had an aromatic flavor and enough natural sugar to sweeten a cup of tea or coffee. He also confirmed the effectiveness of a brew of *caaguazú* bark, called *guina*, which was used widely in the yerbales to fight fevers and as a tonic. This bark was identified as *Pecaraena vellozi* and closely resembled *Pecaraena excelsa*, widely known as Jamaica quassia.[26]

Yerba and the Yerbales

Yerba mate, consumed by the millions of kilos in the Platine countries and Brazil, was one of Paraguay's principal sources of wealth. Yerbales, or stands of yerba trees, were scattered widely over the country. The best and most abundant yerba trees grew well north of Asunción near the center of the country and in the northeast, especially along the upper Paraná. An inferior yerba grew in Argentina's Misiones and in Brazil. Bourgade's authoritative map of 1889 shows yerbales in all southeastern Paraguay.[27] The Jejuy river system in north central Paraguay, with San Pedro as the principal town, provided fairly good waterways for yerba-loaded chatas to make their way to centers of distribution.

In an effort to prevent wasteful exploitation and destruction of the yerbales, President Salvador Jovellanos issued a decree on December 23, 1874, that gave the Junta Económica Administrativa in each department control over concessions to yerbateros. This decree prohibited the destruction of the trees, limited harvesting to the first eight months of the year, and required a waiting period of three years before the branches could again be cut. Until the great land giveaway after 1885, the government kept control of the northern yerbales, permitting yerbateros to lease them at very nominal prices.[28]

A typical establishment in the yerbales consisted of a shed to store supplies and processed yerba, huts for the workers, and *barbacuas* (drying frames). The barbacuas were constructed

> of poles and withes, from 15 to 20 feet square, with arched or angular roofs, and firm, even floors, made of clay, extending 6 or 8 feet beyond the frames on all sides, for the convenience of pulverizing the material after it is dried. Near each *barbacua* is erected a stand or elevated seat, from which the foreman may watch the drying process and make such changes in the disposition of the material as he may deem necessary. Each worker climbs a tree, and with a large knife or facón cuts off all the small branches bearing leaves until the tree is quite stripped. These branches, made up into small bundles, are borne to the drying frame and lightly heaped on top. Under this is then lighted a clear, though not very hot fire [of aromatic wood], under the influence of which the yerba mate is gradually dried.[29]

When the leaves were dry after fifteen to twenty hours of roasting, workmen put out the fires, swept the floor, and beat the dried branches to make the leaves fall to the floor where they were pounded with flat flails, reduced to a powder, and then packed into bales bound with wet leather skins. The leather contracted as it dried, producing a tight bale or *tercio* that weighed from 200 to 250 pounds. In some yerba operations, the dried yerba was ground in a mill, producing a mixture of powder, twigs, and bits of leaves. Skilled workers could produce large quantities of dried yerba: "In a couple of days, a few men, accustomed to the task, can dry between 3,000 and 4,000 kilograms of yerba."[30] Although cultivated yerbales, especially in the agricultural colonies, steadily increased production, the wild yerba accounted for most of the crop. Huge quantities were exported to the Platine ports despite strong competition from Brazil. In a good year in the 1890s, total production would exceed 8,000,000 kilos, one-half of which would be consumed locally. From a total of 1,512,110 kilos in 1873, worth $124,910 gold, exports rose to a peak of 6,318,816 kilos in 1900, worth $758,258 gold. The average yearly export from 1900 to 1920 was about 4,000,000 kilos.[31]

Paraguayan yerba not only suffered from Brazilian competition in foreign markets but also from adulteration by the yerbateros. This adulteration became so notorious that the term *paraguaya* came to mean the lowest grade of yerba. To end this condition, various commissions were established in Asunción, Concepción, and Encarnación in 1896 to inspect exports. Lessees of government yerbales were also guilty of other frauds including theft of yerba from unleased lands.[32]

In seeking ways to make money, the Paraguayan enterpriser inevitably would consider exploitation of natural resources, among which yerba ranked high. Thus it was not difficult for President Bareiro to be rid of Patricio Escobar, his minister of war and marine, by the promise of a concession to exploit the very rich yerbales of Tacuru-pucú on the Alto Paraná due east of Asunción. Congress granted the ten-year concession in 1879 with the stipulation that he was to construct roads and bridges at his own expense. In 1883, probably in anticipation of the act of May 28, 1885, Congress revoked the concession and paid Escobar an indemnity of $f125,000.[33] Three years later, in the year that Escobar became president, native and foreign capitalists founded La Industrial Paraguaya, which was by far the largest, richest, and most influential of Paraguayan companies. The list of its shareholders was also "the list of the most important business men whose resources and intelligence promoted the commercial development of the Republic."[34] Taking advantage of the 1885 land act, the founders bought 855,000 hectares of yerbales and 2,647,727 hectares of forests and campos. La Industrial's yerbales alone produced 800,000 arrobas in 1890, worth about £133,000. By 1904, the company was exporting 400,000 arrobas annually, which were processed in its three mills, one each in Asunción, Corrientes, and Buenos Aires. This gigantic enterprise—gigantic, that is, for Paraguay—capitalized at $f4,000,000 in 1886, was so profitable that it paid large dividends annually and increased its capital to 30,000,000 pesos in 1906 when more than 2,000 men were employed in its haciendas, sawmills, and yerbales. Its five estancias had more than 15,000 animals: 10,640 cattle, 2,537 oxen, 329 horses, 660 mules, 380 sheep, and 500 hogs. Motorboats, chatas, carts, and wagons moved its yerba to market. Brand names of its mate, like Cerro Corá, are still to be found in Paraguayan and Argentine stores. The company prospered through the wise management and guidance of an extremely capable board of directors. In 1906, when the company declared an 18 percent dividend, Oscar Erck was general manager, Juan B. Gaona was president of the board of directors, and Antonio Plate, of the Banco Mercantil, was vice-president. On the board were wealthy bankers and merchants, all of whom had contributed much to Paraguay's economic recovery: Félix de los Ríos, Rodney B. Croskey, Jorge Casaccia, and Gregorio Urrutia. Seven years later, the Farquhar interests acquired La Industrial, and another prominent Paraguayan, José Fasardi, became chairman. Among the directors was Christian G. Heisecke, whose energetic measures to improve agriculture have never received just recognition in Paraguay.[35]

The chief rival of La Industrial was the Brazilian Matte Larangeira, which operated in Mato Grosso, northern Paraguay, and in yerbales east of the Paraná River. Founded by Tomás Larangeira in 1879, the company leased and then bought huge areas, like the Malheiros concession in Mato Grosso. A rival of Matte Larangeira in northern Paraguay was Patri, Navarro y Cía., whose owners had numerous interests in Paraguay. This rivalry caused a very sharp increase in the price of yerbales as both companies bid for lands auctioned under the act of 1885. By 1890, Matte Larangeira was producing 2,000,000 kilos of yerba annually which were exported to Buenos Aires and Rosario to compete with La Industrial. To gain access to its yerbales, the company built a narrow gauge railway to which caravans of fifteen two-wheeled carts, each drawn by four yokes of oxen, brought 300 tercios of yerba for shipment to the Paraguay River. In 1902, Matte Larangeira became Larangeira, Méndez y Cía., with Tomás Larangeira, Hugo Heyn, and Francisco Méndez Gonçalves as principal owners. Capitalized at $40,000,000, the company operated four estancias with 50,000 head of cattle. A fleet of thirty chatas on the rivers and 500 carts on forest trails carried its yerba.[36]

Since nearly all prominent Colorados had an interest in La Industrial, Congress was under constant pressure to handicap Matte Larangeira by levying transit duties on the yerba that crossed Paraguayan frontiers and to prevent Paraguayans from signing labor contracts abroad, a measure which, the Brazilian minister observed, would kill "the great extractive and animal husbandry enterprises of the State of Mato Grosso, which come here to find the necessary workers, since one may say, our compatriots of that rich and vast Brazilian region are interested almost exclusively in politics."[37] President Escurra, not wishing to antagonize Brazil, prevented the labor measure from being discussed in Congress, but the rivalry of the two great companies continued for many years.

Processing and Manufacturing

Paraguay's industries were almost entirely extractive in nature. True manufacturing was severely limited by natural and human resources. The Brazilian consul could report truthfully in 1885 that industry, except for making soap, liquor, and processing mate, was unknown. Cottage industries took the place of factories in producing *ñandutí* lace, cigars, leather goods, furniture, and a large variety of utensils. These were produced by women who worked at home and periodically loaded surplus goods in baskets to be carried on their heads as they walked barefoot to market, or rode a plodding, ear-flopping, tail-twitching burro along the sandy trails and tracks. In all Paraguay there were fewer than 850 commercial and industrial houses and a large percentage of these were in the hands of foreigners. Mulhall noted two sugar mills, three soap factories, and one brick kiln in 1885.[38] Near the end of the century, there were plants for processing yerba, timber, tobacco, fruits, hides, and coconuts, and distilleries to produce *caña*, an alcoholic beverage distilled from sugar. Flour mills, tanneries, match factories, a soap factory, and the brick and tile industry were reasonably prosperous. There was a ready market for the entire production of brooms, palm leaf hats, ice, soda water, cigars and cigarettes, and candles. A comparison of newspaper advertisements in the 1870s with those of a decade later reveals the great progress that had been made in Asunción, Villa Rica, and other towns.

Fernando Saguier built the first postwar sugar mill of any consequence under a very favorable concession of 1878. With other capitalists, Saguier began operations near Ypané in 1879, but lost interest in the enterprise after his small son drowned in the flume. General Caballero joined forces with Doña Anastasia Escota de Bareiro and others to start a small mill called La Perseverencia near Zeballos-cué, just north of Asunción.[39] The next effort was made by Ortlieb Hermanos under a concession of September 1893 to start a mill near Ybytimí on the Tebicuary. Alberto Brun built a small mill at Luque at about the same time and enjoyed much better success than did the Ortliebs, whose enterprise was acquired by La Empresa Azucarera.

Plans for expansion of sugar production led the Banco Agrícola to import considerable machinery from the United States: then a disastrous fall in prices discouraged both growers and the mill owners, leaving the bank with unused equipment. Market recovery in 1897 improved the fortunes of La Azucarera del Paraguay de Ybytimí, also known as La Empresa Azucarera del Paraguay. Located on the Tebicuary River, it was connected by a spur to the Paraguay Central Railway. The mill opened in May 1898 with new English machinery in place.[40] The Banco Agrícola, attempting to reduce Paraguay's dependence on imported sugar, had invested more than 400,000 pesos, or one-sixth of its capital, in unsuccessful sugar enterprises. La Empresa Azucarera del Paraguay, liquidated in 1901, was acquired by Vicente Nogués for 950,000 pesos, 800,000 of which was owed to the Banco Agrícola. After a few lean years, the enterprise began to show a profit, and during the first part of the Liberal era, La Azucarera Paraguay, S.A., was flourishing with a production in 1907 that reached 120,000 arrobas.[41]

Numerous small enterprises, many of them begun by immigrants, revealed opportunities open to industrious craftsmen and small capitalists. Andrew Scala, born in Genoa in 1831, learned shipbuilding in that storied seaport before emigrating to Buenos Aires in 1851 where he directed shipbuilding in La Boca for three decades. Seeking to improve his health, he went to Asunción in 1882 and was soon operating a steam sawmill and shipyard, an enterprise that employed seventy workers in the 1890s and produced large numbers of vessels, among them steam launches, chatas, pilot boats, and steamers. Another Italian, Aurelio Fiori, also built steamers and "all kinds of carts and vehicles."[42]

The Italian taste for vermicelli, spaghetti, and other forms of pasta was met by Marcos Quaranta, whose mill and factory began operation in 1866 at Tuyuty. Quaranta survived the war, moved to Asunción in 1869, and opened his factory in 1885. Twelve years later, he had three stores to sell his daily production of 2,900 pounds of pasta. The first and most important flour mill in the country was begun by Fernando Saguier y Cía. in 1892. This Molino Nacional, which produced 14,000 kilos of flour daily, became the property of Martín y Cía. in 1894.[43]

Another thriving enterprise begun by Italians was the versatile factory owned by Pecci Hermanos y Cía. which operated under a concession of 1880. For ten years the firm produced ice to supply an insatiable market. In 1891 Pecci Hermanos built a factory in Asunción to produce ginger ale, ice, carbonated water, and pasta. This factory turned out from 1,000 to 1,500 bottles of beverages and from 1,000 to 2,000 kilos of pasta daily, and 150 kilos of ice hourly.[44] A descendant of this family, Victor Pecci, gained international recognition in 1979 as one of the world's fine tennis players.

Paraguayans had to depend upon the produce of many small *trapiches*, (crude sugar mills) to satisfy their desire for sweets until José R. Quevado opened his *fábrica de dulces* in February 1897. The first and only one of its kind during the Colorado era, this factory made twenty-two kinds of jellies, jams, preserves, and other sweets. The first meat salting and drying plant was opened by Héctor F. Bado at Pueblo de Cangó along the route from Encarnación in 1892. Great activity in the yerbales of the upper Paraná and in lumber camps created a demand for better meat than the *charque* (dried meat) imported from Argentina and Brazil. Bado, born in Argentina, maintained a continuous open house at Cangó where travelers to and from Encarnación found a hospitable welcome. The enterprise prospered so well that in 1896 some 9,000 cattle were slaughtered to provide from 1,000 to 1,500 arrobas of charque monthly. Two hundred workers found employment at this *establecimiento saladeril* (meat-drying plant).[45] Hides were a by-product that found a ready market in Buenos Aires, where buyers shipped them to Europe.

Numerous kilns turned out a large volume of bricks and tiles but still could not meet the demand. Among the many enterprisers who entered the business, frequently with concessions from Congress, was Francisco Jounger, whose 1876 concession authorized him to manufacture bricks, to operate sawmills, and to operate plants to process coffee, sugar, cotton, and other products. Nothing ever came of this project. Another concessionaire was João Freitas de Travassos, the Brazilian sutler who, with Luís Patri and other partners, was so prominent in the Paraguayan economy during the Colorado era. Travassos y Cía. began to manufacture bricks at Areguá in 1880 under a concession that waived customs duties on all machinery and building materials imported for the enterprise.[46]

There was a good market for candles and matches, nearly all of which had been imported through Buenos Aires until November 15, 1890, when Casal Correa y Cía. officially opened their factory. Using machinery imported from France, the factory employed forty-five workers by 1897 and produced 70,000 candles and 8,000 boxes of matches daily. Soap, too, was an early product of foreign enterprise. In 1881, the Frenchman Esteban Mendiondon, obtained an exclusive ten-year concession to manufacture coconut oil and soap within a league of La Recoleta on the edge of Asunción. This Industria Nacional won a gold medal at the Buenos Aires Continental Exposition in 1882.[47]

Many experiments were made to obtain fiber from the *ibira* and *caraguatá* (wild pineapple) plants. During the Paraguayan War, caraguatá fiber was made into paper, and the Polish military engineer, Robert A. Chodasiewicz, drew some excellent maps for the Allies on sheets of this paper that had a parchmentlike quality.[48] Two enterprisers, Braulio Artecona and Luís L. Lenguas, began a factory at Arroyos y Esteros in 1879 to produce caraguatá paper. The enterprise failed. Artecona tried again in 1889 with better machinery and had a contract with an Argentine company for all he could produce. This time it was poor management that wrecked a very promising enterprise. Ibira gave a finer fiber than caraguatá, but the process of separating and cleaning was too expensive for profitable exploitation.[49]

One of the first significant efforts by American capitalists to invest in Paraguay, after the confiscation of Hopkins's United States and Paraguay Navigation Company in 1854, was made by the Paraguay Development Company, incorporated in Philadelphia on July 26, 1900, with a capital of $500,000. The company's charter authorized it to engage in a wide variety of enterprises: street lighting, yerba processing, textile manufacturing, construction of water works, operation of sawmills, construction of harbor and dock works, building railways, and so forth. Obviously, its $500,000 capital would not go far. Carlos Rodríguez Santos, a nephew of General Caballero, was Paraguay's delegate to the Philadelphia International Commercial Congress and Export Exposition in 1899. He was a leader in organizing the company, whose treasurer wrote that it was organized "with the direct sanction and support of his Government, which would study the needs of our sister republic and obtain the right, upon the most favorable terms, to take up successively those industries down there which would provide opportunities for the safe and remunerative investment of American capital."[50] The first fruit of the company's labor was a concession granted to its subsidiary, the Asunción Electric Lighting and Traction Company, to install street lights and electric streetcars by 1903.[51] The company's ideas were good but its resources were unequal to the multitude of tasks undertaken. Unable to attract sufficient capital, the company faded away.

A report from the Brazilian minister in Asunción in April 1887 should have attracted immediate attention from Baron Cotegipe, who had been so important in postwar relations with Paraguay. Operating in the supposedly useless Chaco, Carlos Casado had "founded there a large steam sawmill and opened a port on the Río Paraguay, three leagues from the mouth of the Apa, where he exports a large quantity of woods for construction, and, above all, of sleepers for the Argentine railways, of which he is the principal supplier, thus using the essential wealth existing in the forests on his property, which measures 3,000 leagues."[52]

Carlos Julián Niceto Casado del Alisal was born on March 16, 1833, in Villada, Spain. A graduate of the Bilboa Naval School and the Universidad Literaria de Valladolid, he had a brief naval career that included two shipwrecks before he went to Buenos Aires late in 1857 and finally settled in Rosario where he prospered in foreign trade. In 1865, Casado married Ramona Sastre Aramburu, daughter of a famous Uruguayan educator, and in the same year started the Banco Casado, which he later sold to the Bank of London. With the proceeds he became a very successful colonizer and railway builder in Santa Fe province, served as director of several banks, and introduced modern methods and machinery to wheat production. As a result of his efforts, Rosario exported the first cargo of wheat to Europe in 1878, thus beginning an extremely important trade.

Casado was an imaginative entrepreneur, daring but practical, who saw opportunities missed by lesser men. Attracted to Paraguay by the Colorado land sales of 1885, he sold most of his property in Argentina and left for Asunción in June 1886. The 3,000 leagues that he bought in the Chaco cost so little that he had ample resources to build a tannin factory equipped with French machinery. By October 1887 his headquarters at Puerto Casado was a town of more than six hundred. The factory, which began operation in 1889 under the direction of Julio Dutrellaux, was the first in the world to produce quebracho extract. The enterprise profited from the start and by 1903 was producing 600 tons of extract monthly. Two powerful tugs towed huge rafts loaded with tannin from Puerto Casado to Buenos Aires. To carry other products, Casado bought two steamers and twelve sailing vessels. All the Casado enterprises prospered: lumbering, tannin, shipping, and investments in Asunción.

Before he died in 1899, Casado turned his empire over to his son, José Casado Sastre, who greatly expanded the company's operations. He built Puerto Sastre, laid 250 kilometers of narrow gauge railway into the interior, and devoted considerable attention to cattle raising. The original 3,000 leagues were reduced by one-half through gifts and sales, but there was plenty of land left to support the huge cattle herds that eventually grew to 50,000 animals.[53] Perhaps the most lasting influence of the Casado enterprise will be the Mennonite colonies begun in the 1920s with the enthusiastic cooperation of José Casado Sastre.

The Lure of Gold

Paraguay is richly endowed with such common minerals as lime, marble, building stone, oxide of manganese, and significant deposits of iron—but no coal, petroleum, or precious minerals. Bearing in mind the successful prewar iron works at Ybicuí, Mariano Gutiérrez in 1872 obtained a concession for exclusive exploitation of iron mines for sixty years. This enterprise failed for lack of capital. A short time later came the Mayer-Mansilla fiasco in search of gold. Much more practical was the effort made by James Horrocks to open a trade with the United Kingdom in Paraguayan oxide of manganese, which also failed.[54]

Magnificent rainbows often arch their splendor in the Paraguayan skies, but no one ever found a pot of gold where they touch the earth in gorgeous color. One can well imagine that every square foot of Paraguay has at some time been the foot of a rainbow. Two of the legends most cherished by Paraguayans concern gold—the secret gold mines of the Jesuits and the buried treasure along the route of the final and disastrous retreat of Francisco Solano López. Living in a country rich in base minerals, Paraguayans also persisted in the belief that there was gold in the sierras that mark the boundary with Brazil. A report that gold had been found had such wide circulation in 1877 that a company, the Sociedad Anónima de Minerales en las Serranías de Amambay y Maracayú en el Paraguay, was formed to exploit the "discovery."[55]

Colonel Lucio V. Mansilla, a politically powerful porteño, and Mauricio Mayer were the prime movers in this venture. Their interest had been aroused by Colonel Francisco Wisner de Morgenstern, who supposedly had discovered gold during the López regime. Wisner's secret had been kept. One guesses that Wisner had convinced Mansilla and Mayer by taking them to the site, probably an area rich in iron pyrites. Whatever it was, Mansilla was satisfied and made frequent trips to Paraguay over a period of three years "to organize a society for exploration of gold mines in the sierras of Amambay and Maracajú, claiming to know the place, discovered in the time of López, and kept in absolute secrecy, where it is said there are fabulously rich deposits of precious metals."[56] In April 1877 a group of men gathered at the Hotel de la Paz in Buenos Aires to hear about Mansilla's trip to the mines with Wisner. The sincerity with which he described the prospects so impressed the audience that on July 15, at another meeting in the same hotel, an enthusiastic group organized the company, approved the proposed articles of incorporation, elected a board of directors, and authorized an expedition to the mines. Mayer and Mansilla had obtained a twenty-five-year concession from Paraguay which they transferred to the company for 2,000 shares, leaving 800 shares to be sold in Buenos Aires and 200 in Paraguay at 2,500 Argentine pesos per share. By September 30, Argentine investors had paid 1,942,500 pesos into the Banco de la Provincia for 777 shares. Among Paraguayan investors were Benjamín Aceval, Cándido Bareiro, José Segundo Decoud, Juan Francisco Decoud, Adolfo Decoud, Patricio Escobar, Bernardino Caballero, and many more prominent politicians and business leaders. Altogether there were 299 shareholders who invested 1,943,343 pesos. Mayer put in 57,736 pesos and Morgenstern advanced 29,000 pesos.[57]

Mayer led the first expedition, which sailed from Buenos Aires on the *Venezia* on August 8, 1877. In Asunción, he registered the articles of incorporation, spent 850,568 pesos to buy five chatas, fifteen carts, and supplies to support eighty-six men and twenty women for nine months. Leaving Asunción on August 26, the expedition reached Tobatí after some difficulty in crossing the hills. Mayer wrote that he expected to reach the mines in thirty days. Going by way of Caraguatay and San Estanislao, the Mayer expedition required ten days to cross the Tacuarí swamp and expected to reach its destination early in October. Additional information on the Mayer expedition is lacking, except that it found no gold. Mansilla persisted until interest died away in 1881. Ten years later an Englishman led an expedition into Mato Grosso, where gold mines did exist in the Cuyabá area, without making new discoveries. Nor were any finds made as a result of prizes offered by the government in 1889 for the discovery of gold, silver, or precious stones.[58] Like the hope of finding oil in the Chaco, the dream of precious minerals has no more substance than the pot of gold at the foot of the rainbow. Far more wealth was to be found in promoting trade in basic forest, agricultural, and animal products.

15

Foreign Trade

Foreign trade was extremely important to Paraguay, a country that depended upon customs duties as a major source of government income and as a means of obtaining specie. Only through trade could Paraguay acquire the many products needed to supplement its own crude economy. Exports, of course, had to pay for imports, and in this Paraguay suffered severe disadvantages. Far removed from their principal markets, shippers were forced to pay exorbitant transportation costs, poor marketing methods resulted in large losses of perishable products, and natural catastrophes drastically reduced products available for export. Although some European markets were opened in the 1890s, Argentina dominated Paraguayan trade. Paraguay's principal exports competed with Argentine and Brazilian products and inevitably suffered from tariffs that were levied in response to pressures exerted by foreign producers.

Woefully inadequate records preclude accuracy in any discussion of Paraguayan trade, and the almost uniformly successful efforts of smugglers to avoid registration with customs officials contribute another factor of unknown dimensions. Although exactitude will forever elude the economic historian, existing evidence is sufficient to provide a general understanding of Paraguay's foreign trade.

"We Cannot Use Statistics"

Every attempt to present reliable statistics about Paraguay in the Colorado era—and for many years thereafter—has been an exercise in frustration and futility. As late as 1912, a writer complained: "For Paraguay we cannot use statistics, as they exist only in very primitive form and for the city of Asunción alone; in fact the population census has still to be taken."[1] Lacking reliable statistics, officials found it impossible to prepare adequate budgets, or to conduct ordinary government business, in anything but a most haphazard manner. Merchants had to guess at how much of a given product could be sold; treasury officials could not estimate income with any degree of accuracy, and consuls were forced constantly to advise their governments that figures in their reports were not reliable. The Brazilian consul in 1883 warned his superiors that the figures he reported were only approximations for "a country that has hardly begun to organize its various public services," compiled from records of official agencies, treasury reports, and consular records.[2] To be sure, individual enterprisers, such as the Paraguay Central Railway, La Industrial Paraguaya, and various banks, presumably kept fairly accurate records to form the bases of reports to stockholders. But the national government had no consistent policy of assembling such reports for current analysis and future reference.

In 1885, near the end of his administration, General Caballero had Congress create the Mesa Estadística General (General Statistical Office), which was to gather statistics; all offices were to send copies of reports to the Mesa which in turn would make an annual summary. The Mesa's first director, J. Jacquet, submitted his first report on December 1, 1887, with the explanation that "the delay in publication of this work is due to the recent creation of this office and the almost complete lack of former documents." Unable to collect much needed data, he did his best to present an exact idea of the country. In his official report of 1885, the minister of hacienda could generalize about improvement in trade since 1880, note the considerable increase in public wealth since 1870, and look forward hopefully to future prosperity, but he presented no statistical evidence. The 1885 Mesa was closed because "no one could be found capable of undertaking the management of it," and merchants understandably, were reluctant to give information about their businesses. Statistics obtained from the *aduana* (customs house) were entirely unreliable.[3] The unusually capable Cecil Gosling gave up in despair as he apologized for the thinness of his 1900 report because of "the lack of official statistics and the great difficulty of obtaining information of any kind." At the end of the Colorado era, the Brazilian consul again reported the impossibility of providing accurate statistics.[4] The figures provided in the following discussion of Paraguayan trade are, therefore, to be considered as no more than approximations.

Foreign Trade and Smuggling

Paraguay's foreign trade was limited to a small number of houses, most of them located in Asunción or Villa Rica, which sold to small merchants and to rural outlets. These same houses bought tobacco, yerba, hides, oranges, and a few other products that could be sold in Buenos Aires. Exports of all products in 1879 were valued at $f1,579,152 and imports at $f952,447. On this trade the government collected $f212,274 in duties.[5] The value of imports, which exceeded $1,000,000 gold in 1880, tripled by 1888, fell to less than $2,000,000 in 1891, and did not reach $3,000,000 again until 1901. Exports nearly doubled during Caballero's presidency, from $1,163,417 in 1880 to $2,103,010 in 1886. In the banner year of 1891, exports were over $3,000,000, dropped by one-half two years later, then began a slow recovery to over $3,000,000 in 1900 and reached a peak of over $4,000,000 in 1903. For the 25 years from 1880 to 1904, Paraguay had a favorable balance of trade of $4,001,629 (see table 9).

Trade involving money was confined primarily to Asunción and the larger towns. The campesino, whether he lived on a chacra or small rancho, rarely raised enough surplus to sell. Subsistence farmers and residents of small towns bartered tobacco, sugar cane products, maize, or whatever a local merchant would accept, for imported necessities. In this way were gathered many of the cattle hides, and capybara, deer, nutria, and pig skins that found their way into the export market. Paraguayans manufactured very little and all of them raised practically the same things. Merchants frequently provided the farmer with necessities between harvests, a system that could never be profitable for the producer and was very risky for the merchant. The interior merchant, in turn, was supplied by one of the few houses in Asunción or Villa Rica and paid for his goods with more produce than cash. At each stage in the trading process the danger of fraud or deception was very real. After having been in the doldrums through most of the 1890s, trade was improving slowly toward the end of the Colorado era. New buildings and homes, the demand for good clothes and fine furniture, were visible signs of a growing prosperity that was limited to Asunción and the larger towns, "for outside people are miserably poor," the British consul reported, "and their wants still restricted to the barest necessities."[6]

Treasury dependence upon duties increased the gravity of losses through smuggling and thievery at the customs houses. Officials regularly falsified accounts, accepted bribes from both importers and exporters, and made it utterly impossible to obtain accurate statistics on trade. About one-fourth of the duties collected in Asunción reached the treasury, according to one Paraguayan critic, and practically none came in from other customs houses.[7] This condition prevailed throughout the Colorado era and improved little if at all under the Liberals. Indeed, cynics insist with good reason that the smuggling business still thrives in Paraguay, whose officials connive with the contrabandistas, especially in the remote border town of Pedro Juan Caballero.

Paraguayans needed no lessons in how to evade the customs collector, but none were more brazen than the sutlers who served the allied occupation forces. The Brazilian foreign office sternly rebuked its officials in Asunción for allowing sutlers to import free of duty goods that immediately were offered for sale in the stores. Evacuation of Paraguay in 1876 brought no relief. Six years after the last

Table 9

Foreign Trade of Paraguay, 1880–1904

	Imports			Exports		
	£	$ Gold	$f Paper	£	$ Gold	$f Paper
1880	206,081	1,030,408	1,030,408	232,683	1,163,417	1,163,417
1881	258,625	1,293,125	1,293,125	385,710	1,928,550	1,928,550
1882	283,496	1,417,480	1,417,480	330,136	1,650,680	1,650,680
1883	208,068	1,040,340	1,040,340	353,095	1,765,495	1,765,495
1884	289,626	1,423,130	1,423,130	314,459	1,572,295	1,572,295
1885	295,319	1,476,595	1,594,722	332,105	1,660,525	1,793,367
1886	383,501	1,917,505	2,377,706	420,602	2,103,010	2,607,732
1887	488,776	2,441,380	3,295,863	430,080	2,154,000	2,907,900
1888	657,951	3,289,755	4,967,530	517,722	2,588,610	3,908,801
1889	639,633	3,198,165	4,989,137	436,676	2,183,380	3,406,072
1890	544,289	2,721,445	4,544,813	580,146	2,900,730	4,844,219
1891	360,400	1,802,000	8,721,680	633,200	3,166,000	15,323,440
1892	497,371	2,486,855	15,120,078	571,598	2,857,990	17,376,579
1893	506,660	2,533,300	15,579,795	319,792	1,598,960	9,833,600
1894	440,441	2,222,205	13,644,338	444,000	2,220,000	13,630,800
1895	492,504	2,462,520	13,730,112	509,145	2,545,225	14,253,260
1896	257,267	2,786,335	18,383,811	490,000	2,450,000	16,170,000
1897	468,661	2,343,305	16,403,135	434,148	2,170,740	15,195,180
1898	564,487	2,822,435	20,866,019	481,492	2,407,460	17,815,204
1899	429,567	2,142,835	14,999,845	580,000	2,900,000	20,300,000
1900	531,148	2,655,740	21,909,855	641,415	3,207,675	26,463,318
1901	600,731	3,003,655	27,032,595	685,336	3,426,680	30,840,120
1902	466,459	2,332,295	23,322,950	778,132	3,890,660	38,906,600
1903	710,365	3,441,825	34,204,074	850,730	4,253,650	40,962,649
1904	713,146	3,565,731	29,223,041	639,252	3,196,261	35,158,871
Totals	11,298,572	57,960,364	352,037,182	12,382,374	61,961,993	339,779,149

Sources: DCR No. 3007, *Paraguay 1902,* p. 7; DCR No. 4086, *Paraguay 1907,* pp. 2, 4; PRO-FO Miscellaneous Series No. 358 (1895), p. 16; *Memorias* of the Ministerio de Hacienda; presidential messages. Figures given in various memorias and presidential messages frequently are at variance with this table. There is also considerable variation from the table in Schurz, *Paraguay,* p. 157.

Brazilian troops had embarked, the Brazilian chargé reported that the monthly income of 30,000 pesos from the Asunción aduana could be doubled if smuggling were stopped, a difficult task because the documents had been stolen.[8] In the same year, José Segundo Decoud and Victorino de la Plaza, the Argentine minister of foreign affairs, signed an agreement to unite their efforts to combat smuggling. Plaza and Decoud hoped to include Bolivia, Brazil, and Uruguay in a five-power pact, an effort that failed because opponents saw an attempt by Argentina to extend its hegemony over Uruguay and, probably, Paraguay. After the Caballero government, desperate for revenue, bore down on thievery at the Asunción aduana, monthly customs receipts doubled to 60,000 pesos. Still, the problem simply would not go away. Smuggling across the Río Paraná was so absurdly easy that Caballero was obliged to reestablish many military and police posts. In all, *El Heraldo* asserted in 1885, the treasury lost 546,323 pesos on smuggled goods valued at 1,220,000 pesos. The editor's remedy was to reduce the tariff, since under rates then in existence, goods worth 500,000 pesos would pay 225,000 pesos in duties.[9] One wonders how the editor could be so exact in stating the losses.

Exports and Tariffs

Argentina and Paraguay were inseparable commercially. During the Colorado era, Argentina provided most of the capital for large enterprises, and Argentine cities were the principal markets for Paraguayan yerba, tobacco, timber products, tomatoes, hides, and other exports. Yerba mate consistently was the most valuable of all exports. Two classes of yerba entered the trade: *mborouiré* (rough mate) which was beaten by flails after drying, and *molida* or milled mate. La Industrial Paraguaya accounted for about one-half of Paraguay's mate exports. In 1895, 9,024 tons went through customs and was sold for about £16,845 (about $84,225 gold or 471,668 Paraguayan pesos). The export duty on molida was 10¢ gold per arroba, and one cent less on mborouiré.[10] A close rival to yerba was tobacco in bales and cigars. In 1886, 442,940 arrobas of yerba and 416,000 arrobas of tobacco were exported.

Tariffs seriously affected Paraguayan prosperity and could be used as a potent political weapon in the struggle between Brazil and Argentina for the control of Paraguay. The Brazilian minister in Buenos Aires asserted that tobacco from Rio Grande do Sul was much better than the Paraguayan product, and Brazilian yerba was equal to Paraguay's best. He was, therefore, understandably disturbed when Argentina in 1877 made slight reductions in duties on Paraguayan products.[11] Argentina's tariff policy was a major concern of Paraguayan diplomats, merchants, and producers. Although

Paraguay denounced the commercial treaty of 1876, its 1883 replacement was little better. Argentina simply did not have to make significant concessions to Paraguay. She could import noncompetitive Paraguayan products free of duty but charge ruinous rates on tobacco and yerba. The tariff in effect in 1890 allowed Argentina to change its rates at will since the trade was much more important to Paraguay than to Argentina. In 1895, for example, Paraguay's exports to Argentina were valued at $1,824,312 gold, but imports from Argentina were valued at only $100,000 gold.[12]

Responding to pressures from Argentine producers and also, probably, to exert political pressure on Paraguay, Argentina increased the duty on Paraguayan tobacco in 1894. This increase, combined with low prices in Europe, was disastrous to Paraguayan tobacco growers, who reduced production to meet local demand, and many of them sought work in the yerbales. This crisis demonstrated conclusively that Paraguay was dependent upon Argentine markets, and the Argentine policy had been oppressive. Paraguay managed to persuade Argentina to reduce the tobacco duty in 1896, an act that brought much rejoicing in Paraguay and which increased Argentine political influence. Continuing Paraguayan efforts resulted in a reduction of tariffs on tobacco, yerba, quebracho extract, and other products by 50 percent or more in 1896. However, severe droughts and locust plagues in 1896 and 1897 reduced the production of both tobacco and yerba so much that Paraguayan farmers benefitted little from the reduced duties.[13]

The Argentine concessions of 1896 did improve relations with Paraguay and greatly increased the influence of the Liberals, who already were planning the revolt of 1904 in which Argentine aid was to be decisive. At the same time, Brazil showed little inclination to permit free trade between Paraguay and Mato Grosso, whose principal products, primarily cattle and yerba, competed directly with Paraguay.

There was very little change in the kinds of products exported by Paraguay for more than twenty years after the Paraguayan War. As the country slowly recovered, supplies of yerba, tobacco, dried hides, and skins of wild animals were accumulated. Argentine and Uruguayan markets could always take various wood products, from logs to bark used in tanning. Sweet oranges, too, were readily available (see table 10). By 1881 there were small surpluses of sugar cane, starch (from mandioca), indigo, and coffee for export.[14] These products steadily increased in volume. As animal husbandry recovered, the number of dried and salted hides and other animal products increased dramatically. In the 1890s, foreign enterprise began to produce quebracho extract, railway sleepers, beams, and logs for the insatiable Argentine market.

Table 10

Exports of Sweet Oranges in Selected Years

	No. of Oranges	Value in Gold $
1873	3,089,000	6,168
1881	47,917,700	47,917
1909	173,149,150	421,444
1915	216,996,750	330,423

Sources: Vansittart, "Report," p. 148; Freire Esteves, *El Paraguay constitucional*, p. 131.

Exports to Argentina for selected periods in 1899 are fairly representative of the trade. In April there were 588 sacks of coco bran, 9,774 hides, 484 logs, 2,081 pounds of quebracho extract, 11,421 planks, 1,491 palm logs, 655 bales of tobacco, 8,400,000 loose oranges, 2,083 sacks of oranges, and 10,021 sacks of yerba. In June there were also shipments of cattle horns, and hooves, starch, tomatoes, limes, horsehair and coconuts.[15] These exports were in sharp contrast with the imports that entered Paraguay legally.

Imports

Except for the unrecorded trade across the Paraná and Paraguay from Argentina and from Mato Grosso on the northern frontier, practically all Paraguay's imports came by river craft from Montevideo, Buenos Aires, and Corumbá. Some products, such as wheat, originated in Argentina, but most of the imported goods came from Europe and were transhipped at Montevideo or Buenos Aires, where agents supplied the merchants in Paraguay. Some of the shipments were consigned to retailers in Pilar, Humaitá, Concepción, and other river ports, but most of them were destined for Asunción.

An impressive variety of imported goods entered the trade. During the first postwar years, live animals—cattle, horses, mules, and sheep—were numerous as Paraguay replaced stock lost during the war. Various foods made up a large volume of duty-free imports: flour, meal, vegetables, maize, potatoes, cheese, oils, and sugar.[16] For many years all the sugar sold in Paraguay and Mato Grosso came from Europe, mainly from France. In 1895, Paraguay imported about 2,300,000 pounds of sugar. The greater portion of imports, whether direct or indirect, were English in origin until the German population outnumbered all foreigners except Italians. Of the important houses in Asunción in 1895, seven were German and one was English. England provided the cheaper cotton goods, such as calico, gray cloth *(lienzo),* and cotton prints; the best quality shawls, ponchos, suitings, and drills were German. Hardware, cutlery, and kitchen utensils, china, and glass came from Germany and Austria. The United States provided agricultural implements, axes, carriages, and windmills. Rice came from India and Italy, coffee from Brazil, candles from the Netherlands, kerosene from the United States. Outside of Asunción and the larger towns, there was little demand for kitchen utensils. Nearly every kitchen, more properly described as a cooking shed, had the bare minimum of equipment, and only the wealthier campesinos possessed a wide range of cutlery, china, and glassware. Considering Paraguay's agricultural potential, it seems the height of folly for the country to import alfalfa, rice, sugar, coffee, onions, soap, butter, beans and cheese. Wheat did not grow well in the country, so imports of that cereal and flour were necessary.[17]

Imports from Germany increased steadily in the 1890s. By 1896, the German consul reported that neither the United States nor Germany appeared to have a clear advantage. German imports threatened to supplant "those of British manufacture, owing to the lower prices at which they are sold," but British tools and machinery were still preferred in 1898. British knives, especially the "Sheffield blade with a brown wooden handle studded with brass nails," cotton goods, and cashmeres continued to be favored by Paraguayans, although American cotton goods were offering competition in 1899. In that year, the British consul reported, "the bulk of the foreign trade with Paraguay both in exports and imports, was in the hands of Germans." German merchants handled the goods, but in 1900 imports of British goods were valued at £167,710, French goods at £81,519, and German imports a poor third at £71,933. Spain, the United States, Italy, and Brazil contributed only £40,082. In 1902, seven countries provided most of Paraguay's imports. The United Kingdom led with £172,778, France was second with £82,491, and Germany was third with £65,037. Argentina, Italy, the United States, Spain, and eleven other countries contributed a total of £146,153.[18] The British consul's summary of imports for the year 1901 holds for the rest of the Colorado era:

> Rice, for which there is a large demand, is imported principally from Bremen. Petroleum, another important item in a country dependent entirely upon lamps for artificial light, comes from North America. Sugar is imported from France and the Argentine Republic. Wines and spirits come from Spain and Italy. There is a small though perhaps growing demand for British spirits such as refined gin and whisky. The amount of beer imported from Europe is small, the cost being too great to compete with the local brewery which does a fairly good business. Hardware and machinery come chiefly from the United States and Germany. The latter country, however, sells a cheaper article and consequently gets a greater proportion of the trade. Earthenware and

glass come from Holland, the United Kingdom, and Germany; china comes from Germany and Austria; window glass from Belgium; table glass from Germany; clocks from the United States and Switzerland. The leather trade is almost entirely in the hands of Germany. Rifles and revolvers come principally from the United States, Belgium, and Germany. Bent wood furniture is imported from Austria and a small amount from the United States. The most important article of import, namely cotton goods, is still entirely in British hands. Germany has, however, monopolized the trade in ponchos and to some extent also that in cloths.[19]

There was no direct trade between Paraguay and the United States, despite sporadic efforts by ministers and consular officers to arouse the interest of government officials and merchants. In arguing for a raise in rank, Judge Bacon in 1887 pointed to the increasing importance of Paraguayan trade, especially in cotton goods which the United States could supply. Because Paraguayans preferred American cottons, some British textile manufacturers affixed the American eagle and an American trade-mark to their goods. Not counting Montevideo and Buenos Aires, Bacon anticipated a market for at least 20 million yards of cotton goods of American manufacture.[20] Five years later the American consul in Asunción also praised the superiority of American over European imports, but reported that no business had been transacted at the consulate for the quarter ending June 30, 1892. When Dr. Eben M. Flagg took over as vice-consul on January 1, 1894, he could find no record of any direct trade between the United States and Paraguay. Attempting to arouse the interest of exporters, Flagg persuaded Paraguayans to export $9,000 worth of "ostrich feathers, angrette plumes, ox hides, stag hides, carpincho hides, orange oil and tobacco, all of which products have turned out profitably to the dealers with the exception of tobacco." There was a great opportunity for tobacco manufacturing in Paraguay, for "no where in the world can finer tobacco be found for certain purposes."[21]

The most persistent and popular promoter of United States–Paraguayan trade was Dr. John N. Ruffin, who saw a great market for American goods in Paraguay. In 1900, Ruffin visited the United States, where he spoke at trade fairs and meetings. In August 1901 he was Mark Hanna's guest in Cleveland and delivered an autographed photograph of President Aceval to Senator Joseph B. Foraker in Cincinnati. He gave lectures at the Buffalo Pan American Exposition. It may have been a coincidence that the Paraguayan Development Company was organized in Philadelphia in 1900. Another enterprise, the Yerba Mate Tea Company, was incorporated in New Jersey in 1899 with $100,000 capital. Despite much advertising, the company failed to make mate a popular drink with Americans.[22] Paraguay's trade with the United Staes was very slow in developing, as was

American investment in the country. The situation was vastly different in the case of Mato Grosso.

The Mato Grosso Trade

The exchange of goods between Paraguay and Brazil's remote province of Mato Grosso was significant. Incomplete records for the years 1891–1893 show that from 10 percent to 15 percent of all Paraguayan exports went to Mato Grosso and 5 percent to 6 percent of all imports came from Mato Grosso.[23] Considering the thriving smuggling trade, the percentages undoubtedly were much higher. Economically, Mato Grosso was much more closely tied to Paraguay than to the rest of Brazil. The round trip from Rio de Janeiro to Corumbá required a tedious two months or more, not counting the time spent in such ports as Montevideo, Buenos Aires, Rosario, Asunción, and Concepción. Much of the cargo shipped from Brazil's Atlantic ports had to be transhipped at Montevideo or Buenos Aires, and again at Asunción, since few ocean-going vessels could sail up the Paraná beyond Rosario. Vessels drawing more than six feet rarely ventured into the Paraguay River, and beyond Asunción, except at high water, vessels of more than three feet draft were in danger of being stuck on shifting sand bars. Most of the craft in the Asunción-Corumbá trade were steamers of small tonnage and a few sailing vessels, several of which were built at Asunción.

After the trade had recovered slowly through the 1870s, thirty or more vessels were involved. For the year 1880–1881, of the thirty-two craft that entered from Corumbá, twenty-three were Brazilian and nine were foreign. In 1892, more than forty vessels engaged in the trade.[24] During the 1890s, the *Diamantino*, at 476 tons the largest serving Mato Grosso, made three round trips annually between Montevideo and Corumbá via Asunción. Some vessels made the run between Porto Murtinho and Concepción or Asunción. The *Dom Thomas*, 116 tons, carried yerba from Murtinho to Asunción, making the voyage in two weeks. Many vessels, like the *Salto* (178 tons), the *Fortuna* (181 tons), the *Leda* (270 tons), the *Diana A* (294 tons), and the *Posadas* (132 tons) took from four to six weeks to do the round trip from Asunción to Corumbá, calling at Murtinho.[25]

Mato Grosso provided northern Paraguay with livestock, but there are no reliable statistics of this trade because there were no customs houses at the Apa River crossings, and smugglers would have avoided them in any case. Cattle from the Malheiros estancia below Fuerte Olimpo found a good market in Asunción. All of the lime and much of the tallow, dried beef, and sugar consumed in Paraguay came from Mato Grosso. Many of the products exported from Asunción to Mato Grosso were reexports from Montevideo and Buenos Aires and included food, mattresses, brooms, machinery, iron and steel products, and dry goods. The Mato Grosso trade reflected Argentine and Paraguayan economic crises. When commercial houses failed in Asunción, Buenos Aires, or Montevideo, the shock waves were felt in Coimbra and Corumbá. Incomplete statistics show a generally unfavorable balance of trade for Mato Grosso, but the figures are deceptive because the number of cattle smuggled into the Concepción area was probably large enough to more than balance the trade account.[26]

Importance of the Asunción–Mato Grosso trade was demonstrated in 1899–1900 when plague caused Brazil to order its ports closed to ships from Paraguayan ports. This action gave rise to contraband on a grand scale, as ships that used to be in the Asunción-Corumbá trade, continued in operation to Bahía Negra, the last Paraguayan port across from Mato Grosso, which was a thirty-six-hour run from Corumbá. From Bahía Negra, goods were shipped to the Bolivian port of Piedra Blanca, which was only three hours from Corumbá, and from there it was easy to smuggle goods into Mato Grosso. Moreover, the entire Paraguayan shore was so close to Brazilian towns that the distance could easily be covered by canoes. During the quarantine, many fazendeiros and merchants visited Asunción without bothering to register at the Brazilian consulate. They came to buy goods for their enterprises, to hire workers for their industries, and to buy salt and other supplies for their fazendas. The lack of salt caused heavy losses of cattle, which fazendeiros were determined to minimize regardless of regulations.[27] After the plague ended, Brazilian officials imposed so many annoying regulations on Paraguayan shipping that many captains refused to enter Brazilian ports. Ships bound for Corumbá had to anchor at the mouth of the Apa and wait for an hour or two until a customs official deigned to come aboard. If the ship arrived at Porto Murtinho after 6:00 P.M., it could not proceed until the next day, when the first official landed and another boarded the vessel for the trip to Corumbá. No vessel could dock there after 5:30 P.M., so the crew "had to spend the entire night on board, fighting like crazy men with the swarms of mosquitoes." After a thorough examination by a doctor in the morning, the ship could dock.[28] Brazilian regulations, however annoying, were inspired by concern for public health and not by a perverse bureaucracy determined to hamper a necessary and profitable trade.

Paraguay's foreign trade, insignificant when compared with that of Brazil or Argentina, was vital to the country's economic health, political stability, and social progress. Any decrease in the volume of products for export caused hardship throughout the country, and, by reducing customs receipts, seriously disrupted government finances.

16

The Wonderland of Government Finance and Banking

Colorado leaders displayed very little skill in managing Paraguay's finances. Neither legislators nor executives were able to devise measures and policies which would meet the demands of the present and fit into a long-range plan, an ideal impossible to realize in postwar Paraguay. The country had barely existed during the allied occupation of nearly a decade when revenues were always inadequate to meet the most elementary needs. Even if postwar officials had been reasonably honest, they would have been unable to restore solvency to the treasury. Argentina and Brazil, far more interested in checkmating each other than in helping the ruined country to recover, provided no economic assistance. Turmoil in their own political and economic conditions would have seriously limited the amount of financial aid that the victors might have offered, and the benevolent idea that a conqueror should help to restore life to the conquered was not to be accepted in the European world for nearly another century. Paraguay had to depend upon its own limited resources and upon the hazy vision of its own leaders.

Only the most rudimentary features of a fiscal policy had emerged in Paraguay dring the years before Cándido Bareiro's regime began the first Colorado era in 1878. Bareiro's tenure was too short to permit development of an integrated fiscal policy. His successors, even when they listened to José Segundo Decoud, were satisifed with keeping the country from sinking beneath a horrendous debt. Only by selling its considerable assets to foreign interests was Paraguay able to maintain a precarious financial existence. Despite extremely unfavorable conditions, daring entrepreneurs did provide the foundations for a banking system during the Colorado era, foundations that survived during the Liberal era.

Sources of Government Income

Regular revenues of the national government consisted primarily of customs duties. To this relatively reliable source were added postal and telegraph revenues, a controversial head tax, sale of stamped paper, fees, license taxes, and considerable sums from the sales and rentals of the public domain (see table 11). Receipts from a modest land tax, imposed in 1896, increased revenues at the end of the century. In the postwar decade, there had been some revenue from the London loans and a loan from the Banco Nacional in Buenos Aires. Colorados increased national revenues through sale of the railway and investment in banking. Expenditures usually exceeded income. On these recurring occasions, the government resorted to the issue of paper money, treasury obligations, bonds, payment certificates and promissory notes, and tinkered with the tariff. The only reason that the various instruments of debt were marketable at all was because they could be purchased at a fraction of their face value and were accepted at par in payment for land and of various imposts. Although ministers of hacienda, with the exception of Decoud, had only the most rudimentary grasp of government finance, all of them understood the need for a balanced budget and the danger of huge issues of paper money. All of them struggled vainly against the lack of a system of taxation.

Although all statistics relating to finance and trade are inaccurate, often grossly so, they are at least indicative of what officials thought to be the case. Total revenues for 1873 were $67,274 and expenditures were $153,486, the deficit having been caused by the revolution of 1873–1874. For several years, until 1881, revenues stayed in the $200,000–$250,000 range. A general increase in trade brought customs revenues to about $500,000 in 1881.[1]

Customs duties were the most consistent source of revenue. This was natural, as the Brazilian chargé observed: "In a pastoral country like this, where agriculture is insignificant and industry unknown, it is not strange that import duties should be the most important source of income.[2] The *Reglamento* of 1873 established regulations for the entry of foreign vessels, cargo manifests, port charges, and customs duties. The first duties, entirely on imports, were set at 25 percent ad valorem, with the exception of a few products. Tobacco and yerba imports paid 40 percent. Dissatisfied with the customs revenues and administration of aduanas, President Gill on June 15, 1877, created a commission of merchants and prominent citizens, including Dr. William Stewart, to revise the tariff. This commission recommended an increase of the tariff on all foreign merchandise to 42 percent ad valorem, of which at least 26 percent had to be paid in gold or silver,

Table 11

Estimated Revenues of Paraguay, 1881–1903

(in *pesos fuertes* $f, nominally equal to $1.00 U.S.)

	Customs	Land Sales	Other[a]	Total
1881	441,678	?	354,750	796,428
1882	477,621	6,621[b]	386,139	870,381
1883	501,032	7,036	42,174	550,242
1884	723,564	53,750	62,658	839,972
1885	826,359	609,510	62,031	1,437,900
1886	1,206,333	2,055,087	1,750,407	5,011,827
1887	1,358,317	1,686,253	11,523	3,056,093
1888	1,389,112	1,788,302	294,740	3,472,154
1889	1,419,882	815,304	1,889,490	4,124,676
1890	1,185,077	324,873	227,814	1,737,764
1891	1,196,315	175,969	275,433	1,647,717
1892	2,131,506	364,355	235,646	2,731,507
1893	4,309,232	938,631	611,402	5,859,266
1894	3,813,619	497,850	599,003	4,910,472
1895	4,519,812	119,660	480,771	5,120,243
1896	5,080,622	488,409	283,836	5,832,867
1897	4,950,311	310,889	491,641	5,752,841
1898	5,059,588	113,688	3,909,859	9,083,135
1899	5,759,895	113,446	3,296,971	9,170,312
1900	8,428,705	280,739	1,147,519	9,856,963
1901	9,930,348	—	1,482,398	11,412,746
1902	9,479,624	—	1,538,692	11,018,316
1903	12,960,674	—	2,432,030	15,392,704

Sources: British and Brazilian trade reports, memorias of Paraguayan ministers of finance and interior, messages of Paraguayan presidents to Congress, Paraguayan newspapers, and diplomatic despatches of Brazilian ministers and chargés.

Notes: Estimated expenditures are not given because even a close approximation is impossible. The budget, as adopted by Congress, generally included only the costs of the presidency and the five administrative departments, and was usually merely a salary budget. Other expenditures often were given by ministers of hacienda under the blanket term "ordinary," but this term covered special appropriations, appropriations for continuing expenses, or "entitlements," and sometimes the total expenditures were arrived at by adding the budget and ordinary expenditures together. "Ordinary" expenditures varied from $f777,395 in 1881 to $f11,803,969 in 1903, while "budget" expenditures for the same years were $f245,555 and $f11,531,068, respectively.

a. Special circumstances account for the surges in income in the 'Other' column. In 1886, there was a great increase in rentals from yerbales; the figure for 1889 includes proceeds from the railway sale.

b. Sales of public lands and yerbales were made under the 1876 law; however, the memoria of the minister of hacienda for the year 1898 erroneously states that there were no sales from 1881–1884.

and 2 percent in copper. No export duties were levied until May 1880, when each hide was taxed 40¢ and each arroba of yerba from 10¢ to 30¢ depending on its quality.[3]

In a desperate move to increase revenues, President González in June 1892 ordered a 100 percent increase of duties on many imports, and a 300 percent increase on such luxury items as porcelain, crystal, cut glass, jewelry, and musical instruments; cards, wax matches, cigars, and alcohol had to pay a 400 percent increase. These duties, effective July 1, 1892, did little to improve revenues.[4] Congress frequently increased the duty on certain imports to benefit a school, to finance public works, to retire paper money, or to aid an enterprise. Typical was the act that increased export duties to benefit the Banco Agrícola: 2¢ per arroba on yerba and tobacco, 2¢ on each hide, 1.5¢ on each vara of hardwood measuring 10″ × 10″, 1/2¢ per vara on boards 1″ or more thick, 3¢ on each railway sleeper, and 50¢ on every beef butchered for public consumption. The American vice-consul observed cogently:

> What benefit the Government is to derive from the tax gathering powers accorded to the Banco Agrícola it is difficult to see—unless it is supposed to find its compensation in the improvement of the agricultural business which the bank is expected to "stir up" & "protect." However, Paraguay is not the only country whose people are supposed to be "stirred up" and "protected" by having burdens laid upon them, and probably it does not make much difference to the people so long as they are "protected" whether they are prevented from buying or whether they are prevented from selling.[5]

In his memorial of 1883, the minister of hacienda, Juan de la C. Giménez, recommended changes in customs laws which Congress approved. The ad valorem duty on imports was reduced to 25 percent, of which 23 percent was payable in gold or silver and 2 percent in copper. A few items paid 50 percent; firearms, gunpowder, ammunition, alcohol, fine wines, liqueurs, and tobacco products. A 40 percent duty was levied on ready-made clothes, hats, saddlery, harnesses, carriages, fireworks, and matches; various cheap wines, beer, and silk paid 30 percent; jewelry, items of gold, precious stones, and lapidary tools paid 10 percent. The free list included industrial machines, steam vessels, blooded animals, fresh fish, fresh fruit, grains, cement, pitch, tar, furniture, agricultural tools brought in by immigrants, gold and silver coins, live plants, steel rails, iron sleepers, and a long list of hardware and exotic products. The tariff act of August 1891 imposed a 10 percent duty on flour and provided that 20 percent of ad valorem duties could be paid in gold or its equivalent in paper. Exports of yerba paid 25¢ to 30¢ per arroba, tobacco 15¢ to 25¢ per arroba. An earlier act, June 3, 1891, had levied duties of 2¢ to 80¢ per kilo on several exports.[6]

License fees provided a small income. These widely resented fees were collected from all who worked at a trade or profession: "no one was exempt. Physicians, dentists, carpenters, down to boatmen, porters & washerwomen were all taxed as though industry were so heinous a crime that if it dare to show itself it must be immediately punished by a fine."[7] Income from stamped paper, roughly equivalent to internal revenue stamps, and receipts from postal and telegraph operations, completed the ordinary sources of revenue.

Extraordinary sources of income included sales and rentals of public lands, and the sale of the Paraguay Central Railway. Fairly accurate statistics begin in 1882, when sales under the 1876 act yielded 6,621 pesos. The acts of 1885 brought a great increase in this income for the rest of the decade, the peak being reached in 1886. This income kept Colorado governments more or less solvent, although recurring depressions seriously affected the economy. Income from land sales ended in 1900, but the state continued to receive rent from yerbales.

The extraordinary income from land sales carried the Caballero and Escobar administrations through difficult times, and Decoud's agreement with the Council of Foreign Bondholders temporarily restored Paraguayan credit abroad. Then came economic troubles throughout the Plata area in the early 1890s which required drastic measures if Paraguay were to remain relatively solvent. President Juan Gualberto González, facing a deficit of $1 million or more, urged economy, reform of the financial system, and additional taxes. Congress did little to meet the president's request. The minister of hacienda informed Congress in June 1894 that interest on the foreign debt was overdue for 1892 and 1893, the debt could not be serviced in 1894, nor could the government meet its obligations to the Paraguay Central Railway.[8] When the minister of hacienda reported a continued gloomy pictured in 1895, no great wisdom was needed to conclude that Paraguay desperately needed other sources of income.

José Segundo Decoud, in his *Cuestiones políticas y económicas* of 1877, had forcefully advocated an economic policy to develop Paraguay's resources. However accurate his analysis and proposed remedies, long-range planning was extremely difficult without a political consensus. Decoud showed, on becoming the guiding intellect of the Colorado party, a clear understanding of the Paraguayan character. Knowing that economic progress and fiscal responsibility were possible only if political peace prevailed, he actively supported the Colorado dictatorship and, as adviser to all Colorado presidents, played a significant role in developing financial policy. His proposal for a land tax aroused determined opposition but was finally passed by Congress in December 1890 and thus was the first direct tax levied in Paraguay other than the unenforceable head tax that had been abolished in 1890. A small inheritance tax, varying from 2 to 15 percent, depending on the closeness of relationship of the legatees, was levied in 1892. It fell to Agustín Cañete, minister of hacienda under President González, to organize collection of the land tax, or *contribución directa*. Experience with the contribución directa was unsatisfactory, but the tax did promote a clearer definition of boundaries as landowners hastened to survey their claims. The original levy was so low that in 1897, taxes of 129,063 pesos were collected at a cost of 85,397 pesos from property valued at 44,397,504 pesos.[9]

The minister of hacienda, observing in 1898 that Paraguay had no genuine system of taxation, admitted that the country was still too immature to devise one. Customs, which yielded at least two-thirds of the revenues, continued to be the most productive source of income and should be improved. His successor in 1900 found the tax laws very inefficient; tax evaders escaped punishment, and the contribución directa needed drastic revision.[10] In that year, this tax yielded only 276,570 pesos, including fines of 28,161 pesos. The reason for failure of this direct tax is clear: 25,280 properties, comprising about 2,500,000 acres, were valued at 1,775,515 pesos, or about 70¢ per acre!

Paraguay's financial situation worsened under President Escurra as ministers of hacienda continued to rely almost entirely on customs revenues and issues of paper money. A bold critic of the government vainly called for an equitable tax system. Congress responded by raising export duties on hides from 40¢ to 65¢ and on yerba from 13¢ to 16¢ per arroba, the increases to be paid in gold. The increased rates reduced rather than increased revenue. Obviously, the words "equitable" and "system" when applied to taxes meant absolutely nothing to Congress. The gold premium rose from 700 in January to 1,000 on April 5. With prices fluctuating rapidly, one would think that Congress would move slowly, but its response was to raise export duties another 10 percent. Lack of confidence in the government's ability to redeem the 11 million paper pesos in circulation caused the gold premium to reach 1200 in May 1903.[11] Clearly efforts to accumulate gold through customs levies had failed.

Paraguayan governments resorted to several devices to meet recurring deficits. The first postwar regime tried desperately to borrow and to sell church ornaments. A member of the Provisional Government, entrusted with selling church ornaments in Buenos Aires, sold the treasure but was unable to find his way back to Asunción, or to find a bank where he could deposit the proceeds to Paraguay's credit. Unfortunately, President Salvador Jovellanos and unscrupulous foreign agents managed to float two disastrous loans in London in 1871 and 1872. Bonds with a face value of £1,562,000 were sold before the inevitable crash of the Latin American bond market.[12]

Paraguayan governments, desperately short of cash, sold public buildings, parcels of land, the prewar arsenal, and issued numerous forms of treasury obligations, paper money, promissory notes, public credit bonds, and a variety of debt certificates, to meet budget deficits.

The first issue of paper money, authorized on December 29, 1870, was for $f100,000. This was followed by an issue of $f300,000 on July 15, 1871, to pay salaries. Then the whole $f400,000 was refunded in a new issue guaranteed by proceeds expected from the sale of the railway. A description or listing of paper money and other issues would be an exercise in futility, as the practice continued with monotonous regularity. Occasionally, enough metallic money was accumulated to permit the amortization of treasury obligations and the burning of some paper. The *cedulas territoriales* (land certificates), paper money, and treasury certificates were all accepted in payment for public lands under the law of December 15, 1876. Under later laws, especially in 1885, the government accepted 50 percent of the purchase price in paper.

The amount of paper money in circulation was kept under control for several years, and its value did not depreciate seriously in terms of gold until 1885. The Banco Nacional del Paraguay, organized in 1884, was authorized to issue notes. By 1892, after the government had been operating the bank for two years, the paper issues had reached 8,800,000 pesos, worth about £215,000 sterling. The amount was reduced somewhat in 1893, but the public had no confidence in paper money. As one journalist observed, if the paper was worth anything it was because there was no other medium of exchange. President Egusquiza optimistically informed Congress in 1895 that government finances were in order, paper in circulation had declined to only $f5,000,000, and there would be no new issues. Congress, refusing to be restrained, authorized an increase to $f8,000,000 in 1896 and to $f10,000,000 in 1897.[13] The gold premium in 1896 was 695—a gold peso cost nearly seven paper pesos. Since lack of confidence kept people from accepting Paraguayan paper, most business transactions were carried on with foreign currencies or on credits obtained from the few strong private banks and the public Banco Agrícola.

The National Debt

An accurate view of Paraguay's domestic and foreign debts is impossible, although the British consul, Cecil Gosling, presented an acceptable estimate near the end of the Colorado era (see table 12). Official reports fail to state the dates for which figures are given, and

Table 12

Paraguay's Public Debt, 1881–1902

(in pounds sterling)

	Internal Debt				External Debt				Total Public Debt
	Bonds etc.	Promissory Notes	Issues of Paper Money	Various	London Loans	Argentine War Debt	Brazilian War Debt	Various	
1881	2,944	123,521		4,069	1,353,551	8,158[a]	1,975,293		
1882		94,345		1,290	1,353,551				3,432,997
1883	57,926	95,144		1,414	1,353,551			177,681	3,669,527
1884	78,591	68,462		384	1,353,551			422,221	3,907,020
1885	87,180	46,062		268	1,353,551			943,965	4,414,837
1886	225,696	35,887		31,914	850,000			1,547,891	4,675,199
1887	95,787	11,038		134	850,000			1,737,659	4,678,429
1888	75,980	641			850,000			1,801,272	4,711,707
1889					807,700				2,791,511
1890	21,694	357	227,778	17,994	843,600	1,897,616	1,975,293	1,912,798	5,008,032
1891	15,036	12,717		39,414	842,200	1,897,616	1,975,293	2,170,190	5,063,368

1892	44,766	26,875	162,568	44,766	842,200	1,897,616	1,975,293	2,478,731	5,583,717
1893		12,616			930,629	1,897,616	1,975,293	1,912,798	5,405,787
1894	27,959	5,767	170,734		930,629	1,897,616	1,975,293	1,912,798	5,567,631
1895	13,473	3,251	178,571		841,000	1,897,616	1,975,293	1,912,798	5,497,837
1896	14,479	11,170	198,567	4,738	994,640	1,897,616	1,975,293	1,912,798	5,686,136
1897	21,275	7,034	262,933	6,068	994,640	1,897,616	1,975,293	2,684,685	5,960,445
1898	91,029	21,682	257,500	10,610	994,640	1,897,616	1,975,293	2,684,685	6,046,957
1899	33,762	31,966	253,461	47,000	994,225	1,897,616	1,975,293	2,684,685	6,028,910
1900	20,083	54,040	284,283		998,852	1,897,616	1,975,293	2,684,685	6,022,754
1901	19,466	50,861	248,616		957,415	1,897,616	1,975,293	2,684,685	5,944,854
1902	12,752	28,837	251,400		952,442	1,897,616	1,975,293	2,684,685	5,913,927

Source: DCR No. 3007, *Paraguay 1902*, p. 6.

Notes: The paper money issues approximately reflect the amount of paper actually in circulation. Presumably, Cecil Gosling, author of this report, used the gold premium in effect at the end of 1902 to arrive at his figures. The total in circulation in 1903 was 12,569,999 pesos. Gosling offered no explanation for omission of figures relating to paper money in the 1880s, 1891, and 1893.

a. The Argentine War Debt figure is misleading. The figure £8,158 represents the pre-1880 loan of $50,000 from the Banco National of Buenos Aires, which was carried constantly from 1881 to 1902 at $24,589 gold and was not a war debt. Gosling's figure for the Argentine war debt does not consider the final settlement of claims carried at $13,423,423 gold from 1897 to 1902. Brazilian polizas were carried at $9,876,465 gold for the entire period 1881–1902. Neither of these war indemnity debts was ever paid.

accounts were kept so haphazardly that all figures are suspect. The British consul reported an interesting accounting practice in 1898: "It is also stated that the public debt on December 31, 1897, amounted to $33,198,585 dol., but these figures can hardly be taken as correct, as in the general balance from which they are taken, gold and paper money are added together, without any allowance being made for the great difference in their values."[14] Not only were gold and paper added together, to the complete confusion of would-be statisticians, but also accounts were kept by various departments in legal tender (curso legal), national money (moneda nacional), and hard pesos (pesos fuertes), pounds sterling, and gold dollars. The standard was the British pound sterling, and matters would have been immensely simplified if all accounts had been converted into that universal standard. Curso legal was all money that was legal tender, and this included coins from many countries. The moneda nacional was paper issued by the treasury, the Banco Nacional del Paraguay, and the Caja de Conversión,[15] and, briefly, quantities of copper and nickel coins. Pesos fuertes generally were silver, usually at a discount in terms of gold and often confused with gold dollars in financial statements.

Efforts to borrow abroad failed after President Gill obtained the loan of $50,000 from the Banco Nacional of Buenos Aires in 1876. The Colorado regimes made no payments on this loan, which was carried at $24,589 gold in treasury accounts. Nevertheless, Congress in 1882 authorized an attempt to borrow $250,000 from the same bank.[16] Although the effort failed, Argentine authorities were mildly interested. Dr. Victorino de la Plaza, an Argentine financier, sent Adolpho P. Carranza to Asunción in March 1883 to assess the situation and to explore the possibility of linking a loan with establishing a branch of the Banco Nacional de Buenos Aires. Carranza's discussion with Decoud proceeded satisfactorily. He offered a loan of $100,000 at the exorbitant rate of 8 percent monthly, with 10 percent annual amortization. According to Decoud's estimate, this loan would have cost Paraguay $45,000 annually but he was enthusiastic about the prospect of a branch bank and anxiously awaited the arrival of Rafael de la Plaza to complete negotiations. While Carranza was in Asunción, Enrique Kubly arrived as head of the Uruguayan legation. Kubly received a chilly reception, probably because he was irritating both Argentina and Brazil with proposals for cancellation of war debts.[17] This complication may explain in part why the Carranza mission failed to result either in a loan or establishment of a branch bank.

Although financial management and fiscal policies improved somewhat in the 1890s, budgetary and accounting methods were far from providing an accurate view of the treasury's condition at any given time. The minister of hacienda usually knew, or pretended to know, how much was in the treasury and how large the deficit would be. Nevertheless, very loose accounting practices, lack of uniformity in reporting, and congressional irresponsibility made the term of every minister of hacienda a nightmare and his reports the despair of foreign observers and future historians.

Paraguayan economic activity was handicapped by the lack of an adequate monetary system and of sound banking institutions. Metal reserves could be accumulated slowly through favorable trade balances and customs receipts, while the creation of banks depended upon the intricate and difficult process of capital formation in an economy in which the majority of transactions were carried on by barter. Paraguay, forced to depend upon foreign coins and currency for its monetary supply, slowly developed its own monetary system but in the process experienced periods of distress caused by the emission of paper money backed only by the country's physical assets. This paper inevitably caused the gold premium to rise astronomically, and imported goods were priced far beyond the reach of most consumers. Toward the end of the 1880s, the monetary and banking situation showed definite improvement, despite economic crises. Private banking institutions, founded on profits from exports of forest and animal products, made up for the bumbling efforts of mixed government-private banks. Infusions of foreign capital and enterprise played a significant role in Paraguay's financial experience.

The Banco Nacional

Paraguay's experience in banking during the first Colorado era was one of grand but frustrated plans. Indicative of the future was the fate of the Asociación General del Comercio, which dated from September 19, 1874. The president ordered all government funds to be deposited in this embryonic bank. Then, on May 29, 1875, three national officials were appointed to liquidate its affairs. Lacking banking resources of any kind, merchants in the larger centers, especially Asunción and Villa Rica, were forced to perform such functions as extending credit, discounting commercial paper, and determining the rate of exchange. Immediately after the war, the Provisional Government made futile efforts to create a bank, and under President Gill, Congress approved plans to create a powerful Banco Nacional. When this proposal failed to attract English investors, a very favorable concession was granted in 1878 to Joaquín Obejero of Buenos Aires, but he was unable to carry out his plans. Congress tried again in 1883 to create a Banco Nacional del Paraguay in cooperation with

English capitalists. Again the effort failed. However, two enterprisers did start a small Banco del Paraguay in 1881 with a capital of
£10,000.[18]

Persisting in its effort to have a national bank, Congress on June
14, 1881, authorized creation of the Banco Nacional del Paraguay, to
be capitalized at $f500,000 with the government subscribing one-
fourth of the shares. Sale of shares to the public was so disappointing
that Congress tripled the bank's capital to $f1,500,000 and took two-
thirds of the shares. In addition to dividends, the government would
receive 5 percent of the bank's profits. The bank began operations on
January 2, 1884, and enjoyed an apparently successful career for a few
years. Using its power to issue paper money, the bank had $f820,000
in circulation in 1887. On paper, at least, its assets were $f4,619, 211.
Unfortunately, economic depression in Argentina severely affected
Paraguay and partly caused the Banco Nacional's paper to depreciate
by 50 percent. Many of its loans had been made to land speculators
who simply refused to pay.[19] Directors of the bank had also been
guilty of indefensible practices. Luís Patri and his associates had
deposited $f25,000 in the bank, the government had paid in its
$f1,500,000, and British capitalists who had bought the Paraguay
Central Railway in 1889 had loaned £50,000 to the bank. Fears for the
solvency of the Banco Nacional and the Banco del Paraguay y Río de
la Plata caused such heavy runs on both institutions that Congress
authorized the Banco Nacional to suspend specie payments and
reorganized it in July 1890. Capital for the reorganized bank came
from several sources. Following the advice of his counselors, President Escobar assembled all the government's resources to back the
reorganized Banco Nacional, and Congress authorized a loan of
$5,000,000 gold. The government put in its stock in the Banco del
Paraguay y Río de la Plata and the Paraguay Central Railway Company, and assets of the Banco Agrícola, which had been founded in
1887. The reorganized bank had broad powers to promote colonization, immigration, and commerce.[20]

These desperate measures failed to save the Banco Nacional.
When José Segundo Decoud became minister of hacienda in 1890, he
informed Congress that the bank's capital was largely fictitious, with
little to back the $f894,565 of bills in circulation. He urged Congress
to enact a series of measures that included payment of land purchases
in gold, a revised customs schedule that required one-eighth of the
duties to be paid in gold, and direct taxation. Congress failed to
accept Decoud's principal proposals and the bank's directors engaged in ludicrous accounting practices, one of which was to carry
Argentine and its own paper money, silver, and gold at the same
value! Finally recognizing the futility of trying to save the bank,

Congress placed it in liquidation on May 18, 1890, and reestablished the Banco Agrícola.[21]

The Banco Agrícola

Of the three banks established in 1887 in which the government was involved, only the Banco Agrícola survived, despite occasionally poor administration. After President Escobar gave his approval, Congress authorized the bank on September 24, 1887. Its capital of $f2,000,000 came from a series of small taxes. The Banco Agrícola made loans to finance crop production, to facilitate exports, to import blooded stock, and to introduce new strains of crops.It started an agricultural school in what is now the beautiful Jardín Botánico of Asunción, and improved rural roads and bridges. To improve the production and marketing of tobacco, the bank imported Cuban experts. The Banco Agrícola did not begin as a true bank since its funds were deposited in the Banco Nacional and in the private Banco de Comercio. Beginning its operations on July 7, 1887, the Banco had only two years to function before Congress unwisely made it a section of the Banco Nacional; fortunately, the bank was reestablished on July 30, 1892, when the Banco Nacional was being liquidated.[22] Under the skillful guidance of Estéban Rojas as president and Ezequiel Recalde as general manager, the reconstituted Banco Agrícola expanded its activities to promote construction of sugar mills and to increase general agricultural production. This activity was especially important because so much of Paraguay's food was imported from Argentina. A Consejo de Agricultura e Industrias, presided over by Christian G. Heisecke, advised the Banco Agrícola. There is little doubt that this institution was the Colorado party's greatest contribution to Paraguay's agricultural development.

Banco del Paraguay y Río de la Plata

This institution, which opened in December 1889, was forced into liquidation in October 1895. Graft, political favoritism, and incompetence marked its entire career. Thomas Duggan, president of the Anglo-Paraguay Land Company, organized a syndicate in Buenos Aires to establish the Banco del Paraguay y Río de la Plata. Congress granted the necessary concession on June 28, 1889. The bank was capitalized at $f8,100,000 divided into 80,000 shares, of which the government agreed to buy 20,000, a purchase which made it a 25 percent owner. The syndicate was to buy 30,000 shares and received 10,000 shares free, while the general public was offered 20,000 shares. The bank's powers were almost as broad as those of the Banco Nacional. It could issue bearer notes, actually paper money, to the amount of 300 percent of its paid-in capital. These notes, supposedly backed by one-third specie, eventually reached a total of more than $f600,000. The government attempted to sell a bond for £400,000 in London to raise money to pay for its shares. When the agent charged with selling this bond could find no takers, the government canceled the bond in 1893 and withdrew its promise to buy 20,000 shares. This action, of course, caused the bank to fail, and English investors claimed to have lost £250,000 in the fiasco.[23]

Private Banks

Daring enterprisers had no difficulty in establishing privately owned banks. They applied to Congress, "stating the object of the corporation, and the internal organization which is to govern it and which should not contravene any organic law of the Republic and permission will be issued to the banking company to establish itself under full recognition by the law." An annual fee of $f1,000 was assessed against each bank.[24]

The first private bank, after the unfortunate experience of the Asociación General del Comercio in 1875, was the Banco de Comercio. A prime mover in this institution was Luís Patri who, with several associates, had bought the railway in 1877. Some of the Patri group wanted to sell the railway back to the government and use the proceeds to start a bank. The majority prevailed and in 1885 established the Banco de Comercio with government paper received in payment for the railway. The bank had the unusual privilege of issuing paper money, but was so cautious that in 1890 its paper totaled about $f40,000 and was backed by $16,000 in gold and silver. Unfortunately, the bank's success attracted too much attention. In an effort to strengthen the Banco Nacional, Congress confiscated the Banco de Comercio on July 19, 1891, and paid for it with nearly worthless Banco Nacional certificates.[25]

Other private banks fared much better. The Banco Milleres y Cía. survived the economic distress of the 1890s. Most of its business was with suppliers of yerba. The Banco de los Ríos y Cía., founded by Vicente Nogues and Guillermo de los Ríos on January 4, 1895, based its prosperity on the thirty-six leagues of yerbales its workers exploited. The bank did a general banking business and was considered second in importance to the Banco Nacional.[26]

The Banco Territorial del Paraguay enjoyed great success under the Colorados, not as a result of political favoritism but because of careful management. Such prominent business and professional men as Juan B. Gaona, Ramón Zubizarreta, Cirilo Solalinde, Marcos Quaranta, Christian G. Heisecke, José Urdapilleta, and Luís Patri were officers or directors. Organized primarily to speculate in land and to conduct a general banking business, it was founded on September 1, 1887. The government had no control over it other than the general concession under which it operated. One of its leaders, Juan B. Gaona, aided the Liberals in their successful revolt of 1904.[27]

Another private bank that prospered until caught in the worldwide depression of 1920, was the Banco Mercantil del Paraguay. Antonio Plate, a native of the Netherlands who had become one of Asunción's leading merchants, started the bank in 1891. Associated with him were Gaona and leaders of La Industrial Paraguaya, which had been organized five years earlier. The Banco Mercantil had branches in Concepción, Encarnación, Pilar, and Villa Rica. During the decade 1894–1904, it paid dividends of 14 percent to 20 percent. This highly respected institution performed all banking functions except the emission of paper money. Closing briefly in 1920, it reopened in 1928 and was the strongest bank in Paraguay.[28]

Private banks, obviously, were far more efficient than the mixed institutions. Those that made the best records were founded on Paraguay's greatest resources—land and yerbales. Their leaders were either important political figures or exercised considerable control over politics. Whatever their social contributions may have been, there is no doubt that they contributed significantly to Paraguay's precarious economy during the Colorado era. The Banco Agrícola was especially useful in promoting agricultural colonies.

Part IV

THE SOCIAL WAY

Paraguayan leaders generally looked to European immigration to solve the country's many problems. Their faith in this solution was unrealistic when so many other countries offered much greater attractions. A flood of immigrants probably would have changed the country's society in dramatic ways but the flood did not come. All the Colorado presidents attempted to lure immigrants into agricultural colonies and all had very limited success. The few hundred who came from abroad had little influence on Paraguayan institutions. True, many descendants of immigrants have risen to high positions. Alfredo Stroessner, who began his long dictatorship in 1954, is the son of a German immigrant and a Paraguayan mother, but his entire career has been pure Paraguayan.

Too little attention has been given to studying rural Paraguay. Indeed, there are those who insist that to know Paraguay one must go to the country, visit the small farmer, become intimately acquainted with the villages and their people. While it may be true that Asunción is not Paraguay, it is also true that the capital is the center of Paraguayan political, economic, and social life. Colorado regimes neglected rural areas in education, public health, and concern for the worker.

Society in the Paraguay of the Colorados was undergoing many significant changes, changes that were to mature under the Liberals—but not because of them—after 1904. Intellectuals began a truly national literature, and the church recovered its autonomy. The clergy continued to be indifferent in quality, and much of rural Paraguay had no regular religious services. Educational improvements in the major cities were not matched by progress in rural areas, where illiteracy was the rule. If one counts the number of newspapers published during the Colorado era, it would appear that journalism flourished. Despite a glaring lack of journalistic responsibility and editorial restraint, Colorado presidents did permit an exceptional degree of freedom of the press. Although journalists stridently opposed many Colorado policies, all of them supported the effort to attract immigrants.

17

Immigration and Colonization

In the great work of regeneration awaiting Paraguay after the war, politicians could not wait for Paraguayans to repopulate their country. They were in a hurry to carry out Alberdi's famous dictum: "Gobernar es poblar" ("To govern is to populate"). Fill the land with people, with industrious workers to clear the forests, to till the soil, and to tend vast herds of cattle yet to come. The formula, reduced to essentials, was simple: bring in immigrants and colonize them on the empty land. Politicians wanted to start with a ready-made agricultural population who needed only the land to create a thriving rural economy upon which Paraguay's future would be built. Paraguay would provide practically everything but the people and their skills.

Official policy, a bumbling and uncertain thing for many years, became more sophisticated as Colorados learned from experience. They recognized the need for efficient propaganda, but never were able to mature their advertising efforts. They changed colonization and immigration laws to rectify mistakes until Paraguay had almost ideal immigration laws that covered the individual immigrant, the colonizing entrepreneur, the colonizing society or company, and the cooperative society. The rugged individualist, the profit-seeking enterpriser, the religious refugee, and the socialist could all find opportunities in Paraguay.

The Need for Immigrants

Paraguayan agriculture and animal husbandry desperately needed an influx of workers. Exploitation of forest resources also depended upon the growth of an adequate labor force. Compounding the problem was Paraguay's failure to retain thousands of her own workers who emigrated to neighboring provinces of Argentina and Brazil.

243

One historian reports that by June 1877 at least twelve thousand Paraguayan families had migrated to Corrientes to escape from grafting officials, compulsory military service, and the general economic stagnation.[1] During the depression of the 1890s, many families went to the Argentine Chaco, Corrientes, and across the Paraná to Posadas. Emigration to Mato Grosso caused Paraguayan journalists to assert that the Brazilian consul was fomenting the movement,[2] as indeed he was. Several Italian and French laborers, unable to find work in Asunción, were among the applicants for aid in going to Mato Grosso. These were "strong and healthy men, very well suited to work in the fields."[3]

There was general agreement among editors, politicians, and informed observers that Paraguay needed agricultural immigrants to prosper: "Above all, we desire colonization because it will strongly influence the habits and customs of our social masses who need to be regenerated by dedication to work by [encouraging] thrift among the workers who need to see the growth of their capital by concentration of their efforts on becoming independent, thus assuring their well-being."[4] This sanguine editor was advancing the interesting thesis that immigrants would be the catalyst to transform Paraguayan society. Colorado presidents, while not subscribing to this sociological concept, sought to solve Paraguay's economic problems by promoting European immigration, continuing the effort begun in the postwar decade. President Caballero hoped for great results from the very liberal immigration act of 1881 and emphasized colonization by private groups instead of a general effort to attract individual immigrants. President Escobar informed Congress in 1889 that the lack of workers prevented agriculture from developing and that the best remedy was to increase the number of immigrants and encourage them to become landowners. In the period from 1881 to 1888, only 2,495 immigrants had come to Paraguay, a record that must be improved. President González, while able to report on five flourishing colonies in 1892, was equally dissatisfied with the small number of immigrants. President Egusquiza in 1896, repeating the complaint, informed Congress that Paraguay must look to Europe for immigrants to "invigorate the American race with their blood, and to increase national production with their labor."[5]

Paraguayan officials held a very low opinion of the native farmer, as did foreign observers, whose comments generally differed little in substance from those of a British diplomat:

> The easy conditions of life, which the very fertility of the soil must produce, have contributed toward making the native one of the most indolent in the world. A patch of ground sufficient to cultivate the maize and tobacco, &c., he requires for the year and a grove of orange trees are enough for his simple wants, and he is perfectly content if the

surplus is large enough to buy just the few articles which are indispensable for the daily life of himself and his family, and he even regards with suspicion and mistrust this ingress of foreigners as being the forerunner of that energy and activity which are enough to cause feelings little short of despair as he idly reclines in his hammock and watches his women at work. For some time, therefore, the efforts of most Paraguayan statesmen have been directed toward devising all possible means to infuse new life into their country by the introduction of labour and capital, and every inducement has been held out for the purpose of attracting immigrants to Paraguay.[6]

Promotion of Immigration

Every Colorado regime made efforts to advertise Paraguay abroad. Participation in international expositions and preparation of handbooks about Paraguay were a part of this continuing propaganda campaign. Paraguay charged its consuls to increase their publicity efforts. In 1884, José Segundo Decoud reported that these efforts were having good results and cited a pamphlet by Auguste Meulemans, consul general in France, as a good example. To coordinate these efforts, Congress in 1898 created the Oficina General de Inmigración, which was charged with publishing a monthly review or bulletin to advertise Paraguay and to establish information offices abroad.[7] One of the first fruits of this act was publication in 1889 of the *Guide de l'immigrant au Paraguay*, which provided general information about the country and its existing agricultural colonies. Invariably, Paraguay was portrayed as an almost ideal place for the agricultural immigrant to prosper. Good features of the climate were emphasized, the unfavorable generally received short shrift. Another attraction was the low price of land and the government's policy of giving land to the colonist.

Foreign travelers and diplomats helped the government in its promotion efforts by enthusiastic reports. Dr. Eben M. Flagg, an American vice-consul well established as a dentist, wrote that "the country, besides possessing rare beauty in the way of natural scenery has most abundant natural wealth requiring only the application of labor to develope it."[8] Another American consular officer vowed that Paraguay had "the finest climate in the world, taking this summer [1898–1899] as the basis. I cannot say the weather is enervating, but rather soothing and balmy. . . . The climate might well be compared with that of Texas or Florida."[9] Here was a country, an Argentine journalist enthused, where the immigrant with small resources "could double his capital in a year with no effort." There were great opportunities for "production of tobacco, yerba, coffee, sugar cane, and cotton; especially for coffee that equals the richest of Brazil, and for tobacco of a quality as rich as in the island of Cuba itself."

Stretching the truth a bit, he wrote that in Paraguay the immigrant would find complete freedom and personal security. "So," the writer concluded, "we invite the industrious working men of small resources to look toward Paraguay and to consider for a while the advantages that country offers them."[10] British ministers to Argentina added their praises, but the observant Vansittart was more realistic as he noted Paraguay's relative inaccessibility, the difficulty of reaching world markets, and the great heat of the summers. Vansittart, however, reported that Paraguay would welcome British agricultural immigrants for whom "the country is admirably adapted in many respects" and superior to Argentina in cost of land, fertility of the soil, and security of life. Still, it would be a long time before memory of the "Lincolnshire farmers" fiasco in 1873 failed to impede British immigration. This ill-conceived effort brought nearly eight hundred immigrants to Paraguay, nearly all of whom left after a few months.[11]

The agricultural immigrant to Paraguay not only faced the vagaries of nature and a very unstable government, but also a lingering xenophobia. True, the occasional traveler met a warm welcome and open hospitality from rural people; but this did not automatically extend to the foreigner who might wish to make his home among them. Decoud indignantly charged in 1877 that irresponsible local authorities were "the most powerful hindrance to the country's progress and development" because of their violation of personal liberties. The rise of powerful landowners also discouraged immigration and should therefore be restrained.[12] The conclusions of a scholar who studied Japanese colonies in Paraguay in 1958 are equally applicable to the Colorado era: "Foreigners have discovered also that Paraguayan society is highly resistant to penetration. It may be argued with some conviction that few immigrants have viewed assimilation as advantageous or desirable. Nevertheless, the barriers to acceptance appear formidable. . . . Neither intermarriage nor acquisition of the Guaraní language seems to temper the reserve that characterizes Paraguayans in their relationships with outsiders."[13] This ethnocentrism probably did not initially affect the flow of immigrants to Paraguay.

Realistic observers reminded their governments of the basic disadvantages: Paraguay's isolation, uncertain markets, political instability, weak financial structure, and governmental inability to protect the immigrant. Immigrants who came with some capital to tide them over the first two or three years, who were determined to work, and were reasonable in their expectations, could succeed.[14] Among the causes of failure were "a lack of a real knowledge of the Spanish language and of the national susceptibilities and prejudices,

and a half disguised contempt for a partially coloured race is responsible for many misconceptions; and, it may be added, for the dislike
with which foreigners are so frequently held by natives of these [Latin
American] countries."[15]

Colorado leaders realized the need for coordination of efforts to
promote immigration and for laws to encourage the European emigrants to settle in Paraguay. An act of Congress on June 7, 1881,
created the Departamento General de Inmigración, headed by a
comisario general, in the ministry of interior. This act authorized
establishment of agricultural colonies, with grants of land to each
colonist, free passage from the point of embarkation, and maintenance for a maximum of one year. Heads of families could receive
about twenty-nine acres (sixteen cuadras, or squares), a single adult
would receive eight cuadras. Each adult could buy from one to four
additional lots at auction. Government of the colony rested in an
intendant, or general manager, who must be able to speak the colonists' language. His principal duties were to distribute land grants,
maintain order, keep the streets clean, take the census, and serve as
general adviser. Seeds, tools, and furniture were to be admitted free of
duty, and colonists were exempt from taxation for ten years. A very
generous provision of the law granted twelve square leagues (about
fifty-one thousand acres) to any company or private enterpriser who
would introduce 140 agricultural families within a two-year period.
Each of the families was to receive about one hundred acres free, and
the colonizer would provide housing, tools, animals, seeds, and
maintenance for one year at not more than a 20 percent premium
over cost. Colonists would repay these loans over a ten-year period,
beginning three years after their arrival. The Paraguayan government would transport the colonists from their port of disembarkation
to the colony. To obtain the necessary land, the government would use
the power of expropriation with compensation to the owners.[16]

Immigrants were subject to the Rural Code, first enacted in 1887
and changed from time to time. This code provided protection for all
rural establishments, from the smallest chacra to the largest estancia. A few provisions are interesting: the government could not expropriate entire herds of cattle; burning of fields to kill weeds and
insects could be done only in July and August; the Juntas Económicas
were required to promote extermination of jaguars, and pigs could
not be kept in town centers.[17]

Under the regime of President Escurra, last of the first Colorado
line, Congress enacted two major laws affecting immigration. The
capstone of Colorado immigration policy, these laws corrected previous errors and omissions. The first, proclaimed on October 6, 1903,
dealt specifically with immigrants. An immigrant was one who en-

tered the country for the first time, was under fifty years of age, was a farmer, worker, professional, craftsman, electrician, or any kind of engineer. The executive power could prevent immigration of undesirables: "In no case will consulates or immigration agencies issue certificates or immigrant passage to individuals of the yellow or black races, to persons ill with infectious diseases, to mendicants, loafers, or gypsies, or to convicts or persons involved in litigation abroad."[18] Single adults must have $50 in gold; each head of family must have $30 for each adult in the family. In addition to free passage from any Río de la Plata port, all expenses were paid by the Immigration Office for eight days after landing in Paraguay. All personal goods, farm machinery, tools, seeds, blooded animals, and one firearem for each adult were admitted free of duty. There were generous provisions for repatriation of Paraguayans. All matters connected with immigration were placed in the Oficina General de Inmigración y Colonización in the ministry of foreign affairs.[19]

The Colonization and Homestead Law, proclaimed June 25, 1904, completed revision of the immigration laws. This was a detailed, liberal, fair, and very advantageous act for the serious settler, which shows that Paraguay had profited from experience. The executive power could establish agricultural or pastoral colonies, preferably along the railway or adjacent to a navigable stream, on public land, or on private land to be expropriated at a fair price. Land assigned to a colony was to be surveyed, cleared, and subdivided into lots. A town site was to be reserved in a central location, divided into squares and building lots. Land was reserved for public uses, houses had to be built away from the street, with trees planted in front. Industrious settlers could acquire additional lots. Pastoral colonies could be established only on public lands unfit for agriculture. The colonies could acquire title after five years of continuous occupation and crop production. Colonists could not mortgage or sell their holdings, nor transfer them except to heirs at death. To ensure assimilation, the law required the use of Spanish for all official acts. Paraguayan history and Spanish had to be taught in all schools.[20]

In addition to aid provided by the Immigration Office, the agricultural immigrant could obtain assistance from the Banco Agrícola, which used its considerable resources freely to promote agriculture. The bank's director in 1897, G. Pereyra Cazal, urged the settlement of farmers near the Paraguay River on sites ready for occupancy: the land surveyed, divided into lots, and a house built on each lot, with an intendant in residence ready to advise the immigrant. Although these recommendations were not followed, Paraguay's laws were sufficiently liberal to have attracted far more immigrants than came to this poorly advertised "paradise" in the heart of South America.

The Immigrant Flow

Like all Paraguayan statistics in the nineteenth century, those relating to immigration are admittedly very inaccurate. Many immigrants, as well as emigrants, failed to register. The count of those who enjoyed free passage from Buenos Aires was also inaccurate for the same reason. Repatriated Paraguayans sometimes were counted as immigrants and not at other times. Children born in Paraguay to foreign parents were counted as Paraguayans and so were omitted from the census of foreigners. In general, incomplete returns showed most of the immigrants to be German, Italian, French, Spanish, or Argentine. The leading nationality changed from time to time with the arrival of small contingents for newly founded agricultural colonies.

Numerous immigrants came to Paraguay in the early 1880s with little governmental inducement. More might have come had it not been for "the war waged by the Argentines against immigration to Paraguay."[21] Nevertheless, the number of Italian, French, Argentine, and English immigrants in Asunción increased notably in the 1880s. By 1883, more than 1,000 European immigrants were in the city, nearly all of them German and Italian farm workers and skilled laborers who were unemployed because of the economic depression.[22] This figure is deceptive because most of the Germans were en route to the recently founded colony of San Bernardino. The census of 1886 showed 7,896 immigrants in the country, of whom 1,529 lived in Asunción. Listed by country of origin, Argentina led with 4,895; Italy was a poor second with 825, followed by Brazil (520), Germany (476), Spain (321), France (228), Uruguay (198), Portugal (116), Switzerland (112), and a sprinkling from fourteen other countries. An unreliable count made in 1887 showed 1,028 Italians, 812 Germans, 547 Spaniards, 389 French, 195 Swiss, 168 English, and 94 Austrians. It is fairly certain that Italians, Germans, Frenchmen, and Spaniards made up the majority of the 5,495 immigrants counted during the period 1881–1890.[23]

Paraguay did not receive the industrious European farmers in the numbers so ardently desired. In 1888, for example, there were 1,064 counted immigrants, of whom only 171 were farmers. The director general provided more information about immigrants for the year ending March 31, 1897. Of the 184 immigrants, 72 were married, 62 were single, and 50 were children. There were 120 males and 64 females. Only 75 were farmers. Of the 340 arrivals in 1899–1900, about one-half (168) were farmers.[24]

The first fairly honest but still very inaccurate report on immigration was published in 1908 by Giuseppe de Stéfano Paternó, then director general of the Office of Immigration and Colonization.

Paternó combed the archives and official documents in an effort to obtain accurate figures. He included only those whose passage had been paid by the government, eliminating seasonal workers. Nor did he try to count those who entered at ports other than Asunción. Paternó gave the honor of being the first genuine immigrants to five German families of eleven persons who arrived on August 24, 1881, en route to San Bernardino—the Siedow, Wache, Degenhardt, Stenzel, and Schonfeld families.[25]

The Paternó report accounted for 12,241 immigrants from August 1, 1881, to March 31, 1907 (see table 13). Compared with immigration into Argentina, Brazil, Uruguay, and the United States for the same period, this figure is microscopic. Even if it were tripled, as well might have been the case, it is certain that Paraguay was not attracting many foreigners.[26] Approximately 74 percent of the registered immigrants were males, a fact that augured well for intermarriage with Paraguayans and assimilation into Paraguayan society. Nearly one-fourth of the immigrants settled in Asunción, while the others went to smaller towns and, especially, to the agricultural colonies.

Beginning of Agricultural Colonies

Individuals, commercial companies, and ethnic groups all sought to take advantage of Paraguay's liberal immigration laws. The government, too, participated in establishing colonies, or groups of settlers, on designated plots of forested land and campos. Colorado governments, generous though they were, could not provide as much aid as the law promised. However, the small number of immigrants did not press too severely upon limited resources. Immigrants came to Paraguay either as individual settlers, or as members of an organized group.[27] Most of the agricultural colonies were family type, and families were preferred for these colonies over individual settlers; others were industrial enterprises like Casado, Risso, and Puerto Max. The industrial colony invariably was established by a capitalist or a company formed for the purpose. A settlement inevitably grew up around Carlos Casado's enterprise, centering at Puerto Casado and forming a clearly defined industrial colony. The same was true of Colonia Risso, on the left bank of the Paraguay River east of Casado, and its meat processing plant, Saladero Risso, a few miles to the south.

In order to be successful, an agricultural colony had to be composed of genuine farmers, young enough to withstand the rigors of the Paraguayan subtropical climate, and reasonably industrious. Ethnic uniformity, while not necessary, appears to have been a factor in success, although some of the most notable failures were ethnically uniform in composition. The colony, of course, had to have access to markets for its products, so its location was extremely important. Even after the close of the Colorado era, Liberals sponsored several colonies that failed miserably. Lessons from the Colorado experience were learned slowly.[28] Agricultural colonization in Paraguay after 1880 began with one notable success and one near failure.

San Bernardino

During the presidency of Cándido Bareiro, the executive office received an inquiry about immigration policy from Jacob Schaerer, a wealthy German. Encouraged by the president's reply and the Immigration Act of 1881, several German families prepared to emigrate to Paraguay. Formally organized on June 14, 1881, San Bernardino received its first settlers when eleven immigrants arrived at Asunción on August 24 and were sent to the north side of Lake Ypacaraí.[29] In addition to free passage from Buenos Aires and temporary housing in a fine guest house in Asunción, the settlers received aid from the newly created Department of Immigration. George F. Metzler, its first director, was pleased with the progress of the colony, whose settlers bought land at cost in an area expropriated by the government. Within a year the colony had grown to about three hundred people, with new immigrants "arriving by almost every steamer."[30] Other Germans came to reconnoiter, encouraged by Metzler and Christian Heisecke, the consul general for Germany and Austria-Hungary. One of the visitors, Ernst Mevert, met Edward Augustus Hopkins, who had a farm near San Bernardino where he grew tobacco, coffee, and bananas.

These industrious farmers quickly established a model colony. Although the land was not as fertile as advertised, by 1887 there were 363 settlers and a cultivated area of 800 acres at San Bernardino. A variety of crops and fruits were flourishing: sugar cane, corn, beans, mandioca, pineapples, strawberries, currants, alfalfa, asparagus, sweet potatoes, and rice.[31] San Bernardino grew slowly but steadily as the settlers diversified their activites and more immigrants arrived. Taking advantage of the lake, they constructed tourist facilities that attracted many people from Asunción who were delighted with the thirty-five-mile rail trip to Areguá, followed by the launch ride across the lake. By 1891, the colonists had many cattle, horses, hogs, and chickens; these, as well as dairy and meat products, were marketed in Asunción. An English visitor in 1893 commented that "the colonists had found life too easy, and had gradually accommodated their wants to the simple standard of comfort prevailing in Paraguay."[32] Obviously, the settlers had adapted readily to the Paraguayan milieu. The colony quickly outgrew its original boundaries and had to be enlarged for new arrivals. By 1897, the settlers had

Table 13

Registered Immigrants Entering at Asunción, 1882–1907 (years ending March 31)

| | By Sex | | | By Age | | | By Principal Countries of Origin | | | | | | |
	Total	Male	Female	0–12	13–50	50 plus	Italy	Germany	France	Spain	Argentina	Switzerland	England
1882	100	73	27	19	81		2	96				2	
1883	236	137	99	73	163		3	197			12	5	
1884	218	138	80	57	155	6	2	141	23		22	22	1
1885	284	179	105	96	170	18		152	53		10	48	
1886	47	24	23	15	26	6	2	21	4		7	12	
1887	115	84	31	25	83	7	2	67	3			25	3
1888	807	744	63	40	749	18	261	141	92	54	18	30	17
1889	1,119	858	261	169	911	39	277	193	184	264	15	40	26
1890	1,886	1,590	296	238	1,594	54	710	200	351	280	44	74	33
1891	823	643	180	198	605	20	292	90	165	120	31	15	13
1892	368	268	100	77	280	11	104	64	85	64	4	10	8

1893	512	321	191	162	325	25	43	92	239	38	28	10	34
1894	458	294	164	136	303	19	53	46	177	49	27	42	9
1895	205	136	69	51	145	9	19	44	41	7	20	36	3
1896	270	155	115	82	175	13	18	92	24	3	36	38	32
1897	200	131	69	53	136	11	55	25	35	12	17	13	20
1898	187	126	61	50	127	10	25	19	15	16	36	10	52
1899	400	263	137	159	229	12	326	17	17	6	2	3	21
1900	320	225	95	75	239	6	104	15	34	63	15	13	50
1901	140	95	45	31	102	7	25	18	23	25	18	2	12
1902	471	318	153	151	306	14	158	26	33	91	75	7	17
1903	584	411	173	153	409	22	215	45	17	72	127	7	15
1904	316	227	89	81	226	6	63	35	7	51	69	1	8
1905	350	226	124	93	243	14	88	33	32	51	73	7	16
1906	599	399	200	172	418	9	138	83	18	70	86	2	8
1907	1266	988	238	232	994		377	131	64	206	98	5	15
Total	12,241	9,053	3,188	2,691	9,194	356	3,360	2,083	1,736	1,542	890	479	413

Source: MRE, *Memoria de la oficina de inmigración y colonización correspondiente a los años 1905–1906—1906–1907*, pp. 18–25.

Notes: Figures for 1881–1882 are from August 1, 1881–March 31, 1882. Glaring omissions include at least 350 Australians who arrived in the 1890s.

fenced nearly 600 acres and were cultivating 930 acres. Peter Herken's brewery was operating by 1886, and other enterprisers produced wine, jams, jellies, coconut oil, soap, and caña. San Bernardino prospered to such an extent that on August 31, 1901, it became a municipality and thus was fully assimilated into the Paraguayan political structure.[33]

A truly remarkable event for the development of San Bernardino occurred in December, 1902, and forever put to rest the question of navigability of the Río Salado, which drained Lake Ypacaraí into the Río Paraguay. People crowded the shore of the lake to look in wonder at the SS *Victoria*, a British sternwheeler whose crew had brought her up the Salado into the lake:

> After 15 weeks of incessant hard work, during which time 26 dams were built, a canal cut, and the vessel actually lifted over a portion of the outskirts of the forest, Lake Ypacaray was finally reached. The achievement showed considerable pluck and endurance on the part of those concerned, as, owing to the fact of the river being entirely overgrown with aquatic plants, it was impossible to steam, and the crew had to get into the water and push the vessel along—a performance which was rendered all the more unpleasant by the presence in the water and mud of innumerable crocodiles, boas and poisonous reptiles.[34]

The two Englishmen and their Paraguayan crew, after an incredibly difficult and dangerous effort, had demonstrated that the short Salado was not navigable. The *Victoria* found profitable use on the San Bernardino–Areguá run.

Villa Hayes

Carlos Antonio López, although dubious about the outcome, began group settlements in the Chaco by admitting French immigrants to an outpost on the right bank of the Paraguay River some twenty-five kilometers north of Asunción. In 1855, the French recruits, 400 of them, arrived to become settlers of Nuevo Burdeos. The French were all gone in 1856, happy to be out of the inhospitable Chaco. This fiasco, fully as bad as the "Lincolnshire farmers" in 1872–1873, was the result of bad planning, recruitment of nonfarmers, inadequate support, and a hostile environment. Little had changed at the site in 1879. Renamed Villa Occidental, it had been held by Argentina until an arbitral decision by President Rutherford B. Hayes in 1878 awarded the southern Chaco Boreal to Paraguay. A grateful congress renamed the place Villa Hayes (pronounced "áh-jayce" by the Paraguayans). President Bareiro was anxious to strengthen this Chaco outpost. To do so, Congress in 1879 encouraged settlement in the Departamento Occidental, of which Villa Hayes was the administrative center. An area of about 125 square kilometers was set aside to be awarded to colonists who would be protected from Indians by a line of military posts on the north.[35]

Colonists were slow to accept the challenge of Chaco pioneering. In 1881, Villa Hayes was still unoccupied except for a few Italian peasants and a detachment of troops whose armament included artillery entirely useless against gangs of marauding Indians hovering nearby. Sixteen convicts were working on redoubts, barracks, and houses. President Caballero saw that success at Villa Hayes would indicate "the probability of colonizing the rest of our country, largely unoccupied and unproductive because of the lack of workers and capital."[36] By 1885 there were only 41 foreign settlers; a year later the colony counted 155 Austrians, Italians, Spaniards, Swiss, Argentines, French, and Belgians, many of whom soon left for more attractive areas. Nevertheless, the colony did grow slowly, and the settlers produced sugar cane, coffee, corn, alfalfa, onions, sorghum, and various other vegetables and had 4,000 animals in 1891. The population, which had reached 321 in 1891, dropped to 287 in 1896.[37]

Villa Hayes definitely was not a model colony, but it was reasonably successful in the long run. Contrasted with San Bernadino, which began at about the same time, it was an official rather than a private colony, heterogeneous in population, and started with a pueblo, or organized town. Although only a short distance from Asunción, Villa Hayes was a frontier community, threatened constantly by thieving Guaycurú Indians. Livestock produced by the settlers was especially attractive to these survivors of the stone age. Maintaining a settlement at Villa Hayes was very important to Paraguay in its contest with Bolivia over ownership of the Chaco Boreal. Continuous occupation, not economic success, was the principal goal. The amazing success of Germans at San Bernardino more than compensated for the weakness of Villa Hayes and encouraged the establishment of many other agricultural colonies in eastern Paraguay.

18

The Growth of
Agricultural Colonies

San Bernadino and Villa Hayes were the only colonies started by the Colorados before they began to sell off the public domain. During the rest of the Colorado era, from 1885 to 1904, there were some notable successes and several well publicized failures. Critics of Colorado colonization efforts, expecting too much too soon, blamed failures on misgovernment, exaggerated promises, poor location, and undesirable immigrants. There was much truth in all these accusations.

Among the reasonably successful colonies were Villa Sana, Colonia Elisa, and Colonia González, widely separated geographically and very diverse in origin and composition. Each of these had its troubled years; each eventually succeeded. Villa Sana was a corporate enterprise; Elisa, begun by a bank, was sold to a daring entrepreneur; González, sponsored by the government, failed initially and then prospered as Colonia Nacional. Three socialistic experiments failed: Nueva Germania, Nueva Australia, and the latter's offshoot Cosme. None of these could get beyond the stage of struggling settlements before 1904. Whether successful or not, each colony provided valuable lessons and demonstrated that agricultural colonies could achieve the great objectives set for them.

Nueva Germania

German interest in founding colonies in South America was intense in the 1880s. The historian Heinrich von Treitschke (1834–1896) and other champions of German imperialism saw in Brazil, Chile, and the Platine republics fertile fields for German colonization. Had the millions who went to the United States been directed to South America, they might have founded a new German empire.[1]

Three prominent Germans were in Paraguay in 1883 to study

colonization prospects. Dr. Bernhard Förster, whose wife Lisbeth was a sister of the philosopher Friedrich Nietzsche, was a leader of the anti-Semitic group in Prussia, and "his idea of founding a new Germany on this continent," the British chargé in Buenos Aires reported, "to the absolute exclusion of all Jewish elements has been repeatedly canvassed in various portions of the German press."[2] Far less capable was Heinrich Quistorp, who wanted a land grant of 150 leagues, upon which he promised to colonize 20,000 immigrants in five years. Nothing came of Quistorp's grandiose scheme. The last of the trio was Baron Karl von Gülich of Leipzig who represented the Empresa Colonizadora Alemana of Leipzig. Förster and von Gülich, apparently representing the same group, probably disagreed on where a settlement could be made. Von Gülich, after spending two years in reconnoitering prospective sites, proposed a family-type colony along the Itá-Ypané-Guarambaré axis south of Asunción. As finally constituted, von Gülich's colony was somewhere on the Río Capybary southeast of Villa Rica. A few families settled there but soon moved away.[3]

Bernhard Förster had better success for a while with his colony of Nueva Germania between the Aguaray-mi and the Aguaray-guazú, tributaries of the Río Jejuy, ninety kilometers southeast of Concepción. Founded in 1887 on a grant of twelve leagues, Nueva Germania made little progress. Förster insisted on each family's being separated from its nearest neighbor by a mile or more. The heavily wooded area required back-breaking effort to prepare ground for planting coffee trees, mandioca, cotton, sugar cane, and other crops. To reach market, produce had to be loaded on flat-bottomed boats for floating down the Río Jejuy, then to San Pedro and on to the Río Paraguay. The cost was prohibitive. In 1890 there were 193 persons in ninety families scattered through the colony. They finally found their salvation in cultivating yerba, a process developed by Fritz Neumann of Breslau.

Desertions from Nueva Germania steadily eroded the colony's strength. Dr. Förster, ill and discouraged, committed suicide in 1889, and Lisbeth sold her interest to a corporation two years later. Nueva Germania's population, which dropped to 85 in 1898, had increased to 171 in 1904, about one-half of whom were Germans. Despite the efforts of Oscar Erck, a successful merchant in Asunción, the colony barely survived.[4]

Colonia Villa Sana

Dreams of wealth waiting to be gathered attracted the efforts of two companies to form proprietary colonies in the late 1880s. The Sociedad Anómina Colonizadora del Paraguay revealed an impressive roster of wealthy men, including Carlos Casado, Adeodato Gondra, Ricardo Mendes Gonçalves, Jorge Casaccia, Juan G. González, and Emilio Aceval. In May 1888 these men proposed a far-reaching plan to found a string of colonies along the Paraguay Central Railway, and others near ports of the Río Paraguay. They proposed a mixed company, with the Paraguayan government subscribing one-fourth of the 2 million pesos capital. Although President Escobar recommended the proposal to Congress, nothing came of it.[5]

Far more successful was a Frenchman, J. Valentin, who organized the Société Générale Paraguayo-Argentina in Buenos Aires in 1887. Much of the capital was subscribed in France. Profiting from errors of its predecessors, the society provided guidance at the port of embarkation and a resident agent-adviser who would lay out the colony in advance and provide necessities for the colonists. All cattle and horses, marked with the owner's brand, would graze together, to be separated at an annual roundup. The society bound itself to provide numerous services and privileges: purchases at wholesale from the society's store, aid in the sale of products, promotion of cultural and industrial projects, and the guidance of a "representative who should be considered by every inhabitant as his adviser, his friend, and his brother."[6] Colonists could buy land on easy terms from the society's 900 leagues of magnificent forests and lush pastures in the northwestern corner of eastern Paraguay. After reconnoitering the property in September 1889, Valentin returned a year later with twenty-five colonists and equipment to begin an agricultural colony. After resting a day at Concepción, the party proceeded to establish a town, Villa Sana, and began to prepare for planting. Within a few years the colony was thriving. G. Richoux, Delbeaf y Cía. established coffee plantations on the society's land in 1892 and five years later had 23,400 trees which produced 740 arrobas of dried beans.[7] Villa Sana continued as a village after the society sold its holdings to the Société Fonciére du Paraguay in 1902.

Colonia Elisa

The Banco del Paraguay y Río de la Plata founded Colonia Elisa at San Antonio on the Río Paraguay fifteen kilometers south of Asunción. The site had been selected by Edward Augustus Hopkins for various enterprises in 1853–1854. The land was good, a market for the colony's products was close, and the river offered a good transportation route to supplement the rutted road to Asunción. The bank had a grant of 1,000 cuadras to be sold in lots of 16 cuadras at 1,600 pesos, each lot to be ready for planting. Each colonist could borrow up to 500 pesos from the bank at 10 percent. By the end of 1891, there were 81 colonists in twenty-four families at Elisa, producing a variety of crops and huge amounts of charcoal. The bank in 1895 sold the colony to a Swede, Dänen Emil Johannsen, who obtained a loan from the Banco Agrícola. Johannsen brought in more farmers—Swedes, Danes, Paraguayans, and other nationalities—until by 1903 the colony counted 360 persons. Under Johannsen, the enterprise was more of a profitable real estate operation than a true colonizing venture.[8]

Colonia Presidente González

A French explorer, the Marquis du Bois du Tilleul, came to Paraguay in 1887 and became interested in starting a French colony near Yegros. This, apparently, was the origin of Colonia Presidente González, later called Colonia Nacional, which was created by presidential decree on December 17, 1891. The site was an area of twelve leagues of virgin forest on fertile, red soil about ten kilometers south of Yegros between the Río Pirapó and the Paraguay Central Railway. The founding act provided very generous terms for settlers. Widely advertised in Europe, the colony attracted people of many nationalities. More than four hundred French settlers had arrived by 1893 and were clearly a majority. Ideally, it was expected that timber sales would pay for the cost of clearing the land which would then be planted to sugar cane, tobacco, wheat, corn, potatoes, peanuts, grapes, coffee, rice, alfalfa, and other crops.[9] Hardy indeed were the immigrants who were not dismayed by the density of the forest: "They had been unable to commence cultivation until a clearance had been made of the underscrub, the trees had been felled, chopped and burnt, and the humidity owing to the dense virgin forest made this a very difficult operation, so that it was impossible . . . to put up a house and clear a sufficient amount of ground to get a crop in six months." They were also discouraged by failure of the government to provide the promised cows and by exorbitant prices at the commissary.[10] Mr. M. de C. Findlay, second secretary of the British legation in Buenos Aires, visited the colony in December 1893 in company with the manager, who met him at the railway with horses. A short distance from the station, the riders turned into one of several narrow *picadas* (trails) through the forest that led to clearings planted to maize and mandioca. The first little farm they visited belonged to a hardy Frenchman who had cleared ten acres in thirteen months. Findlay was deeply impressed: "When we looked at the dense forest of hardwood trees towering above a mass of creepers and undergrowth, it seemed incredible that so much could have been accomplished by a single man . . . whose principal instruments had been an axe and a box of matches. The little rancho was surrounded by maize, mandioca, maní (peanut) tobacco, beans, sugar-cane, alfalfa, melons, and every sort of vegetable." There were also patches of wheat and a miniature rice paddy. Findlay found that German, Polish, and French settlers were doing well, despite having lost their first crop to drought and locusts.[11] Many seceders from the nearby Australian colony, after spending three weeks at Villa Rica, received plots near Perry Station adjoining the colony. The cash allowance promised by the government was in "bonds" or payment certificates, which storekeepers accepted at a discount.

After President González was overthrown on June 9, 1894, no one would accept the payment certificates, so the Australians had to leave. In September and October, forty-five of the seceders from Nueva Australia left Colonia González and made their way to Buenos Aires where they expected Australia to pay their way back to Adelaide. There was also much discontent among the French settlers. They complained bitterly to Charles François, their consul in Asunción, who urged them to give up and to leave for Argentina on the *Saturno*, scheduled to sail on March 20, 1895. The colonists left en masse, the government lost its cash advances, and François lost his exequatur.[12] This exodus of disillusioned French colonists caused the American consul to comment: "The colonies in this country . . . have always proved a failure, and even the last one named for the president and backed by his power, if that goes for anything, has been a dead failure."[13]

González, renamed Colonia Nacional, succeeded because of hard work by the settlers who persisted; they were rewarded with aid from the Banco Agrícola, which provided a sugar mill, tobacco driers, tanneries, various shops, and two schools. After the Banco Mercantil assumed its management in 1896, the colony prospered. Settlers of various nationalities continued to arrive. The population grew from 408 in 1896 to 930 in 1900 and to 1305 in 1906. Fourteen countries were represented, with Paraguayans, Germans, French, and Italians making up the majority.[14]

Nueva Australia, Cosme, and 25 de Noviembre

The areas north and south of Villa Rica, drained by affluents of the rivers Manduvirá and Tebicuary, held rich potential for industrious colonists. The most widely publicized of all agricultural colonies was the socialistic experiment by the New Australian Cooperative Settlement Association, which was begun in this area.[15] The last two decades of the nineteenth century were years of severe economic troubles in Australia, years that spawned radical labor leaders who led their followers on a prolonged but unsuccessful general strike. In the words of the British minister to Buenos Aires:

> It was a time when banks were breaking and hard-earned savings lost, and when heavy depression and deep commercial gloom appeared to

be settling down all over Australia, and there were many who thought they could better their lot, but it is surprising what confidence was felt, what reliance was placed in the accounts of the happy future in store for them in Paraguay, and how many were so far influenced by the consideration that for a minimum subscription of 60£, they would be fed, clothed, and housed, and see their children receive an excellent education as to give up their little all, sell what they had, hand over what they might possess for the benefit of the association.[16]

William Lane, an English journalist, was the leading labor agitator in Australia and a major force in forming the association in 1893. Lane was a Communist who sought first to establish his Utopia in Australia. When the association failed to obtain land at home, they sent two agents to investigate prospects in Brazil, Argentina, and Paraguay. These men, William Saunders and Alfred W. Walker, were so impressed by what they saw in Paraguay that on January 6, 1893, Saunders applied for a grant of land on which to establish an agricultural and pastoral colony. Walker clarified this request in a petition dated March 4, in which he asked for 100 leagues of unoccupied land upon which the association would settle 1,200 families having a total population of more than 4,000 persons. Walker's proposal actually became the contract between Paraguay and the association. An initial grant of 50 leagues was to be followed by another of equal size when 600 families had been settled. The association would deposit a bond of 6,000 pesos, to be returned upon arrival of the first 100 families. To acquire the land Walker wanted between Villa Rica and Caaguazú, Congress appropriated 200,000 pesos and raised an additional 250,000 pesos by selling yerbales. *El Centinela*, never friendly toward the González government, observed cynically that although the treasury was empty and public employees had not been paid, the country must have colonies.[17]

The association in Australia actively recruited volunteers for the grand experiment in communism. Its newspaper, the *New Australia*, featured an article by the Rev. T. E. Ash, whose experience in Uruguay, if not his clerical status, should have prevented him from writing such outrageous nonsense as these gems: "In Paraguay civil war is unknown. . . . Paraguay is destined in the near future to be selected as the seat of central government for a federalist republic of the whole of the South American nations . . . [Asunción] would be the capital of the greatest Republic the world has ever yet seen—greater by numbers and extent and riches than France or America."[18] A few naive Australians may have been lured into paying £60 into the general treasury of the association by this ridiculous propaganda. On July 16, 1893, William Lane and 254 men, women, and children sailed from Sydney on the *Royal Tar*, which dropped anchor at Asunción in mid September. On the next day, September 16, Lane sent the unmarried men by train to Villa Rica, to be followed by the others a day

later. There was no road to the site of Lane's Utopia. High-wheeled ox
carts, loaded with personal belongings and those unable to walk,
bumped along a trail through the forest and across the campos to the
two sites chosen by Lane where the colonists would build their
ranchos. No tents had been provided for temporary shelter, but the
men worked willingly to erect thatched huts, and, when their tools
finally arrived, showed equal enthusiasm for clearing the land for
planting. To mollify the 300 squatters who had to be displaced, the
association surrendered three leagues of its land,[19] an area that eventually became Colonia 25 de Noviembre north of Ajos (see map 5).

To give the Australians complete freedom in managing their own
affairs, a presidential decree of September 23 made William Lane
intendant of the colony. Lane was a petty dictator, an uncompromising zealot who demanded unquestioning obedience. Although regulations adopted by the group required many questions to be submitted to the community for decision, Lane often resorted to unilateral
decisions. He particularly abhorred alcohol. Several of the men had
sampled this forbidden beverage at Villa Rica, and two of them
indulged much too freely in caña. Lane expelled them. While there
was little sympathy for such miscreants, there were many other
causes for complaint. The women grumbled about their diet of mate,
mandioca, and maize. Many of the settlers knew absolutely nothing
about farming, resented the restrictions imposed by the communist
structure, and objected strongly to holding everything in common.
With only two unmarried women in the group, and isolated from
Paraguayan society, the young men found little solace in gazing upon
the beauty of their surroundings, in contemplating the shapely forms
of tall trees draped with graceful vines. When summer set in, discontent increased. Soon after Lane had expelled the two inebriates,
eighty-two others seceded. After a short stay at Villa Rica, the malcontents went to Colonia González or to Asunción where they asked
Dr. William Stewart, the British consul, to help them return to Australia. Fred White, a leader of the dissidents, assured the government
that they liked Paraguay and wanted to stay, but they objected to
isolation and the colony's policy of exclusiveness.[20] Several of the
seceders urged British officials to warn their friends in Australia not
to emigrate to Paraguay. To counteract this unfavorable publicity,
Alfred Walker hurried to Asunción where he assured Stewart that
Lane was a good administrator and the complaints came from persons undesirable as immigrants. Defending the colony in the press,
Walker wrote: "The very raison d'etre of New Australia is a protest
against the wrong engendered by the reign of capitalism and the
cut-throat scramble of competitive industrialism."[21]

Pakenham decided it was time to have an unbiased report on
New Australia, so he sent his second secretary, Mr. M. de C. Findlay, to

Map 5. Agricultural Colonies in the Colorado Era

reconnoiter the colony and look over the country. Findlay arrived at the colony on New Year's Eve, 1893, during the most uncomfortable part of the Paraguayan summer. No holiday festivities interfered with his visit, nor did Lane make any effort to prevent him from talking freely with the colonists. Lane, of course, had little to fear, since nearly all the malcontents had left. Although Findlay agreed that Lane ruled with a heavy hand, he concluded that complaints to Stewart were greatly exaggerated. Colonists who were willing to work hard could succeed in establishing a very large and prosperous community, and "if they fail it will be owing to the independent character of the men, and the rigid views of their chairman, and not to any want of fertility in the land or of generosity on the part of the Paraguayan government."[22]

Undeterred by reports from the first settlers, a second group sailed from Adelaide on the very day that Findlay arrived at New Australia. They reached Asunción on March 7, 1894. Lane met the ship and before anyone could land he threatened reprisals against everyone who discussed affairs of the association. Lane's conduct was enough to cause considerable concern among the latest recruits, who could not be kept from speculating as to what lay ahead. Lane's threats served only to bring about his downfall in April, when many of the newcomers joined with the remaining colonists to force his resignation. After the coup of June 1894 forced President González to resign, the government took little interest in the colony. Still, prospects were not at all unfavorable as a new manager guided the 250 who remained. Nueva Australia had 250,000 acres of very fertile land in campos and forests and could support 70,000 cattle. After only a year, there were more than 1,800 cattle, 170 horses, and many pigs and chickens. The colonists had cleared about 70 acres, and had planted 213 acres to a variety of crops. There were plans for a brickyard and a tannery.[23]

Dissension wrecked Nueva Australia. One of the colonists, Alexander K. MacDonald, who later wrote a book about Paraguay, explained the colony's failure: "We were townspeople, mechanics, clerks, stockmen, and land surveyors, etc., etc., anything and everything but back-woods men." The cooperative scheme offered little incentive. The colonists lacked the tools, experience, and skills to succeed. MacDonald concluded that "although most of us admit that we have failed comunistically, there is no reason why we should not form the nucleus of a successful colony in this fair land."[24]

Nueva Australia struggled on as a cooperative for a few more months. Finally, in December 1896, when only fifty men, twenty women, and eighty children were left, thirty-one colonists signed a petition asking the British consul in Asunción to intervene and bring about the dissolution of the New Australia Cooperative Settlement

Association. The Paraguayan government agreed, and early in 1897 Nueva Australia became an open colony with little more than its name on the maps to mark the place where communism had failed.[25]

Colonia Cosme

After his forced resignation, Lane bought 9,375 hectares midway between Caazapá and Yegros (see map 5). Saunders and fifty-two other colonists joined him in this second secession from Utopia. When Walker reported to Stewart in Asunción on April 27, 1894, the consul-doctor was hopeful that harmony might be restored among the Australians. Formally founded on May 12, 1894, Colonia Cosme was governed by a constitution, a copy of which was available to all who were interested. This document described the colony as being dedicated to communism and stated clearly the difficulties to be encountered by colonists. William Saunders left the colony on August 5, 1894, to seek recruits in Australia, armed with a letter signed by fifty-two adults who again declared their loyalty to communism and to William Lane. Saunders had small success on his mission, since only five recruits from New Zealand and four from Australia joined Cosme in 1896. Subtracting seven who withdrew, the colony numbered forty-nine men, eighteen women, and twenty-six children. In its second year, Cosme had promising crops of grapes, bananas, coffee, sugar cane, mandioca, maize, sweet potatoes, alfalfa, beans, and peanuts and an experimental plot of wheat. Still, the group was on basic subsistence rations.[26]

Reported to be by far the best conducted colony in Paraguay, the settlement showed little progress. Cosme desperately needed an influx of dedicated communists. Lane published the *Cosme Monthly* which he distributed widely in Australia and New Zealand. On July 27, 1901, the faithful at Cosme gathered to bid farewell to Lane, who set out for Australia in a vain effort to entice others into his wilderness paradise. He could do no better than Saunders as a recruiter among people who evinced great interest in Cosme and an equally great desire not to emigrate. Paraguay could expect no significant Australian immigration. Nevertheless, 187 immigrants went to Cosme from 1896 to 1905, more than went to any other colony except 25 de Noviembre, which attracted 395 during the years 1895–1906.[27]

25 de Noviembre

Far more successful than either of the Australian colonies, 25 de Noviembre was founded by a decree dated December 19, 1893, "with the laudable plan of bringing together in one place and in their own homes all the native settlers who were scattered within the zone

ceded to the 'Compañía Cooperativa Colonizadora Nueva Australia,' " with all the privileges granted under the colonization act of
1881.[28] The colony began with three leagues of excellent land a few
miles north of Ajos. As settlers moved in, they were grouped into
small communities around which were the cultivated fields,
pastures, and woodlands. Within four years there were 912 inhabitants who had about 1,900 acres under cultivation. Livestock included
2,500 cattle, 360 horses, 180 sheep, 100 hogs, and 70 goats. The colony
grew rapidly: to 1,481 in 1899; 2,496 in 1902, and 6,000 in 1910 divided
into twenty communities.[29] Animal husbandry combined with diversified agriculture and horticulture explained the colony's success (see
table 14). Agricultural practices were so poor that Paternó had recommended establishment of an agricultural school and experimental
farm in the colony. Finally approved on December 30, 1905, the
project was so poorly supported that the agronomist in charge resigned in October 1907. The experimental farm he had started soon
became overgrown with weeds. Colonists supplemented their income by stealing timber from the public domain, a practice common
in all colonies near forests. Within one year, 1909–1910, over three
thousand dressed logs were delivered to the railway for shipment to
Asunción. To supply the two privately owned petit-grain oil factories,
colonists cut off branches of the bitter orange trees instead of strip-
ping the leaves, a practice that nearly killed off the orange groves. As
usual in the colonies, settlers complained that the manager was a
grafter.[30]

Colonia Hohenau

Of the last three colonies begun under Colorado auspices—Hohenau,
Esperanza, and Trinacria—only Hohenau prospered. Interest in the
Alto Paraná area above Encarnación slowly increased as more and
more enterprisers came to recognize its great potential. Heavily
forested, with rich yerbales and fertile campos, the region could
easily become the richest in Paraguay. Two enterprisers, Wilhelm
Closs of Rio Grande do Sul and Carlos Reverchon of Encarnación,
asked for a concession in 1898 to establish a colony on the upper
Paraná thirty-five miles north of Encarnación.[31] In approving their
petition, Congress promised the partners one league of land free for
each thirty families brought in, with a limit of sixteen leagues. The
proprietors in turn could sell the land to colonists in lots of forty
hectares (about ninety-five acres.)

The first recruits for Hohenau were Brazilian-Germans who arrived in 1899. A malaria epidemic discouraged some of the original
settlers, and Closs was glad to sell out to Ambrosio Schöller.[32] After a

Table 14

Field and Fruit Crops, Colonia 25 de Noviembre, in 1910
(total acreage = 4,498)

Crop	Acreage	Crop	Acreage	Fruit Trees and Plants	
Maize	1,117	Rice	205	Sweet orange trees	21,248
Mandioca	635	Potatoes	163	Banana plants	23,920
Tobacco	655	Peanuts	133	Pineapple plants	6,566
Coffee	519	Sugar cane	128	Peach trees	738
Beans	477	Onions	52	Lemon trees	306
Cotton	214			Miscellaneous	460

Source: Genaro Romero, *Informes sobre las colonias "Trinacria," "Nueva Italia," "25 de Noviembre" presentados al ministerio de relaciones exteriores*, pp. 50–51.

very shaky beginning, Hohenau attracted numerous frontier-hardened Germans from Rio Grande do Sul whose dogged persistence inspired immigrants to come from Germany and northern Italy. Building their substantial homes on either side of a well-maintained road, the settlers cleared enough land to grow crops that supported several industries. In the first years of the Liberal era, Colonia Hohenau's future was in doubt, but later developments fully justified the faith of Reverchon and Closs as the colony grew rapidly in population and prosperity. With good reason, the surveyor-inspector Angel Battilana reported in 1909: "This colony is indisputably the foremost colony in the country." More than one hundred twenty families had settled by 1909 and supported a brewery, four water-powered mills for processing corn, mandioca, wheat, rye, and other grains, two distilleries, bakeries, shops, and meat markets. The colony produced practically everything grown in Paraguay except tobacco.[33]

Colonia Esperanza (Gaboto)

A proprietary colony that failed and was taken over by the government was Colonia Esperanza, located about 24 kilometers east of Villa Franca and 105 kilometers south of Asunción. Juan Antonio Amado persuaded the government to expropriate four leagues at a cost of $f69,300. His contract or concession of February 27, 1899, required him to pay $1,000 gold per league and to introduce several hundred colonists. The first settlers arrived in the middle of 1899 and almost at once began to complain so much about the administrator that Amado himself took charge at the end of the year. By that time there were 43 colonists, 30 men and 13 women, representing eight nationalities. One house with a zinc roof had been built and twelve more were under construction. The colonists could not meet payments for the land, and so few were settled that Amado asked to be released from his contract. President Carvallo's government agreed on February 26, 1902, and established a colony and town on the site of Esperanza. Renamed Gaboto, the colony appeared to have a chance to survive. Jacob Wavrunek, director of the department of immigration, reported that "without doubt, because of its good location [Gaboto] is destined to be one of the most important colonies in the country." But it was not to be. Gaboto, always in danger of flooding, had only 183 persons in 36 families by 1906 and a realistic appraisal admitted that it would never amount to anything.[34]

Colonia Trinacria

At about the same time that hopeful settlers were moving to Esperanza and Hohenau, immigrants from Sicily were arriving to take up land in the wilderness forty kilometers east of Villa Rosario and sixty kilometers south of the ill-fated Nueva Germania. Dr. Giuseppe de Stéfano Paternó organized the Sociedad Colonizadora Italo-Paraguaya in Catania, Sicily, in November 1897. After the society approved his program, Paternó left for South America in March 1898 and was in Asunción a month later, where he enjoyed a cordial welcome from General Egusquiza.[35]

To arouse support for his plans in Asunción, the enthusiastic Sicilian gave two public lectures in which he developed a logical philosophy of colonization. He emphasized Paraguay's need for European immigrants to develop the country's great natural resources, the need to locate colonies on transportation routes to give access to markets, and the advisability of planting crops best suited to the country. To avoid being victimized, colonists must resort to cooperative marketing which could also control quality. With all colonists contributing to the cooperative the society would finance construction of buildings and the purchase of machinery.[36]

Enthusiasm in Paraguay was not matched in Catania, where *Il Corriere* strongly opposed Paternó's plan in an effort to discourage emigration, printed letters from disillusioned Italian immigrants in Paraguay, charged that Paternó would be a dictator, condemned the site selected as entirely unsuitable, asserted that there were no successful colonies in Paraguay, and cited poor markets, poor transportation, low prices, a bad climate, lazy natives, and xenophobia as reasons for failure.[37] To counterattack, Italian residents in Asunción met and resolved unanimously that Paraguay was a wonderful place to live, where the industrious worker would "always see his efforts crowned with success."[38] President Egusquiza had already recommended that Congress grant the concession requested by Paternó on May 24, 1898. Dutifully the Congress gave its approval. The law of July 29 made an initial grant of fifteen to twenty leagues south of Asunción along the river, the land to be expropriated. The government would continue to deliver parcels to the society until a total of fifty leagues had been turned over. The society was to establish thirty families per league within two years and engage in industrial, pastoral, and agricultural activities.[39]

Having secured the desired action from Congress, Paternó traveled south of Asunción to select the land, but owners held out for such high prices that Paternó, faced by the imminent arrival of the first contingent of colonists, was forced to select another site. He chose sixteen leagues east of Villa Rosario, north of Asunción, owned by Vicente Nogues, for which the government paid $f295,986. The first group of colonists left Naples on September 7, 1898, and arrived at Asunción on October 15. As the 237 newcomers disembarked from the *Villafranca*, they received a warm welcome from the capital's large Italian colony. If they expected a life of ease, they were disillusioned almost immediately upon reaching Trinacria. Soon many had been expelled or had left voluntarily. As in the case of Nueva Australia, the malcontents began a campaign to discredit the colony's manager.[40] Paternó accumulated debts of more than sixteen thousand pesos in settling the colonists. He left for Italy in 1899 to raise more capital and to enlist more immigrants, encouraged by the government's promise to pay the debt if another group arrived by November 30, 1900. The promised expedition did arrive in February, but of the sixty-two immigrants, only three had the required $200 gold in capital. The presence of plague in Asunción put an end to further immigration for some time, and, with Paternó in Italy, Trinacria disintegrated. Most of the colonists went to Asunción to seek work. When the government canceled his contract on October 26, 1900, Paternó received two leagues on which he could try to start another colony.[41]

Future efforts in the Trinacria area were also discouraging. The South American Lumber Company of California received a concession of part of Trinacria's original grant in 1907 and started a colony called Santa Clara or Nueva California. After importing some machinery and settlers, the company gave up. The government took over the colony, renamed it General Aquino, and threw it open to general settlement. The result of grants to Trinacria and Nueva California was a tangle of claims and counter-claims as the courts sought to clarify land titles. The Brazilian minister's report to his government when Congress made the original concession to Paternó proved to have been entirely accurate: people in the know said that Paternó's scheme was a pipe dream.[42]

Balance Sheet

What could Paraguay show for the many thousands of pesos spent to pay fares from Buenos Aires, to provide subsistence allowances, tools, seeds, and oxen? Where were the thousands of industrious European farmers who, working the country's *tierras de labor* (farm land), would transform Paraguayan economy and society? A decade after Germans began the successful Colonia San Bernardino, a thoughtful editor looked at Argentina's Colonia Bouvier a few miles south of Asunción on the west bank of the Paraguay, and asked what did Paraguay have that was comparable. Answering his own question, he observed gloomily: "Nothing, unfortunately, because not only do European immigrants shun Paraguay, but also natives emigrate because of persecutions and outrages committed by political authorities in rural areas. Agriculture is almost completely abandoned: here is the cause of the lack of production, the country's misery, the government's insolvency, and the acute commercial crisis that has paralyzed all mercantile transactions." A month later, the same writer resumed his lament: "European immigration will not be directed to Paraguay while there are no guarantees for its own inhabitants, while lands are not offered to the farmers. . . . To govern is to populate, Alberdi has said; but our leaders have put the opposite maxim into practice: to depopulate is to misgovern—and this is why their jefes políticos have declared war *á outrance* upon the country people."[43]

Nearly a decade later, the dean of the diplomatic corps, clear-headed after his magnificent New Year's reception, warned his superiors that "if these colonization efforts fail, as nearly all have thus far failed in this country, the [economic] ruin will be frightful."[44] Commenting on Paternó's contract, *La Patria Paraguaya* urged a careful study of colonization problems and warned that "artificial immigration," as occurred in the colonization schemes, almost always resulted in exaggerated claims, followed by inevitable disillusionment." Paraguay should put its trust in spontaneous immigration.[45] From the vantage point of time and distance, the young Eligio Ayala, whose great abilities carried him to the presidency of Paraguay, while studying in Switzerland condemned agricultural colonies as a stupid waste of money when native workers were being forced to emigrate in order to make a living.[46]

These critics, justified in their harsh judgments, unerringly pointed to the major causes for failure in Colorado colonization efforts. Not until the 1920s and 1930s, when the cousins Eligio and Eusebio Ayala were prominent leaders of the Liberal party, did sturdy, determined, and well-financed Mennonite and Japanese colonists vindicate the Colorado policies. Liberal governments could claim the credit, although Colorado experience was indispensable.

19

People and Society

No attempt to re-create a nation's social experience can be more than partially successful, especially when the effort is made by an outsider who tries to assess a country's unrecorded social life. Unfortunately, Paraguayans who were becoming increasingly literate devoted most of their literary efforts to political polemics, mediocre poetry, and tiresome essays. No great, or even interesting, novels appeared during the Colorado era to mirror the life of any social group. One must depend primarily upon brief glimpses provided by foreign reporters, mostly consular or diplomatic agents, and a few travelers. Occasionally a cabinet officer would lift a corner of the curtain in a revealing paragraph of a memoria. While social activities of the wealthier classes often received effusive descriptions in the press, the rural classes were largely ignored except by writers who excoriated them for laziness and improvidence and exhorted them to work, work, work. Intellectuals never tired of proclaiming "Manos a la obra!" ("Hands to the task!") as a worthy motto for others to follow. [1]

Guaraní Heritage?

The visitor to Paraguay today cannot fail to be impressed by the apparent heterogeneity of the people, especially if the Mennonite and Japanese colonies are included in the itinerary. But this heterogeneity was lacking when the Colorados assumed control in 1878. The people of the Colorados' Paraguay were ethnically homogeneous. There were few "pure" Indians, except in the Chaco and in remote forests, and also few of undiluted European blood. Paraguay was predominantly a mestizo nation, its people a mixture of Europeans and Guaraní-speaking Indians. Although respected scholars[1] found that the twentieth-century Paraguayan in a small rural community displayed little of his Guaraní ancestry other than the language, a widespread belief that the Indian heritage was extremely important prevailed in the nineteenth century and is still very widely believed. Near the end of the Colorado era, a writer asserted that "wherever one goes in Paraguay he finds, vivid and indelible, the stamp of the Guaraní race and he finds unimpeachable evidence that this race has resisted every misfortune of destiny, has formed a single type from indigenous varieties, their congenerics, and . . . has conquered all the ethnic elements that, with and after the conquest, immigrated into the country."[2]

Just how much of the Paraguayan folklore, folk medicine, and other cultural traits were Guaraní-based is difficult to determine, but there is no doubt about the language. Guaraní, modified by four and a half centuries of intimate contact with Spanish, was almost universally spoken by Paraguayans. A very difficult language for a foreigner to learn, this expressive Indian tongue surely exerted a tremendous influence on thought patterns while serving as a barrier against foreign penetration into Paraguayan society, especially in rural areas where many people spoke only Guaraní. This language was considered to have been the agent for diffusion of the common culture, "the depository of the old and new traditions and great sorrows of the country. . . . When Paraguayans are abroad, they feel a common brotherhood only when speaking in Guaraní."[3]

A somewhat supercilious Brazilian believed that the language was filled with savagery and idolatry: "That is why the traveler is impressed by the mongoloid features of the people, by the discordant and guttural sounds of the dialect, and by a conjunction of barbaric customs, found only in inferior races of oriental extraction."[4] A more sympathetic observer suggested that rather than being an obstacle to be overcome, the Guaraní language was better adapted to esthetic, religious, and individual needs than Spanish. An English traveler from Buenos Aires was very favorably impressed: "The Paraguayans are the happiest people I have ever met: they only become grave and serious when they talk Spanish and this transition from merriment to gravity is remarkable. Even the educated Paraguayan abandons restraint the moment he talks Guaraní, but he is as serious as a judge when talking Spanish."[5] Guaraní remained almost entirely a spoken language and appeared rarely in newspapers.

Women, Family, and Home

For more than a century after the close of the War of the Triple Alliance in 1870, observers commented on the effects of the dreadful conflict that destroyed the first Paraguayan republic. The impact of the war on all aspects of Paraguayan life was indeed devastating, but many characteristics of the social milieu had roots in the colonial period that had lasted for nearly three centuries and into a half century of dictatorships. The prevalence of concubinage, emphasis upon *machismo* (male virility and sexual prowess), and the resulting dominant role of the woman in family life, especially among the lower classes, continued after the war. These characteristics were greatly exaggerated as a result of the practical elimination of adult males during the conflict. Typical of writers who attributed weaknesses in family life to the war was Justo Pastor Benítez (1895–1962), one of Paraguay's finest and most prolific authors, who concluded:

> Perhaps the most terrible and lamentable effect of the war of 64–70 was destruction of the Paraguayan home. More than material destruction, more than territorial spoliation, it caused Paraguay's misfortune by its consequences, the disappearance of that strong and healthy cell that the family was before that great disaster.
>
> The country was left without the home. Homeless and sorrowing women were the ones who rebuilt the race . . . and they continue being its support after more than fifty years. . . . The formation of families is almost an exception, the percentage of natural children is alarming . . . because the natural child in our country is a creature abandoned to the weak protection of the woman. Almost never can it count on paternal protection.[6]

Another essayist wrote with poetic license:

> Hope extinguished in your hearts, and curiosity in your minds, you adjust to the desert, to the desperate nakedness of your huts and of your instincts. Because diffidence, fear and blind submission weigh on your flesh. Because the memory of nameless disaster presses upon you. Because you have been begotten from wombs shaken by horror, and you wander stupefied in the old theater of the most destructive war in history. . . . You are the survivors of the catastrophe, the errant specters of the night after battle.[7]

Fifteen years before Barrett wrote his compassionate essay, the Brazilian consul general, although not a very sympathetic witness, reported that "the principal feature of the social order, and on which the organization of the family rests, is not religious and Catholic marriage but the concubinage of almost all of its inhabitants. Even in the lack of other enumerated causes, this fact would reveal and explain the weakness and backwardness of the nation condemned to perish if a strong influx of civilization does not rescue it from the moral decadence that prevails."[8]

The Paraguayan War has been held accountable for undermining moral values as well as nearly destroying the family. Vansittart found that morality "was at a very low ebb," without specifying what conduct he included under the term. Drunkenness was common among men and was recognized as a vice.[9] Sexual promiscuity continued to prevail and was even defended as resulting in a vigorous race: "In Paraguay, fortunately, as yet there are no barriers to legitimate love, to the unions that irresistibly attract and enslave the heart."[10] There was, nevertheless, a double standard. Men, to prove their machismo, notoriously violated the marriage vow. Consensual marriage was too common to be worthy of comment. Whether formally married or just living with a man, a woman was subject to gossip, at least, if she had more than one sexual partner at a time.

Despite the innumerable accolades bestowed upon women by uncritical writers, Paraguayan women fell far short of presiding over ideal homes. The outspoken and fearless Teodosio González (1871–1932) characterized home conditions as deplorable. Even in bourgeois families, disorder, grossness, violence, obscenity, and vice prevailed.[11] That there was crudeness in the postwar home cannot be denied, but all men were not unchivalrous brutes and the virtuous woman was not a rarity. Travelers found the rural family hospitable and kind in the midst of poverty. Dr. Bernhard Förster, founder of Nueva Germania, traveled widely in Paraguay in the early 1890s and, although he had a poor opinion of the men, praised the women: "A comparison between the Paraguayan women and men will be unfavorable to the latter. The women are helpful, pleasing, very good natured and much more industrious than the men: It is not unusual for the men to take advantage of them in a way that would appear to us Germans as mistreatment. The woman not only keeps the house, the kitchen, and the men's clothes in order, . . . but also works in the fields, carries in the water and wood, milks the cow, etc."[12] Add to these tasks childbearing and infant care, and one can hardly fault women for not maintaining ideal homes. At the same time that Förster wrote, European and American farm women were performing similar tasks. The British minister, on a visit from Buenos Aires in 1881, made a short trip into the interior where he found that "the women do all the work—the war having destroyed most of the male population—This excess of women is naturally very pleasant for the lords of creation. It is singular, though, that as a rule generally faithful to their men, a large proportion of the women prefer not marrying—as that entails working for a husband as well as children."[13] What the traveler Molins found in 1914 was equally true in the Colorado era. He was deeply impressed by the swarms of women who labored in so many capacities, "in the streets, and in the market, on the piers and in the country, always with a load on the head, in never ending vertebral gymnastics that gave a truly elegant bearing to the body. . . . The Paraguayan woman is admirable: frugal, enduring to the point of sacrifice, kind and brave." Lover, mother, weaver, cook, soldier, nurse, "without being mannish she has won to a large degree . . . , the man's place and openly assumes the man's privilege of smoking. The paraguaya is a professional smoker. . . . The cigar is an incentive and a pastime; it is like chica for the Bolivians and sweet caña to the peon of the mill: it distracts and pleases."[14]

The place of women in society was not enviable. There were no women in such professions as law and medicine. There were, of course, midwives. Women, qualified or not, filled most of the teaching positions at extremely low pay. Married women could testify in court but could not witness legal documents. While not forbidden by law to do so, women did not attend public political meetings nor did they vote. They did have their own societies, especially those devoted to charity, but they had no church offices and no voice in the management of church affairs. Under the criminal code, women could not be sentenced to death. Divorce was permitted, but neither party could remarry while the other was alive.[15]

The marriage law of 1899 contained some articles that protected the wife as well as many that made her, in modern parlance, a second-class citizen. All married couples resident in Paraguay were subject to Paraguayan law. Close relatives could not marry, although first cousins often did so after paying an official or priest to ignore the ban. Females could marry at the age of twelve, males at fourteen. Marriage licenses were issued by the official in charge of the civil register, before whom the marriage must take place. A religious ceremony could follow this universally required civil ceremony, but in practice the cost of church marriages precluded all but the wealthier classes from enjoying this luxury. The husband and wife were required to live in the same house, the husband to pay household expenses. Lacking a nuptial contract, the husband was legal administrator of all goods owned by the couple, and the wife could enter into no financial contract without the husband's consent. Unless he announced his opposition publicly, the husband could not prevent his wife from entering a profession or working in industry. In practice, women operated hundreds of scantily stocked stores.

Divorce, as noted, did have some restrictions and consisted "only in the personal separation of the spouses, without dissolution of the matrimonial tie." Legal causes included adultery, assault with intent to kill, attempt to persuade a spouse to commit adultery or any crime, excessive cruelty, and desertion for more than one year. In the event of a divorce, the couple's goods were to be divided equally. Children under the age of five remained with the mother; custody of older children was awarded by judicial discretion. The wife received alimony if the husband caused the divorce or if she had no means of support.[16]

Impressions of Rural Life

Paralleling the generous sentiments about women was the almost universal belief in male laziness, promiscuity, and general lack of

moral standards. Satisfied with the bare necessities of life, men had
no incentive, and no desire to better themselves—if one believes the
conventional wisdom. Vansittart in 1881 found Paraguayan men "little given to work" and as lazy as before the war when the dictators
had to force them to grow bananas, oranges, cotton, and tobacco. In
the postwar years, young liberals constantly urged their countrymen
to be more industrious. A decade later, writers were playing the same
theme: there was too much aversion to work.[17] Early in President
Escobar's term, a frequent visitor from Buenos Aires wrote of Villa
Rica: "With all due regard to the fair sex, women are utterly unable to
build alone the future of this magnificent country. I shall not mention
the men, because they are quite out of the question: smoking cigars,
eating oranges, chewing sugar chunks, and performing all their functions like somnambulists." Only a large number of immigrants could
make Villa Rica anything but "a garden of pleasure, of indolence and
of ease, but nothing more."[18] Natives and foreigners alike agreed that
Paraguayan men were incurably lazy. During the depression of the
1890s, an editor blamed the people for widespread hunger in rural
areas: "It is also known that the inhabitant of our country, with
exceptions of course, is by nature viciously lazy, that he never has
worked for his daily subsistence, because he is satisfied with the
mandioca and the orange, the first planted with little labor, and the
second found everywhere. When he works it is not to satisfy his
hunger but to feed his vices, he has no more ambition than that he
never seeks to improve himself nor looks to the future."[19] These were
the reasons, the writer insisted, why employers could not find workers, and when they received cash advances peons would spend the
money and not keep their contracts. Peons worked when they wanted
to, but preferred to be in the shade, having women bring mate to
them. There was work for thousands in the yerbales and processing
plants but no workers. Another critic, Teodosio González, held that
"thousands of able-bodied people prefer to live almost naked, to sleep
on the ground and to eat what they can reach, like a haltered horse,
before picking up a work tool."[20] No writer has been more severe in
condemning his countrymen than this lawyer, who found laziness
and lying to be universal. Everyone lies, he wrote, from the president
to the lowest peasant, and moral cowardice, apathy, and spiritual
degeneration were common.[21] This harsh judgment seems to confirm
that of the Brazilian consul general who reported in 1885: "I do not
believe that the present hierarchy will be able to regenerate the
country. It lacks the vitality and energy imparted by long and legitimate exercise of liberty, and certainly a century will pass before these
people can emerge into the light of civilization to take a distinct place
among the American nations."[22]

Not all observers of Paraguayan society indulged in such sweeping denunciations. Rey de Castro found great respect in rural society

for the skilled craftsman and a democratic spirit that led sons of the wealthiest ranchers and merchants to seek the company of daughters of storekeepers, artisans, carpenters, and other skilled workers.[23] One is tempted to ask if these young men were motivated solely by "democratic spirit."

Rafael Barrett (1874–1910), a Spanish essayist of social protest, lived in Paraguay for five years, married a Paraguayan girl, and traveled widely in the country before returning alone to his native Spain shortly before his death. Deeply sympathetic toward the Paraguayan people, he condemned the cruelty of La Industrial Paraguaya toward its workers, the gross cheating of the minero, the widespread social injustice that he found, and the excessively high prices charged by merchants. A much better observer than the diplomats, he penetrated to the causes of the Paraguayan malaise. In the countryside, the peón was "a miserable prisoner of a patch of earth. He has nowhere to take his harvests, which perhaps he wrenches from the soil in a desperate effort. . . . Beyond, under the squalid orange groves left by the Jesuits, the farm hut of mud and cane rises, a hole where one languishes in the shade. Enter: you will find no glass nor a chair; you will sit on a piece of wood, you will drink muddy water from a gourd, you will eat maize boiled in a dirty pot, you will sleep on leather straps tied to four posts. And remember that we speak of the rural bourgeoisie." People did not work, Barrett continued, because they were sick, stricken with tuberculosis, diarrhea, and other diseases with no medical attention other than that of a *curandero* (healer). Men were driven by the lash and the sword into military barracks. Profoundly saddened by the fate of people of all ages, Barrett cried out against the burdens that they bore, the sickness and malnutrition that weighed upon them. He could not blame the men for seeking escape in alcohol and gambling.[24]

Paraguayans generally were desperately poor. González castigated his fellow citizens for not saving, for not anticipating illness, old age, or unemployment, for wasting everything on one extravagant fling. More than half the rural population lived in miserable mud-and-thatch huts of one or two unfloored rooms, without comforts of any kind, eating little, sick and half naked. There was no privacy within a family.[25] A bad impression of rural life might be gained by "the excursionists who incidentally come to a place in the country and find the masters of modest homes occupied in taking maté, dancing, strumming the guitar, and singing, or more likely sleeping in the hammock, or asleep on their ponchos. . . . These travelers spread the belief that the Paraguayan rural class is lost, that it does not work, that it is steeped in laziness and vices."[26] Rey de Castro protested that this was not a true picture, since all the people, including the very young and old of both sexes, hurried to their fields at dawn to work for four or five hours before lunch. Later in the evening, when the heat of the day lessened, they returned to their tasks to work another three or four hours. After a short siesta, the women were busy preparing food, sewing, weaving, and making simple clothes.

As economic depression continued in the 1890s, vagrancy, begging, and theft became more common. One editor expressed a widely held belief that vagrants should be forced to work. Referring to the Guaraní heritage, he wrote: "But we do not refer to this inveterate custom that we have inherited from our primitive race and which culture is erasing little by little, but the growing tendency to abandon the axe for the beggar's rags."[27] To meet the problems of vagrancy and begging, President Egusquiza announced in 1894 that shops would be established "where the vagabonds and delinquents could acquire the habits of work, the only way to stimulate moral regeneration of persons useless or dangerous to society."[28]

Problems of Health

Paraguay's reputation as being a healthful place to live was certainly grossly exaggerated. The climate itself, by no means the best in South America, did offer advantages that were more than offset by deplorable public health conditions, profound ignorance of personal hygiene, and inadequate or nonexistent medical care throughout the republic. Asunción, the most important commercial and cultural center, lacked adequate hospitals and suffered from a chronic shortage of doctors, dentists, and nurses. The most basic personnel and facilities were completely lacking in villages and towns. There were no public sewers or water systems anywhere in Paraguay. Disposal of garbage and human wastes was left to the individual household, a problem less serious in sparsely settled rural areas than in towns and cities. Toward the end of the century, an editor deplored the lack of sanitation in Asunción: "All of our doctors agree in attributing so much of the illness that afflicts us to the lack of hygiene. For more than three and a half centuries the streets and land of the capital have been the never cleared depository of filth thrown by the people. In the good times of don Carlos A. López [1840–1862] some sewers were opened which have been ruined by neglect. These emptied into the Laguna Lucha, whose waters were then daily renewed and which today are stagnant because the old canal is blocked."[29] Most of the city, especially the outlying barrios, had almost no garbage collection in 1900, causing one observer to remark: "No doubt that garbage is the worst source of venomous miasmas."[30]

Paraguay and Paraguayans were not unique in having these problems. Large and small cities everywhere were far from being ideal in public health and sanitation. Public hygiene and public health were among the first of a multitude of problems that the young Paraguayan liberals attacked in 1869. They asked that the government's first attention be devoted to public hygiene: fines should be levied for throwing filth, dirty water, and the contents of slop buckets into the streets.[31] The occupation forces did little to improve conditions. When Vansittart was drafting his invaluable report in 1882, he asked Dr. William Stewart to provide a memorandum on health. Stewart, a well-qualified physician, insisted that "the principal zymotic diseases, yellow fever, typhus and typhoid, diphtheria, cholera and dysentery" were almost unknown in Paraguay. Goiter and elephantiasis were endemic. There was surprisingly little malaria, but intermittent fevers did appear. Far ahead of his time, Dr. Stewart held that "the abuse of tobacco is also a prolific cause of disease, producing tissue changes of the blood-vessels and of the viscera to an alarming extent." Poor diet made natives "prone to dyspepsia and diarrhoea." With smallpox vaccination mandatory, that disease had been eradicated.[32] Despite his long residence in Paraguay, the doctor ignored a few ailments, especially leprosy and venereal disease, and he was wrong about smallpox, cases of which appeared frequently.

Animals roamed freely through the streets, adding to accumulated filth that remained until a heavy rain washed it away. Especially annoying and dangerous were the packs of dogs which not only acted as scavengers but also threatened pedestrians and howled constantly. Every gentleman carried a stout *bastón* (cane) which served the dual purpose of protection and completion of the wardrobe. The plague of dogs continued for several decades. George L. Kreeck, U.S. minister in the 1920s, once referred to the country as "Perroguay."

In the 1890s, when Asunción suffered severely from epidemic diseases, sanitary conditions had improved very little. A journalist complained that every kind of disease was spread in the unclean markets. Milk was still being sold from door to door by vendors whose utensils were rarely inspected, and stores that sold food and drink escaped supervision. A decade later, there were still complaints about the bad quality of bread, "of the bad conditions in which it is distributed" and of the dirty bottles in which milk was sold.[33] Fortunately, milk generally was scalded before being used.

The government and public were not indifferent to public health problems, but did very little to provide effective remedial measures. The first postwar governments had appointed boards of health that had little power. Dr. William Stewart was head of the Council of Medicine and Public Hygiene appointed by President Gill in 1876 and became chairman of the Medical Council created in 1883. Composed of four medical doctors, two pharmacists, and one chemist, the council was to propose public health measures and to supervise the practice of medicine, pharmacy, surgery and "allied arts." No one could exercise these professions without the council's permission, which was given only after an examination, although those already practicing could continue. In towns that lacked professional medical care, the council could authorize one or more to be curanderos. The Vaccination Office, which had been created in 1880 under Dr. Stewart's direction, held smallpox in check. This clinic was attached to the Medical Council in 1898 when a National Health Council replaced the Medical Council.[34] Paraguay still lacked adequate medical facilities. So few students registered in the School of Medicine that it was closed in 1892 for six years. The country, therefore, had to depend upon doctors trained abroad, and there were very few of them. Cities and rural areas offered so few incentives that doctors also became politicians, writers, administrators, and businessmen. Nearly all Paraguayans who bore the title of "doctor" were lawyers.

Paraguay's first postwar public hospital was the Hospital de Caridad, supported by the Sociedad de Beneficencia, with some help from the national government and the city of Asunción. Women of the capital were active in promoting asylums for orphans and the indigent. Spurred by an epidemic in the early 1890s, Congress approved funds for these institutions at the behest of José Segundo Decoud, whose concern for public health never lessened after his service with the Provisional Government in 1869.[35]

General lack of sanitation caused a high incidence of disease, frequently reaching epidemic proportions. The dreadful cholera scourge that devastated Buenos Aires in 1886 also struck Paraguay. The first cases appeared on November 19, followed by a steadily increasing number. By December there were six to eight new cases daily and three or four deaths. The Public Health Council denied the existence of a cholera epidemic. Nevertheless, panic set in as the disease spread. More than ten thousand people fled from Asunción to rural areas to escape the pestilence. Ships could not call at the port, leaving the telgraph as Asunción's only link with other countries. As people fled to the country, the city council opened a quarantine station below Asunción, organized neighborhood committees, and continued the distribution of free medicines and disinfectants to the poor. The council ordered that the thatched huts in the city's center be burned, the occupants paid and moved to other localities; belatedly, the council also ordered the markets to be cleaned. High temperatures and the dreaded north wind added to discomfort that was finally relieved by heavy rains.[36]

An influenza epidemic and scattered cases of smallpox increased the distress of economic depression in 1890. Malaria and stomach disorders were widespread in December 1896 and continued until the following winter. Bubonic plague at the end of the century added to Paraguay's misery. The plague outbreak occurred when four crew members of the *Centauro* out of Buenos Aires landed at Asunción on April 28, 1899. Although three of the men died, doctors refused to admit that they had plague until Dr. Stewart made the diagnosis. There were at least twenty-five deaths from confirmed cases of plague between September 4 and October 21, with many more suspected. Dr. Facundo Insfrán, who had studied in Buenos Aires, replaced Dr. Stewart as head of the health council. He enlisted the aid of an Argentine medical mission and of the Pasteur Institute of Paris, which sent Dr. Michel Elmaisian to establish a laboratory and a biological institute in the hospital.[37] Before the outbreak could be contained, 60 of the 124 cases ended in death.

News of the plague in Paraguay caused so much attention in Buenos Aires that ships from Asunción were quarantined at Martín García. The Paraguayan government had closed ports on the Paraguay River on September 19, 1899, causing goods to accumulate at Corrientes, Formosa, and other ports. The resulting economic distress led the Brazilian minister to lament: "This unfortunate country is in the arms of a thousand troubles, which, if they persist for some time will probably cause the complete ruin of Paraguay, of which already there are terrible indications, such as misery and hunger that prevail throughout the republic, where a prolonged drought made a bad situation worse."[38] By mid March 1900 the plague appeared to be over. After several months of quarantine, the people were ready for a national fiesta to celebrate the country's eighty-ninth anniversary of independence with dances, receptions, parades, a Te Deum in the cathedral, and an extended holiday.[39]

The celebration was premature. The plague broke out again in July, and the Public Health Council recommended that President Aceval close all ports but Asunción and order a thorough disinfection of passengers, cargo, and baggage. Dr. Benjamín Aceval, brother of the president, rector of the National University, and Paraguay's representative at the Chaco arbitration in 1878, died of plague on July 25, 1900. This new outbreak was considered over by August 12, although trade to Mato Grosso was prohibited by Brazil for another fortnight. Bubonic plague continued to appear with distressing regularity in Paraguay. Since public health statistics were nonexistent, there is no way to determine its incidence throughout the country. The exceptionally cold winter of 1902 brought an epidemic of pulmonary influenza for which there are no reliable statistics.[40]

Another exercise in futility would be an effort to present accurate mortality statistics for Paraguay or any of its urban communities.

Cholera was given as the cause of 82 deaths in Asunción in 1886, followed by pneumonia (27), and tubercolosis (20). For Asunción and its suburbs, 200 causes were given for 979 deaths from 1898 to 1899, led by infantile tetanus (138), enteritis (71) tuberculosis (53), and a variety of real and imaginary diseases diagnosed as dysentery, tetanus, fever, and *falta de energía* (general debility).[41] There was also a falta de energía in law enforcement.

Public Safety and Law Enforcement

That crime should flourish and criminals go unpunished was to be expected in the postwar decade. In succeeding years, however, the Colorados failed to create a nationwide police force; nor did they, by personal example, encourage law observance. Colorados regularly rigged elections and resorted to extremes of violence to keep opponents from the polls. With this example, one may well ask how the people could be expected to be law-abiding. Men carried concealed weapons, especially knives and firearms, wherever they went, be it in church, at fiestas, or in sessions of Congress. The unarmed man was a fool. Paradoxically, Paraguayan society as a whole was not violent, although the incidence of crime cannot be determined because statistics are either lacking or are completely unreliable. There were cases in which the department's jefe político was unable to maintain order, as in Barrero Grande and Caraguatay in 1878, when there were numerous crimes against Brazilians who had settled in those communities.[42]

Public safety appears to have improved somewhat during the years immediately following allied evacuation in 1876. Five years later, the British minister to Argentina and Paraguay thought that life and property were much safer in Paraguay than in Argentina, especially in the province of Corrientes.[43] The minister of justice reported a significant decrease in criminal trials in 1880 as well as a decrease in misdemeanors (see table 15). Nearly all cases of homicide and wounding occurred at fiestas "owing to abuse of strong drinks, and to the negligence of the police in not prohibiting revellers from carrying arms."[44] Perhaps it was the universal custom of carrying arms that justified this report in 1882: "Crimes of violence are very rare, and in no part of South America is life and property more secure than in Paraguay. Robbery and theft are almost unknown, and a stranger may ride unarmed from one end of the country to the other without fear of molestation."[45] One might, indeed—if he were extremely lucky and had a very fast horse.

Paraguay's police forces were altogether too small and too poorly trained. There were no rural police of any consequence during the Colorado era. Criminals usually were not apprehended, and when

Table 15

Trials in Criminal Courts in Asunción, 1880

Type of Crime	No. of Cases	Type of Crime	No. of Cases
Homicide	38	Sedition	3
Wounding	36	Attempt to murder	2
Slander and calumny	21	Disrespect of authority	2
Robbery	18	Letter stealing	2
Cattle-lifting	10	Abandoning children	2
Forgery	8	Piracy	1
Abuse of authority	8	Suicide	1
Offenses against modesty	6	Bigamy	2
Housebreaking	7	Gang robbery	1
Libel	6	Crimes against health	1

Source: Vansittart, "Report," p. 112.

arrested they could use close ties with influential persons to escape punishment. This was true for all but the vagabonds who lacked protection of the *compradazgo* system.[46] For one author, proof of the law-abiding nature of rural people was their quick response to a law that required help for twenty days to fight the locust scourge in 1898. On this occasion, 90,153 men, 11,716 women, and 6,354 children fought locusts for more than two months without pay.[47] They were, of course, serving their own interests.

Only one gang of outlaws disturbed the country during the Colorado regime. This band was assembled by the brothers Juan and José López and Constantine Valiente. Natives of San Pedro, they appeared early in 1889 and eventually led some five hundred well armed and mounted bandits. To escape their raids and vandalism, so many people fled that San Pedro was practically deserted. The gang attacked neighboring villages and finally caused President Escobar to send troops to restore order. The López brothers escaped, and as late as October 1892 they were still terrorizing settlers along the Apa.[48]

Violent crimes, especially against foreigners, increased somewhat in the 1890s. This was also the decade in which Paraguay was making strong efforts to attract agricultural immigrants, despite recurring droughts, locust plagues, epidemics, quarantines, and economic depression. The increase in banditry coincided with hard times and led President Escobar to establish more military posts, a practice continued by his successors.[49] None of the agricultural colonies were seriously hampered by criminal activity.

Police protection in Asunción was never adequate. The official Colorado press organ complained that the city was at the mercy of thieves and cutthroats. Another paper accused the police of complicity in crime, as "bands of poncho-clad men wearing red bandannas, carrying knives and pistols, roam the streets and public places, threatening everyone without the police ever seeing them."[50] Asunción had a city government, but the minister of interior was responsible for public safety. The city's Departamento General de Policía, headed by a chief of police, was divided into two sections. The larger was the military section, commanded by army officers. A sergeant-major headed this force of 170 soldiers and 67 officers who were distributed among eighteen commissaries.[51] A reorganization in 1890 did little to improve the force. The military section was then renamed the Cuerpo de Vigilantes. Recruits for this corps, drafted for four-year terms, received the bare minimum of training beyond basic drill and instruction in weapons. The 94 officers and 222 soldiers in the corps had nothing but contempt for the score or more of civilian police. The chief of police, Zacarías Jara, complained about the corps's inefficiency and asked for a permanent, trained civilian force. Constant complaints about police brutality, indifference to public welfare, and spying activities of the investigative section caused Francisco Bogarín, minister of interior in 1894, to reform the police department. A Guardia Civil replaced the Cuerpo de Vigilantes. Initially composed of 250 men, some of whom were taken from the Vigilantes, the Guardia was increased to 275 by 1898, and to only 310 in 1900.[52]

In an effort to improve conditions in Asunción, the chief of police issued a sweeping order on October 8, 1894. Weapons could not be carried openly in the streets; public demonstrations against authorities and foreign diplomats, or disturbing meetings, were punishable by jail terms. The chief also warned against public blasphemy, insults to females, nasty comments to passersby, the sale or showing of obscene books and pictures, appearing improperly clothed, practicing sorcery and selling charms, begging, exhibiting deformed creatures to get charity, inducing children to beg, throwing garbage and dirty water in streets and public places, or getting drunk in public. At the end of the century, the minister of interior complained that "vagrancy, gambling, begging, and every kind of vice that permeates society, and, worst of all, drunkenness, are principal social plagues, and until these evils are fought effectively by public authorities, laws, and society itself, these sins and crimes will not decrease."[53] Shortly after this admonition, Stephen Forbes Cunningham, an Englishman who with two associates had tried to start a rope factory in 1896, was murdered at Arroyos y Esteros. Although he had lost a large sum in his business venture and had gone back to England, Cunningham returned to Paraguay and unwisely rented a room from a drunkard who conspired with a young Frenchman to rob and kill him. In reporting this incident, Consul Cecil Gosling observed: "It is not that the people in general are bad or antagonistic to foreigners, but that the Government is too weak to insist that crime shall be adequately punished." Criminals frequently were freed as a favor to some influential person—the compradazgo system at work. In return for the favor, the criminals "promising to lend their services in controlling the elections—knife and pistol in hand, and, failing this, the worst criminals are always liable to be released on public feast days, on the President's birthday and others. Again, if possessed of a little money, they suffer but small inconvenience in jail, being allowed to gamble and drink at leisure."[54]

All too often newspapers carried stories of citizens being attacked in public places in Asunción. Itiberê da Cunha, dean of the diplomatic corps, despaired of seeing improved conditions without a drastic change in a government whose authorities always had excuses for not acting.[55] He concluded that life and property were not safe in Paraguay as the Colorado era drew to a close.

Social Diversions

Arturo Bray looked back with nostalgia from the early twentieth century to the last two decades of the nineteenth. Mule-drawn tram cars, police with "red pompoms and imposing swords," and the lamplighter with his ladder making his rounds at nightfall to light the kerosene lamps, were fond memories. Deep ditches, sandy streets, no pavements, the servant going from door to door offering savory chipá, the water carrier with his cask in a little cart, and young men serenading their sweethearts, the president and his ministers going to their offices on horseback, all belonged to an unsophisticated era. It was a leisurely and amiable life, of parties in chandeliered parlors crowded with sunburned damask-covered furniture, where homemade liquor was sampled "while the girl in high headdress, tight corset, and rustling skirts attacks the piano with Schubert's serenade, alternating it with schottiches, mazurkas, and gavottes." And there were theatricals, sumptuous and exclusive balls, where beautiful girls in silks and jewels danced gracefully. At home, mothers sewed or told stories of the late war, "girls, studying piano, talk with the stars and recite madrigals." Well-dressed men wore narrow-waisted frockcoats "and sported imposing mustaches drooping over aggressive beards." The rougher men wore ponchos, sharpened knives at the waist. The *chacarita*, a slum area on the edge of the bay, was the scene of brawling and bloodshed on Sundays. "Men continued the saintly custom of asking the benediction of the mother, the master, or the priest; they uncovered their heads at the passing of a teacher, an officer, or the Eucharist; everyone crossed himself when the evening bells sounded the hour of prayer." Progress had not ruined the tempo of life in a society where no one was very rich or very poor.[56]

Social events in the Colorados' Paraguay showed little change over the years. There were the usual late afternoon *tertulias* (tea parties) and the informal contacts among close friends. Occasionally a troupe made the trip upriver from Buenos Aires. The first of these troupes was a circus that arrived in 1882 and whose members stayed on to train Paraguayan acrobats. Another circus came in 1888, and in 1894 the Gran Compañía Imperial presented various dramatic performances. Numerous native *comparsas*, or theatrical groups, performed during the Christmas season. Several theatrical groups performed in the Teatro Nacional, today the Teatro Municipal. Although the theater was in disrepair, the Compañía Dramática Española performed there in December 1881 and again in 1902. A musical comedy company, the Compañía de Zarzuela, came in 1883. Several other companies entertained the asuncenos in the 1890s, and in 1902 the Compañía de Operas brought grand opera to Asunción. These traveling groups invariably found a warm welcome in the city.[57] Parents who could afford the small fees provided private music lessons for their children. Favorite instruments were the harp, guitar, and piano. In Asunción as well as in rural areas, church marriages and religious celebrations featured prominently among diversions.

Parades marked special days, such as the day of San Blas (February 3), Corpus Cristi in June, and on May 14, Paraguayans celebrated their independence day with great enthusiasm. On October 12, 1892, Paraguay marked the four hundredth anniversary of Columbus's discovery of America with "fairs, military parades, parades of school children, and brilliant fiestas."[58] The anniversary of the founding of Asunción, August 15, was always an occasion for great festivities, as was December 8, day of the Virgin of Caacupé, when crowds descended upon that small village, combining a religious pilgrimage with more mundane activities. There were neighborhood fiestas to mark saints' days, lower-class marriages in families that could not afford the church ceremony, and the inevitable informal gatherings to watch gambling and cock fights. The consumption of huge amounts of caña resulted in drunkenness and many fights. Officially approved gambling could be had by buying lottery tickets for the benefit of the Charity Hospital.[59]

Excursions on the tramway to Recoleta church and cemetery were popular Sunday outings. Another popular resort was Lambaré, which could be reached only on foot or horseback until well after 1890, since there were no carriages in Asunción. One could rent an excellent horse for three pesos a day. This trip was "far more picturesque than that to the Recoleta; lanes are narrow and you gallop under the shade of forest trees nearly all the time; at the foot of every hill you cross small streams, and the ride in the shade is delightful even with the thermometer at 90° F.," an English visitor wrote in 1887.[60]

Music played a large role in Paraguayan life. Numerous travelers commented on the ubiquitous guitar, which might be called the Paraguayan national instrument. Harps, violins, mandolins, and lutes also found favor among musicians. *Conjuntos*, or groups playing the guitar, harp, and violin are still a major feature of Paraguayan music. In 1892 several music teachers and amateurs organized a "magnificent orchestra" which was much in demand for dances and concerts.[61]

The four diplomats in Asunción entertained lavishly to celebrate their major national holidays. Typical was the Brazilian celebration on September 7, 1898. Brazil's minister held an official reception for the cabinet, diplomatic and consular corps, prominent foreigners, and leaders of the business community. President Egusquiza sent a band to play Brazil's national anthem. A dance that ended at 3:30 A.M. concluded the festivities. To celebrate Brazil's birthday as a republic, the minister also gave a grand ball attended by the best of Asunción's society.[62]

The formation of clubs and societies increased considerably after 1880. The first important cultural society was El Ateneo, organized by a small group of intellectuals in 1883.[63] Although El Ateneo lasted only a short time, it did publish Paraguay's first intellectual journal, *Revista del Ateneo Paraguayo*. More enduring was the Instituto Paraguayo, founded in May 1895. The institute had several sections; its *Revista* emphasized music, art, and literature. Juan Francisco Pérez Acosta kept the institute alive until it merged with the Gimnasio Paraguayo in 1933.[64] Among other groups were El Agrícola Tabaclera, organized in March 1892 by natives and foreigners as an agricultural society, and several clubs formed by persons of the same nationality. Of these "national" clubs, the Centro Español de la Asunción was the most important. Organized on September 22, 1895, the club had broad purposes: to promote closer ties among Spaniards and with Spain, to create a library of books and periodicals, to encourage commerce, to provide public lectures and unusual events, to promote recreational activities, and, eventually, to erect a building for the use of its members and visitors. Active membership was limited to Spaniards, others could be associate or honorary members. The Centro, inaugurated with much fanfare on February 9, 1896, listed 481 active and associate members, and 16 honorary members a year later. Twenty nations were represented in the membership,[65] which was a "who's who" of important Paraguayans. The Centro Español was the prototype of national clubs, and engaged in practically all the activities later undertaken by such clubs, which, by the end of the Colorado era, had become an integral part of Paraguayan culture.

20

Literature, Education, and Religion

Paraguayans of the Colorado era did not distinguish themselves as artists, writers, dramatists, actors, or musicians. Thriving folk arts demonstrated the Paraguayan love for things of beauty, their folk music was an integral part of daily life, their organized and spontaneous fiestas always included graceful dancing, and, unfortunately, disgraceful drinking and brawling. These activities were a part of that very real web of life called "culture," realities that distinguished the nation. Life is of one piece, a vast tapestry of threads that run from pattern to pattern, inextricably entangling economics, politics, law, literature, education, and religion with the multifarious activities in which people engage. As was the case with economics, politics, and law, the Colorados were in a position to exercise powerful influence on literature, education, and religion. Except for a small number of notable publications, literature was intimately connected with journalism. Freedom of the press, therefore, was necessary to promote literary expression. Except for a few private and parochial schools, education was a function of government, a responsibility met with very limited success. Religion, while important in Paraguayan life, lacked the significance it had enjoyed during the colonial era. The church failed to recover from the blows it suffered under Francia and the two Lópezes, and as an institution was relatively powerless.

Literature

"We have said and repeated that the literary and scientific production in Paraguay has not been as abundant as one might expect from the many individuals who are fully prepared to place their names on works worthy of acclaim within and outside of the country."[1] While this judgment by a native Paraguayan is altogether just, and although the Paraguayan environment may not seem to have been conducive to scholarly pursuits, there were some pioneers in the Colorado era whose work encouraged the slowly increasing intellectual community. Paraguayan writers naturally turned to history and to poetry far more than to other literary forms. So close to the War of the Triple Alliance and deeply involved with Bolivia in a dispute over the Chaco Boreal, Paraguay produced intellectuals who felt compelled to explain and to defend their country while responding vigorously to condescending or hostile works produced in Argentina and Brazil. The result was numerous polemics, most of which appeared serially in newspapers.

Several writers who had appeared in the postwar decade continued to be active. Centurión finds only seven authors worthy of note for the 1870s. Of the thirteen works listed, two are documents, four are concerned with the religious question, two describe Paraguayan resources, two are attacks on President Gill's administration, and two are collections of editorials and essays. A translation of a book on government completes the list. Twenty-nine publications are listed for the 1880s. Three are issues of the *Almanaque nacional del Paraguay*, seven are school texts or discourses on curricula, and one is an anonymous drama.[2] Compared with previous output, a flood of works appeared in the last fifteen years of the Colorado era. Histories, biographies, memoirs, essays, travel accounts, scientific studies, and textbooks predominated. An occasional volume of verse appeared, but for the most part poets found their best outlet in the newspapers, as did essayists.

Literary figures in the Colorado era fall easily into two chronological groups. First to be considered are those born before 1860 and who survived to lead active lives in the postwar decades These writers were concerned for the most part with economic, social, and political problems. Some of them were historians of a sort, and all of them held important positions in government, education, or religion. In addition to the ones selected for brief notice, there were many more who published essays and poetry, or who produced work of little lasting merit. Most of the second group were born in the period 1860–1880, and were just beginning their political and literary careers at the end of the Colorado era. All of them were journalists, most attempted poetry, and, with one exception, produced their finest work after 1900.

Oldest and most controversial of the first group was Fidel Maíz (1828–1920), a bellicose priest who contributed significantly to religious turmoil in the postwar decade.[3] A teacher as well as a polemicist of the first order, Maíz wrote textbooks for his school in Arroyos y

Esteros, biographical sketches of the López family, and, finally his memoirs, *Etapas de mi vida* (1919) to refute charges of Juan Silvano Godoi.

Gregorio Benítez (1834–1910) served Francisco Solano López and postwar governments as a diplomat in Europe and South America. Also a jurist and journalist, he wrote on politics, finance, and military and diplomatic history. His best work is the *Anales diplomático y militar de la guerra del Paraguay* (1906). Another survivor of the Paraguayan War who had served López faithfully was Juan Crisóstomo Centurión y Martínez (1840–1903) whose principal work is the *Memorias o reminiscencis sobre la guerra del Paraguay* (3 vols., 1894–1897). One of the most respected of all Paraguayan intellectuals was Dr. Benjamín Aceval (1845–1900), educator, jurist, diplomat, and historian. This native of Asunción contributed his exceptional talents unselfishly to the service of his country. His *República del Paraguay, apuntes geográficos e históricos* (1893), while slender, is an excellent work.[4]

The brothers Decoud, so prominent in the 1870s as young liberals and vigorous opponents of lopizmo, made significant contributions to Paraguayan letters. José Segundo (1848–1909) won prominence as editor of *La Regeneración* and wrote penetrating studies in economics, sociology, history, and government. He assembled a fine library which, after his death, was lost to Paraguay. His bibliography, *A List of Books, Magazine Articles and Maps Relating to Paraguay* (1904), was widely distributed. More important as a literary figure was his brother Héctor Francisco (1855–1930), whose *Compendio de geografia de la República del Paraguay* (1901) went through several editions. Most of his significant work was published after 1904. Like Aceval, he was bitterly opposed to the cult of lopizmo.

Juan Silvano Godoi (1850–1926), architect of the plot that resulted in the murder of President Juan Bautista Gill, was a minor literary figure who accumulated a major library during his eighteen-year exile in Buenos Aires. For nearly a quarter of a century (1902–1926) he was the director of the Biblioteca, Museo y Archivo de la Nación, of which Godoi's own library of 20,000 volumes and important art collection were the nucleus. His principal works were on various aspects of military and political history, the best of which is a collection of essays, *El Barón de Rio Branco* (1912).[5]

To the formation of organized political parties in 1887 has been attributed the origin of modern Paraguayan intellectual life. An even more important event was the moving of Dr. Moisés S. Bertoni (1858–1929), a Swiss scientist, from Argentina to southeastern Paraguay, where he built a fine home and laboratory on the upper Paraná to study Paraguay's flora, fauna, and Indians. His reputation grew with the publication of numerous scientific studies that resulted from his investigations and explorations. President González summoned him to Asunción to become director of the agricultural school. In 1893, while serving in this post, he recruited a number of Swiss colonists to settle at Puerto Bertoni in a colony named Guillermo Tell after his young son, who bore the name of the legendary Swiss patriot.[6]

Another fine intellect was Dr. Alejandro Audibert (1859-1919), who was educated in Buenos Aires and served in high judicial positions in Paraguay for many years after 1883. It was he who kept the Chamber of Deputies from persecuting Manuel Curuchet, a Spanish editor of *El Heraldo*, in 1885. Audibert later was professor of law, editor of *El Independiente*, and a noted historian.

Leading intellectuals of the second group, born in the 1860–1880 period, were Cecilio Báez, Manuel Domínguez, and Manuel Gondra. A contemporary called them "the highest trilogy of Paraguayan intelligentsia."[7] Báez (1862–1941), vehement in his denunciation of López, was primarily a writer of superficial history whose bibliography contains upward of fifty titles, most of which were published after 1900.[8] Domínguez (1869–1935), foremost literary figure of the Colorado era, was a product of the Paraguayan educational system. A school administrator, professor, archivist, journalist, and politician, he served both Colorado and Liberal regimes. Many of his publications were devoted to Paraguay's title to the Chaco. His exceptional command of Spanish, beautiful and vigorous prose, earned him a leading place in Paraguayan letters.[9] Gondra (1871–1927) was an insatiable scholar who assembled the library later purchased by the University of Texas, where it forms the nucleus of a major Paragūayan collection. A fine stylist and master of Spanish, he is remembered internationally for the Gondra Convention adopted by the Fifth Pan American Conference in 1923. Although his major work was to come after the August Revolution of 1904, in which he played a leading role, Gondra's early articles and essays marked him as one of Paraguay's brilliant young men.

Juan Emiliano O'Leary (1879–1968) used his formidable literary skill to glorify Francisco Solano López. The apotheosis of this controversial dictator was O'Leary's principal accomplishment, the major goal of a man who certainly did become a legend in his own time. As "Pompeyo González" he collaborated with Enrique Solano López, the dictator's son, who published *La Patria*. Journalist, poet, historian, and diplomat, he was for many years director of Paraguay's Biblioteca Nacional and Archivo Nacional.

Also educated in Paraguay was Dr. Blas Manuel Garay (1873–1899) who held various government positions, including diplomatic posts in London, Paris, and Madrid. Charged with searching the Archivo General de las Indias for proof of Paraguay's title to the

Chaco, he compiled the valuable *Colección de documentos relativos a la historia de América–particularmente a la historia del Paraguay* (1899). In his brief life he also wrote histories of Paraguay based on archival research, founded *La Prensa*, and edited several other papers before his tragic death in a duel at the age of twenty-six on December 19, 1899.[10]

Alejandro Guanes (1872–1925), educated in Asunción and at the Colegio de San José in Buenos Aires, was one of the few poets whose verses are worth preserving. He collaborated with many of his fellow writers in editing various newspapers. Juan Francisco Pérez Acosta (1873–1967) published very little of importance until the Liberal era. Pérez Acosta's early career gave little indication of the literary prominence that he won later in life. As a young man he wrote for *La Democracia*, the Liberal party's dignified voice, *El Independiente*, and other papers. Eventually he was to be recognized as "dean of contemporary Paraguayan writers,"[11] an accolade fully deserved by his patient labors in archives and libraries. He was one of the first Paraguayan historians to make excellent use of the extraordinarily rich resources of Paraguay's Archivo Nacional.

Most of these writers participated in organizing literary clubs where they could entertain one another with their essays and poems, enjoy lively conversation, and forget the political arena in which many of them were bitter enemies. They founded reviews and literary journals, which generally died after a few numbers. Successful or not, these pioneers and their fellows laid the foundations for the literary renaissance that gave luster to the Liberal era.

Although very few newspapers have survived the Colorado era, journalists were very active. Newspapers were the principal outlet for poets, rhymsters, essayists, and political polemicists. A very notable feature of the Colorado era was freedom of the press. Most of the sixty or so newspapers that appeared in Asunción during the 1878–1904 period were party organs. As the fortunes of political factions changed, so did their journalistic endeavors. Most papers survived for a few months, or, at best, a few years—and deserved their fate. By far the best of all the newspapers was *La Democracia*, founded by Ignacio Ibarra on March 1, 1881, and which survived until 1904. Only occasionally did Colorado officials intervene to close an irresponsible paper. Plácido Casaús, or Casajús, master of vituperative satire, entertained a limited audience with the Sunday *La Verdad Autógrafa*, which first appeared on March 15, 1885. This weekly soon changed into *El Látigo* and then to *El Látigo Inmortal*. That Colorados endured its biting sarcasm and wild exaggerations until September 20, 1892, is a tribute to their genuine interest in a free press, or perhaps a measure of their indifference.

"Let her go to church to SEE the Mass,
since she does not understand it"

After the tumultuous 1870s, there was very little excitement in the church. The Paraguayan clergy had regained their religious independence with the appointment of Padre Pedro Juan Aponte as bishop on October 15, 1879. To be certain that no foreigner would ever again be in a dominant clerical position, Congress in 1882 required that all vicars-general be native Paraguayans. When the papal delegate to the Platine republics precipitated an argument in Argentina over religious instruction in normal schools, José Segundo Decoud said that if he tried it in Paraguay, the delegate would receive his passports promptly.[12] There would be no more outside dictation to the Paraguayan church! Nevertheless, one day a week was reserved for religious instruction in Paraguay's normal schools, but attendance was voluntary. Decoud held a justifiably low opinion of the rural clergy and was reported as having said:

> They are not only ignorant, and therefore quite incapable of imparting religious knowledge; but also grossly immoral, and therefore equally incapable of setting a good example, in the way of virtuous living, to their parishioners. They, as a rule, live in open concubinage with their mistresses; . . . in fact, the enforced celibacy of the clergy in this Country especially, was the greatest of all evils; and he himself, good Catholic as he trusted he was, could only hope that the day would come when its obligation would be legally annulled.[13]

To improve the quality of the clergy, governmental subsidies enabled young men to study at the Colegio Pio Latino Americano in Rome and at the Seminario Conciliar in Asunción. The minister of justice, worship, and public instruction attributed much of the harmonious church-state relationship to Bishop Aponte's wise leadership. At the same time he regretted that the budget had allowed the ministry to start repairs on only six churches and to build one new one at the newly founded Villa Florida.[14]

Rural Paraguay was very poorly served by the church. Even relatively large towns lacked regularly assigned priests, a neglect that imposed minimal hardships upon a people who regarded religious obligations lightly. Religious services were attended indifferently, and then usually by women and children; occasionally a man would slip inside to stand just beside the church door in order to make a quick departure. Religious holidays, usually accompanied by fiestas, were noted for the boisterous behavior of men who consumed large quantities of fiery caña. The little village of Caacupé, site of an annual pilgrimage on December 8, took on all the aspects of a carnival and market to serve the hundreds of pilgrims who came to pray to the richly attired Blue Virgin on whose beautiful gown they pinned thousands of paper pesos.

The death of Bishop Aponte on September 14, 1891, left the church without a bishop for four years, during which time Padre Claudio Arrua was ad interim administrator of the diocese of Paraguay. A good man, Arrua was far from being as capable as the wise, tolerant, and progressive Aponte, who was deeply mourned throughout the republic. As Aponte's successor, government officials and leading clergymen finally selected a truly remarkable man, the learned and universally respected Juan Sinforiano Bogarín (1863–1939), whom His Holiness accepted as bishop on June 30, 1895. Under Bishop Bogarín, the church won widespread support, at least in nuclear Paraguay. A firm believer in the separation of church and state, and an uncompromising advocate of Catholic doctrine, Bogarín nevertheless exercised a strong influence in government.

Bogarín welcomed the efforts of Protestant missionaries among wild Indians of the Chaco, a field in which Catholics had done almost nothing after the colonial period. England's South American Missionary Society had six missionaries in the Chaco in 1896, and early in 1897 the Reverend Mr. William Barbrooke Grubb and two companions sailed from England to join them. Grubb, an old hand at missionary work in South America, had arrived in Paraguay for the first time in 1889 to succeed a missionary to the Lengua Indians who had died at his station near Concepción. Because of his daring and success in the Chaco, the Paraguayan government gave him the imposing title of Comisario General del Chaco y Pacificador de los Indios. Grubb's work, as well as Chaco settlement, was made much easier by the presence of reinforced military outposts near Bahía Negra and Olimpo. President Escurra was well pleased with the progress of the English mission which had been entrusted with converting the Lenguas.[15]

Methodist missionaries were active in Asunción in the 1890s. They established model schools and were so successful in avoiding controversy with the Catholics that Bishop E. W. Warren of Colorado received a very warm welcome when he visited Asunción in April 1898. Dr. John N. Ruffin, the American consul, added importance to Warren's visit by meeting him at the dock with a carriage, one of only three or four such vehicles in the capital.[16] Warren's speech before an appreciative audience in the Italian Salon on April 12 emphasized development of resources and education as the foundations for future greatness. Missionaries of the Methodist Episcopal Church were an important part of the small American colony in Asunción for many years.

At the end of the century there was a flurry of dissension as the Masons assailed the fanaticism of Catholic women. Many prominent

Paraguayans, including José Segundo Decoud, were Masons, and, in view of anticlerical sentiment during the postwar decade, the polemics of 1899 were not remarkable. A pseudonymous critic, signing himself "Tancredo," published a series of polemics in *La Reforma* to attack religious fanaticism which, he asserted, held Paraguayan women in its devilish grasp. Ignorant of natural philosophy that clearly explained certain religions to the human spirit, women were increasingly victimized. Tancredo condemned women for seeking solace in religious activities that caused them to "postpone the laborious but sweet satisfactions of the many domestic tasks demanded by care of the family; but women, terrorized by fears of eternal damnation, of purgatory and hell, with which they are threatened in the confessional, and under the influence of priests, neglect their natural duties in an effort to live eternally in God's presence."[17] Tancredo was disturbed by the frantic reception given by crowds of women to Bishop Bogarín when he returned from Rome after his consecration: "neither the fear of bubonic plague nor the orders of police, city authorities, and the Council of Public Health could contain that feminine avalanche of Asunción, that crazy, grotesque, ridiculous female uproar." The tumultuous greeting was a triumph of planning by the clergy, an outpouring of fanaticism that should be fought endlessly, Tancredo insisted, by every father who loved domestic peace and order. What man could keep a woman from the confessional? Tancredo also advised men to spend more time at home instead of wasting hours in coffee houses or clubs. He concluded his diatribe by urging that women be forbidden to confess: "Let her go to church to SEE the mass, since she does not understand it because she does not know Latin."[18]

This Masonic attack was an aberration, a hangover from the extreme liberalism of the postwar decade. Paraguay's Catholicism was innocuous; while women found comfort in the church, men generally gave only nominal allegiance to an institution tolerated if not revered.

"Until Not a Single Child Lacks the Benefits of Education"

Brave attempts to create an educational system began even before the Paraguayan war ended. The talented Doña Asunción Escalada opened her Escuela Central para Niñas (Central School for Girls) on November 7, 1869. This was followed quickly by the Escuela Municipal para Niños (Municipal School for Boys), directed by Francisco Valeti. In March 1870 the Triumvirate ordered jefes políticos and comandantes in all departments to set up elementary schools and decreed compulsory attendance. These efforts, however well intentioned, were pathetic. Rural areas lacked all the essentials for a school system except pupils. Probably a typical experience was that of Justo P. Flecha, who attempted to teach a score of boys at Laureles, near Humaitá, who were growing up in abysmal ignorance. He importuned the Bareiro government to send him paper, slates, erasers, arithmetic books, and clothes for his nearly naked charges. Pupils in Asunción fared much better and had opportunities for more than the rudiments of an education. The city government opened its *colegio*, a combination high school and junior college, on April 1, 1870. A Colegio Nacional, supported by the national government, opened on December 1, 1870, and the Colegio Nacional de Enseñanza Superior (National School of Higher Education), authorized in December 1876, opened in 1877. The Seminario Conciliar, to train clergymen, started on April 4, 1880, and had a much longer life than many of the other schools. Padre Julio C. Montagne, its first director, served until 1921.[19]

Prodded by Paraguay's few intellectuals, especially José Segundo Decoud, the Colorados made commendable efforts to improve education. Nearly everything remained to be done, from creating an educational policy to providing teachers, buildings, and equipment. Despite idle boasts, Paraguayans generally were far less interested in education than in creature comforts and pleasures, and there was very little economic surplus that could be directed into the improvement of social institutions. The national government was always in a precarious financial condition, venal politicians squandered limited resources, ignorant buffoons generally headed rural governments, and there was no firm tradition or commitment to education among the people.

The Caballero regime made some efforts to improve education. Caballero's advisers, concerned with cultural life, caused the general to sponsor colegios and normal schools, to subsidize students studying abroad, and to import foreign teachers. An ambitious Ateneo Paraguayo, founded privately in 1883, attempted to promote science, letters, and the arts.[20] Paraguay's School of Law was created in 1882 and attached to the Colegio Nacional. Prominent among its teachers were Ramón Zubizarreta, Domingo Giménez y Martín, and Leopoldo Gómez y Terán. The Colegio Nacional was noted for its lax discipline. The school, a journalist charged, was a "model of demoralization. This must be true when a policeman must be stationed there to prevent collegiate brawls. This must be true when the young men educated there emerge as examples of bad behavior." The writer blamed parents for not controlling their rowdy sons, who defied their professors and grouped themselves into militant political parties to the detriment of their studies. One professor who survived the ordeal of teaching in the Colegio was Padre Facundo Bienes y Girón, a graduate of the University of Salamanca, who came to Paraguay in

1877 and taught philosophy, theology, and letters for twenty-four years.[21]

President Caballero was justly proud of his efforts to promote education and was pleased to announce the opening of new schools. In his annual message of April 1, 1884, he proclaimed that "education is the basis of a people's prosperity and so long as it is not widely spread, we shall experience major difficulties in our political reorganization." One year later he announced that the government had spent 30,000 pesos on 99 public schools which enrolled 6,376 pupils. At the same time there were 1,272 pupils in 50 private schools.[22] The public schools received less than five pesos per pupil. The minister of justice, worship, and public instruction invariably requested more support for public education in his annual reports. Journalists, too, frequently urged larger appropriations, as did *La Nación* on the arrival of Domingo Faustino Sarmiento, whose fame as an educator was probably greater than his renown as a politician.

To escape the bitter winter in Buenos Aires, Sarmiento decided to visit Asunción. The famous Argentine enjoyed a hero's welcome when he arrived on July 25, 1887. More than three thousand people are said to have met his ship, while a committee of notables, headed by Senator José Segundo Decoud, welcomed him officially. Although Sarmiento had been president of Argentina during the last two years of the Paraguayan War, he was not considered an enemy. Paraguay welcomed him as an apostle of liberty, education, and human dignity. In November he went back to Buenos Aires but returned to Asunción in May 1888. He continued his literary contributions to *El Independiente*, articles he had begun during his first visit, and constantly urged the government to make greater efforts on behalf of education. Sarmiento died in Asunción on September 11, 1888, sincerely mourned wherever his name was known.[23]

Sarmiento's arrival in Paraguay coincided with congressional consideration of President Escobar's recommendation that two normal schools, one for men and one for women, be established.[24] Congress responded with a comprehensive law of October 24, 1887, that created the Departamento General de Educación, controlled by a Consejo Superior de Educación, within the ministry of justice. The new department and council were given broad powers over personnel, finances, curricula, texts, libraries, and equipment. Districts or departments that would subscribe 500 pesos for a library would receive matching funds from the government. Once more the law made education compulsory for boys from seven to fourteen and for girls from six to twelve.

This basic law was concerned principally with primary education. Decoud, Paraguay's foremost champion of education in the Colorado era, presented a bill on September 24, 1889, to improve secondary and higher education. He proposed colegios nacionales for Villa Rica, Villa del Pilar, and Villa Concepción, a university for Asunción, and greater financial support for all schools. An enthusiastic Congress passed Decoud's "Ley de Enseñanza Secundaria" over President Escobar's veto. In addition to providing for colegios, the law created the Universidad Nacional in Asunción. The immediate result of this law was a surge in public education as the Council subsidized more than one thousand schools with an enrollment of 28,526 students, more than double the 1887 enrollment of 13,346. The total cost was only 289,968 pesos, of which 103,461 pesos went to the Colegio Nacional in Asunción.[25] Support for rural schools obviously continued to be extremely niggardly.

President González failed to enforce the Decoud law vigorously. Two colegios, he believed, would suffice to provide students for the university which, because of the depression of 1890, should be closed for a year. Students enrolled would be given subsidies to continue their studies abroad.[26] A year later, González reversed his attitude toward education as he lectured Congress on the need for better schools: "Public education is a concern of the most transcendental importance in a democratically ruled country. It requires sacrifices and a persevering consecration but its results fully repay the efforts that a Nation makes in pursuit of its moral and intellectual rebirth. It is not possible to create a civilized and republican nation without educated citizens, and to achieve this worthy goal, we need to increase our schools until not a single child lacks the benefits of education."[27] González had been alarmed by educational statistics for 1890: there were 292 rural elementary schools with 448 teachers and 18,944 pupils. The majority of children were not in school.

Asunción continued to fare far better than the rural areas. In 1901, for example, 25,247 pupils were enrolled in public schools in all of Paraguay. In Asunción alone there were 205 teachers for 5,147 pupils; in the rest of the country there were 547 teachers for 20,100 pupils. The shortage of qualified teachers was chronic. In an effort to alleviate the shortage, pedagogy was added to the curricula of the colegios, whose graduates could then teach in primary schools.[28]

José Segundo Decoud's dream of a university was realized when President Escobar on December 31, 1889, issued a decree to create the Universidad Nacional. The School of Law, which had been closed from 1883 to 1886, was absorbed into the School of Law and Social Sciences, where Dr. Ramón Zubizarreta in law, Dr. Alejandro Audibert in political economy and history, and Dr. Ramón de Olascoaga in literature, were noted teachers. There were four graduates in 1893, the first lawyers to come from the Paraguayan educational system. Addition of a School of Medicine was an expression of hope rather than recognition of reality, since it was closed in 1892. The new university had a very uncertain beginning. At the end of 1899, there were only 24 students in law, 26 in medicine, and 387 in the Colegio Nacional.[29]

Higher education in agriculture fared no better. The first school of agriculture, provided for by a law of September 24, 1887, was to be established in Colonia Presidente González. Under the direction of Carlos von Gülich, the school finally opened in 1892. Interest in the school and government support were so low that the institution was stillborn. Pressure for a school of agriculture continued to be exerted by private interests in the 1890s. When President Egusquiza gave his approval, Congress in October 1895 provided for the Escuela de Agricultura Práctica y Granja Modelo (School of Practical Agriculture and Model Farm) to be established near the capital and staffed with experts. The school, which began officially in October 1896 in Trinidad, was forced to close by the plague epidemic in 1897. Reopened in the same year under the direction of Dr. Moisés S. Bertoni, the school enrolled fifty-seven students who studied meteorology, agriculture, arboriculture, horticulture, botany, zoology, chemistry, and such cultural subjects as Spanish grammar, morality, and religion.[30]

The Colorados' efforts on behalf of education must be termed at best only a limited success. A few prominent teachers, lawyers, and medical doctors held degrees from the Escuela Normal, Colegio Nacional, and Universidad Nacional in Asunción. Far more preferred to complete their education abroad, especially in Argentina. Throughout the Colorado era appropriations for education were grossly inadequate. Teachers were scarce, poorly trained, badly underpaid, and compelled to work with minimal materials while attempting to teach indifferent pupils who often were undernourished and suffering from various diseases. Of course, illiteracy was the rule rather than the exception. Unable to read even the biased newspapers published in the principal towns, the campesino was ignorant of national issues. Politically he was at the mercy of the local party apparatus, whose functionaries could exploit inherited loyalties not in the least endangered by education.

In Retrospect

Failures and mistaken policies aside, the Colorados must be given credit for having revived the Republic of Paraguay. When Cándido Bareiro became president in 1878, the country was little more than a geographical expression, an international derelict cast aside by the conquerors, of so little consequence that no country maintained a fully accredited minister in Asunción. Under Colorado rule, Paraguay slowly recovered its position in the family of nations, at least in South America, where both Brazil and Argentina by the 1890s were once more seriously concerned about the Paraguayan stance in international affairs.

Condemnation of Colorado political practices is inevitable if one balances them against the constitution of 1870. The most charitable of judgments holds that Colorados violated the constitution only to the extent necessary to ensure their continued domination of the government. Measures used to defeat opponents were crude, brutal—and effective. Practices followed by Caballero, Escobar, and their successors were not unique to Paraguay. Stolen elections, terrorism to prevent electoral opposition, bribery to assure dependable majorities, and even assassination were by no means unknown even in the most advanced republics, and Paraguay was a backward nation unschooled in democracy, held together only by a primitive drive to survive. A few Colorados, especially José Segundo Decoud, Juan Crisóstomo Centurión, and Gregorio Benítez, were well acquainted with the political histories and practices of France, Great Britain, the United States, and other nations. Just how much of that knowledge was reflected in advice to Colorado leaders is impossible to determine.

Isolated and parochial as it undoubtedly was, Paraguay did not exist in a vacuum. While by no means a blanket pardon for Colorado political practices, the example of Argentina, with which a great many Paraguayans felt a natural affinity, must have been significant. Brazil, too, showed scant respect for Paraguayan sovereignty. Colorados at least maintained a precarious political peace during very critical years, a peace that, despite Liberal revolts in 1891 and 1904, was even more remarkable in view of the turmoil that followed the end of their first period of dominance.

José Segundo Decoud emerges with enhanced prestige from a close study of the Colorado era. Decoud's ideas were centerpieces in many presidential messages and policies. A Colorado for convenience, a pragmatic politician, Decoud never deserted major tenets of his liberal philosophy. Paraguayan historians have been too hasty in attributing to Bernardino Caballero the major role in developing coloradismo, a term that means little more than the Colorado system or methods of government. In shifting credit to Decoud, one must also charge that statesman with some glaring mistakes. Decoud's willingness to sacrifice much of Paraguay's claim to the Chaco Boreal detracts considerably from his luster as a diplomat and patriot, and his willingness to sell off the public domain for immediate financial advantage resulted in long-range ill effects on Paraguay's land system by creating a new class of latifundistas, by making acquisition of land for agricultural colonies unnecessarily expensive, by imposing insurmountable obstacles to creation of a class of small landowners.

Bernardino Caballero had the prestige, the well-deserved popularity so necessary for political leadership. Decoud, tainted in public view as a legionario, could never alone have exercised decisive influence in Paraguayan affairs. Paraguayans understood and trusted Caballero; they tolerated Decoud but were skeptical of his patriotism. A consistent champion of improved education, Decoud never relaxed his efforts to promote Paraguay's school system at all levels. Colorado economic policies, for which Decoud bears a large measure of responsibility, did result in a great influx of much-needed foreign capital, especially after 1900, and encouraged native capitalists to invest in their own country. One must not be too hasty in attributing sale of the public domain primarily to Decoud. Pressure for this policy undoubtedly came from many sources and Decoud could not have prevented the process. Obviously, there were many more men whose ideas helped to shape Colorado policies and to guide Colorado leaders. The influence of these men, identifiable through their economic activities, needs to be assessed much more carefully before a valid judgment can be entered confidently in the ever changing historical record.

Prominent though it was, Argentine-Brazilian rivalry for control of Paraguay can be easily overemphasized. Brazil's gross interference in Paraguayan politics in 1894, more than balanced by Argentine support of the 1904 rebellion, did little to change the direction of Paraguayan political development. And, in view of the tumultuous years of Liberal rule after 1904, Argentine statesmen could not have been proud of their country's role in the August Revolution. The surge in foreign investment that came after 1900 was the result of Colorado policies, the availability of venture capital in foreign countries, the obvious advantages of investment in a country whose government was friendly to enterprisers, and a slow realization abroad of opportunities waiting to be seized. Politically, Argentina and Brazil played to a stalemate; economically, Argentina emerged the clear victor. But the game was not over, and one sees in the present tremendous hydroelectric power developments a continuation of the old Luso-Hispanic rivalry.

Colorado emphasis on agricultural colonization was perfectly sound, and much of the country's contemporary progress can be attributed to extensive colonization, especially on the Alto Paraná where pioneering German colonists at Hohenau set a notable example. Paraguay's success in agricultural colonies fully vindicates the Colorado faith in that means of promoting economic development.

While Paraguay surely appeared to be a cultural wasteland to the casual observer during the Colorado era, there were important beginnings that were eventually to bear fruit in literature and the arts. The quality of life, at best a precarious thing, improved very slowly. Still, an impartial, sympathetic observer looking back over the years from the vantage point of December 1904, would have been deeply impressed by Colorado achievements in guiding Paraguay through an apparently interminable morass.

Abbreviations
Notes
Bibliography
Index

Abbreviations

AGJIG	Archivo del General José Ignacio Garmendia
AGM-DC	Archivo del General Mitre. Documentos y correspondencia
AGN-BA	Archivo General de la Nación, Buenos Aires
AHI-MRD	Arquivo Histórico de Itamaraty, Ministério das Relações Diplomáticas
ANA-SH	Archivo Nacional, Asunción, Sección Histórica
AVP	Archivo de Victorino de la Plaza
CCAP	Colección de Carlos Alberto Pusineri Scala, Asunción
CE	Coleções Especiais
Col. Cot.	Coleção Barão de Cotegipe
Cen.	Central (in Brazilian despatches)
Conf.	Confidencial, confidential
DCR	Diplomatic and Consular Reports
DDA	Diplomatic despatches from United States Ministers to Argentina
DDPU	Diplomatic Despatches from United States Ministers to Paraguay and Uruguay
DIPU	Diplomatic Instructions of the Department of State, 1801–1906. Paraguay and Uruguay
DO	Diario Oficial
DUSCA	Despatches from United States Consuls in Asunción
ENCL.	Enclosure
GC-UCR	Godoi Collection, University of California-Riverside
GP	Juan Bautista Gill Papers
HAHR	Hispanic American Historical Review
IAEA	Inter-American Economic Affairs
JIASW	Journal of Inter-American Studies and World Affairs
MDBA-D	Missões Diplomáticas Brasileiras, Assumpção, Despachos
MDBA-OR	Missões Diplomáticas Brasileiras, Assumpção, Oficios Recebidos
MDBBA-OR	Missões Diplomáticas Brasileiras, Buenos Aires, Oficios Recebidos
MEVA	Missões Especiais Visconde de Arinos
MH	Ministerio de Hacienda, Paraguay
MI	Ministerio del Interior, Paraguay
MRE-A	Ministerio de Relaciones Exteriores, Argentina
MRE-P	Ministerio de Relaciones Exteriores, Paraguay
NPFO	Notes from the Paraguayan Foreign Office
NPL	Notes from the Paraguayan Legation in the United States to the Department of State
PMR	Paraguay Monthly Review

PRO-FO   Public Record Office—Foreign Office (FO 6, Argentina; FO 13,
                 Brazil; FO 59, Paraguay)
RADI   *Revista Argentina de Derecho Internacional*
RCBA-O   Repartições Consulares Brasileiras Asunção, Oficios
Res.   Reservado (in Brazilian despatches)
RIP   *Revista del Instituto Paraguayo*
RM   *Revista Mensual*
RO   *Registro Oficial*
RP   *Revista del Paraguay*
RPCD   República del Paraguay, Cámara de Diputados
RPCS   República del Paraguay, Cámara de Senadores
RPS   *Revista Paraguaya de Sociología*
Sec.   Secção (in Brazilian despatches)

Notes

Preface

1. Several months after having completed the manuscript of this study, I learned of a doctoral dissertation by Ricardo Caballero Aquino, "The Economic Reconstruction of Paraguay in the Postwar Period: Politics and Property in the Era of General Caballero, 1869-1904," which was completed at Southern Illinois University in December, 1980. This dissertation by a native Paraguayan contains valuable insights that supplement the present work. Neither Dr. Caballero Aquino, former editor of the Cultural Supplement of *ABC Color* in Asunción, nor I knew that we were working on the same period.

Chapter 1. The Land, the People, the Towns

1. Joseph Pincus, *The Economy of Paraguay*, p. 7.
2. Emmanuel de Bourgade la Dardye, *Paraguay, the Land and the People*, p. 14.
3. See figure 3 in Norman R. Stewart, *Japanese Colonization in Eastern Paraguay*, p. 5.
4. Adlai F. Arnold, *Foundations of an Agricultural Policy in Paraguay*, p. 7.
5. For an excellent description of Paraguayan geography, see Stewart, *Japanese Colonization*, pp. 25–28.
6. Arthur G. Vansittart, "Report by Mr. Vansittart on the Commerce, Finances &c. of Paraguay," *Sessional Papers, Accounts and Papers, Commercial Reports*, LXXI, 89. Hereafter Vansittart, "Report."
7. José Pedro Werneck Ribeiro de Aguilar to C. Francisco Diana, 1ª Sec. No. 38, Asunción, Oct. 22, 1889, MDBA-OR 201/2/3.
8. Henrique Mamede Lins de Almeida to Felippe Pereira, 2ª Sec. No. 19, Asunción, Sept. 14, 1893, MDBA-OR 201/2/5.
9. DCR No. 2121, *Paraguay 1897*, p. 3.
10. *La Nación*, Jan. 3, 1899.
11. Bourgade, *Paraguay*, p. 101.
12. John Hoyt Williams, "Observations on the Paraguayan Census of 1846," pp. 425, 436, and his *The Rise and Fall of the Paraguayan Republic, 1800–1870*, pp. 116–17; Harris Gaylord Warren, *Paraguay and the Triple Alliance*, pp. 31–33; *Anuario estadístico de la República del Paraguay*, Libro primero, p. 6.
13. M. G. and E. T. Mulhall, *Handbook of the River Plate* (5th ed., 1885), p. 626. Registration of vital statistics did not begin until January 1, 1889 (Decree No. 10,004, Oct. 33, 1888, *DO*, Oct. 26, 1888; Castello Branco to

Rodrigo Augusto da Silva, 1ª Sec. No. 4, Asunción, Nov. 20, 1888, RCBA-O 238/3/8). Response to this decree was spotty at best. In 1897, the Registro Civil registered only 84 births in Asunción, and 4,823 in 1898 (MI, *Memoria, 1898–99*, p. 8).

14. W. L. Schurz, *Paraguay: A Commercial and Industrial Handbook*, p. 11.

15. Ernst Mevert, *Reisebriefe aus Paraguay*, p. 18.

16. Vansittart, "Report," p. 84.

17. W. F. Mulhall and P. A. Freund, *Letters from Paraguay*, No. 30 (dates and pagination are irregular in this volume).

18. *La Democracia*, Dec. 29, 1891.

19. Frank G. Carpenter, "Undeveloped Empire," *Boston Globe*, Feb. 19, 1899, clipping in John N. Ruffin to David J. Hill, No. 88, Asunción, June 17, 1899, DUSCA T 329/5.

20. Gabriel Carrasco, *Cartas de viaje por el Paraguay, los territorios nacionales del Chaco, Formosa y Misiones y las provincias de Corrientes y Entre Rios*, p. 93; *Almanaque nacional del Paraguay para el año de 1886*, pp. 123, 190, 264.

21. *El Paraguayo*, Jan. 27, 1887.

22. Carrasco, *Viaje*, pp. 87–93; Jaime Molins, *Paraguay*, pp. 22–25.

23. Mulhall and Freund, *Letters*, No. 5, p. 14.

24. *Guía general de la República del Paraguay* (1907), p. 64.

25. MI, *Memoria, 1888*, pp. 43–46; MI, *Memoria, 1890*, pp. 6–7; *La Prensa*, Jan. 1, 1890; DCR No. 2121, *Paraguay 1897*, p. 11.

26. José Almeida e Vasconcellos to Villa Bela, 1ª Sec. No. 2 Res., Asunción, Dec. 31, 1878, MDBA-OR 201/1/15.

27. Héctor Francisco Decoud, *Geografía de la República del Paraguay*, p. 77; *El Paraguay*, April 19, 1887; DCR No. 2275, *Paraguay 1897*, p. 7; Cecil Gosling to Lansdowne, No. 12 Commercial, Asunción, June 22, 1904, PRO FO 59/62.

28. Francisco Regis de Oliveira to Cotegipe, Sec. Cen. No. 10, Asunción, June 24, 1887, MDBA-OR 201/2/2. The sign for the *peso fuerte*, or strong peso, was an *F* superimposed on an *S*. Since many printers lacked this character, the symbol $f (or $F) was frequently used.

29. *La Nación*, July 29, 1877.

30. Alexander F. Baillie, *A Paraguayan Treasure*, p. 180.

31. DCR No. 792, *Paraguay 1890*, p. 1; *La Democracia*, Sept. 24, 1891; *La Libertad*, May 23, 1893.

32. RPCD, *Actas de las sesiones del período legislativo del año 1871*, p. 30; José Auto da Silva Guimarães to Cotegipe, Asunción, Jan. 15, 1873, Col. Cot. 29/38; *Nación Paraguaya*, Oct. 4, 1873.

33. *Almanaque nacional del Paraguay para el año de 1886*, pp. 105–07; *La Nación*, Aug. 25 and Oct. 2, 1887; *El Independiente*, May 7, 1888.

34. Mulhall, *Handbook of the River Plate* (6th ed., 1892), p. 649; DCR No. 1006, *Paraguay 1892*, p. 17; DCR No. 2215, *Paraguay 1898*, p. 8.

35. Mulhall and Freund, *Letters*, No. 8.

36. Ibid.

37. Eben M. Flagg to Edwin F. Uhl, encl. in No. 143, Asunción, June 30, 1895, DUSCA T 329/3.

38. Mulhall and Freund, *Letters*, No. 8.
39. Vansittart, "Report," p. 86.
40. John N. Ruffin to David J. Hill, No. 76, Asunción, Jan. 11, 1899, DUSCA T 329/4.

Chapter 2. The Government

1. For an analysis of the constitution of 1870, *see* Warren, *Paraguay and the Triple Alliance*, pp. 77–92.
2. Pedro Ribeiro Moreira to Francisco de C. Soares Brandão, 2ª Sec. No. 5, Asunción, Aug. 16, 1883, RCBA-O 238/3/7.
3. Moreira, "Relatorio commercial e politico do anno findo de 1884," encl., Moreira to Manuel Pinto de Souza Dantas, 2ª Sec. No. 2, Asunción, Feb. 20, 1885, ibid.
4. Contemporary descriptions of Congress are in José de Almeida e Vasconcellos to Antônio Moreira de Barros, Sec. Cen. No. 34, Asunción, Aug. 21, 1879, MDBA-OR 201/1/15, and in Vansittart's "Report," p. 98.
5. Moreira to João da Matta Machado, 4ª Sec. No. 12 Conf., Asunción, Dec. 29, 1884, RCBA-O 238/3/7.
6. Brasilio Itiberê da Cunha to Castro Cerqueira, 2ª Sec. No. 8, Asunción, June 4, 1895, MDBA-OR 201/2/6.
7. Eligio Ayala, *Migraciones, ensayo escrito en Berna en 1915*, p. 54.
8. *El Centinela*, July 23, 1893; Decoud, *Geografía de la República del Paraguay*, pp. 70–71.
9. L. S. Sackville West, "Report on the Present Political, Financial, and Social State of the Republic of Paraguay," encl., West to Derby, No. 109 Conf., Buenos Aires, Oct. 30, 1875, PRO-FO 6/328.
10. Eben M. Flagg to Edwin F. Uhl, Asunción, June 30, 1895, DUSCA T 329/3.
11. Rafael Barrett, *El dolor paraguayo*, p. 223.
12. Teodosio González, *Infortunios del Paraguay*, pp. 62–64; Fernando Viera, *Colección legislativa de la República del Paraguay, 1842–1895*, passim.
13. *El Triunfo*, Oct. 12, 1903; González, *Infortunios del Paraguay*, pp. 423–24.
14. José Pedro Werneck Ribeiro de Aguilar to Justo Leite Chermont, 2ª Sec. No. 26, Asunción, Sept. 1, 1891, MDBA-OR 201/2/4; Edmund Shaw to Josiah Quincy, No. 89, Asunción, June 1, 1893, DUSCA T 329/3.
15. Shaw to W. F. Wharton, No. 46, Asunción, July 30, 1892, DUSCA T 329/3.
16. RO, 1870, pp. 84–85, 1872, pp. 321–23, and 1882, pp. 844–52.
17. MI, *Memoria 1890*, pp. 4–5, and *1898*, pp. 45–49; Gómes Freire Esteves, *El Paraguay contemporáneo*, p. 70.
18. Freire Esteves, *El Paraguay contemporáneo*, pp. 54–55; Vansittart, "Report," pp. 113–14.
19. F. Pakenham to Earl of Rosebery, No. 32, Buenos Aires, June 7, 1893, PRO-FO 59/50.
20. *Infortunios del Paraguay*, p. 52.
21. Ibid., p. 102.

22. Francisco Regis de Oliveira, "Histórico dos principães assumptos tratados pela legação do Brasil no Paraguay, durante o anno de 1886," encl., Oliveira to Cotegipe, 1ª Scc. No. 4, Asunción, Feb. 7, 1887, MDBA-OR 201/2/2.

23. *El Centinela*, May 28, 1893.

24. Issue of Feb. 16, 1893.

25. Juan Bautista Egusquiza, *Mensaje* (April, 1898), p. 4.

26. *El dolor paraguayo*, p. 185.

27. William Stewart, "Historia del Paraguay por el Dr. William Stewart," MS. CCAP.

28. *El Semanario*, July 16, 1859, p. 2.

29. Juan Carlos Mendonça, "La cronología de las generaciones paraguayas." The first Colorado era ended in 1904. Although Higinio Morínigo (1940–1948) was more of a Colorado than anything else, the second Colorado era began in 1954 with the ascendency of Alfredo Stroessner.

30. *Hombres y épocas del Paraguay*, I, 118–19.

31. The same attitude prevailed in the 1960s. See Frederic Hicks, "Interpersonal Relationships and Caudillismo in Paraguay."

32. *El Centinela*, April 3, 1893.

33. Itiberê da Cunha to Castro Cerqueira, 2ª Sec. No. 7 Res., Asunción, Nov. 4, 1898, MDBA—OR 201/2/6.

34. *El Paraguayo*, Jan. 28, 1887; Florentino del Valle, *Cartilla cívica: proceso político del Paraguay 1870–1950*, p. 59; *La Patria Paraguaya*, Sept. 7, 1900.

35. [Cecilio Báez], "Liberal manifesto," Oct. 18, 1891, *El Tiempo*, Nov. 2, 1891.

Chapter 3. Bareiro and the Colorado Triumph, 1878–1880

1. Gómes Freire Esteves, *El Paraguay constitutional*, p. 50.

2. Decree of Nov. 25, 1878, *RO* 1878, p. 16.

3. *La Reforma*, Nov. 27, 1878; Almeida to Villa Bella, 1ª Sec. No. 2 Res., Asunción, Dec. 31, 1878, MDBA-OR 201/1/15.

4. *La Reforma*, Dec. 13, 1878.

5. RPCS, *Actas* 1878, pp. 302–03.

6. *La Reforma*, Dec. 4, 1878, and May 1, 1879; Ramón Zubizarreta, "La cuestión de la moneda," p. 141.

7. La Reforma, Feb. 1879–June 30, 1880.

8. Zubizarreta, "La cuestión de la moneda," p. 142; *La Reforma*, Aug. 8, 1879.

9. Zubizarreta, "La cuestión de la moneda," p. 143; *La Reforma*, May 23, 1880.

10. Vasconcellos to Villa Bella, Sec. Cen. No. 4, Asunción, Aug. 8, 1878, and 1ª Sec. No. 2 Res., Asunción, Dec. 31, 1878, MDBA-OR 201/1/15; *La Reforma*, April 11 and June 8, 1880.

11. Vasconcellos to Villa Bella, Sec. Cen. No. 1 Res., Asunción, Jan. 3, 1879, MDBA-OR 201/1/15; Bray, *Hombres y épocas del Paraguay*, I, 103–04.

12. Vasconcellos to Villa Bella, Sec. Cen. No. 2 Res., Asunción, Jan. 21, 1879, MDBA-OR 201/1/15.

13. Same to same, Sec. Cen. No. 3 Res., Asunción, Feb. 8, 1879, ibid.

14. Vasconcellos to Antônio Moreira de Barros, Sec. Cen. No. 1 Res., Asunción, Jan. 25, 1880, MDBA-OR 201/l/16.

15. Nicanor Godoi to Juansilvano Godoi, Corrientes, Feb. 1, 1880, GC-UCR; Moreira de Barros to Vasconcellos, Sec. Cen. No. 1. Res., Rio de Janeiro, Feb. 24, 1880, MDBA-D-201/1/10.

16. Cándido Bareiro, *Mensaje* (April, 1879), passim; *RO* 1879, p. 224; Vasconcellos to João Lins Vieira Cansanção de Sinimbú, 1ª Sec. No. 5 Res., Asunción, May 1, 1879, MDBA-OR 201/1/15. For the religious question, see Warren, *Paraguay and the Triple Alliance*, pp. 169–75.

17. Vasconcellos to Sinimbú, 1ª Sec. No. 15, Asunción, June 12, 1879, MDBA-OR 201/1/15; Francis Clare Ford to Salisbury, No. 66, Buenos Aires, June 15, 1879, PRO-FO 6/353; Héctor Francisco Decoud to Adolfo Decoud, Asunción, Dec. 27, 1877, GC-UCR.

18. The *Galileo* had reached Corrientes on June 6 (*El Porteño*, June 6, 1879, copy in GC-UCR).

19. *RO*, 1879, pp. 511–14; *El Comercio*, June 12, 14, 21, and 24, 1879; Vasconcellos to Sinimbú, 1ª Sec. No. 6 Res., Asunción, June 30, 1879, MDBA-OR 201/1/15.

20. "Inventario del armamento y equipos militares tomados al vapor 'Galileo' y trasbordados al vapor de guerra argentino 'Resguardo'," GC-UCR.

21. *Boletín oficial*, July 5, 1879; Bareiro, *Manifiesto*, July 5, 1879, copies in MDBA-OR 201/1/15; *El Comercio*, June 14, 1879; Vasconcellos to Moreira de Barros, 1ª Sec. No. 21, Asunción, Aug. 5, 1879, *El Comercio*, June 14, 1879.

22. Law of July 4, 1879, *RO*, 1879, pp. 521–23.

23. M. M., "Paraguay. 25 de noviembre de 1882," p. 34.

24. Cándido Bareiro, *Mensaje* (April, 1880), passim.

25. Vasconcellos to Souza, 1ª Sec. No. 1 Res., Asunción, Sept. 8, 1880, MDBA-OR 201/1/16.

26. *La Reforma*, Sept. 5, 1880.

Chapter 4: Bernardino Caballero, 1880–1886

1. Freire Esteves, *El Paraguay constitucional*, p. 53; M. M., "Paraguay. 25 de noviembre de 1882," p. 33; Brizuela to Cotegipe, Montevideo, Sept. 17, 1880, Col. Cot. 11/45.

2. Freire Esteves, *El Paraguay constitucional*, p. 54. A copy is in GC-UCR.

3. *Hombres y épocas del Paraguay*, I, 94.

4. Vasconcellos to Pedro Luiz Pereira de Souza, 1ª Sec. No. 1 Res., Asunción, Sept. 8, 1880, MDBA-OR 201/1/16.

5. Brizuela to Cotegipe, Montevideo, Sept. 17, 1880, Col. Cot. 11/45.

6. *La Reforma*, Sept. 6, 1880. For more on journalism, see Harris Gaylord Warren, "Journalism in Asunción under the Allies and the Colorados, 1869–1904."

7. Hipólito Sánchez Quell, *Proyección del General Caballero en la ruta de la patria*, p. 28.

8. Rio Branco to São Vicente, Buenos Aires, Jan. 9, 1871, "Cartas do

Visconde do Rio Branco," *Anuário do Museu Imperial* (Petropolis, 1951), XII, 37; Henri Pitaud, *El General Caballero*, p. 81.

9. Sánchez Quell, *Proyección del General Caballero*, p. 31.

10. Vasconcellos to Souza, 1ª Sec. No. 1 Res., Asunción, Sept. 18, 1880, MDBA-OR 201/1/16; George Glynn Petre to Granville, Asunción, No. 14, June 20, 1882, PRO-FO 59/39.

11. Edwin A. Egerton to Granville, No. 50, Buenos Aires, July 31, 1881, PRO-FO 6/364.

12. Bray, *Hombres y épocas del Paraguay*, I, 105.

13. Juan Silvano Godoi, *Mi misión a Rio de Janeiro*, p, 83; *La Reforma*, Nov. 27, 1878; Egerton to Granville, No. 50, Buenos Aires, July 31, 1881, PRO-FO, 6/364.

14. Bacon to Bayard, Montevideo, No. 193, Oct. 19, 1887, DDPU 128/7.

15. Brasilio Itiberê da Cunha to Olynthe de Magalhães, 2ª Sec. No. 3, Asunción, March 15, 1900, MDBA-OR 201/2/7.

16. *El Diario*, March 6, 1909.

17. Efraím Cardozo, *Hace cién años*, VI, 174.

18. Carlos R. Centurión, *Historia de la cultura paraguaya*, I, passim.

19. Pedro Ribeiro Moreira, "Relatorio commercial e politico do anno findo de 1884," RCBA-O 238/3/7.

20. *La Reforma*, June 9, 1881.

21. Harris Gaylord Warren, "The Paraguay Central Railway, 1856–1889," pp. 15–16.

22. *El Diario*, Sept. 4, 1881; *La Democracia*, Nov. 8, 1881; Vasconcellos to Souza, Sec. Cen. No. 25, Asunción, Nov. 9, 1881, MDBA-OR 201/1/16.

23. *La Reforma*, Aug. 10, 1881; Vasconcellos to Franklin Americo de Meneses Doria, Sec. Cen. No. 34, Asunción, Dec. 21, 1881, MDBA-OR 201/1/16.

24. *La República* (Buenos Aires), Feb. 13 and May 10, 1881; *La Reforma*, Dec. 14, 1881.

25. *La Democracia*, Oct. 11, 1881; Vasconcellos to Souza, 1ª Sec. No. 15, Asunción, Oct. 12, 1881, MDBA-OR 201/1/16.

26. Henrique Mamede Lins de Almeida to Felippe Franco de Sá, 1ª Sec. No. 3, Asunción, March 10, 1882, and 1ª Sec. No. 1 Conf., Asunción, March 30, 1882, MDBA-OR 201/2/1; Franco de Sá to Almeida, 1ª Sec. No. 1 Conf., Rio de Janeiro, April 28, 1882, MDBA-D 201/4/10.

27. See Cavalcanti de Lacerda's despatches to Franco de Sá in April and May, 1882, MDBA-OR 201/2/1.

28. Bernardino Caballero, *Mensaje* (April, 1882), p. 4.

29. Brizuela to Cotegipe, Montevideo, Sept. 2, 1882, Col. Cot. 11/46.

30. Florentino del Valle, *Cartilla cívica*, p. 59.

31. Hipólito Sánchez Quell, *Falando do Paraguai ao Brasil*, p. 44.

32. Edmund Monson to Granville, No. 7 Paraguay Conf., Assumption, Oct. 14, 1884, PRO-FO 59/41.

33. Caballero, *Mensaje* (April, 1885), p.5.

34. July 26, 1885; *La Verdad*, March 22, 1885.

35. Caballero, *Mensaje* (April, 1886), p. 507.

36. *El Paraguayo*, April 12, 1887; *La Palabra* (Montevideo), July 16, 1887; *La Nación* (Buenos Aires), July 27 and 28, 1887.

Chapter 5. Escobar and Party Formation, 1886–1890

1. Bray, *Hombres y épocas del Paraguay*, I, 108.
2. Juan Silvano Godoi, *Monografías históricas*, p. 108 n.
3. Henri Pitaud, *El General Caballero*, p. 169; Bray, *Hombres y épocas del Paraguay*, I, 109.
4. Pedro Candido Affonso de Carvalho to João Lustosa da Cunha Paranaguá, 1ª Sec. No. 20, Asunción, July 29, 1885, MDBA-OR 201/2/2.
5. Centurión, *Historia da la cultura paraguaya*, II, 334–36; *El Orden*, July 29, 1885.
6. Carvalho to Paranaguá, 1ª Sec. No. 20, Asunción, July 29, 1885, MDBA-OR 201/2/2; *El Orden*, July 29, 1885.
7. Francisco Regis de Oliveira to Cotegipe, Sec. 1ª No. 11, Asunción, Nov. 26, 1886, MDBA-OR 201/2/2; *El Paraguay*, Nov. 26, 1886; *La Democracia*, Nov. 26, 1886.
8. Harris Gaylord Warren, "Banks and Banking in Paraguay, 1871–1904."
9. *El Sud-Americano* (Buenos Aires), Aug. 5, 1888; *La Prensa* (Buenos Aires), Jan. 1, 1890.
10. MI, *Memoria, 1888*, p 10.
11. José Werneck Ribeira de Aguilar to Quintana Bocayuva, Sec. Cen. No. 9, Asunción, March 27, 1890, MDBA-OR 201/2/4.
12. José de la Cruz Ayala, Cecilio Báez, Manuel Curuchet, and Domingo Giménez y Martín were associates (Centurión, *Historia de la cultura paraguaya*, I, 530).
13. *El Látigo Inmortal*, Nov. 27, 1887.
14. *La Cotorra*, Feb. 13 and March 6, 1887.
15. *El Látigo Inmortal*, Jan. 8, 1888.
16. Harold F. Peterson, "Edward A. Hopkins, a Pioneer Promoter in Paraguay"; Warren, "The Hopkins Claim Against Paraguay and the Case of the Missing Jewels," pp. 23–44.
17. Pablo Max Ynsfran, *La expedición norteamericana contra el Paraguay, 1858–1859*, I, 161–246.
18. Juan F. Pérez Acosta, *Carlos Antonio López, obrero máximo: labor administrativo y constructivo*, pp. 433–38; Pablo Max Ynsfran, "Sam Ward's Bargain with President López of Paraguay."
19. Bayard to Bacon, No. 12, Washington, Dec. 26, 1885, DIPU 77/128.
20. Bacon to Bayard, No. 188, Montevideo, Oct. 5, 1887, DDPU 128/7.
21. Decoud to Caldwell, Asunción, June 19, 1881, NPFO 603/3.
22. Frederick T. Frelinghuysen to Williams, No. 41, Washington, March 25, 1884, DIPU 77/128.
23. Oliveira to Cotegipe, 1ª Sec. No. 9, Asunción, Aug. 5, 1887, MDBA-OR 201/2/2.
24. Hopkins to Bacon, Buenos Aires, Oct. 22, 1887, encl., Bacon to Bayard, No. 193, Montevideo, Oct.19, 1887, DDPU 128/7.
25. Victor C. Dahl, "The Paraguayan 'Jewel Box'."
26. John Hay to William R. Finch, Washington, No. 140, Nov. 27, 1889, DIPU 11/45; Blaine to George Cheney, No. 102, Washington, Nov. 30, 1889, ibid.

27. Carlos Pastore, *La lucha por la tierra en el Paraguay*, pp. 249–51.

28. Epifanio Méndez Fleitas, *Lo histórico y lo anti-histórico en el Paraguay—carta a los Colorados*, p. 16.

29. Warren, *Paraguay and the Triple Alliance*, pp. 196–214; F. Arturo Bordón, *Liberales ilustres*, pp. 18–20; Justo Pastor Benítez, *Ensayo sobre el liberalismo paraguayo*, pp. 9–17; Cecilio Báez, *Cuadros históricos y descriptivos*, p. 241.

30. Benítez, *Ensayo sobre el liberalismo paraguayo*, p. 17.

31. *El Paraguayo*, Feb. 8, 1870.

32. Mulhall and Freund, *Letters*, p. 34.

33. *El Paraguayo*, Feb. 18, 1887.

34. Ibid., Feb. 18 and 24, March 3 and 25, April 2, May 3, 1887.

35. Oliveira to Cotegipe, 1ª Sec. No. 5, Asunción, April 2, 1887, MDBA-OR 201/2/2.

36. Valle, *Cartilla cívica*, pp. 14–15; Báez, *Cuadros históricos*, p. 242; *La Democracia*, July 11, 1887.

37. Valle, *Cartilla cívica*, p. 20. Names of the founding members are in Báez, *Cuadros históricos*, p. 247; Benítez, *Ensayo sobre el liberalismo paraguayo*, pp. 12–14; and Bordón, *Liberales ilustres*, passim.

38. *La Nación*, Aug. 27, 1887.

39. Henry D. Ceuppens, *Paraguay año 2000*, p. 45; *La Nación*, Aug. 27 and Sept. 4, 1887; Valle, *Cartilla cívica*, p. 21; Bordón, *Liberales ilustres*, p. 6.

40. *La Nación*, Sept. 4, 10, and 11, 1887.

41. Carvalho to Cotegipe, 1ª Sec. No. 19, Asunción, Dec. 16, 1887, and 1ª Sec. No. 24, Asunción, Dec. 31, 1887, MDBA-OR 201/2/2.

42. *El Sud-Americano* (Buenos Aires), June 15, 1888.

43. Carvalho to Rodrigo A. da Silva, Sec. Cen. No. 15, Asunción, Oct. 7, 1888, MDBA-OR 201/2/3.

44. *La Nación*, Aug. 30 and Sept. 8, 1887.

45. See issues of Aug. 28, Sept. 11, Oct. 30, and Nov. 4, 18, 20 and 27, 1887.

46. Freire Esteves, *Historia Contemporánea*, p. 66.

47. *La Razón*, Sept. 19, 1889; *La Democracia*, Sept. 20, 1889.

48. Aguilar to D. Francisco Diana, 1ª Sec. No. 36, Asunción, Oct. 8, 1889, and 1ª Sec. No. 42, Asunción, Nov. 13, 1889, MDBA-OR 201/2/3.

49. *La Razón*, Nov. 8, 1889.

50. Antonio Taboada to Juan Silvano Godoi and Benigno Ferreira, Asunción, Oct.30, 1889, GC-UCR.

51. *El Látigo*, Oct. 11, Nov. 17, Dec. 6 and 8, 1889.

52. Ibid., Jan. 5, 1890.

53. [Antonio Taboada], *Memoria* (Centro Democrático, 1890), passim.

54. *La Razón*, April 8, 1890; *La Democracia*, April 18, 1890; Aguilar to Quintana Bocayuva, 1ª Sec. No. 11, Asunción, April 9, 1890, MDBA-OR 201/2/4.

55. Patricio Escobar, *Mensaje* (April, 1890), p. 9.

56. José Irala to Nicanor Godoi, Asunción, Jan. 25, 1890, GC-UCR; Irala to Benigno Ferreira, Asunción, Feb. 2, 1890, ibid.; Centurión to Martín García Merou, Asunción, Feb. 15, 1890, *DO*, Feb. 27, 1890.

57. Aguilar to Bocayuva, 1ª Sec. No. 13, Asunción, May 13, 1890, and 1ª Sec. No. 17, Asunción, June 18, 1890, MDBA-OR 201/2/4.

58. (Fernando Uriburu?) to Fereira, Asunción, Feb. 14, 1890, GC-UCR.

59. *La Razón*, July 22, 1890; Aguilar to Bocayuva, 1ª Sec. No. 21, Asunción, July 16, 1890, MDBA-OR 201/2/4.

60. H. F. Pakenham to Salisbury, Paraguay No. 5 Conf., Asunción, Aug. 8, 1890, PRO-FO 59/48.

Chapter 6. The Trials of González, 1890–1894

1. José Pedro Werneck Ribeiro de Aguilar to Bocayuva, 1ª Sec. No. 35, Asunción, Nov. 28, 1890, MDAB-OR 201/2/3; *DO*, Nov. 27, 1890.

2. Aguilar to Bocayuva, 2ª Sec. No. 36, Asunción, Jan. 19, 1891, MDBA-OR 201/2/4.

3. Same to same, 1ª Sec. No. 36, Asunción, Dec. 10, 1890, ibid.

4. *La Democracia*, March 14, 1891; Aguilar to Tristão Alencar Araripe, 2ª Sec. No. 11, Asunción, March 24, 1891, MDBA-OR 201/2/4; *DO*, Sept. 1, 1891.

5. *La Democracia*, Aug. 29, 1892; *La República*, Sept. 27, 1892; *DO*, Oct. 1, 1892; Almeida to Custodio José de Mello, 3ª Sec. No. 8, Asunción, Oct. 5, 1892, and 3ª Sec. No. 9, Asunción, Oct. 14, 1892, MDBA-OR 201/2/4.

6. Aguilar to Araripe, 2ª Sec. No. 10, March 10, 1891, MDBA—OR 201/2/4.

7. Aguilar to Justo Leite Chermont, 2ª Sec. No. 14, Asunción, April 21, 1891, ibid.

8. *La Democracia*, April 13, 1891. Documentation relating to the revolt is in GC-UCR.

9. *La Democracia*, April 6, 1891; Aguilar to Leite Chermont, 2ª Sec. No. 13, Asunción, April 21, 1891, MDBA-OR 201/2/4. The official title was Presidente de la Comisión Directiva del Centro Democrático.

10. *La Democracia*, Aug. 18 and 22, Sept. 9, 24, and Oct. 7, 1891.

11. *El Tiempo*, Oct. 26 and 31, 1891.

12. Ibid., Nov. 2, 1891; Báez, *Cuadros históricos*, pp. 249–65.

13. *El Tiempo*, Oct. 31, 1891.

14. Edmund Shaw to William F. Wharton, No. 19, Asunción, Oct. 20, 1891, DUSCA T 329/3; Aguilar to Leite Chermont, 2ª Sec. No. 30, Asunción, Oct. 20, 1891, MDBA-OR 201/2/4; Luiz Antônio Correa de Sá to Leite Chermont, 2ª Sec. No. 1, Asunción, Oct. 20, 1891, RCBA-O 238/3/9; Higinio Arbo, *Política paraguaya*, p. 36; *El Tiempo*, Oct. 26, 1891; Efraím Cardozo, *Efemérides de la historia del Paraguay*, pp. 395–96.

15. Aguilar to Leite Chermont, 2ª Sec. No. 30, Asunción, Oct. 20, 1891 and 2ª Sec. No. 31, Asunción, Oct. 24, 1891, and 2ª Sec. No. 32, Asunción, Oct. 31, 1891, MDBA-OR 201/2/4.

16. *The Standard* (Buenos Aires), Oct. 23, 1891.

17. Estrada to Leite Pereira, 2ª Sec. No. 11, Asunción, March 22, 1892, MDBA-OR 201/2/5.

18. Juan Gualberto González, *Mensaje* (April, 1892), p. 21. González rewarded Egusquiza by promoting him to general.

19. Almeida to Mello, 2ª Sec. No. 8 Res., Asunción, Aug. 6, 1892, MDBA-OR 201/2/5; *DO*, Aug. 5, 1892.

20. Almeida to Mello, 2ª Sec. No. 9 Res., Asunción, Aug. 18, 1892, MDBA—OR 201/2/5; *El Tiempo*, Aug. 8, 1892; *El Independiente*, Aug. 18, 1892. On Nov. 17, 1893, Tattersall, Funes, Logos y Cía. in Buenos Aires sold at auction munitions that brought $45,062.20 gold to Godoi (inventory in GC-UCR).

21. *La Democracia*, Aug. 31, 1892.

22. Almeida to Mello, 2ª Sec. No. 17, Asunción, Nov. 12, 1892, MDBA—OR 201/2/5.

23. Same to same, 2ª Sec. No. 41, Asunción, Nov. 22, 1892, ibid.

24. Same to same, 2ª Sec. No. 43, Asunción, Dec. 6, 1892, ibid.

25. *El Independiente*, Dec. 14, 1892; *La Democracia*, Dec. 14, 1892; *El Tiempo*, Jan. 9, 1893; Almeida to Antônio Francisco Paula Souza, 2ª Sec. No. 2, Asunción, Jan. 16, 1893, MDBA-OR 201/2/5.

26. F. Arturo Bordón, *Historia política del Paraguay: era constitucional*, p. 194.

27. Almeida to Paula Souza, 2ª Sec. No. 5, Asunción, Feb. 16, 1893, MDBA-OR 201/2/5; *La Democracia*, Feb. 16, 1893; *La Libertad*, March 4 and 5, 1893.

28. Almeida to João Felipe Pereira, 2ª Sec. No. 19, Asunción, Sept. 14, 1893, MDBA-OR 201/2/5; Almeida to Cassiano do Nascimento, 2ª Sec. No. 3, Asunción, Feb. 3, 1893, ibid.; Almeida to Paula Souza, 2ª Sec. No. 8, Asunción, April 6, 1893, ibid.; *La República*, Sept. 15, 1893.

29. *La Democracia*, Oct. 4, 1893.

30. For Ferreira, see Bray, *Hombres y épocas del Paraguay*, II, 125–62.

31. Bacon to Bayard, No. 47, Montevideo, Feb. 16, 1886, DDPU 128/5.

32. Almeida to Paula Souza, 2ª Sec. No. 3 Res., Asunción, Jan. 31, 1893, MDBA-OR 201/2/5; *La Libertad*, April 3, 1893. Decoud toyed with the idea of an armed revolt and wrote to Godoi to inquire about arms. Godoi replied that arms would cost $25,300 gold (Godoi to Decoud, Buenos Aires, Jan. 12, 1893, GC-UCR).

33. Almeida to Paula Souza, 2ª Sec. No. 1 Res., Asunción, April 12, 1893, MDBA-OR 201/2/5.

34. Almeida to Filisberto Firmo de Oliveira Freire, 2ª Sec. No. 14, Asunción, June 2, 1893, ibid.

35. Almeida to Felippe Pereira, 2ª Sec. No. 32, Asunción, Oct. 4, 1893, ibid.

36. Almeida to Oliveira Freire, 2ª Sec. No. 13, Asunción, May 16, 1893, ibid.; *El Centinela*, June 4, 1893.

37. *El Centinela*, March 12, 1893.

38. Almeida to Barão de Cabo Frio, 2ª Sec. No. 9, Asunción, June 15, 1893, MDBA-OR 201/2/5.

39. *El Centinela*, June 11, 1893.

40. *La Democracia*, May 24 and 28, 1893.

41. Almeida to Oliveira Freire, 2ª Sec. No. 15, Asunción, June 30, 1893, and 2ª Sec. No. 16, Asunción, July 17, 1893, MDBA-OR 201/2/5.

42. *La República*, Nov. 22, 1892; Almeida to Felippe Pereira, 2ª Sec. No. 22, Asunción, Oct. 4, 1893, MDBA-OR 201/2/5.

43. Bernardino Caballero, *Carta programa*, Nov. 25, 1893, encl. Almeida to Nascimento, 2ª Sec. No. 26, Asunción, Nov. 22, 1893, ibid.

44. Almeida to Felippe Pereira, 2ª Sec. No. 22, Asunción, Oct. 4, 1893, ibid.

45. Almeida to Nascimento, 2ª Sec. No. 17, Nov. 30, 1893, ibid.

46. Cavalcanti to Nascimento, 2ª Sec. No. 3, Asunción, March 10, 1894, ibid.

47. Same to same, 2ª Sec. No. 1 Res., Asunción, March 17, 1894, ibid.

48. Nascimento to Cavalcanti, 2ª Sec. No. 4 Res., Rio de Janeiro, May 10, 1894, MDBA-D 201/4/11; Cavalcanti to Nascimento, 2ª Sec. No. 5, Asunción, May 31, 1894, and 2ª Sec. No. 2 Conf., Asunción, June 10, 1894, MDBA-OR 201/2/5.

49. Cavalcanti to Nascimento, 2ª Sec. No. 5, Asunción, May 31, 1894, MDBA-OR 201/2/5.

50. For further details, see Harris Gaylord Warren, "Brazil and the Cavalcanti Coup of 1894 in Paraguay," pp. 221–36.

51. Cavalcanti to Nascimento, 2ª Sec. No. 10, Asunción, Aug. 21, 1891, MDBA-OR 201/2/5.

52. Juan Gualberto González, *Manifiesto del presidente de la República del Paraguay D. Juan G. González a sus conciudadanos, June 30, 1894*, pp. 1–9.

Chapter 7. Egusquiza and the Politics of Conciliation, 1894–1898

1. Bray, *Hombres y épocas del Paraguay*, I, 123.

2. Ibid.

3. Frank G. Carpenter, "Underdeveloped Empire," *Boston Globe*, Feb. 19, 1899, clipping in John N. Ruffin to David J. Hill, No. 88, Asunción, June 17, 1899, DUSCA T 329/3.

4. Angel Martínez in interior, Héctor Velázquez in foreign affairs, Emilio Aceval in war and marine, Agustín Cañete in hacienda, and Rufino Mazó in justice.

5. Antônio Nunes Gomes Pereira to Carlos Augusto de Carvalho, 2ª Sec. No. 15, Res., Asunción, MDBA-OR 201/2/5.

6. Henrique Carlos Ribeiro Lisboa to Carvalho, 2ª Sec. No. 8, Asunción, March 22, 1895, MDBA-OR 201/2/6.

7. Juan B. Egusquiza, *Mensaje* (April, 1895), pp. 5–7.

8. Lisboa to Carvalho, 1ª Sec. No. 11, Asunción, April 2, 1895, MDBA—OR 201/2/6.

9. Same to same, 2ª Sec. No. 16, Asunción, May 15, 1895, and 2ª Sec. No. 17, Asunción, May 25, 1895, ibid.

10. *El Eco del Paraguay*, June 5, 1895; Lisboa to Carvalho, 2ª Sec. No. 18, Asunción, June 6, 1895, MDBA-OR 201/2/6.

11. Lisboa to Carvalho, 1ª Sec. No. 1 Conf., Asunción, Jan. 2, 1896, MDBA-OR 201/2/6.

12. Same to same, 2ª Sec. No. 28, Asunción, Oct. 28, 1896, ibid.

13. Juan B. Egusquiza, *Mensaje* (April, 1896), pp. 3–4.

14. Freire Esteves, *El Paraguay constitucional*, p. 80; Manuel Bernardez, *El tratado de la Asunción*, p. 22.

15. *El Diario* (Buenos Aires), Feb. 12, 1896.

16. Stuart to Richard Olney, No. 103, Montevideo, Jan. 13, 1897, DDPU 128/9.

17. Arbo, *Política paraguaya*, p. 36.

18. Gómes Freire Esteves, *Historia contemporánea del Paraguay*, p. 77.

19. Ibid.

20. Lisboa to Carvalho, 2ª Sec. No. 4 Res., Asunción, Dec. 3, 1895, and 2ª Sec. No. 32, Asunción, Dec. 19, 1895, MDBA-OR 201/2/6.

21. Carlos R. Centurión, *Historia de las letras paraguayas*, II, 48.

22. Freire Esteves, *Historia contemporánea*, p. 79.

23. *El Rayo*, Nov. 8, 1896.

24. "Contrato entre D. Enrique López y el Presidente del Paraguay Juan B. Egusquiza sobre cuestión de los campos de Mato Grosso (Brasil) y perdidos en la guerra de la Triple Alianza. Año 1895." Dec. 31, 1895. Copy in GC-UCR.

25. Juan Romero Gómez in "Reclamación del Señor Enrique S. López al gobierno del Brasil," MS. in GC-UCR; Egusquiza to Godoi, Asunción, Jan. 4, 1896 (note on Egusquiza's calling card), ibid.

26. José Segundo Decoud to Adolfo Decoud, Asunción, Jan. 24, 1878, ibid.

27. Fern. A. Berghmans to Godoi, Buenos Aires, Aug. 31, 1897, ibid.

28. Decoud to Egusquiza, Asunción, Aug. 10, 1897, *RM* 2 (Sept. 15, 1897), 221; same to same, Asunción, Sept. 4, 1897, ibid.; Egusquiza to Decoud, Asunción, Sept. 7, 1897, ibid.; Itiberê da Cunha to Castro Cerqueira, 1ª Sec. No. 8, Asunción, Aug. 6, 1897, MDBA-OR 201/2/6; *La Opinión*, Aug. 10, 1897; *La Democracia*, Aug. 11, 1897; *El Cívico*, Aug. 11, 1897; *El Pueblo*, Aug. 12, 1897; Itiberê da Cunha to Castro Cerqueira, 2ª Sec. No. 8, Asunción, Oct. 28, 1897, and 2ª Sec. No. 6, Asunción, May 6, 1898, MDBA-OR 201/2/6.

29. Juan Bautista Egusquiza, *Mensaje* (April 1897), pp. 4–5; Itiberê da Cunha to Castro Cerqueira, 2ª Sec. No. 14; Asunción, Dec. 12, 1896, MDBA-OR 201/2/6.

30. *La Democracia*, Oct. 26, 1897.

31. *La Prensa*, Feb. 1, 1898. This was the first issue of the paper.

32. Itiberê da Cunha to Castro Cerqueira, 2ª Sec. No. 1, Asunción, Jan. 3, 1898, MDBA-OR 201/2/6.

33. Itiberê da Cunha's despatches detailing these developments are preserved in MDBA-OR 201/2/6.

34. Juan Bautista Egusquiza, *Mensaje* (April, 1898), pp. 2–4.

35. Itiberê da Cunha to Castro Cerqueira, 2ª Sec. No. 5 Res., Asunción, May 28, 1898, MDBA-OR 201/2/6.

36. Ruffin to Chas. W. Gridler, No. 18, Asunción, Feb. 17, 1898, DUSCA T 329/4. According to Ruffin, "The *Temerario* was a light draft boat sent out to the River Plate to destroy American vessels and commerce. The *Oregon* was sent out to attack her" (Ruffin, "The *Temerario* at Asunción," p. 636).

37. Itiberê da Cunha to Castro Cerqueira, 2ª Sec. No. 4 Res., Asunción, April 20, 1898, and 2ª Sec. No. 14, Asunción, Sept. 26, 1898, MDBA-OR

201/2/6; R. B. Croskey to Edward Thornton, No. 8, Asunción, Oct. 13, 1898, PRO-FO 29/56; Thornton to Salisbury, Paraguay No. 2, Buenos Aires, Dec. 10, 1898, ibid.

Chapter 8. Aceval and the Failure of Conciliation, 1898–1902

1. *El Paraguayo*, June 6, 1898; *RP* 1 (1898), 273; Itiberê da Cunha to Olynthe de Magalhães, 2ª Sec. No. 1 Res., Asunción, Jan. 27, 1900, and 2ª Sec. No. 8, Asunción, June 29, 1900, MDBA-OR 201/2/7.
2. Encl. No. 2, Ruffin to Hill, No. 77, Asunción, Jan. 14, 1899, DUSCA T 329/4.
3. Trans. of Aceval's inaugural message, encl., W. R. Finch to Hay, No. 10, Montevideo, Dec. 15, 1898, DDPU 128/10.
4. Itiberê da Cunha to Magalhães, 2ª Sec. No. 15, Asunción, Nov. 26, 1898, MDBA-OR 201/2/6.
5. Same to same, 2ª Sec. No. 1, Conf., Asunción, Nov. 30, 1898, ibid.
6. Same to same, 2ª Sec. No. 1, Asunción, Jan. 2, 1899, ibid; *La Democracia*, Jan. 2, 1899; *La Opinión*, Jan. 2, 1899.
7. Emilio Aceval, *Mensaje* (April, 1899), p. 4.
8. Freire Esteves, *El Paraguay constitucional*, p. 73.
9. Itiberê da Cunha to Magalhães, 2ª Sec. No. 1 Res., Asunción, Jan. 27, 1900, and 2ª Sec. No. 1 Asunción, March 2, 1901, MDBA-OR 201/2/7.
10. MI, *Memoria, 1898–1899*, p. 4; Valle, *Cartilla cívica*, p. 25.
11. Itiberê da Cunha to Magalhães, 2ª Sec. No. 1 Res., Asunción, Jan. 27, 1900, MDBA-OR 201/2/7.
12. Finch to Hay, No. 395, Montevideo, March 23, 1900, DDPU 128/10; MI, *Memoria, 1899–1900*, pp. 3–4.
13. Itiberê da Cunha to Magalhães, 2ª Sec. No. 3 Asunción, March 15, 1900, MDBA-OR 201/2/7.
14. Same to same, 2ª Sec. No. 3, Asunción, March 15, 1900, and 2ª Sec. No. 8, Asunción, June 29, 1900, ibid.
15. *La Patria Paraguaya*, Sept. 7, 1900.
16. Itiberê da Cunha to Magalhães, 2ª Sec. No. 10, Asunción, Sept. 12, 1900, and 2ª Sec. No. 1, Asunción, March 2, 1901, MDBA-OR 201/2/7.
17. Fabio Queirolo to Aceval, Asunción, March 19, 1901, GC-UCR.
18. Itiberê da Cunha to Magalhães, 2ª Sec. No. 2, Asunción, April 2, 1901, and 2ª Sec. No. 1 Res., Asunción, April 18, 1901, MDBA-OR 201/2/7.
19. Valle, *Cartilla cívica*, p. 25.
20. Francisco Ysidro Resquín, "Breves relaciones históricas de la guerra . . ." ANA-SH 366, passim; Katharina von Dombrowski, *Land of Women*, pp. 316–23.
21. Francisco Pinheiro Guimarães, *Um voluntário da patria*, p. 38; R. C. Kirk to Fish, No. 15, Buenos Aires, Aug. 22, 1869, DDA 68/19; *La Regeneración*, Oct. 1 and 21, Nov. 21, 1869, March 6, April 20, and May 28, 1870.
22. Félix Farías to Mariano Varela, Santiago, May 12, 1870, Correspondencia confidencial da la legación argentina, 1869–1870–1871, AGN BA.
23. *La Democracia*, March 1, 1885; *La Verdad*, March 22, 1885.

24. *La República* (Buenos Aires), Feb. 11, 1870; José Auto de Guimarães to Rio Branco, Asunción, Aug. 1, 1871, Col. Cot. 29/26.

25. M. L. Forgues, "Le Paraguay; fragments de journal et de correspondances, 1872–1873," pp. 385–86.

26. *El Paraguayo*, April 24, 1888.

27. Juansilvano Godoi, *El Barón de Rio Branco*, p. 269 n. 4; Aguilar to Leite Chermont, 2ª Sec. No. 20, Asunción, July 21, 1891, MDBA-OR 201/2/4.

28. J. Wavrunek to Finch, Asunción, Dec. 5, 1901, encl., Finch to Hay, No. 507, Montevideo, Jan. 11, 1902, DDPU 128/14.

29. On April 3, the Liberal papers *El Pueblo* and *La Opinión* severely criticized Garay for having instigated the near riot; Juan B. Egusquiza, *Mensaje* (April 1898), p. 4.

30. Itiberê da Cunha to Castro Cerqueira, 2ª Sec. No. 5, Asunción, April 4, 1898, MDBA-OR 201/2/6; Itiberê da Cunha to Magalhães, 2ª Sec. No. 2, Asunción, June 14, 1901, MDBA-OR 201/2/7; *El Estudiante*, July 28, 1901.

31. Itiberê da Cunha to Magalhães, 2ª Sec. No. 1 Res., Asunción, Oct. 2, 1902, MDBA-OR 201/2/7.

32. Campos to Aceval, Asunción, Aug. 16, 1901, GC-UCR; Abilio Cesar Borges to Magalhães, 2ª Sec. No. 6, Asunción, Aug. 23, 1901, MDBA-OR 201/2/7.

33. Finch to Hay, No. 507, Montevideo, Jan. 11, 1902, DDPU 128/14; "Manifiesto del Comité Revolucionario," boletín de *La Patria*, Jan. 9, 1902; Ruffin to H. D. Peirce [*sic*], No. 129 Conf., Asunción, Jan. 17, 1902, DUSCA 329/5.

34. Congreso Nacional, República del Paraguay, *Sesión extraordinaria del 9 de enero del año 1902*, p. vi.

35. Ibid., pp. vii–ix, xi.

36. *La Tribuna* (Montevideo), Jan. 11, 1902, and *El País* (Montevideo), Jan. 10, 1902, quoted in Finch to Hay, No. 507, Montevideo, Jan. 11, 1902, DDPU 128/14.

37. Borges to Magalhães, 2ª Sec. No. 1, Asunción, Jan. 10, 1902, MDBA-OR 201/2/7.

38. Same to same, 2ª Sec. No. 3 Res., Asunción, March 25, 1902, ibid.

39. Same to same, 2ª Sec. No. 2 Asunción, April 3, 1902, ibid.; *PMR* 2, no. 4 (April, 1902), 89–96.

40. Cecil Gosling to Lansdowne, No. 1 Treaty, Asunción, April 7, 1902, PRO-FO 59/60.

41. *PMR* 2, no. 4 (April, 1902), 117–18.

42. Itiberê da Cunha to Magalhães, 2ª Sec. No. 5, Asunción, June 17, 1902, MDBA-OR 201/2/7.

43. Same to same, 2ª Sec. No. 7, Asunción, Sept. 4, 1902; 2ª Sec. No. 1 Res., Oct. 2, 1902, and 2ª Sec. No. 2 Res., Asunción, Oct. 19, 1902, ibid.

44. Itiberê da Cunha to Magalhães, 2ª Sec. No. 8, Sept. 9, 1902, MDBA-OR 201/2/7.

Chapter 9. End of the First Colorado Era

1. *La Patria*, Nov. 25, 1902.

2. Peña returned to Rio de Janeiro in April 1903. In May, Antolín Irala

became minister of foreign affairs, Antonio Sosa replaced Moreno in hacienda, and Francisco Chaves took over justice (Eduardo Fleytas to Finch, Asunción, Nov. 27, 1902, encl., Finch to Hay, No. 602, Montevideo, Dec. 8, 1902, DDPU 128/15).

3. Juansilvano Godoi, *El Coronel don Juan Antonio Escurra*, pp. 5–14.

4. Pictures of these and other public figures are in Arsenio López Decoud, ed., *Album gráfico de la República del Paraguay*, passim.

5. Godoi, *El Coronel don Juan Antonio Escurra*, p. 15.

6. Itiberê da Cunha to Magalhães, 2ª Sec. No. 1 Conf., Asunción, Sept. 4, 1902, MDBA-OR 201/2/7.

7. Itiberê da Cunha to Rio Branco, 2ª Sec. No. 12, Asunción, Dec. 23, 1902, and 2ª Sec. No. 10, Asunción, Dec. 1, 1902, ibid.; *El País*, Dec. 15, 1902.

8. Itiberê da Cunha to Magalhães, 2ª Sec. No. 2, Asunción, March 18, 1903, MDBA-OR 201/2/7.

9. Same to same, 2ª Sec. No. 1 Res., Asunción, Jan. 10, 1903, ibid.

10. Same to same, 2ª Sec. No. 2 Res., Asunción, Feb. 2, 1903, and 2ª Sec. No. 4, Asunción, April 8, 1903, ibid.

11. Same to same, 2ª Sec. No. 2, March 18, 1903, and 2ª Sec. No. 5, Asunción, May 15, 1903, ibid.; *Boletín quincenal de la Cámara de Comercio de la Asunción*, June 16, 1903, passim; Itiberê da Cunha to Rio Branco, 2ª Sec. No. 8, Asunción, July 2, 1903; and 2ª Sec. No. 9, Asunción, Aug. 26, 1903, and 2ª Sec. No. 11, Asunción, Oct. 2, 1903, MDBA-OR 201/2/7.

12. *La Bastilla*, Aug. 6, 1902.

13. Ibid.

14. López Decoud, *Album gráfico*, passim.

15. Ricardo Brugada, *Política paraguaya: Benigno Ferreira*, pp. 7–15.

16. Benigno Riquelme García, *Cumbre en soledad; vida de Manuel Gondra*, passim.

17. Harris Gaylord Warren, "The Paraguayan Revolution of 1904," pp. 365–84. Juan Carlos Herken Krauer, "La revolución liberal de 1904 en el Paraguay," accurately emphasizes economic factors in causing the revolt.

18. Haggard to Lansdowne, Paraguay No. 5, Buenos Aires, Aug. 10, 1904, PRO-FO 59/62; *El Siglo* (Montevideo), Aug. 13, 1904.

19. Finch to Hay, No. 786, Montevideo, Aug. 12, 1904, DDPU 128/17, enclosing clippings from *El Día* (La Plata) and the Montevideo *El Siglo* and *Diario Nuevo*; Haggard to Lansdowne, Paraguay No. 5, Buenos Aires, Aug. 10, 1904, PRO-FO 59/62.

20. "Manifiesto del Partido Nacional Republicano á sus correligionarios," *El Paraguay*, Aug. 9, 1904, copy in John N. Ruffin to Loomis, No. 160, Asunción, Aug. 11, 1904, DUSCA T 329/6. One of the recruits was Gustavo Sosa Escalada, who recorded his memoirs of the revolt in *El buque fantasma* (Asunción, 1905), reissued as the July 1982 Paraguayan Book-of-the-Month.

21. Haggard to Lansdowne, Paraguay No. 6 Conf., Buenos Aires, Aug. 12, 1904, PRO-FO 59/62; Ruffin to Loomis, No. 160, Asunción, Aug. 11, 1904, DUSCA T 329/6. A *surubí* is a large fish commonly found in the Río Paraguay.

22. Rafael Barrett, "Paraguay: The Last Revolution and Present Politics," encl., Edward C. O'Brien to Elihu Root, No. 64, Montevideo, Dec. 12, 1905, DDPU 128/18.

23. *La Constitución*, Oct. 19, 1904, and *La Tarde*, Aug. 24, 1904, published the exchange of notes. In rebel hands, the *Pollux* became the *Patria*. Elías Ayala commanded the *Constitución*, while Duarte continued to command the *Libertad*.

24. "Al pueblo," manifesto of the Revolutionary Committee, Aug. 15, 1904, encl. No. 4, Ruffin to Loomis, No. 163, Asunción, Sept. 8, 1904, DUSCA T 329/6.

25. "Manifiesto del Presidente de la República Coronel Juan A. Escurra," Asunción, Aug. 16, 1904, encl., Ruffin to Loomis, No. 161, Asunción, Aug. 16, 1904, DUSCA T 329/6.

26. "Manifiesto de la Junta Revolucionaria de la capital," Asunción, Aug. 30, 1904, *El Grito del Pueblo*, Feb. 2, 1905; Manuel Domínguez, "Manifiesto del Vice-Presidente de la República del Paraguay," Oct. 15, 1904, encl. No. 1, Korab to Loomis, No. 172, Asunción, Nov. 26, 1904, DUSCA T 329/6; *La Constitución*, Oct. 19, 1904.

27. Gosling to Haggard, No. 28, Asunción, Aug. 26, 1904, encl. No. 1, Haggard to Lansdowne, Paraguay No. 9, Buenos Aires, Sept. 23, 1904, PRO-FO 59/62; *La Constitución*, Oct. 8, 1904.

28. Gosling to Haggard, No. 38 Conf., Asunción, Sept. 30, 1904, encl., Haggard to Lansdowne, Paraguay No. 11 Conf., Buenos Aires, Oct. 7, 1904, PRO-FO 59/62.

29. "Al pueblo. Manifiesto del general en jefe del ejército revolucionario, Sept. 25, 1904," encl., Korab to Loomis, Asunción, Dec. 4, 1904, DUSCA T 329/6.

30. Itiberê da Cunha to Rio Branco, 2ª Sec. No. 11, Asunción, Oct. 11, 1904, and 2ª Sec. No. 12 Res., Asunción, Oct. 21, 1904, MDBA-OR 201/2/8; Gosling to Haggard, No. 41, Asunción, Oct. 10, 1904, and Haggard to Lansdowne, Paraguay No. 12, Buenos Aires, Oct. 30, 1904, PRO-FO 59/62.

31. Itiberê da Cunha to Rio Branco, 2ª Sec. No. 13 Res., Asunción, Oct. 29, 1904, MDBA-OR 201/2/8.

32. Same to same, 2ª Sec. No. 14 Res., Asunción, Nov. 5, 1904, ibid.

33. Same to same, 2ª Sec. No. 15 Res., Asunción, Nov. 18, 1904, ibid.

34. Same to same, 2ª Sec. No. 16 Res., Asunción, Nov. 26, 1904, and 2ª Sec. No. 17 Res., Asunción, Dec. 2, 1904, ibid.

35. "El tratado de Pilcomayo, acta de paz," encl., Gosling to Lansdowne, No. 4, Asunción, Dec. 29, 1904, PRO-FO 59/62; Korab to Loomis, No. 175, Asunción, Dec. 19, 1904, DUSCA T 329/6; *El Triunfo*, Dec. 25, 1904; *El Grito del Pueblo*, Dec. 25, 1904.

36. Gosling, "Report on the Political Situation in Paraguay in 1905," encl., Gosling to Gray, No. 3, Asunción, March 7, 1906, PRO-FO 371/10.

Chapter 10. Sparring with Old Enemies

1. See above, pp. 66–69.

2. Carvalho to Cotegipe, 1ª Sec. No. 3, Asunción, March 27, 1886, MDBA-OR 201/2/2.

3. Edmund Monson to Granville, Paraguay No. 7 Conf., Assumption, Oct. 15, 1884, PRO-FO 59/41.

4. José de Almeida e Vasconcellos to Pedro Luiz Pereira de Souza, 1ª Sec. No. 1 Conf., Asunción, Dec. 17, 1880, MDBA-OR 201/1/16.

5. *La Democracia*, June 10, 1882; Henrique de Barros Cavalcanti de Lacerda to Philippe Franco de Sá, Sec. Cen. No. 15, Asunción, June 25, 1882, MDBA—OR 201/2/1.

6. Petre to Granville, No. 56, Buenos Aires, Aug. 4, 1882, PRO-FO 6/368.

7. Brizuela to Cotegipe, Montevideo, Sept. 2, 1882, Col. Cot., 11/46, and same to same, Montevideo, Oct. 25, 1882, ibid., 11/48.

8. Henrique Mamede Lins de Almeida to Franco de Sá, 4ª Sec. No. 1, MDBA-OR 201/2/1; Decoud to Franco de Sá, encl., Lacerda to Cotegipe, Asunción, July 30, 1882, 4ª Sec. No. 1, MDBA-OR 201/2/2; Héctor Alvarez to Victorino de la Plaza, Asunción, July 30, 1882, AVP AGN-BA 7/4/5/10.

9. "Treaty of Friendship, Commerce and Navigation between Brazil and the Republic of Paraguay, June 7, 1883," encl., Dering to Granville, No. 9, Asunción, July 11, 1883, PRO-FO 59/40; *Colección de tratados celebrados por la República del Paraguay*, pp. 119–39; William A. Barrington to Granville, No. 4 Commercial, Buenos Aires, Feb. 1, 1884, PRO-FO 59/43.

10. Alvarez to Plaza, Asunción, May 2, 1882, AVP AGN-BA 7/4/5/10; MRE-A, *Memoria, 1882*, pp. xxxviii–xxxix; Alvarez to Ministro de Relaciones Exteriores, Asunción, May 4, 1882, AVP AGN-BA 7/4/5/10.

11. MRE-A, *Memoria, 1884*, pp. 150–70.

12. Charles J. Kolinski, *Independence or Death! The Story of the Paraguayan War*, pp. 220–21.

13. Dering to Granville, No. 4, Asunción, July 3, 1883, PRO-FO 59/40; Monson to Granville, No. 84 Conf., Buenos Aires, Nov. 10, 1884, PRO-FO 6/380.

14. MRE-A, *Memoria, 1877*, II, 647–50; MRE-A, *Memoria, 1889*, pp. 251–60.

15. Carlos Carneiro de Campos, Vizconde de Caravellas, to Araujo Gondim, 1ª Sec. No. 22, Rio de Janeiro, May 13, 1874, MDBA-D 201/4/8; Vasconcellos to Souza, 1ª Sec. No. 2 Res., Asunción, May 17, 1881, MDBA-OR 201/1/16; *La Reforma*, Aug. 11, 1881.

16. Saguier to Juan Bautista Gill, Buenos Aires, Jan. 17, 1877, GP CCAP.

17. Vasconcellos to Moreira de Barros, 1ª Sec. No. 11 Res., Asunción, Oct. 1, 1879, MDBA-OR 201/1/15; Eduardo Callado to Cotegipe, Asunción, Nov. 28, 1876, 1ª Sec. No. 8 Conf., Asunción, Nov. 28, 1876, MDBA-OR 201/1/14.

18. Jara to Vasconcellos, Asunción, April 26, 1878, MRE-P, *Memoria, 1879*, pp. 65–72; Vasconcellos to Barão de Villa Bella, 1ª Sec. No. 17, Asunción, May 9, 1878, MDBA-OR 201/2/2; *La Reforma*, May 9, 1878; Vasconcellos to Pedro Luiz Pereira de Souza, 1ª Sec. No. 16, Asunción, July 10, 1880, MDBA-OR 201/1/16.

19. Rufino Elizalde to Mitre, Buenos Aires, Sept. 23, 1867, AGM-DC, V, 173.

20. MRE-P, *Memoria, 1883*, encl., Dering to Granville, Buenos Aires, June 13, 1883, PRO-FO 6/374; *Ratificación y canje del tratado de paz[,] amistad y reconocimiento de deuda . . .* (Montevideo, 1883), passim; *La Democracia*, April 21, 1883; Brizuela to Cotegipe, Private, Montevideo, June 27, 1885, Col. Cot. 11/51.

21. Thomas Fortunato de Brito to Alberto Flangini, Montevideo, Nov. 27, 1867, MEVA-AHI 272/1/19/2; Flangini to Brito, Montevideo, Nov. 30, 1867, ibid.; Ministro de Relaciones Exteriores to Brito, Montevideo, July 13, 1867, ibid.; Brito to João Custosa da Cunha Paranaguá, Buenos Aires, Dec. 31, 1867, ibid. The basic Brazilian currency unit was the *rei* (Spanish *real*), too low in value to be coined. There were, however, coins of larger denomination, especially 100, 400, 500, and 1,000 reis. The silver coin of 1,000 reis was the *milreis*, popularly called a *patacón*. One thousand milreis made a *conto*. This unit was written 1:000$000. The conto was worth about £50 sterling (about $247.50 U.S.) in the 1880s. Any silver dollar was popularly called a patacón in Paraguay.

22. Francisco L. Bareiro, *El Paraguay en la República Argentina: la condonación de la deuda de guerra: nobles iniciativas*, pp. 14, 19–22; Coferino Luque to Mitre, Buenos Aires, Aug. 25, 1903, AGJIG AGN-BA 7/17/3/6; Luque to Alejandro Montes de Oca, Buenos Aires, June 20, 1903, ibid.; Itiberê da Cunha to Rio Branco, 2ª Sec. No. 4 Res., Asunción, April 24, 1903, MDBA-OR 201/2/1.

23. Lacerda to Albuquerque, Sec. Cen. No. 9 Res., Asunción, Nov. 25, 1882, MDBA-OR 201/2/1; Francisco J. Ortiz to Decoud, Buenos Aires, June 2, 1886, encl., Oliveira to Cotegipe, 1ª Sec. No. 4 Res., Asunción, July 3, 1886, MDBA-OR 201/2/2.

24. Itiberê da Cunha to Magalhães, 2ª Sec. No. 1 Conf., Asunción, March 4, 1889, MDBA-OR 201/2/2; Ruffin to Hill, Asunción, April 4, 1899, DUSCA T 329/4.

25. Flagg to Finch, Asunción, Feb. 28, 1899, encl., Finch to Hay, No. 154, Montevideo, March 10, 1899, DDPU 128/10.

26. Itiberê da Cunha to Magalhães, 2ª Sec. No. 11, Asunción, Oct. 28, 1900, MDBA-OR 201/2/7; *RADI*, VI, 24–28; César Gondra, *La deuda de la guerra de 1865*, passim.

27. Vera Kelsey, *Brazil in Capitals*, pp. 217–42; Affonso de E. Taunay, *História das bandeiras paulistas*, II, 13–24.

28. Bourgade, *Paraguay*, p. 31.

29. Itiberê da Cunha to Magalhães, 3ª Sec. No. 14, Asunción, Oct. 31, 1902, MDBA-OR 201/2/7.

30. *El Cívico*, March 8, 1897; Gomes Pereira to Castro Cerqueira, 2ª Sec. No. 3, March 11, 1897, MDBA-OR 201/2/6.

31. *La Prensa*, March 12, 1901; *La Patria*, July 12, 1902; Itiberê da Cunha to Magalhães, 3ª Sec. No. 10, Asunción, July 23, 1902, MDBA-OR 201/2/7; Itiberê da Cunha to Rio Branco, 3ª Sec. No. 2, Asunción, Feb. 23, 1903, ibid.

32. Ruffin to Hill, No. 92, Asunción, Aug. 26, 1899, DUSCA T 329/5; Itiberê da Cunha to Ruffin, Asunción, Aug. 24, 1899, encl., Ruffin to Hill, No. 93, Asunción, Sept. 29, 1899, ibid.

33. Itiberê da Cunha to Magalhães, 2ª Sec. No. 116, Asunción, Dec. 9, 1898, MDBA-OR 201/2/6.

34. Serge Correia to Duque Estrada, 2ª Sec. No. 14, Rio de Janeiro, May 10, 1892, MDBA-D 201/4/11; Estrada to Leite Pereira, 2ª Sec. No. 23, Asunción, May 28, 1892, MDBA-OR 201/2/5.

35. Borges to Magalhães, 2ª Sec. No. 7, Sept. 30, 1901, and 2ª Sec. No. 1 Res., Asunción, Dec. 15, 1901, MDBA-OR 201/2/7; *La Patria*, Sept. 30, 1901;

Borges to Magalhães, 2ª Sec. No. 10, Asunción, Nov. 16, 1901, MDBA-OR 201/2/7.

Chapter 11. Colorados and the Chaco Boreal

1. Cecilio Báez and Juan C. Centurión, "Límites con Bolivia," p. 84; Luís G. Benítez, *Historia diplomática del Paraguay*, pp. 164–65.

2. MRE-A, *Memoria, 1878*, pp. 10–31. Bolivia's Dr. Mariano Donato Muñoz had protested against the territorial provisions of the treaty of May 1, 1865 (Augusto Tasso Fragoso, *A paz com o Paraguai depois da guerra da Tríplice Aliança*, p. 18 n.1).

3. MRE-A, *Memoria, 1873*, pp. xvi–xviii.

4. Manuel Francisco Correia to Joaquim Maria Nascentes de Azambuja, Sec. Cen. No.– Res., Rio de Janeiro, Aug. 16, 1872, MDBA-D 201/4/8.

5. José del Carpio to the President of Argentina, La Paz, April 1, 1878, MRE-A, *Memoria, 1878*, pp. 10–31. the quotation is at p. 31.

6. Audibert's long study was published in *El Independiente*, Jan.–Feb., 1891, and reprinted in 1901 as *Questión de límites entre el Paraguay y Bolivia*, and as *Los límites de la antigua provincia del Paraguay* in 1892. See also Blas Garay, in *La Prensa*, Feb. 3, 1898; Cecilio Báez, *Paraguay y Bolivia: la cuestión de límites;* Eusebio Ayala, "La significación del laudo arbitral del Presidente Rutherford Hayes," in Eduardo Amarilla Fretes, *El Paraguay en el primer cincuentenario del fallo arbitral*, pp. 53–64.

7. Vansittart, "Report," p. 80.

8. *La Reforma*, May 23, 1880.

9. Bareiro to the Congress, Asunción, July 11, 1879, *El Diario*, July 16, 1879. Significantly, Bareiro reflected the general opinion that Bahía Negra marked Paraguay's northern frontier and that the boundary should run due west from there.

10. Antônio Moreira de Barros to José de Almeida e Vasconcellos, Sec. Cen. No. 22, Rio de Janeiro, Aug. 9, 1879, and Sec. Cen. No. 24, Rio de Janeiro, Sept. 1, 1879, MDBA-D 201/4/10.

11. *La Reforma*, Oct. 7, 1879.

12. Ibid., May 23, 1880; Vasconcellos to Souza, Sec. Cen. No. 24, Asunción, April 21, 1880, and Sec. Cen. No. 38, Asunción, May 24, 1880, MDBA-OR 201/1/16.

13. *La Reforma*, Sept. 26, 1879.

14. MRE-P, *Memoria, 1880*, p. 5; Valle, *Cartilla cívica*, p. 33.

15. Vasconcellos to Moreira de Barros, 1ª Sec. No. 12 Res., Asunción, Oct. 19, 1879, MDBA-OR 201/1/15; Moreira de Barros to Vasconcellos, 1ª Sec. No. 12 Res., Rio de Janeiro, Nov. 17, 1879, MDBA-D 201/4/10.

16. Under the constitution of 1870, a treaty had to be approved by both houses of Congress before the president could ratify.

17. MRE-P, *Memoria, 1883;* Ribeira Moreira to Sousa Dantas, Sec. Cen. No. 2, Asunción, Feb. 3, 1885, RCBA-O 238/3/7.

18. *La Democracia*, June 20, 1885.

19. Carvalho to Cotegipe, 1ª Sec. No. 35, Asunción, Oct. 27, 1885, MDBA-OR 201/2/1; *La Democracia*, Nov. 14, 1885; *El Orden*, Nov. 18, 1885.

20. Castello Branco to Silva Prado, Asunción, Dec. 3, 1885, RCBA-O 238/3/7.

21. Oliveira to Cotegipe, Sec. Cen. No. 16, Asunción, May 20, 1886, MDBA-OR 201/2/2.

22. Bacon to Bayard, No. 257, Montevideo, Oct. 17, 1888, DDPU 128/7; Oliveira to Cotegipe, 1ª Sec. No. 5 Res., Asunción, July 10, 1886, MDBA-OR 201/2/2; Cotegipe to Oliveira, 1ª Sec. No. 5 Res., Rio de Janeiro, Sept. 23, 1886, and 1ª Sec. No. 6 Res., Rio de Janeiro, Sept. 28, 1886, MDBA-D 201/4/10.

23. Among the many sources for the treaty are José Aguirre Acha, *The Arbitration Zone in the Bolivian-Paraguayan Dispute through the Diplomatic Negotiations*, p. 21; Benítez, *Historia diplomática*, pp. 84–85; and Oliveira to Cotegipe, 1ª Sec. No. 3 Res., Asunción, Feb. 20, 1887, MDBA-OR 201/2/2. Escobar recommended approval in his *Mensaje* (April, 1887), p. 11.

24. *La Democracia*, Jan. 18 and 19, 1888; Carvalho to Cotegipe, 1ª Sec. No. 2, Asunción, Jan. 19, 1888, MDBA-OR 201/2/3.

25. Notes exchanged between Pinilla and Decoud in 1888 are in MRE-P, *Memoria, 1889*.

26. Ibid., pp. 18–36. Centurión's note of Nov. 3, 1888, is at pp. 24–36. See also Carvalho to Silva, 1ª Sec. No. 28, Asunción, Oct. 16, 1888, MDBA-OR 201/2/3; *El Independiente*, Oct. 15, 1888; Benítez, *Historia diplomática*, pp. 322–30.

27. Carvalho to Silva, 1ª Sec. No. 23, Asunción, Sept. 28, 1888, and Sec. Cen. No. 11, Asunción, April 3, 1888, MDBA-OR 201/2/3; *La Democracia*, Sept. 28, 1888. *El Paraguayo*, Oct. 7, 10, and 12, 1888, attacked the treaty vigorously.

28. *El Sud-Americano* (Buenos Aires), Nov. 5 and Dec. 5, 1888.

29. Carvalho to Silva, 1ª Sec. No. 3 Conf., Asunción, Oct. 22, 1888, MDBA—OR 201/2/3.

30. *El Paraguayo*, Oct. 21, 1888; Carvalho to Silva, 1ª Sec. No. 31, Asunción, Nov. 21, 1888, MDBA-OR 201/2/3.

31. Carvalho to Silva, 1ª Sec. No. 1, Asunción, Jan. 15, 1889, and 1ª Sec. No. 2, Asunción, Jan. 26, 1889, MDBA-OR 201/2/3; *La Democracia*, Jan. 24, 1889.

32. Among numerous diplomatic despatches, one may note especially Aguilar to Silva, 1ª Sec. No. 12, Asunción, April 22, 1889, MDBA-OR 201/2/3; Barão de Alencar to Silva, 1ª Sec. No. 8, Buenos Aires, March 21, 1889, and 1ª Sec. No. 19, Buenos Aires, May 4, 1889, MDBA-OR 206/2/2; Centurión to Pinilla, Asunción, Sept. 13, 1889, encl. No. 4 in Aguilar to Diana, 1ª Sec. No. 35, Asunción, Sept. 27, 1889, MDBA-OR 201/2/3. Pinilla's "manifesto" is also in *La Nación* (Buenos Aires), Jan. 14, 1890.

33. Pakenham to Salisbury, Paraguay No. 1, Buenos Aires, Jan. 20, 1890, PRO-FO 59/48.

34. DCR No. 792, *Paraguay 1890–1891*, p. 5.

35. *La Democracia*, Jan. 17, 1891; *El Independiente*, Jan. 19, 1891; *El Nacional*, Feb. 5, 1891; *DO*, July 28, 1891.

36. *La República*, Aug. 4, 1891; *La Democracia*, Sept. 26, 1891 and Dec. 13, 1892; Juan G. González, *Mensaje* (April 1892), p. 22.

37. Aguirre Acha, *The Arbitration Zone*, p. 28; Fulgencio R. Moreno, *Diplomacia paraguayo-boliviana*, pp. 42–43.

38. *El Pueblo*, Nov. 21 and 27, 1894; *El Centinela*, Oct. 28, 1894.

39. Antonio Gomes Pereira to Carvalho, 2ª Sec. No. 5 Res., Asunción, Nov. 15, 1894, MDBA-OR 201/2/5.

40. Juan B. Egusquiza, *Mensaje* (April 1896), p. 1; *El Pueblo*, Feb. 9, 1896; *La Opinión*, Feb. 3 and 13, 1896.

41. Itiberê da Cunha to Castro Cerqueira, 2ª Sec. No. 12, Asunción, Nov. 14, 1896, MDBA-OR 201/2/6.

42. William A. C. Barrington to Salisbury, Paraguay No. 2, Asunción, July 26, 1897, PRO-FO 59/55; *La Opinión*, July 12, 1897; *La Democracia*, July 10 and 12, 1897; Itiberê da Cunha to Castro Cerqueira, 2ª Sec. No. 2 Res., Asunción, July 12, 1897, and 2ª Sec. No. 3 Res., Asunción, July 20, 1897, MDBA-OR 201/2/6.

43. Gómez to Decoud, Sucre, Aug. 21, 1897, MRE-P, *Memoria, 1898*, pp. 12–14; Decoud to Gómez, Asunción, Sept. 21, 1897, ibid., p. 16; "Datos sobre la cuestión de límites entre Bolivia y el Paraguay: estado de la cuestión," encl. No. 2 in John N. Ruffin to Thomas W. Cridler, No. 3, Asunción, Nov. 18, 1897, DUSCA T 329/4.

44. Itiberê da Cunha to Castro Cerqueira, 2ª Sec. No. 7 Res., Asunción, Feb. 25, 1898, MDBA-OR 201/2/6.

45. Ibid.

46. Ibid.

47. MRE-P, *Memoria, 1899–1900*, pp. 21–25.

48. Ruffin to Hill, No. 10 bis, Asunción, Jan. 4, 1900, DUSCA T 329/5; Itiberê da Cunha to Magalhães, 2ª Sec. No. 9, Asunción, Aug. 1, 1900, MDBA-OR 201/2/7.

49. Quijarro to Azevedo, Buenos Aires, Sept. 28, 1900, encl., Azevedo to Magalhães, 1ª Sec. No. 4 Res., Buenos Aires, Oct. 22, 1900, MDBBA-OR 206/1/2.

50. *El Municipio* (Concepción), Oct. 9, 1900; Quijarro to Itiberê da Cunha, Asunción, Jan. 16, 1901, encl., Itiberê da Cunha to Magalhães, 3ª Sec. No. 1, Asunción, Jan. 18, 1901, MDBA-OR 201/2/7.

51. Itiberê da Cunha to Magalhães, 3ª Sec. No. 2, Asunción, Feb. 22, 1901, MDBA-OR 201/2/7.

52. Manuel Domínguez, "Memoria, June 20, 1902," *PMR* 2 (June, 1902), 188–90.

53. Itiberê da Cunha to Magalhães, 2ª Sec. No. 2, Asunción, June 14, 1901, MDBA-OR 201/2/7.

54. MRE-P, *Memoria, 1903*, pp. 14–16.

55. Antolín de Irala to Brazilian Minister of Foreign Affairs, Asunción, April 29, 1904, NPL 350; Itiberê da Cunha to Rio Branco, 2ª Sec. No. 6, Asunción, Feb. 29, 1904, MDBA-OR 201/2/8; Rio Branco to Itiberê da Cunha, 2ª Sec. No. 1, Rio de Janeiro, July 28, 1904, MDBA-D 202/1/2.

Chapter 12: The National Patrimony

1. Pastore, *La lucha por la tierra en el Paraguay*, pp. 98–102, 120–60; John Hoyt Williams, "Paraguay's Nineteenth-Century *Estancias de la República*"; Richard Alan White, *Paraguay's Autonomous Revolution, 1810–1840*, lists seventy state estancias in Appendix I, pp. 263–64.

2. Pastore, *La lucha por la tierra en el Paraguay*, p. 129.

3. Ibid., p. 131.

4. Ibid., p. 147.

5. Authorities differ as to the exact area of a Paraguayan square league. The basic unit of linear measure was the *vara*, equal to .866 meters. A league was 5,000 varas, or 4,330 meters (14,205.8 ft), or 2.69 miles. A square league, therefore, was 7.2361 square miles or 4,631 acres. W. L. Schurz, *Paraguay: A Commercial Handbook*, p. 8, gives a square league as 4,632 acres, while Bourgade la Dardye lists one square league as 4,635 acres, but "1 square legua (land measure)" as 1769 hectares of 4,365 acres. Apparently this is a typographical error. I have used 4,632 acres for the Paraguayan square league. One square cuadra was 10,000 sq. varas, or 1.854 acres.

6. Francisco Wisner de Morgenstern, "El Paraguay en 1871, según Wisner," p. 763; Pastore, *La lucha por la tierra en el Paraguay*, p. 178.

7. Raffaele Costaguta, *Cenni storici, commerciali e geografici sul Paraguay*, pp. 39–40.

8. González, *Infortunios del Paraguay*, pp. 149–51.

9. Vansittart, "Report," pp. 94–95. Vansittart equated the Paraguayan league to 4,500 English acres. Viera, *Colección legislativa de la República del Paraguay, 1842–1895*, p. 11.

10. Pastore, *La lucha por la tierra en el Paraguay*, pp. 215–16.

11. Carvalho to Manuel Pinto de Souza Dantas, 1ª Sec. No. 2, Asunción, May 6, 1885, MDBA-OR 201/2/1; RO 1885, pp. 1214–16; *Almanaque nacional del Paraguay para el año de 1886*, p. 312; *El Orden*, June 25, 1885.

12. Class III lands were those fronting the Paraguay to a depth of ten leagues and comprised a band extending from the Pilcomayo north to Concepción; the land in a band to a depth of ten leagues west of the Class III area, and from a point opposite Concepción north to the frontier, was Class IV; the rest of the Chaco was in Class V. Grazing land generally was to be sold in lots no smaller than one-half league.

13. *RO*, 1885, pp. 1229–31; *El Orden*, July 16 and 17, 1885; Viera, *Colección legsilativa*, p. 267.

14. González, *Infortunios del Paraguay*, pp. 147–48.

15. Mulhall and Freund, *Letters*, p. 4.

16. *El Látigo*, Sept. 11, 1887.

17. A detailed list of buyers, prices and areas is in Pastore, *La lucha por la tierra en El Paraguay*, pp. 237–44.

18. Valle, *Cartilla cívica*, pp. 59–60.

19. Oliveira to Cotegipe, 2ª Sec. No. 10, Asunción, April 15, 1887, MDBA-OR 201/2/2.

20. These criticisms are based on a number of contemporary reports, such as Eben M. Flagg to Department of State, Asunción, Oct. 8, 1895, NPFO T 693/1, and DCR No. 792, *Paraguay 1890–1891*, passim.

21. *El Paraguayo*, June 13, 1888.

22. *La Democracia*, Oct. 7, 1891.

23. Flagg, "Information concerning the banking system of Paraguay," Asunción, Oct. 7, 1895, NPFO T 693/1.

24. A good summary of the Lynch claims is in Pastore, *La lucha por la tierra en el Paraguay*, pp. 148–55. Copies of the deeds are in GC-UCR.

25. Harris Gaylord Warren, "Litigation in English Courts and Claims Against Paraguay Resulting from the War of the Triple Alliance."

26. This *venia* was validated at the British consulate in Bordeaux on September 29, 1875, and certified before the French vice-consul in London on Oct. 4, 1875. A copy is in GC-UCR. The power of attorney is dated at London, July 2, 1879, and is signed "E. A. Lynch Lopez." Copy in GC-UCR.

27. Commission from the Paraguayan Committee in Buenos Aires to Juan Silvano Godoy, June 5, 1881. Original in GC-UCR.

28. Edwin A. Egerton to Granville, No. 57 Private, Buenos Aires, July 31, 1881, PRO-FO 6/364.

29. "Bases del empréstito," London, Aug. 27, 1881, MS. in GC-UCR.

30. Godoi to Benigno Ferreira, London, Sept. 24, 1881, ibid.

31. E. López to Juansilvano Godoi, Asunción, Nov. 2, 1883, ibid.

32. Carvalho to Cotegipe, 1ª Sec. No. 1 Res., Asunción, Jan. 11, 1888, MDBA-OR 201/2/3.

33. *El Látigo*, Dec. 25, 1887; Carvalho to Cotegipe, 1ª Sec. No. 1 Res., Asunción, Jan. 11, 1888, MDBA-OR 201/2/3; Oliveira to Cotegipe, 1ª Sec. No. 6 Res., Asunción, July 28, 1887, MDBA-OR 201/2/2.

34. *El Paraguayo*, March 8, 1888. The whole controversy is ably reviewed in *Reclamación temeraria—las pretendidas 3,105 leguas de tierras públicas en el Paraguay de Madama Lynch y sus subrogantes*, and in Ramón Zubizarreta, *Dictamen*. See also "Venta de unos terrenos por Enrique Solano López a Juan Antonio Ayerich, Francisco Cordero y Juan Silvano Godoy," MS. in GC-UCR.

35. *Tribuna Nacional* (Buenos Aires), April 3, 1883; Araujo Gondim to Albuquerque, 1ª Sec. No. 39, Buenos Aires, April 7, 1883, MDBBA-OR 205/4/11; Enrique Solano López, *Revalidación de títulos de terrenos al sud del Pilcomayo*, passim; Andrés Moscarda, *Un caso de prescripción contra el fisco*, pp. 7–10.

36. Warren, *Paraguay and the Triple Alliance*, pp. 264–66.

37. The 500 leagues were to be selected by the Council within five years. (José Segundo Decoud, *Informe del comisionado especial . . . para el arreglo de la deuda precedente de los empréstitos de 1871 y 1872*, passim; Henry Valpy, *Paraguay Land Warrants: Report to the Council of Foreign Bondholders on the Selection of Lands*, p. 25). Lands were to be selected in the departments of Curuguaty, San Salvador, San Estanislao, Alto Paraná, Chaco, and all of the island of Yacyretá.

38. Valpy, *Paraguay Land Warrants; El Paraguayo*, Jan. 5, 1888; *La Democracia*, Jan. 10, 1888; Carvalho to Cotegipe, 1ª Sec. No. 1, Asunción, Oct. 28, 1895, MDBA-OR 201/2/3; RO 1895, p. 110. The company actually received 478 leagues, 632 cuadras, or 2,087,641 acres, worth £1,440,000 (MI, *Memoria, 1896*, pp. 49–50). The discrepancy is accounted for by the payment of £60,000 in interest after the Decoud-Bouverie agreement was signed.

Chapter 13. Foundations of a Capitalist State

1. Petre to Granville, No. 1, Asunción, June 9, 1882, PRO-FO 59/39.

2. Vansittart to Petre, Buenos Aires, Nov. 15, 1882, ibid.

3. MRE-P, *Memoria*, May 31, 1884; Caballero, *Mensaje* (April, 1883), pp. 3–5.

4. Bacon to Bayard, No. 18, Montevideo, Oct. 3, 1885, DDPU 128/14; Pakenham to Salisbury, No. 1 Paraguay, Asunción, July 12, 1890, PRO-FO 59/48.

5. *El Paraguayo*, Feb. 16, 1867.

6. Egusquiza, *Mensaje* (April, 1895), p. 4; Aceval, *Mensaje* (April, 1900), p. 5.

7. Warren, "Banks and Banking in Paraguay, 1871–1904"; Pastore, *La lucha por la tierra en El Paraguay*, p. 252; DCR No. 792, *Paraguay 1890*, p. 1.

8. Arthur Peel, "Report on the Colony of New Australia in Paraguay," p. 18, encl., Pakenham to Kimberly, No. 14 Commercial, Paraguay, Buenos Aires, Nov. 28, 1894, PRO-FO 59/52. Hereafter Peel, "Report."

9. Andrés Héctor Carvallo, *Mensaje* (April, 1902), p. 12.

10. *El Cívico*, Dec. 13, 1899.

11. Moreira, "Relatorio Commercial e politico do anno findo de 1884," encl., Moreira to Souza Dantas, 2ª Sec. No. 2, Asunción, Feb. 20, 1885, RCBA-O 238/3/7.

12. For a list of such concessions, see Bordón, *Historia política del Paraguay*, I, 208–22.

13. *La Reforma*, Nov. 4, 1882; RPCS, *Actas* 1876, pp. 159–60; *RO*, 1878, pp. 384–85.

14. Boletín quincenal de la Cámara de Comercio de la Asunción, June 16, 1903.

15. Carpenter, "Underdeveloped Empire," *Boston Globe*, Feb. 19, 1899, encl., Ruffin to Hill, No. 88, Asunción, June 17, 1899, DUSCA T 329/5; Decree of Jan. 1, 1871, encl., Oliveira to Cotegipe, 1ª Sec. No. 1, Asunción, Jan. 19, 1887, MDBA-OR 201 2/2.

16. *El Paraguayo*, Dec. 1, 1885.

17. Oliveira to Cotegipe, 1ª Sec. No. 1, Asunción, Jan. 19, 1887, MDBA-OR 201/2/2.

18. José Rodríguez Alcalá, *El Paraguay en marcha*, pp. 293–94.

19. *PMR* 1 (1901), 24.

20. Benítez, *Ensayo sobre el liberalismo paraguayo*, p. 88; I.V. Wavrunek "Answers to questions for the International Woman's Suffrage Conference to be Held in Washington, D.C., Feb. 12th–18th, 1902," encl., W. R. Finch to Hay, Montevideo, Dec. 24, 1901, DDPU 128/14.

21. Araujo Gondim to Albuquerque, 1ª Sec. No. 34, Buenos Aires, March 24, 1882, MDBBA-OR 205/4/11; Eduardo Drolhe Fasciotti to Domingos Magalhães, 3ª Sec. No. 13, Asunción, Nov. 30, 1901, RCBA-O 238/3/12; Molins, *Paraguay*, pp. 6–8; DCR No. 1963, *Paraguay 1896*, p. 3; *DO*, July 23, 1892; Peel, "Report."

22. Vansittart, "Report," pp. 81–82.

23. DCR No. 1963, *Paraguay 1896*, p. 3.

24. Valle, *Cartilla cívica*, pp. 112–13.

25. Vansittart, "Report," p. 131. First class passengers paid $45 for the trip to Asunción, and $70 from Asunción to Buenos Aires. Second class fares were 50 percent less.

26. Bourgade, *Paraguay*, p. 129. The Platense Company ran more than one hundred steamers on the rivers after gaining its monopoly.

27. Moreira, "Relatorio commercial e politico do anno findo de 1884," encl., Moreira to Souza Dantas, 2ª Sec. No. 2, Asunción, Feb. 20, 1885, RCBA-O 238/3/7; *El Heraldo*, July 10, 1884.

28. Thomas Joseph Hutchinson, *The Paraná*, pp. 260–61; Edmund Monson to Granville, No. 1 Treaty, Assumption, Oct. 16, 1884, PRO-FO 59/43; Pastore, *La lucha por la tierra en El Paraguay*, p. 252.

29. Lloyd Brasileiro was bankrupt in 1900 (Fasciotti to Magalhães, 4ª Sec. No. 9, Asunción, March 31, 1900, RCBA-O 238/3/2).

30. DCR No. 1006, *Paraguay 1891*, p. 1; DCR No. 1963, *Paraguay 1896*, p. 15; DCR No. 2121, *Paraguay 1897*, p. 14; DCR No. 2275, *Paraguay 1898*, p. 9.

31. Ruffin, "Navigation of the Rio de la Plata," advance sheets of Consular Reports No. 1530, Dec. 27, 1902, DUSCA T 329/6.

32. For its early history, see Warren, "The Paraguay Central Railway, 1856–1889."

33. José Auto da Silva Guimarães to Manoel Francisco Correia, No. 602, Asunción, Aug. 29, 1871, GC-UCR.

34. Albuquerque to Callado, 2ª Sec. No. 4, Rio de Janeiro, May 3, 1877, MDBA-D 201/4/9.

35. João Rodrigues Martins to Souza, 2ª Sec. No. 4, Asunción, Sept. 9, 1881, RCBA-O 238/3/7; *Contrato sobre prolongación del ferro-carril de Paraguarí á Villa-Rica celebrado entre el superior govierno y el Señor Don Luís Patri el 24 de setiembre de 1886*, pp. 3–8.

36. See Warren, "The Paraguay Central Railway, 1856–1889," pp. 16–22.

37. Details of this sordid affair may be followed in ibid., pp. 31–48. A good review of the railway question is in Itiberê da Cunha to Carvalho, 3ª Sec. No. 6, Asunción, Aug. 8, 1896, MDBA-OR 201/2/6.

38. Oliveira to Cotegipe, 2ª Sec. No. 11, Asunción, April 25, 1887, MDBA-OR 201/2/2; *El Paraguayo*, April 19, 1887.

39. E. A. Hopkins, "My Life-Record," in Ynsfran, *La expedición norteamericana contra el Paraguay, 1858–1859*, I, 249–55, at p. 254.

40. The complete concession is in *RO*, 1887, pp. 101–03 and *La Democracia*, Sept. 22, 1887. See also MI, *Memoria, 1890*, p. 14; Oliveira to Cotegipe, 2ª Sec. No. 11, Asunción, April 25, 1887, MDBA-OR 201/2/2.

41. Forgues, "Le Paraguay," p. 400; Vansittart, "Report," p. 118.

42. Bourgade, *Paraguay*, p. 137.

43. Aguilar to Silva, 1ª Sec. No. 4, Asunción, April 16, 1889, MDBA-OR 201/2/3; Aguilar to Chermont, 2ª Sec. No. 25, Asunción, Aug. 28, 1891, MDBA-OR 201/2/4; *DO*, Aug. 28, 1891; Shaw to Wharton, No. 12, Asunción, Sept. 11, 1891, DUSCA T 329/3; DCR No. 1006, *Paraguay 1892*, pp. 16–17.

44. *RO*, 1869, p. 31; Vansittart, "Report," pp. 109–10.

45. Escobar, *Mensaje* (April, 1889), p. 11.

46. Pérez Acosta, *Carlos Antonio López*, pp. 291–93; Vansittart, "Report," p. 118; *La Democracia*, Nov. 8, 1881; *El Diario*, Sept. 4, 1881; Alvarez to Minister of Foreign Affairs, Asunción, Oct. 20, 1893, MRE-A *Memoria, 1884*,

pp. 244–45; DCR No. 792, *Paraguay 1890*, p. 5; González, *Mensaje* (April, 1894), pp. 9–10.

47. Caballero, *Mensaje* (April, 1885), p. 9; Atilio García Mellid, *Proceso a los falsificadores de la historia del Paraguay*, II, 468.

Chapter 14. Basic Industries

1. *DO*, Sept. 24, 1897; DCR No. 2121, *Paraguay 1898*, p. 3; MI, *Memoria, 1898*, p. 16; William Harrison, "Business outlook in Paraguay for the year 1899," encl., Finch to Hay, No. 126, Montevideo, Jan. 19, 1899, DDPU 128/10.

2. DCR No. 2121, *Paraguay 1898*, p. 3; Gosling to Grey, No. 3 Commercial, Asunción, June 4, 1907, PRO-FO 368/118; "La producción del algodón en el Paraguay," *RM* 2 (1898), 358.

3. Giuseppe de Paternó, "La obra del Dr. Paterno," p. 78; Caballero, *Mensaje* (April, 1883), pp. 5–6; José Segundo Decoud, *Cuestiones políticas y económicas*, pp. 4–5, Carlos Rey de Castro, *La clase rural paraguaya*, p. 45.

4. Escobar, *Mensaje* (April, 1889), p. 7; Freire Esteves, *El Paraguay consituticional*, p. 80; González, *Mensaje* (April, 1891), p. 7; Egusquiza, *Mensaje* (April, 1896), p. 51. Decoud led in organizing the Sociedad Agrícola y de Aclimatación del Paraguay in 1877 which published *El Agrónomo* (Pastore, *La lucha por la tierra en el Paraguay*, p. 189).

5. *RO*, 1876, pp. 171–73; José Segundo Decoud, *Plan económico presentado por el poder ejecutivo*, pp. 20–25; Aguilar to Pereira, 2ªa Sec. No. 4, Asunción, Jan. 26, 1892, MDBA-OR 201/2/5.

6. MI, *Memoria, 1898–1899*, p. 5; Freire Esteves, *El Paraguay constitucional*, p. 163.

8. DCR No. 1963, *Paraguay 1896*, p. 3.

9. Act of Aug. 23, 1884, *Almanaque nacional . . . 1886*, pp. 101–02.

10. The Germans at San Bernardino had 200,000 trees bearing fruit in 1896 (DCR No. 1963, *Paraguay 1896*, p. 13; *Revista Comercial*, Aug. 15, 1900).

11. Vansittart, "Report," pp. 141, 148; Schurz, *Paraguay*, pp. 48–50.

12. Mulhall and Freund, *Letters*, No. 8, p. 25.

13. George Maney to Secretary of State, No. 11, Montevideo, July 8, 1890, DDPU 128/8.

14. DCR No. 1963, *Paraguay 1896*, p. 5.

15. MH, *Memoria, 1900*, pp. 459–60; Freire Esteves, *El Paraguay constituticional*, p. 164.

16. Viera, *Colección legislativa*, p. 145; Vansittart, "Report," p. 96.

17. Mulhall and Freund, *Letters*, No. 7. Several of these letters are not paged.

18. DCR No. 2275, *Paraguay 1898*, p. 6; Aceval, *Mensaje* (April, 1901), pp. 10–11; Stewart to Foreign Office, Asunción, April 30, 1886, PRO-FO 59/44; Gosling to Lansdowne, No. 6, Asunción, June 24, 1901, PRO-FO 59/59.

19. Aguilar to Diana, 2ª Sec. No. 2, Asunción, Aug. 11, 189, MDBA-OR 201/2/3; *El Paraguayo*, Aug. 11, 1899; Finch to Hay, No. 290, Montevideo, Feb. 15, 1900, DDPU 128/12; *The Paraguay Review* 3, no. 1 (March, 1903), 1–2.

20. Vansittart, "Report," p. 148; Egerton to Granville, No. 5 Commercial, Buenos Aires, July 31, 1881, PRO-FO 6/365; Schurz, *Paraguay*, pp. 78–80.

21. J. W. Hankin to Foreign Office, No. 13, Asunción, Oct. 31, 1903, PRO-FO 59/62; Arthur Wilson Fox to Foreign Office, London, Feb. 8, 1904, ibid.

22. Dering to Granville, No. 2, Asunción, July 2, 1883, PRO-FO 59/46; Act of Dec. 4, 1884, Viera, *Colección legislativa*, pp. 261–62; Ivan M. Elchibegoff, "The Forest Resources and Timber Trade of Latin America," p. 81.

23. Act of Aug. 29, 1876, *RO*, 1876, p. 127.

24. Gosling to Salisbury, No. 13 Commercial, Asunción, Aug. 7, 1900, PRO-FO 59/58.

25. Gosling to Lansdowne, No. 3 Treaty, Asunción, Oct. 17, 1902, PRO-FO 59/63.

26. Gosling to Director of Kew Gardens, Asunción, May 14, 1901, PRO-FO 59/62; Gosling to Lansdowne, No. 1 Commercial, Asunción, Jan. 12, 1905, PRO-FO 59/63; Director of Kew Gardens to Foreign Office, [London], May 8, 1905, ibid.

27. Charles A. Washburn, *History of Paraguay*, I, 450. The accent is retained on the *e* since the word was invariably written *maté* during the nineteenth century, but it is always pronounced with the accent on the first syllable. Yerbales are located on Bourgade's map accompanying his *Paraguay*.

28. Viera, *Colección legislativa*, pp. 81–83. Congress made yerba a government monopoly by the act of July 4, 1876 (*RO*, 1876, pp. 164–65).

29. E. L. Baker, "Report on Yerba Mate or Paraguay Tea," pp. 99–100; Washburn, *History of Paraguay*, I, 457–61.

30. Vansittart, "Report," p. 145.

31. Meulemans, *La République du Paraguay*, p. 8; Freire Esteves, *El Paraguay constitucional*, p. 165; DCR No. 2275, *Paraguay 1898*, p. 5.

32. Freire Esteves, *El Paraguay constitucional*, p. 78.

33. Ibid., pp. 52, 56.

34. Alcalá, *El Paraguay en marcha*, p. 290.

35. DCR No. 1006, *Paraguay 1890*, p. 19; DCR No. 1963, *Paraguay 1896*, p. 4; Rodríguez Alcalá, *El Paraguay en marcha*, p. 292.

36. Oliveira to Cotegipe, 2ª Sec. No. 10, Asunción, April 15, 1887, MDBA-OR 201/2/2; Rodríguez Alcalá, *El Paraguay en marcha*, pp. 298–302.

37. Itiberê da Cunha to Rio Branco, 3ª Sec. No. 5, Asunción, Aug. 25, 1903, MDBA-OR 201/2/7.

38. Mulhall and Mulhall, *Handbook* (5th ed., 1885), p. 633; Moreira, "Relatorio commercial e politico do anno findo de 1884," RCBA-O 238/3/7.

39. Eugenio Friedmann, *Historia del azúcar en el Paraguay*, 133–34; *La Democracia*, July 12, 1881; Egerton to Granville, No. 5 Commercial, Buenos Aires, July 31, 1881, PRO-FO 6/365.

40. DCR No. 2121, *Paraguay 1897*, p. 13.

41. Friedmann, *Historia del azúcar en el Paraguay*, pp. 145–52.

42. *Almanaque nacional . . . 1886*, p. 173; *RM* 2, no. 24 (Feb. 15, 1898),

367–70; Fasciotti to Magalhães, 3ª Sec. No. 3, Asunción, April 10, 1900, RCBA-O 238/3/12; Nicolás Pinto da Silva Valle to Rio Branco, 3ª Sec. No. 10, Asunción, July 8, 1904, RCBA-O 238/3/13.

43. *RM* 2, no. 20 (Oct. 15, 1897), 238–242, and no. 22 (Dec. 15, 1897), 297–303; *Almanaque nacional . . . 1886*, p. 173.

44. *RM* 2, no. 19 (Sept. 15, 1897), 198–203.

45. *RM* 2, no. 21 (Nov. 15, 1897), 278: *RM* 3, no. 25 (March 1898), 23–28.

46. Act of June 14, 1876, *RO*, 1876, p. 91; act of Aug. 25, 1879, *RO*, 1879, p. 545; RPCD *Actas* 1879, p. 483. The company was prospering in 1881 (Vansittart, "Report," p. 151). Another prominent brick and tile factory was located in the Chaco opposite Asunción. Andrés Porras, the owner, advertised it for sale in 1887 (*La Nación*, Sept. 4, 1887).

47. *RM* 2, no. 16 (Aug. 15, 1897), 178–85. The government was forced to pay damages to Mendiondon after having inadvertently granted another concession to Molina y Cía. which built the Fábrica Nacional in 1885 (*Almanaque nacional . . . 1886*, p. 171).

48. These maps are preserved in perfect condition in MVEA AHI-MRD 272/1/19/5.

49. DCR No. 1006, *Paraguay 1891*, pp. 19–20.

50. William Mill Butler, *Paraguay*, pp. 5–6. Butler was secretary, treasurer, and general manager.

51. *PMR* 1, no. 4 (April, 1901), 116; ibid., no. 5 (May, 1901), 201: Emilio Aceval, *Mensaje* (April, 1901), p. 5.

52. Oliveira to Cotegipe, 2ª Sec. No. 10, Asunción, April 15, 1887, MDBA-OR 201/2/2.

53. Hector M. Lagos, *Carlos Casado del Alisal*, passim; *La Nación*, Oct. 4, 1887.

54. RPCS, *Actas* 1872, p. 79; Horrocks to Petre, Asunción, July 16, 1882, encl., Petre to Granville, No. 7 Commercial, Buenos Aires, Aug. 10, 1882, PRO-FO 6/369.

55. Sackville West to Derby, No. 78, Buenos Aires, Sept. 15, 1877, PRO-FO 6/340.

56. Gondim to Pereira de Souza, 1ª Sec. No. 3 Conf., Buenos Aires, Feb. 4, 1881, MDBBA-OR 205/4/9.

57. *RO*, June 9, 1877, pp. 232–33; *El Economista* (Buenos Aires), Oct. 15, 1877.

58. Gondim to Pereira de Souza, 1ª Sec. No. 3 Conf., Buenos Aires, Feb. 4, 1881, MDBBA-OR 205/4/9; DCR No. 1006, *Paraguay 1892*, p. 3; *DO*, Sept. 22, 1893; Lins de Almeida to Pereira, 3ª Sec. No. 13, Asunción, Sept. 23, 1893, MDBA-OR 201/1/5.

Chapter 15. Foreign Trade

1. *Paraguay* 1, no. 1 (Oct. 1912), 3. Miguel Angel González Erico's "Estructura y desarrollo del comercio exterior del Paraguay: 1870–1918" is concerned primarily with the period after 1904.

2. Moreira to Francisco da C. Soares Brandão, 2ª Sec. No. 5, Asunción, Aug. 16, 1883, RCBA-O 238/3/7.

3. Act of July 20, 1885, *RO*, 1885, pp. 1234–35; Viera, *Colección legislativa*, pp. 272–74; *RO*, 1888, p. 19; MH, *Memoria, 1885*, p. 8; W. J. Holmes to Foreign Office, No. 3 Commercial, Asunción, Sept. 14, 1896, PRO-FO 59/54; DCR No. 2275, *Paraguay 1898*, p. 3; Ruffin to Cridler, No. 9, Asunción, Jan. 31, 1898, DUSCA T 329/4.

4. Silva Valle to Rio Branco, 3ª Sec. No. 2, Asunción, April 25, 1904, RCBA-O 238/3/13.

5. Report of Juan del Molino Torres in MRE-A, *Memoria, 1880*, pp. 91–94.

6. DCR No. 1963, *Paraguay 1896*, p. 2.

7. González, *Infortunios del Paraguay*, p. 155.

8. Manoel Francisco Correia to Francisco Pereira Pinto and José Auto da Silva Guimarães, Rio de Janeiro, April 10, 1872, CE AHI-MRD 246/2/7; Henrique de Barros Cavalcanti do Lacerda to Philippe Franco de Sá, Sec. Cen. No. 1 Res., Asunción, May 21, 1882, MDBA-OR 201/2/1.

9. Araújo Gondim to Albuquerque, Sec. Cen. No. 12, Buenos Aires, Aug. 11, 1882, MDBBA-OR 205/4/10; Lacerda to Albuquerque, Sec. Cen. No. 3, Asunción, , Feb. 18, 1883, MDBA-OR 201/2/1; *El Heraldo*, Nov. 13, 1885; MH, *Memoria, 1885*, p. 10.

10. *La Revista Paraguaya* 1 (July 30, 1882), 12–13; DCR No. 1963, *Paraguay 1896*, p. 4.

11. Gondim to Albuquerque, Sec. Cen. No. 6, Buenos Aires, June 12, 1877, MDBBA-OR 205/4/5.

12. DCR No. 2121, *Paraguay 1897*, p. 6.

13. DCR No. 1963, *Paraguay 1896*, p. 2; Itiberê da Cunha to Carvalho, 2ª Sec., No. 4, Asunción, May 28, 1896, MDBA-OR 201/2/6; Lisboa to Carvalho, 1ª Sec. No. 2 Res., Asunción, Jan. 15, 1896, ibid.; *La Democracia*, Jan. 14, 1896; MRE-P, *Memoria, 1897*, p. 3; MRE-P, *Memoria, 1898*, pp. 3–4; DCR No. 2275, *Paraguay 1898*, p. 3.

14. Vansittart, "Report," p. 140.

15. *The Standard* (Buenos Aires), June 8, 1899, encl. No. 2, Ruffin to Hill, Asunción, June 17, 1899, DUSCA T 329/5; Finch to Hay, No. 222, Montevideo, Aug. 23, 1899, DDPU 128/11.

16. Vansittart, "Report," p. 128.

17. DCR No. 2121, *Paraguay 1897*, pp. 7–8.

18. DCR No. 2275, *Paraguay 1898*, p. 4; DCR No. 2426, *Paraguay 1899*, pp. 4–5; DCR *Paraguay 1900*, pp. 6–7; DCR No. 3007, *Paraguay 1902*, p. 8.

19. DCR No. 2886, *Paraguay 1901*, p. 5.

20. Bacon to Bayard, No. 156, Montevideo, May 25, 1887, DDPU 128/6.

21. "Summary of business at the United States consulate at Asunción, Paraguay, during the quarter ended June 30, 1892," encl., Edmund Shaw to Wharton, No. 43, Asunción, June 30, 1892, DUSCA T 329/3; "Questions between the Government of Paraguay and U.S. Consulate," encl. No. 2, Flagg to Edwin F. Uhl, No. 143, Asunción, June 30, 1895, ibid. Charles H. Chase, an American living in Villa Rica, shipped fifteen bales of jaborandi leaves to New York in 1895 (Samuel W. Thomé to W. W. Rockhill, Asunción, Aug. 7, 1896, DUSCA T 329/4).

22. Ruffin to Cridler, No. 2, Asunción, Nov. 9, 1897, DUSCA T 329/4 Butler, *Paraguay*, p. 60.

23. Francisco Gil del Castello Branco to Quintana Bocayuva, 2ª Sec. No. 21, Asunción, May 27, 1890, RCBA-O 238/3/7; A. Barros Bastos to Aguilar de Carvalho, 3ª Sec. No. 4, Asunción, March 2, 1896, RCBA-O 238/3/10.

24. Rodrigues Martins to Pereira de Souza, 2ª Sec. No. 5, Asunción, Oct. 20, 1881, RCBA-O 238/3/7; Correa de Sá to Paula Souza, 3ª Sec. No. 10, Asunción, June 2, 1893, RCBA-O 238/3/9.

25. "Relação dos navios despachados no vice consulado em Vila Conceição durante o 1º trimestre de 1899," encl., Fasciotti to Magalhães, Asunción, April 10, 1899, RCBA-O 238/3/11; "Relação dos navios despachados no vice consulado em Assumpção no terceiro quartel de 1903," encl., Fasciotti to Rio Branco, 4ª Sec. No. 25, Asunción, Oct. 1, 1903, RCBA-O 238/3/12.

26. Jaime Dias to Cassiano do Nascimento, 3ª Sec. No. 4, Asunción, April 26, 1894, RCBA-O 238/3/9. Joaquim Antônio Malheiros owned the Malheiros fazenda. Correa de Sá to Filippe Pereira, 3ª Sec. No. 15, Asunción, Sept. 15, 1893, ibid.

27. Sinimbú to Vasconcellos, Sec. Cen. No. 5, Rio de Janeiro, March 12, 1879, MDBA-D 201/4/10; Moreira de Barros to Vasconcellos, Sec. Cen. No. 5, Rio de Janeiro, July 16, 1879, ibid.; Fasciotti to Magalhães, 3ª Sec. No. 2, Asunción, Feb. 15, 1900, RCBA-O 238/3/12.

28. *La Patria*, Feb. 16, 1903.

Chapter 16: The Wonderland of Government Finance and Banking

1. Petre to Granville, No. 4, Asunción, June 20, 1882, PRO-FO 59/39.

2. Oliveira to Cotegipe, No. 25, Asunción, July 17, 1886, MDBA-OR 201/2/6.

3. *RO*, 1877, p. 236; Vansittart, "Report," pp. 137, 140; Freire Esteves, *El Paraguay constitucional*, p. 53; Lacerda to Franco de Sá, Sec. Cen. No. 1 Res., Asunción, May 21, 1882, MDBA-OR 201/2/1.

4. Encl. No. 1, Shaw to Wharton, No. 41, Asunción, June 10, 1892, DUSCA T 329/3.

5. Flagg, "Information concerning the banking system of Paraguay," Asunción, Oct. 7, 1895, DUSCA T 693/1, pp. 10–11. Hereafter Flagg, "Banking."

6. Dering to Granville, No. 6 Commercial, Asunción, July 7, 1883, PRO-FO 59/40; *Almanaque nacional . . . 1886*, p. 170; DCR No. 1006, *Paraguay 1890*, p. 21.

7. Flagg to Department of State, Asunción, Oct. 7, 1895, DUSCA T 693/1.

8. González, *Mensaje* (April, 1892), p. 6; Arthur Peel, "Report on the Colony of New Australia in Paraguay," encl., Pakenham to Kimberly, No. 14 Commercial, Paraguay, Buenos Aires, Nov. 28, 1894, PRO-FO 59/52.

9. *RO*, 1895, p. 125; MH, *Memoria, 1894*, pp. 6–7; MH, *Memoria, 1896*, p. 8; *DO*, Feb. 25, 1891; DCR No. 2275, *Paraguay 1895*, p. 110; MH, *Memoria, 1897*, Anexo E; p. 37.

10. MH, *Memoria, 1898*, p. 3; MH, *Memoria, 1900*, p. 8.

11. *El País*, Jan. 30 and July 14, 1892; Fasciotti to Magalhães, 3ª Sec. No. 1, Asunción, Feb. 3, 1902, RCBA-O 238/3/12; Gosling to Lansdowne, No. 5

Commercial, Asunción, Feb. 16, 1902, PRO-FO 59/60, and No. 8, Asunción, May 7, 1903, PRO-FO 59/61.

12. Harris Gaylord Warren, "The Golden Fleecing."

13. *El Centinela*, May 21, 1893; Egusquiza, *Mensaje* (April, 1895), p. 25; DCR No. 2121, *Paraguay 1897*, p. 16; Itiberê da Cunha to Carvalho, 2ª Sec. No. 8, Asunción, Aug. 31, 1896, MDBA-OR 201/2/6; *La Democracia*, Oct. 11, 1896.

14. Zubizarreta, "La cuestión de la moneda," p. 153; DCR No. 2275, *Paraguay 1898*, p. 10.

15. This office was created on July 14, 1903, primarily for the purpose of increasing the amount of money in circulation, to deal in gold, and to perform other transactions. A commercial section, created Sept. 4, 1903, with $f3,000,000 as capital, was to promote commerce through loans at 10 percent, and discounts at 9 percent. It paid the Caja 4 percent on its capital (*El Grito del Pueblo*, Jan. 23, 1904). Severely criticized for being staffed by incompetent young men, the agency was a failure. Most of the employees lacked public confidence, had no financial experience, and were pompous and arrogant (*El Triunfo*, July 14, 1904).

16. Lacerda to Albuquerque, Sec. Cen. No. 10 Res., Asunción, Dec. 6, 1882, MDBA-OR 201/2/1.

17. Adolpho P. Carranza to Plaza, Asunción, March 24, 1883, AVP AGN-BA 7/4/5/10.

18. *RO*, 1874, p. 589, and 1875, p. 757. Warren, "Banks and Banking in Paraguay, 1871–1904" González Erico, "Desarrollo de la banca en el Paraguay"; Mendes Fleitas, *Diagnosis paraguaya*, pp. 263–64; RPCS *Actas 1878*, pp. 279–89, and 1879, pp. 331–32; *RO*, 1878, p. 373; Vansittart, "Report," p. 106; *Estatutos de la Sociedad Anómina Banco del Paraguay*, encl., Vasconcellos to Souza, Sec. Cen. No. 25, Asunción, Nov. 9, 1881, MDBA-OR 201/1/16.

19. *RO*, 1883, pp. 1043–46; Padua Fleury to Soares Brandão, 1ª Sec. No. 2, Asunción, Nov. 10, 1883, MDBA-OR 201/2/1; *Memoria del directoria del "Banco Nacional del Paraguay" correspondiente al año de 1887*, pp. 3–7; Flagg, "Banking," pp. 14–18.

20. Viera, *Colección legislativa*, pp. 461–72.

21. MH, *Memoria, 1890*, passim; DCR No. 1006, *Paraguay 1892*, p. 6; Viera, *Colección legislativa*, pp. 528–30. The Banco Nacional's affairs were finally closed on Aug. 20, 1903.

22. MH, *Memoria, 1888*, p. 6; Viera, *Colección legislativa*, pp. 528–30; *El Independiente*, May 23, 1893.

23. Statement of Alfred Busk, Asunción, Nov. 3, 1895, Document Aa in Thornton to Salisbury, Consular No. 2, Buenos Aires, Jan. 24, 1896, PRO-FO 6/448. The whole affair is recounted in *Bono general de cuatrocientos mil libras esterlinas. Demanda del fiscal general de estado. Contestación del Banco del Paraguay y Río de la Plata* (Asunción, 1895). A copy is in PRO-FO 6/448.

24. Flagg, "Banking," pp. 4–5.

25. *La Democracia*, Dec. 14, 1894; MH, *Memoria, 1890*, p. 5; Zubizarreta, "La cuestión de la moneda," p. 153.

26. Richard von Fischer-Treuenfeld, *Le Paraguay décrit et illustré*, p. 69; Butler, *Paraguay*, p. 11.

27. Flagg, "Banking," passim; Warren, "The Paraguayan Revolution of 1904."

28. DCR No. 2275, *Paraguay 1899*, p. 4; López Decoud, *Album gráfico de la República del Paraguay*, passim; Fischer-Treuenfeld, *Paraguay*, p. 57.

Chapter 17: Immigration and Colonization

1. Freire Esteves, *El Paraguay constitucional*, p. 89. This figure became 20,000 in González, *Infortunios del Paraguay*, p. 89.

2. *El Independiente*, Feb. 16 and 17, 1891; *La Democracia*, Nov. 21, 1891; Dias to Araripe, 3ª Sec. No. 2, Asunción, Feb. 23, 1891, MDBA-OR 201/2/4. In the early 1880s, the Brazilian consul-general had urged his government to help discontented families to emigrate (Francisco Gil del Castello Branco to Antônio da Silva Prado, Asunción, Dec. 3, 1885, RCBA-O 238/3/7.

3. Dias to Francisco Pereira, 2ª Sec. No. 39, Asunción, Dec. 16, 1890, RCBA-O 238/3/8. The outflow of discontended families continued until, according to one writer, Paraguayans made up more than 60 percent of the population of Mato Grosso and Misiones, and 80 percent of Formosa (González, *Infortunios del Paraguay*, p. 367).

4. *La Democracia*, Aug. 31, 1887.

5. Caballero, *Mensaje* (April, 1883), pp. 6–7; Escobar, *Mensaje* (April, 1889), p. 5; González, *Mensaje* (April, 1892), p. 9; Egusquiza, *Mensaje* (April, 1896), pp. 8–9.

6. Foreign Office, Miscellaneous Series No. 358, "Report on the 'New Australia' Colony in Paraguay," p. 14. Hereafter "New Australia Report."

7. MRE-P, *Memoria, May 31, 1884;* decree of June 15, 1888, Viera, *Colección legislativa*, pp. 412–14.

8. Flagg to Department of State, Asunción, Oct. 7, 1895, NPFO T 693/1.

9. Ruffin to Finch, Asunción, Jan. 17, 1899, encl., Finch to Hay, Montevideo, Jan. 30, 1899, DDPU 128/10.

10. *La Pampa* (Buenos Aires), March 20, 1880.

11. Egerton to Granville, No. 5 Commercial, Buenos Aires, July 31, 1881, PRO-FO 6/365; Petre to Granville, No. 1, Asunción, June 9, 1882, PRO-FO 59/39; Vansittart, "Report," passim; Harris Gaylord Warren, "The 'Lincolnshire Farmers' in Paraguay."

12. Decoud, *Cuestiones políticas y económicas*, pp. 5–6.

13. Stewart, *Japanese Colonization in Eastern Paraguay*, p. 77.

14. DCR No. 1537, *Paraguay 1893*, p. 3; Decoud, *Cuestiones políticas y económicas*, p. 3; Fischer-Treuenfeld, *Paraguay*, pp. 40–42.

15. DCR No. 3649, *Paraguay 1906*, p. 3. Paraguayans also entertained a deep dislike for Brazilians (Oliveira to Cotegipe, 2ª Sec. No. 12, Asunción, Nov. 18, 1886, MDBA-OR 201/2/2).

16. Viera, *Colección legislativa*, pp. 171–76; *La Reforma*, June 9, 1881; Vansittart, "Report," pp. 91–92; *RO*, 1881, pp. 742–47. The first director general of immigration was George F. Metzler, a German who had brought 200 colonists to San Bernardino. Metzler was appointed on June 14, 1882 (*RO*, 1882, p. 853). President Escobar had the department of immigration transferred from interior to foreign affairs in 1888 (MRE-P, *Memoria, 1889*,

p. 7). An act of February 28, 1902, combined the information office, the commissary of immigration, and the department of immigration into a Dirección General de Inmigracíon, divided into three sections. The first director was Jacob Wavrunek, a Polish-American immigrant from Wisconsin (Finch to Hay, No. 590, Montevideo, Oct. 11, 1902, DDPU 128/15). Wavrunek was dismissed early in 1904 because of alcoholism (Ruffin to Loomis, No. 151, Asunción, Jan. 16, 1904, DUSCA T 329/6). Four years later, when the Colorados decided to sell off the public domain, the law was revised to give twenty-five leagues of Chaco land to any company that would establish 140 families in the land within four years (Act of July 15, 1885, *Almanaque nacional . . . 1886*, pp. 224–30.

17. Ibid., pp. 174–86.

18. Japanese were permitted to enter the country by laws of 1924 and 1925; immigrants were permitted by the Decree of April 30, 1936 (Carlos A. Rolón, comp., *Compilación de leyes y decretos ordenados por Carlos Pastore*, p. 82).

19. MRE—P, *Leyes de inmigración, colonización y reducción de tribus indijenas*, pp. 3–7. Hereafter *Leyes de inmigración.*

20. Ibid., pp. 9–20. See also Lyra Pidoux de Drachenberg, "Inmigración y colonización en el Paraguay, 1870–1970."

21. Lisboa to Carvalho, 1ª Sec. No. 1 Conf., Asunción, June 2, 1895, MDBA-OR 201/2/6.

22. Moreira to Affonso Penna, Asunción, June 28, 1883, RCBA-O 238/3/7.

23. *Anuario estadístico de la República del Paraguay* (1888), p. 42; DCR No. 1006, *Paraguay 1892*, p. 83; MI, *Memoria, 1890*, p. 69.

24. MRE-P, *Memoria, 1889*, pp. 140–41; MRE-P, *Memoria, 1897*, p. 14; MI, *Memoria 1899–1900*, p. 159.

25. MRE-P [José de Stéfano Paternó], *Memoria de la oficina de inmigración y colonización correspondiente a los años de 1905–1906 —1906–1907*, p. 15. Hereafter Paternó, *Memoria.*

26. When the Paraguay Central Railway passed into English hands and Luis Patri obtained the concession to extend the railway in 1888, workers were brought in from England and other countries. By 1892 their number had reached 360, and during the next ten years only 77 more were added (ibid., pp. 26–27).

27. The sociologist may be concerned with differentiating between group settlements and colonists. For a discussion of this point, see Joseph Winfield Fretz, *Group Settlements in Paraguay*, pp. 23–25.

28. For a summary of unsuccessful group settlements, see ibid., pp. 23–27.

29. Christian Heisecke, a German who had been in Asunción since 1872, translated the request (Pitaud, *El General Caballero*, p. 159). For the early development of San Bernardino, see Bernhard Förster, *Deutsche Colonien in dem oberen Laplata-gebiete, mit besonderer Berücksichtigung von Paraguay*, pp. 184–93; Paternó, *Memoria*, p. 15.

30. Vansittart, "Report," p. 15.

31. Mevert, *Reisebriefe aus Paraguay*, passim; MI, *Memoria, 1888*, p. 58.

32. DCR No. 1357, *Paraguay 1893*, p. 11.

33. *RM* 3, no. 25 (March, 1898), 21–22; MRE-P, *Memoria, 1898*, pp. 7–8; Juan Carlos Herken Krauer to author, London, Sept. 28, 1982: Fischer-Treuenfeld, *Paraguay*, p. 46.

34. DCR No. 3007, *Paraguay 1902*, p. 14.

35. Williams, *The Rise and Fall of the Paraguayan Republic, 1800–1870*, pp. 192–93; act of July 4, 1879, *RO*, 1879, pp. 521–23; *Almanaque nacional . . . 1886*, pp. 267–68.

36. Vansittart, "Report," p. 113; Caballero, *Mensaje* (April, 1881), p. 5.

37. There were 10 distilleries, 15 *trapiches* (primitive sugar mills), and 4 brick yards in 1898 (Martins to Pereira de Souza, 2ª Sec. No. 5, Asunción, Oct. 20, 1881, RCBA-O 238/3/7; Vansittart, "Report," p. 90; Pastore, *La lucha por la tierra en el Paraguay*, pp. 200, 252; MI, *Memoria, 1888*, p. 58; MRE-P, *Memoria, 1898*, p. 35; *RM*,1, no. 6 [March, 1896], 21ff.).

Chapter 18: The Growth of Agricultural Colonies

1. This was the fear expressed by the American minister to Germany, whose report of March 12, 1883, was sent to Buenos Aires by the Argentine minister in Washington. The Argentine minister of foreign relations published this report as a pamphlet in February, 1885 (Monson to Granville, No. 22, Buenos Aires, March 10, 1885, PRO-FO 6/385).

2. Dering to Granville, No. 20, Buenos Aires, April 7, 1883, PRO-FO 6/374.

3. Ibid.; Quistorp wrote an effusive propaganda pamphlet; *El Orden*, Aug. 8, 1885; Carvalho to Paranaguá, 1ª Sec. No. 24, Asunción, Aug. 9, 1885, MDBA-OR 201/2/11; *La Nación*, Sept. 11, 1887.

4. Fretz, *Immigrant Group Settlements in Paraguay*, pp. 56–58; *La Nación*, Sept. 1, 1887; Aceval, *República del Paraguay, apuntes geográficos e históricos*, p. 33, hereafter Aceval, *Apuntes;* MRE-P, *Memoria, 1898*, p. 35; MRE-P, *Memoria, 1899–1900*, p. 135; *RM* 1, no. 1 (March 15, 1898), 23.

5. *RO*, 1888, pp. 48–51; Carvalho to Augusto da Silva, Sec. Cen. No. 10, Asunción, June 8, 1888, MDBA-OR 201/2/3; *El Paraguayo*, June 6, 1888.

6. Société Générale Paraguayo-Argentina, *Colonies de Villa Sana créés en 1889 par J. Valentin*, p. 17; Aceval, *Apuntes*, p. 35.

7. *RM* 2, no. 19 (Sept. 15, 1897), 213–14.

8. Fretz, *Immigrant Group Settlements in Paraguay*, pp. 35–36, lists Elisa as an unsuccessful Swedish colony. It was not Swedish in origin and never was predominantly Swedish in composition. See also Schurz, *Paraguay*, p. 139.

9. Pitaud, *El General Caballero*, p. 192; *La Democracia*, Dec. 18, 1898; Cabo Frio to Aguilar, 2ª Sec. No. 38, Rio de Janeiro, Dec. 17, 1891, MDBA-D 201/4/11; bylaws of the colony, dated Dec. 29, 1891, are in Bureau of American Republics, *Bulletin* No. 54 (1894), pp. 117–20: *Noticia sobre la colonia "Presidente González" en el departamento de Caazapá*, pp. 11–12.

10. DCR No. 1357, *Paraguay 1893*, p. 10.

11. Ibid., p. 26.

12. "New Australia Report," p. 11; *DO*, 1895, pp. 40–41; Lisboa to

Carvalho, 2ª Sec. No. 9, Asunción, March 22, 1895, and 2ª Sec. No. 1 Res., Asunción, April 11, 1895, MDBA-OR 201/2/6. The French minister in Buenos Aires was so annoyed that consular relations were not restored until Jan. 13, 1898 (*La Opinión*, Jan. 15, 1898; Ruffin to Wheeler, No. 7, Asunción, Jan. 15, 1898, DUSCA T 329/4).

13. "A lottery scheme of Señor Alcorta and Syndicate," encl. Shaw to Wharton, No. 64, Asunción, Jan. 14, 1893, DUSCA T 329/3.

14. MRE-P, *Memoria, 1899–1900*, p. 163; MH, *Memoria, 1899*, Anexo D; *The Paraguay Review* 2, no. 7 (July, 1902), 218–19. Colonia Nacional became part of the Yegros district *(partido)* on Jan. 31, 1902 (Fischer-Treuenfeld, *Paraguay*, p. 49).

15. See Harold V. Livermore, "New Australia."

16. "New Australia Report," p. 3.

17. "Contract between the Government of Paraguay and the New Australia Cooperative Association, March 10, 1893," *DO*, No. 1065, encl. No. 2, Stewart to Foreign Office, Oct. 10, 1893, PRO-FO 59/51.

18. *New Australia*, Sept. 16, 1893, encl., Pakenham to Rosebery, Paraguay No. 4 Commercial, Buenos Aires, Jan. 31, 1894, PRO-FO 59/52.

19. Decree of Dec. 19, 1893, Viera, *Colección legislativa*, pp. 587–88; DCR No. 1357, *Paraguay 1893*, p. 23.

20. Stewart to Foreign Office, Asunción, Oct. 10, 1893, PRO-FO 59/51; Lins de Almeida to Pereira, Asunción, 3ª Sec. No. 12, MDBA-OR 201/2/5; DCR No. 1357, *Paraguay 1893*, p. 22; *La República*, Sept. 23, 1893; Colonists to Commissioner of Emigration, New Australia, Dec. 5, 1893, encl., Stewart to Pakenham, Asunción, Dec. 30, 1893, PRO-FO 59/52.

21. *The Review of the River Plate*, Jan. 13, 1892, encl. No. 4, Pakenham to Rosebery, Commercial No. 4 Paraguay, Buenos Aires, Jan. 16, 1894, PRO-FO 59/52; A. Brittlebank to Stewart, Villa Rica, Dec. 21, 1893, encl., Stewart to Pakenham, Asunción, Dec. 30, 1893, ibid.

22. DCR No. 1357, *Paraguay 1893*, p. 19.

23. "New Australia Report," p. 14.

24. MacDonald to Editor, Colonia Nueva Australia, Feb. 25, 1895, *The Standard* (Buenos Aires), March 13, 1895, encl., Pakenham to Kimberley, Paraguay No. 3 Commercial, Buenos Aires, March 13, 1895, PRO-FO 59/53.

25. W. J. Holmes to Foreign Office, No. 9 Commercial, Asunción, Dec. 26, 1896, PRO-FO 59/54. In 1906, there were 134 people, including 34 Paraguayans, in the area (MRE-P, *Memoria de la oficina general de inmigración y colonización correspondiente a los años 1905–1906 —1906–1907*, p. 99).

26. Stewart to Pakenham, Asunción, May 2, 1894, encl., Pakenham to Kimberley, Commercial No. 14 Paraguay, Buenos Aires, May 7, 1894, PRO-FO 59/52); "The Constitution of Cosme Colony," passim; William Lane, "The Second Yearly Report of Cosme Colony, Paraguay, May 12th, 1896," copy in Gondra Collection, University of Texas-Austin.

27. DCR No. 1963, *Paraguay 1896*, p. 11; Lane to Pedro Peña, Colonia Cosme, Jan. 20, 1903, MRE-P, *Memoria 1903*, pp. 453–54; Gosling to Lansdowne, No. 15 Commercial, Asunción, Sept. 10, 1902, PRO-FO 59/60. Lane had left Australia on Oct. 15, 1902, and returned to Cosme in December (MRE-P, Paternó, *Memoria*, pp. 26–27).

28. Genaro Romero, *Informe sobre la colonia "25 de Noviembre,"* p. 1; *DO*, Nov. 20, 1893; Almeida to Cassiano do Nascimento, 3ª Sec. No. 1, Asunción, Jan. 3, 1894, MDBA-OR 201/2/5; Viera, *Colección legislativa*, p. 588.

29. MRE-P, *Memoria, 1898*, p. 36; Meulemans, *La République du Paraguay*, p. 9. Adolf N. Schuster, *Paraguay*, p. 604, gives only 1,640 for the population in 1921. In earlier reports, many small communities had been attached to the colony for administrative purposes.

30. Romero, *Informe sobre la colonia "25 de Noviembre,"* passim.

31. *PMR* 1, no. 1 (July 1901), 216.

32. *The Paraguay Review* 2, no. 7 (July, 1902), 218. With this issue, *The Paraguay Monthly Review* shortened its name and became a quarterly. MRE-P, Peternó, *Memoria*, pp. 95–96; Angel Battilana, *Informe sobre la colonia "Hohenau,"* pp. 2–13. Battilana was Inspector Agrimensor de Colonias and made his report to the minister of foreign affairs.

33. *PMR* 1, no. 2 (Feb. 1901), 40; MRE-P, *Memoria, 1900–1901*, pp. 39–41; MRE-P, *Colonia Gaboto organización y reglamentación*, pp. 3–9.

34. Wavrunek to Antolín Irala, Asunción, June 18, 1903, in MRE-P, *Memoria 1903*, p. 440; MRE-P, Paternó, *Memoria*, p. 96.

35. Pertinent documents relating to the foundation and early activities of the society, the polemic between its administrative council and *Il Corriere di Cattania*, the protest of Italians in Asunción, Dr. Paternó's defense, and the proposed law authorizing the colony are in Paternó, "Obra."

36. Ibid., pp. 2–31.

37. Ibid., pp. 83–105.

38. Pasquale Pecci to Egusquiza, Asunción, June 30, 1898, ibid., pp. 106–97. Pecci was president of the Sociedad Italiana de Mútuos Socorros.

39. Egusquiza to Congress, June 24, 1898, ibid., pp. 128–29; act of July 29, 1898, ibid., pp. 134–37.

40. Giuseppe de Stéfano Paternó, *Relazione sulla colonizzazione nel Paraguay*, pp. 20–22, 29; Romero, "Informe sobre las colonias 'Nueva Italia' y 'Trinacria,' " pp. 17, 119; DCR No. 2275, *Paraguay 1898*, p. 9.

41. Romero, "Informe," pp. 21–24; *PMR* 1, no. 7 (July, 1901), 218; MRE-P, *Memoria, 1900–1901*, p. 39.

42. Romero, "Informe," pp. 30–34; MRE-P, Paternó, *Memoria*, p. 98; Itiberê da Cunha to Castro Cerqueira, 2ª Sec. No. 12, Asunción, Aug. 14, 1898, MDBA-OR 201/2/6.

43. *La Democracia*, Sept. 11 and Oct. 1, 1891.

44. Itiberê da Cunha to Magalhães, 2ª Sec. No. 1, Asunción, Jan. 2, 1899, MDBS-OR 201/2/6. *La Democracia* and *La Opinión*, in their issues of Jan. 2, 1899, praised the Brazilian's lavish New Year's reception.

45. Issues of Oct. 27 and 29, 1900.

46. Ayala, *Migraciones*, p. 47.

Chapter 19: People and Society

1. See especially Elman R. Service and Helen S. Service, *Tobatí: A Paraguayan Town*, pp. 24–27.

2. Rey de Castro, *La clase rural paraguaya*, pp. 6–7.

3. Ibid., p. 8.

4. Moreira, "Relatorio commercial e politico do anno findo de 1884," encl., Moreira toSouza Dantas, 2ª Sec. No. 2, Asunción, Feb. 20, 1885, RCBA-O 238/3/7.

5. Barrett, *El dolor paraguayo*, pp. 31–32; Mulhall and Freund, *Letters*, p. 11.

6. Benítez, *Ensayo sobre el liberalismo paraguayo*, pp. 82–83.

7. Barrett, *Dolor Paraguayo*, p. 15.

8. Moreira, "Relatorio," p. 7.

9. Bray, *Hombres y épocas del Paraguay*, I, 98: Vansittart, "Report," p. 153.

10. Rey de Castro, *Clase rural*, p. 34.

11. *Infortunios del Paraguay*, p. 446.

12. *Deutsche Colonien in dem oberen Laplata-gebiete*, p. 81.

13. Egerton to Granville, Buenos Aires, July 30, 1881, PRO-FO 6/365.

14. Molins, *Paraguay*, pp. 15–16.

15. Wavrunek, "Answers to questions for the International Woman's Suffrage Conference."

16. *Ley de matrimonio civil*, 1899.

17. Vansittart, "Report," p. 153; *RP* 1 (Aug. 20, 1882), 51.

18. Mulhall and Freund, *Letters*, p. 25.

19. *El Progreso*, Jan. 20, 1894.

20. *Infortunios del Paraguay*, p. 99.

21. Ibid., pp. 542–49. See also Decoud, *Cuestiones políticas y económicas*, p. 4.

22. Moreira, "Relatorio," p. 7.

23. *Clase rural*, pp. 14, 17.

24. *Dolor paraguayo*, pp. 95–97. Although Barrett wrote during the early Liberal era, his description of rural life is valid for the entire Colorado era.

25. González, *Infortunios del Paraguay*, pp. 98–100; Ayla, *Migraciones*, p. 68.

26. Rey de Castro, *Clase rural*, p. 17.

27. *La Patria*, May 18, 1894.

28. Egusquiza, *Mensaje* (April, 1894), p. 10.

29. *La Prensa*, March 2, 1898. The American consul moved the consulate from the center of town to escape "the kitchen water &c.[that] is turned into the streets at night" (Ruffin to Hill, No. 101, Asunción, Dec. 19, 1899, DUSCA T 329/5).

30. *La Patria Paraguaya*, Sept. 5, 1900.

31. *La Regeneración*, Oct. 1, 1869.

32. Vansittart, "Report," pp. 89–90. Smallpox vaccination had been made compulsory on July 30, 1880.

33. *La Democracia*, Feb. 11, 1893; *El País*, Nov. 15, 1901.

34. Decree of Nov. 20, 1883, *RO*, 1883, p. 1063; *MI, Memoria, 1898–1899*, p. 11.

35. *Revista Paraguaya* 1 (Aug. 6, 1882), 28–29; Lins de Almeida to Felippe Pereira, 2ª Sec. No. 22, Asunción, Oct. 4, 1894, MDBA-OR 201/2/5.

36. Oliveira to Cotegipe, 2ª Sec. No. 21, Asunción, Dec. 8, 1886, and 2ª Sec. No. 18, Asunción, Nov. 28, 1883, MDBA-OR 201/2/2.

37. Castello Branco to Bocayuva, 2ª Sec. No. 10, Asunción, Feb. 26, 1890, RCBA-O 238/3/8; DCR No. 1963, *Paraguay 1896*, p. 18; Guillermo Stewart, *La peste*, pp. 3–10; Aceval, *Mensaje* (April, 1901), p. 14. Elmaisian renewed his contract for two years in 1904 (*PMR* 1 [April, 1901], 13).

38. Itiberê da Cunha to Magalhaes, 2ª Sec. No. 2, Asunción, Feb. 18, 1900, MDBA-OR 201/2/7.

39. Same to same, 2ª Sec. No. 7, May 15, 1900, *ibid.;* Gosling to Salisbury, No. 7 Commercial, Asunción, March 19, 1900, PRO-FO 59/58.

40. *La Tribuna*, July 24, 1900; Harrison to Hill, No. 116, Asunción, July 24, 1900, and No. 117, Asunción, July 27, 1900, DUSCA T 329/5; Itiberê da Cunha to Magalhães, 3ª Sec. No. 6, Asunción, Aug. 17, 1900, and 3ª Sec. No. 10, Asunción, Sept. 24, 1900, MDBA-OR 201/2/7; *La Prensa* (Buenos Aires), Sept. 22 and 24, 1900; Fasciotti to Rio Branco, 3ª Sec. No. 9, Asunción, Aug. 5, 1902, RCBA-O 283/3/12.

41. MI, *Memoria, 1898–1899*, Cuadro No. III.

42. Villa Bello to Vasconcellos, 1ª Sec. No. 29, Rio de Janeiro, Nov. 13, 1878, MDBA-D 201/4/9.

43. Egerton to Granville, No. 50, Buenos Aires, July 31, 1881, PRO-FO 6/364.

44. Vansittart, "Report," p. 111.

45. Petre to Granville, No. 4, Asunción, June 20, 1882, PRO-FO 59/39.

46. Parents generally selected *compadres* for their children at baptism. The compadre had important responsibilities toward the child, and even to the entire family.

47. Rey de Castro, *Clase rural*, pp. 23–25.

48. *El Paraguayo*, May 7 and June 2, 1889; *El Independiente*, May 6, 1889; Aguilar to Silva, 1ª Sec. No. 17, Asunción, May 28, 1889, MDBA-OR 201/2/3; Aguilar to Diana, 1ª Sec. Res. No. 1, Asunción, Oct. 23, 1889, ibid.; Almeida to Mello, 2ª Sec. No. 38, Asunción, Oct. 20, 1892, MDBA-OR 201/2/5.

49. Pakenham to Salisbury, No. 2 Paraguay, Asunción, Aug. 8, 1890, and No. 3 Paraguay, Asunción, Aug. 8, 1890, PRO-FO 59/48.

50. Oliveira to Cotegipe, 2ª Sec. No. 12, Asunción, Nov. 18, 1886, MDBA-OR 201/2/2; Escobar, *Mensaje* (April, 1887), p. 5.

51. *El Paraguayo*, Feb. 5, 1887; *El Látigo*, Nov. 27, 1887; MI, *Memoria, 1888*, p. 19.

52. MI, *Memoria, 1890*, Anexo E; MI, *Memoria, 1895*, pp. 73–83; MI, *Memoria, 1899–1900*, p. 11.

53. *DO*, Sept. 24, 1897, p. 2; MI, *Memoria, 1899–1900*, p. 43.

54. Gosling to Salisbury, No. 8, Asunción, Sept. 29, 1900, PRO-FO 59/58.

55. *La Patria Paraguaya*, Aug. 25, 1900; Itiberê da Cunha to Magalhães, 3ª Sec. No. 14, Asunción, Oct. 31, 1902, MDBA-OR 201/2/7.

56. Bray, *Hombres y épocas del Paraguay*, I, 117–19.

57. Centurión, *Historia de la cultura paraguaya*, I, 390–96.

58. Freire Esteves, *El Paraguay constitucional*, p. 73.

59. Act of June 8, 1880, *RO*, 1880, p. 638.

60. Mulhall and Freund, *Letters*, p. 105.

61. *La Democracia*, May 24, 1893.

62. Ibid., Sept. 9, 1898; *El Pueblo*, Sept. 6, 1898; *La Opinión*, Sept. 6, 1898; *La Prensa*, Sept. 8, and Nov. 16, 1898; *La Democracia*, Nov. 16, 1898; *El Cívico*, Nov. 16, 1898.

63. Among them were Alejandro Audibert, Ramón Zubizarreta, Juan Crisóstomo Centurión y Martínez, and Cecilio Báez (Centurión, *Historia de la cultura paraguaya*, I, 407).

64. Ibid., I, 449–50; Freire Estves, *El Paraguay constitucional*, p. 78. Permanent members included Manuel Domínguez, Federico Bogarín, Juan E. O'Leary, Ignacio Pane, Antolín Irala, and Enrique Solano López (*La Patria Paraguaya*, Oct. 29, 1900).

65. Prominent members included the merchants Pedro and Marcelino Jorba, the jurist Ramón Zubizarreta, Dr. Victorino Abente, the Swiss Justín Berthet, the Germans Alfredo and Max Boetner, Johann Quell, and Augusto and Federico Creydt, the Englishmen Rodney B. Croskey and Robert E. Stewart, Italians Luís Patri and Marcos Quaranta. During the Spanish-American War, Consul Dr. John N. Ruffin accused his vice-consul, the dentist Dr. Eben M. Flagg, of disloyalty because of his activities in the Centro.

Chapter 20: Literature, Education, and Religion

1. Rodríguez Alcalá, *El Paraguay en marcha*, p. 323.

2. Centurión, *Historia de la cultura paraguaya*, I, 361–70.

3. Warren, *Paraguay and the Triple Alliance*, pp. 169–75.

4. Five of Aceval's works are noted in David Lewis Jones, *Paraguay: A Bibliography*.

5. Many of Godoi's papers and his diaries are in the Godoi–Díaz Pérez Collection, University of California, Riverside.

6. Centurión, *Historia de la cultura paraguaya*, I, 416–17.

7. Rodríguez Alcalá, *El Paraguay en marcha*, p. 328.

8. Carlos F. S. Fernández-Caballero lists forty-four titles by Báez in his *Aranduká ha kuatiañeé Paraguai rembiapocué: The Paraguayan Bibliography*.

9. Rodríguez Alcalá, *El Paraguay en marcha*, pp. 327–28.

10. *La Prensa*, Dec. 20, 1899, is given over almost entirely to tributes to Garay. See also John Hoyt Williams, "Note on Blas Garay."

11. Centurión, *Historia de la cultura paraguaya*, I, 453.

12. Warren, *Paraguay and the Triple Alliance*, pp. 169–75; act of July 12, 1882, Viera, *Colección legislativa*, pp. 189–90; Monson to Granville, No. 3 Paraguay, Asunción, Oct. 8, 1884, PRO-FO 59/41.

13. Monson to Granville, No. 3 Paraguay, Asunción, Oct. 8, 1884, PRO-FO 59/41.

14. *Memoria del Ministerio de Justicia, Culto e Instrucción Pública*, 1886. This is a single page memoria.

15. *La Democracia*, Sept. 15, 1891; Almeida to Mello, 2ª Sec. No. 45, Asunción, Dec. 30, 1892, MDBA-OR 201/2/5; *La República*, Dec. 23, 1892; *RO*, 1895, p. 55; W. Barbrooke Grubb, *An Unknown People in an Unknown Land*, pp. 17–21; A. J. Simpson to Salisbury, London, Feb. 7, 1897, PRO-FO 59/55;

Barrington to Salisbury, No. 5, Buenos Aires, Feb. 24, 1897, and No. 25, Buenos Aires, May 27, 1897, ibid.

16. *La Democracia*, April 14, 1898.

17. *La Reforma*, Oct. 1, 1899.

18. Ibid.

19. Flecha to Minister of Justice, Laureles, May 22, 1879, GC-UCR; Benítez, *Historia cultural*, pp. 204–05; Warren, *Paraguay and the Triple Alliance*, pp. 167–69.

20. Sánchez Quell, *Falando do Paraguai ao Brazil*, p. 45.

21. *RO*, 1882, p. 855; *El Centinela*, May 21, 1893; *El Grito del Pueblo*, March 13, 1904.

22. Caballero, *Mensaje* (April, 1885), p. 15.

23. *La Nación*, July 26 and Aug. 17, 1887; Carlos R. Centurión, "Sarmiento en Paraguay."

24. Escobar, *Mensaje* (April, 1887), p. 13.

25. Viera, *Colección legislativa*, pp. 393–401; *La Razón*, July 14, 1889; Aguilar to Diana, 1ª Sec. No. 27, Asunción, July 26, 1889, and 1ª Sec. No. 32, Asunción, Sept. 3, 1889, MDBA-OR 201/2/3; *El Paraguayo*, Oct. 1, 1889; Escobar, *Mensaje* (April, 1889), p. 16. The Concejo de Educación in 1888 granted monthly subsidies for sixty children being educated by the Hermanos de Caridad (*El Independiente*, May 7, 1888).

26. Aguilar to Bocayuva, 1ª Sec. No. 37, Asunción, Dec. 24, 1890, MDBA-OR 201/2/4.

27. González, *Mensaje* (April, 1891), p. 14.

28. Ibid., pp. 20–22. The Colorado era ended with 744 teachers in 319 public schools that enrolled 27,858 pupils. Another 1,765 pupils were in 29 private schools (*Mensaje y proyectos financieros del P. E. á las HH. CC. LL.*, 1904, p. 39).

29. González, *Mensaje* (April, 1894), pp. 37–40; *RO*, 1889, pp. 98–99; *El Estudiante*, Nov. 12, 1899.

30. *La República*, Jan. 8 and 9, 1892; Aguilar to Leite Pereira, 2ª Sec. No. 3, Asunción, Jan. 12, 1892, MDBA-OR 201/2/5; MH, *Memoria, 1896*, pp. 10–11; MH, *Memoria, 1897*, pp. 214–55; DCR No. 2275, *Paraguay 1898*, p. 5.

Bibliography

Manuscripts and Printed Documents

Argentina

Archivo del General José Ignacio Garmendia. AGN BA.
Archivo del General Mitre. Documentos y correspondencia. 6 vols. Buenos Aires, 1911.
Escribanía Pública de Registro Civil No. 62 de la Capital de la Nación. *Testimonio del informe pericial del Sr. Calígrafo Fernando Berghmans.* Buenos Aires, 1897.
Félix Frías. Correspondencia confidencial de la legación Argentina [in Chile] 1869–1871. AGN BA.
Ministerio de Relaciones Exteriores. *Colección de tratados celebrados por la República Argentina con las naciones extrangeras.* 3 vols. Buenos Aires, 1884.
———. *Documentos diplomáticas y consulares* (Boletín No. 28, Tomo VI). Buenos Aires, 1904.
———. *Memorias.* 14 vols. 1878–1891. Titles vary slightly.
Ministerio de Relaciones y Culto. *Catálago de la biblioteca y mapoteca y archivo.* Buenos Aires, 1910.

Brazil

"Cartas do Visconde do Rio Branco." *Anuário do Museu Imperial*, Petrópolis, 1951.
Carvalho, Pedro Candido Affonso de. "Histórico dos principães assumptos tratados pelo legação do Brasil no Paraguay durante o anno de 1886," encl., Francisco Regis de Oliveira to Barão de Cotegipe, 1ª Sec. No. 4, Asunción, Feb. 7, 1887. MDBA-OR.
Chodasiewicz, R[obert] A[dolf]. "Copia da carta dirigida ao presidente da República Argentina pelo Sargento-mór R. A. Chodasiewicz, 1867, com dois [tres] mapas em papel vegetal indicando as posições dos exércitos paraguaios." MEVA (1867–1868) (Thomaz Fortunato Brito), Rio da Prata. AHI MRF 272/1/19/5.
Coleções especiais. Guerra do Paraguai. Corespondencia recebida e expedida de José Auto da Guimarães (Barão do Jaguarão) comandante em chefe do exército brasileiro de ocupação. Despachos. Instrucções, 1859–1887. AHI MRD 201/4/7–11.
Missões diplomáticas brasileiras, Buenos Aires. Despachos, 1874–1906, AHI MRD 207/3/13–15.
Missões diplomáticas brasileiras, Buenos Aires. Oficios recebidos, 1869–1905. AHI MRD 205/3/13–15, 206/1/1–14.

Missões especiais (Visconde de Arinos) Fortunato E. Brito. Oficios confidenciais recebidas do chefe da missão, 1867. AHI MRD 272/1/19.

Moreira, Pedro Ribeiro. "Relatorio commercial e politico do anno findo de 1884," encl., Moreira to Manuel Pinto de Souza Dantas, 2ª Sec. No. 2, Asunción, Feb. 20, 1885. RCBA-O, AHI MRD 238/3/7.

Oliveira, Francisco Regis de. "Histórico dos principães assumptos tratados pela legação do Brasil no Paraguay, durante o anno de 1886," encl., Oliveira to Cotegipe, 1ª Sec. No. 4, Asunción, Feb. 7, 1887. MDBA-OR 201/2/2.

Repartições consulares brasileiras asunção, oficios, 1881–1905. AHI MRD 238/3/7–13.

Great Britain

The Public Record Office contains the reports from diplomats and consuls to the Foreign Office, which are filed under various F. O. numbers. There is also an annual series of consular summaries, published under varying titles. These consular reports are identified by country, year, and number. Titles of both groups may vary considerably.

Diplomatic and Consular Despatches, Paraguay. 27 vols. PRO-FO 59/37–63.

Diplomatic and Consular Reports, Paraguay. 12 nos. 1890–1906. Most of these diplomatic and consular reports were published as numbered reports in the continuing *Annual Series*, and most were included in volumes of the *Accounts and Papers* series. Individual country reports were also published separately. A typical title is "Paraguay: Report on the General Condition of Paraguay" (Foreign Office, 1890, Annual Series No. 792), *Accounts and Papers*, 1890–1891, v. 87 (London, 1890), pp. 321–28. This item would be referred to in the notes as DCR No. 792, *Paraguay 1890*. Because of their great importance, the following two reports are listed separately:

"Report on the Present Political, Financial and Social State of the Republic of Paraguay," encl., Lionel L. Sackville West to Derby, No. 109 Conf., Buenos Aires, Oct. 30, 1875. PRO-FO 6/368, folios 76–90.

"Paraguay. Report by Mr. [Arthur G.] Vansittart on the Commerce, Finances &C. of Paraguay." *Sessional Papers, Accounts and Papers, Commercial Reports*, LXXI (London, 1883), 77–154.

Paraguay

Banco Nacional del Paraguay. *Memoria del directorio del "Banco Nacional del Paraguay" correspondiente al año de 1887 presentada a los accionistas en la cuarta asamblea anual el 25 de enero de 1888*. Asunción, 1888.

Bareiro, Cándido, *Manifiesto del presidente de la república al pueblo*. Asunción, 1879.

Boletín oficial de la nación. Asunción, 1871–. Irregular.

Bono general de cuatrocientos mil libras esterlinas. Demanda de fiscal general de estado. Contestación del Banco del Paraguay y Río de la Plata. Asunción, 1895.

Caballero, Bernardino. *Carta programa del General Don Bernardino Caballero, Nov. 18, 1893.* Asunción, 1893.

――――. *Discurso del Jeneral Don Bernardino Caballero al recibirse de la presidencia de la república ante el honorable congreso de la nación, 25 de noviembre de 1882.* Asunción, 1882.

――――. *Manifiesto del Partido Nacional Republicano á sus correligionarios.* Asunción, Aug. 9, 1904.

――――. Proclama del General Bernardino Caballero al tomar el mando de las fuerzas nacionales después de la muerte de Don Cándido Bareiro en 1880." GC-UCR.

Cámara de Diputados, República del Paraguay. *Actas de las sesiones de los períodos legislativos de los años 1873–74–75–76–77–78–79–80.* Asunción, 1910.

――――. *Sesiones del día 2 de abril al 30 de setiembre año 1888.* Asunción, 1889.

――――. *Sesiones del período legislativo.* Irregular holdings for 1871–1880, 1888–1889, 1895–1899, 1901, 1902, 1908–1909. Gondra Collection, Universityof Texas-Austin.

Cámara de Senadores, República del Paraguay. *Actas de las sesiones de los períodos legislativos de los años de 1874–75–76–77–78–79–80.* Asunción, 1908.

"Censo geral da Republica do Paraguay levantado em 12 de março de 1886," encl., Francisco Regis de Oliveira to Barão de Cotegipe, 2ª Sec. No. 15, Asunción, June 28, 1887. AHI-MRD, MDBA-OR 201/2/2.

Centro Democrático. *Manifiesto al pueblo de la nación paraguaya del comite revolucionario del Centro Democrático.* Asunción, 1891.

――――. *Memoria de la comisión directiva del Centro Democrático correspondiente al período reglamentario de 1889 a 1890.* Asunción, 1890.

Código rural de la República del Paraguay. Asunción, 1887.

Colección de tratados celebrados por la República del Paraguay. 3 vols. Asunción, 1885, 1890, 1895.

Congreso Nacional, República del Paraguay. *Sesión extraordinaria del dia 9 de enero del año 1902.* Asunción, 1902.

Constitución de la República del Paraguay sancionada por la honorable convención constituyente en sesión del 18 de noviembre de 1870. Asunción, 1871.

Contrato entre D. Enrique López y el presidente del Paraguay Juan B. Egusquiza sobre cuestión de los campos de Mato Grosso (Brasil) y perdidos en la guerra de la Triple Alianza. Año 1895. GC-UCR.

Contrato sobre prolongación del ferro-carril de Paraguarí a Villa-Rica celebrado entre el superior govierno y el Señor Don Luis Patri el 24 de setiembre de 1886. Asunción, 1888.

Decoud, José Segundo. *Informe del comisionado especial Señor Ministro de Relaciones Exteriores Don José S. Decoud al gobierno de la República del Paraguay, dando cuenta de su misión a Londres para el arreglo de la deuda procedente de los empréstitos de 1871 y 1872.* Asunción, 1886.

――――. "Límites del Paraguay con Bolivia―posesión del Gran Chaco," encl. No. 3, Ruffin to Cridler, No. 3, Asunción, Nov. 18, 1897. DUSCA T 329/4.

――――. *Plan económico presentado por el poder ejecutivo. Colección de leyes sancionadas por el H. congreso de la nación en sus sesiones extraordinarias de noviembre de 1890.* Asunción, 1891.

Departamento de Tierras y Colonias. *Compilación de leyes y decretos ordenados por Carlos Pastore, presidente del departamento y ejecutado por Carlos A. Rolón.* Asunción, 1939.

Departamento Nacional de Higiene. *Reglamentación del ejercicio de la farmacia.* Asunción, 1909.

Documentos relativos a la reclamación norteamericana. Asunción, 1887.

Domínguez, Manuel. *Manifiesto del vice-presidente de la República del Paraguay, Oct. 15, 1904.* Asunción, 1904.

Escritura de Venia supletoria otorgada por Don Javier de Quatrefages en favor de Elisa Alicia Lynch, Buenos Aires, Feb. 7, 1885. Copy in GC-UCR.

Escurra, Juan A. *Manifiesto del presidente de la república Coronel Juan A. Escurra.* Asunción, Aug. 16, 1904.

Estatutos de la sociedad anómina Banco del Paraguay. Buenos Aires, 1881.

Ferreira, Benigno. *Al Pueblo.* [Villa del Pilar?], Aug. 15, 1904.

——. *Al Pueblo. Manifiesto del general en jefe del ejército revolucionario.* Sept. 25, 1904.

Gill Papers. Colección de Carlos Alberto Pusineri Scala, Asunción.

Godoi Collection. Papers of Juan Silvano Godoi. University of California, Riverside. This collection has been reorganized by Mr. Thomas Whigham since the author used it; hence, there are no references in notes to boxes or carpetas.

González, Juan Gualberto. *Manifiesto del presidente de la República del Paraguay D. Juan G. González a sus conciudadanos, June 30, 1894.* Buenos Aires, 1897.

——. *Mensaje y discursos leídos al congreso nacional el 25 de noviembre de 1890 en ocasión del juramento á la constitución prestado por el nuevo presidente de la república, ciudadano Juan G. González.* Asunción, 1890.

——. *Manifiesto del presidente de la República del Paraguay D. Juan G. González a sus conciudadanos, June 30, 1894.* Buenos Aires, 1897.

Lane, William. *The Second Yearly Report of Cosme Colony, Paraguay, May 12th, 1896.* Asunción (?), 1896.

Ley de matrimonio civil [Dec. 2, 1898]. Asunción, 1899.

López, Enrique Solano. *Crédito territorial y agrícola de la República del Paraguay.* Asunción, 1887.

Mendonça, Juan Carlos, ed. *Las constituciones paraguayas y los proyectos de constitución de los partidos políticos.* Colección Cultura Paraguaya. Asunción, 1967.

Mensajes de los presidentes de la República del Paraguay al Congreso. 26 vols. Asunción, 1878–1905. There is no one compilation with this title. For the sake of brevity, the author has placed all the annual messages together. While they differ slightly in wording, and vary in length from one to many pages, a typical entry would be, Cándido Bareiro, *Mensaje del presidente de la República del Paraguay al abrir las sesiones del congreso en abril de 1880,* and would be cited as Bareiro, *Mensaje* (April, 1880).

Ministerio de Hacienda. *Memorias.* 1883–1900. 16 vols. Asunción, 1884–1901.

Ministerio del Interior. *Memorias.* 1888–1900. 7 vols. Asunción, 1889–1902.

Ministerio de Justicia, Culto e Instrucción Pública. *Memoria.* April 30, 1886, in *El Orden,* May 2, 1886.

Ministerio de Relaciones Exteriores. *Colonia Gaboto organización y reglamentación*. Asunción, 1902.

———. *Datos estadísticos sobre el movimiento de inmigración en el Paraguay desde 1882 hasta 1907. Publícalos la Dirección General de Inmigración y Colonización. Autorizado para el efecto por el señor doctor Don Cecilio Báez, ministro de relaciones exteriores*. Asunción, 1908.

———. *Informe sobre la colonia Hohenau*. By Angel Battilana. Asunción, May 10, 1909.

———. *Leyes de inmigración, colonización y reducción de tribus indíjenas*. Asunción, 1913.

———. *Memorias*. 1878–1903. 20 vols. Asunción, 1878–1903.

———. *Reglamento para la colonia "Nueva Italia" en el departamento de "Villeta."* Asunción, 1907.

———. Oficina General de Inmigración y Colonización. *Memoria de la oficina general de inmigracón y colonizacón correspondiente a los años 1905–1906 —1906–1907*. Asunción, 1908.

Noticia sobre la colonia "Presidente González" en el departamento de Caazapá. Asunción, 1891.

Oficina general de etadística. *Anuario estadístico de la República del Paraguay. Año 1886*. Asunción, 1886.

Oficinia general de informaciones. *Guide d' l'immigrant au Paraguay*. Asunción, 1889.

Partido Liberal. *Estatutos. Reglamento interno de la comisión central*. Asunción, 1895.

"Los proyectos rentísicos. Mensaje del P. E. Asunto de emisión—Banco Agrícola—Cloacas y aguas corrientes." *Boletín quincenal de la Cámara de Comercio de la Asunción* 1 (June 16, 1903).

Registro oficial de la República del Paraguay, 1869–1895. 10 vols. Asunción, 1876–1897. Titles vary, and some years are bound together.

"Renuncia de Don Adolfo Saguier 1878." GC-UCR.

Resquín, Francisco Ysidoro. "Breves relaciones históricas de la guerra contra el gobierno de la República del Paraguay, por los gobiernos de la Triple Alianza, brasileiro, argentino, y oriental—Estractado de documentos de la luz pública, y de los sucesos de armas, durante la guerra de mas de cinco años, que sostiene el gobierno de la nación paraguaya, contra los poderes de la Triple Alianza. Asunción del Paraguay, año de 1875." Archivo Nacional, Asunción.

[Romero, Genaro]. *Informe sobre la colonia "25 de Noviembre."* Asunción, 1910.

———. "Informe sobre las colonias "Nueva Italia" y "Trinacria."" Asunción, 1910.

———. *Informes sobre las colonias "Trinacria," "Nueva Italia," "25 de Noviembre" presentados al ministerio de relaciones exteriores*. Asunción, 1911.

———. "Nuestras colonias: la colonia "25 de Noviembre"—informe elevado al ministerio de relaciones por el comisionado señor Genaro Romero, Asunción, 25 de mayo de 1910." Mounted clipping from unidentified newspaper, Gondra Collection, University of Texas—Austin.

Statutes and Laws of the Bank of Paraguay and the River Plate. Buenos Aires, 1889.

Stewart, William. "Historia del Paraguay por el Dr. William Stewart." CCAP.

Tratados celebrados entre las repúblicas del Paraguay y Uruguay. N.p., n.d.

Viera, Fernando. *Colección legislativa de la República del Paraguay, 1842–1895.* Asunción, 1895.

[Wisner von Morgenstern, Francisco]. *Sobre la cantidad de leguas de terrenos públicos aproximadamente, la calidad de ellos, sus producciones, etc. Informe por orden de S. E. el señor presidente de la República del Paraguay.* Asunción, 1871.

United States

Barrett, Rafael. "The Last Revolution and the Present Politics," encl., Edward C. O'Brien to Elihu Root, No. 69, Montevideo, Dec. 12, 1905. DDPU 128/18.

Despatches from United States Consuls in Asunción, 1844–1906. National Archives Microfilm Publications. Microcopy T 329, Rolls 1–6.

Despatches from United States Ministers to Paraguay and Uruguay. File Microcopies of Records in the National Archives, No. 128, 19 vols., Oct. 11, 1858–July 17, 1906.

Diplomatic Instructions of the Department of State, 1801–1906. Paraguay and Uruguay, Oct. 6, 1858–July 26, 1906. File Microcopies of Records in the National Archives, No. 77, Roll 128.

Flagg, Eben M. "Information Concerning the Banking system of Paraguay." Asunción, Oct. 7, 1895. NPFO T 693/1.

Notes from the Paraguayan Legation in the United States to the Department of State, March 12, 1852–May 16, 1906. National Archives Microfilm Publications, Microcopy T 350, Rolls 1–2.

Records of the United States Legation in Paraguay, 1861–1935. Copies of notes sent to the Paraguayan Foreign Office, Nov. 23, 1861–May 10, 1873 and Sept. 22, 1862–May 14, 1907. National Archives Microfilm Publications, Microcopy T 693, Roll 4.

Records of the United States Legation in Paraguay, 1861–1935. Notes from the Paraguayan Foreign Office, Nov. 18, 1865–June 4, 1885. National Archives Microfilm Publications, Microcopy T 693, Roll 3.

Ruffin, John N. "Navigation of the Rio de la Plata," Advance sheets of Consular Reports No. 1350, December 27, 1902. DUSCA T 329/6.

Wavrunek, J. V. "Answers to Questions for the International Woman's Suffrage Conference to be Held in Washington, D.C., Feb. 12th–18th, 1902," Asunción, Dec. 12, 1901, encl., W. R. Finch to John Hay, Montevideo, Dec. 24, 1901. DDPU 128/14.

Books and Pamphlets

Aceval, Benjamin. *República del Paraguay: apuntes geográficos e históricos.* Asunción, 1893.

Aguirre Acha, José. *The Arbitration Zone in the Bolivian-Paraguayan Dispute through the Diplomatic Negotiations.* La Paz, 1929.

Alcorta, Sinforiano. *Antecedentes históricos sobre los tratados con el Paraguay.* Buenos Aires, 1885.

Almanaque nacional del Paraguay para el año de 1886. Asunción, 1886.

Arbo, Higinio. *Política paraguaya.* Buenos Aires, 1947.

Argaña, Luís María. *Perfiles políticos: perfiles doctrinarios e ideológicos de los partidos y de los movimientos políticos en el Paraguay.* Asunción, 1977.

Arnold, Adlai F. *Foundations of an Agricultural Policy in Paraguay.* Praeger Special Studies in International Economics and Development. New York, 1971.

Audibert, Alejandro. *Cuestión de límites entre el Paraguay y Bolivia: artículos publicados por "La Democracia" y "El Pueblo."* Asunción, 1901.

————. *Los límites de la antigua provincia del Paraguay.* Primera parte. Buenos Aires, 1892.

Ayala, Eligio. *Migraciones: ensayo escrito en Berna en 1915.* Santiago de Chile, 1941.

Báez, Cecilio. *Cuadros históricos y descriptivos.* Asunción, 1906.

————. *Paraguay y Bolivia: la cuestión de límites.* Asunción, n.d.

————. *La tiranía en el Paraguay: sus causas, caracteres y resultados: colección de artículos publicados en "El Cívico."* Asunción, 1903.

Baillie, Alexander F. *A Paraguayan Treasure: The Search and the Discovery.* London, 1887.

Bareiro, Francisco L. *El Paraguay en la República Argentina: la condonación de la deuda de guerra: nobles iniciativas.* Buenos Aires, 1900.

Barrett, Rafael. *El dolor paraguayo.* Montevideo, 1911.

Benítez, Gregorio. *Exposición de los derechos del Paraguay en la cuestión de límites con Bolivia sobre el territorio del Chaco, presentada al plenipotenciario boliviano Dr. Telmo Ichazo.* Asunción, 1895.

Benítez, Justo Pastor. *Ensayo sobre el liberalismo paraguayo.* 3rd ed. Asunción, 1932.

Benítez, Luís G. *Historia diplomática del Paraguay.* Asunción, 1972.

Bernardez, Manuel. *El tratado de la Asunción.* Montevideo, 1894.

Bordón, F. Arturo. *Historia política del Paraguay: era constitucional, 1869–1886.* Asunción, 1976.

Bordón, F. Arturo, and Cardozo, Efraím, eds. *Liberales illustres.* Tomo I. *Precursores y fundadores del partido liberal.* Asunción, 1966.

Bourgade la Dardye, Emanuel de. *Paraguay, the Land and the People, Natural Wealth and Commercial Capabilities.* London, 1892.

Bray, Arturo. *Hombres y épocas del Paraguay.* 2 vols. Buenos Aires, 1957.

Brugada, Ricardo. *Política paraguaya: Benigno Ferreira.* Asunción, 1906.

Butler, William Mill. *Paraguay: A Country of Vast Natural Resources, Delightful Climate, Law-Abiding People, and Stable Government: Rightly Called the Paradise of South America.* Philadelphia, 1901.

Calzada, Rafael. *Rasgos biográficos de José Segundo Decoud: homenaje en el 4º aniversario de su fallecimiento, 4 de marzo de 1909.* Buenos Aires, 1913.

Cardozo, Efraím. *Efemérides de la historia del Paraguay.* Asunción and Buenos Aires, 1967.

————. *Hace cién años: crónicas de la guerra de 1864–1870.* 12 vols. Asunción, 1967–1981.

Carrasco, Gabriel. *Cartas de viaje por el Paraguay, los territorios nacionales del Chaco, Formosa y Misiones y las provincias de Corrientes y Entre Rios*. Buenos Aires, 1889.

Centurión, Carlos R. *Historia de la cultura paraguaya*. 2 vols. Asunción, 1961.

————. *Historia de las letras paraguayas*. 3 vols. Buenos Aires, 1948.

Centurión y Martínez, Juan Crisóstomo. *Memorias, o reminiscencias históricas sobre la guerra del Paraguay*. 4 vols. Asunción, 1948.

Ceuppens, Henry D. *Paraguay año 2000*. Asunción, 1971.

Cibils, Manuel J. *Anarquía y revolución en el Paraguay*. Buenos Aires, 1957.

[Cordero, Antonio]. *Reclamación: varios documentos Don Francisco Cordero y otros ciudadanos argentinos pidiendo la intervención del gobierno con motivo de despojo de sus propiedades verificado por el gobierno del Paraguay*. Buenos Aires, 1888.

Costaguta, Raffaele. *Cenni storici, commerciali e geografici sul Paraguay*. Genoa, 1901.

Decoud, Héctor Francisco. *Geografía de la República del Paraguay*. 2d. ed. Asunción, 1896.

Decoud, José Segundo. *Questiones políticas y económicas*. Asunción, 1877.

————. *Exposición presentada por José S. Decoud a la honorable cámara de diputados a propósito de la investigación iniciada en virtud de una denuncia falsa de anexión*. Asunción, 1898.

Dictamenes jurídicos sobre propiedades en el Paraguay pertenecientes a Don Enrique Solano López y otros. Buenos Aires, 1887.

Dombrowski, Katharina von. *Land of Women*. Boston, 1935.

Estatutos del Centro Español fundado el 22 de setiembre de 1895 en la Asunción del Paraguay. Asunción, 1899.

Fernández-Caballero, Carlos F. S. *Aranduká ha kuatiañeé Paraguai rembiapocué: The Paraguayan Bibliography*. Asunción and Washington, D.C., 1970.

Fischer-Treuenfeld, Richard Friedrich Eberhard von. *Le Paraguay décrit et illustré: étude sur le progrès économique du pays*. Brussels, 1906.

————. *Paraguay in Wort und Bild: Eine Studie über den wirtschaftlichen Fortschritt des Landes*. Berlin, 1906.

Förster, Bernhard, *Deutsche Colonien in dem oberen Laplata-gebiete, mit besonderer Berücksichtigung von Paraguay*. Leipzig, 1886.

————. *Dr. Bernhard Försters Kolonie Neu-Germania in Paraguay*. Berlin, 1891.

Freire Esteves, Gómes. "Historia contemporánea de la república." In *El Paraguay constitucional, 1870–1920*, ed. Luís Freire Esteves and Juan C. González Peña, Buenos Aires, 1921.

————. *Historia contemporánea del Paraguay: lucha de cancillerias en el Río de la Plata*. Buenos Aires, 1921.

————. *El Paraguay constitucional, 1870–1920*. Buenos Aires, 1921.

Fretz, Joseph Winfield. *Immigrant Group Settlements in Paraguay: A Study in the Sociology of Immigration*. North Newton, Kansas, 1962.

Freund, P. A., and W. F. Mulhall. *Letters from Paraguay extracted from "The Standard."* Buenos Aires, 1888.

Friedmann, Eugenio. *Historia del azúcar en el Paraguay*. Asunción, 1966.

García Mellid, Atilio. *Proceso a los falsificadores de la historia del Paraguay*. Biblioteca de Estudios Históricos. 2 vols. Buenos Aires, 1963–1964.

Godoi, Juansilvano. *El Barón de Río Branco*. Asunción, 1912. A book of essays written at various times and collected for publication. The author's name appears in various forms: Juan Silvano Godoi, Juan Silvano Godoy, Juansilvano Godoi, and Juansilvano Godoy. He appears to have preferred Juansilvano Godoi.

————. *El Coronel don Juan Antonio Escurra, presidente electo de la República del Paraguay.* Asunción, 1903.

————. *Mi misión a Río de Janeiro.* Buenos Aires, 1897.

————. *Monografías históricas.* Buenos Aires, 1893.

————. *Monographias históricas com um appendice contendo o capitulo viii do livro de Benjamin Mossé sobre a campanha do Paraguay e o depoimento do General D. Francisco Isidoro Resquin.* Rio Grande, 1895. The author's name is printed as Juan Silvano de Godoi, but the presentation copy to General Bartolomé Mitre is signed "Juansilvano Godoi." Copy in Museo Mitre, Buenos Aires.

Gondra, César. *La deuda de la guerra de 1865.* Asunción, 1903.

González, Juan Natalicio. *Geografía del Paraguay.* Mexico City, 1964.

González, Juan Natalicio, and Pablo Max Ynsfran. *El Paraguay contemporáneo.* Paris, 1926.

González, Teodosio. *Infortunios del Paraguay.* Buenos Aires, 1931.

Grubb, W. Barbrooke. *An Unknown People in an Unknown Land: An Account of the Life and Customs of the Paraguayan Chaco, with Adventures and Experiences Met with during twenty Years' Pioneering and Exploration amongst them.* Ed. H. T. Morrey Jones. London, 1911.

Guía general de la República del Paraguay. Asunción, 1907.

Hutchison, Thomas Joseph. *The Paraná; with Incidents of the Paraguayan War, and South American Recollections from 1861 to 1868.* London, 1868.

Jones, David Lewis. *Paraguay: A Bibliography.* New York and London, 1979.

Kelsey, Vera. *Brazil in Capitals.* New York and London, 1942.

Kolinsky, Charles J. *Independence or Death! The Story of the Paraguayan War.* Gainesville, 1965. By far the best account of the Paraguayan War in English.

Lagos, Hector M. *Carlos Casado del Alisal: su biografía; una vida armónica al servicio del progreso nacional.* Buenos Aires, 1949.

López, Enrique Solano. *Revalidación de títulos de terrenos al sud del Pilcomayo.* Buenos Aires, 1885.

López Decoud, Arsenio. *Album gráfico de la República del Paraguay.* Buenos Aires, 1911.

————. *La República del Paraguay: un siglo de vida nacional, 1811–1911.* Buenos Aires, 1911.

Macdonald, Alexander K. *Picturesque Paraguay, Sport, Pioneering, Travel; a Land of Promise, Stockraising, Plantations, Industries, Forest Products, Commercial Possibilities.* London, 1911.

Maíz, Fidel. *Etapas de mi vida: contestación a las imposturas de Juan Silvano Godoy.* Asunción, 1919.

Martínez, Benigno. *El Paraguay: memoria bajo el punto de vista industrial y comercial en relación con los paises del Plata.* Asunción, 1885.

Memoria de la Comisión Directiva de la Sociedad "Centro Español" en su período administrativo desde su fundación hasta el 20 de enero de 1897. Asunción, 1897.

Méndez Fleitas, Epifanio. *Diagnosis paraguaya.* Montevideo, 1965.

————. *Lo histórico y lo antihistórico en el Paraguay—carta a los Colorados.* Buenos Aires, 1976.

Meulemans, Auguste. *La République du Paraguay: étude historique et statistique.* Paris, 1884.

Mevert, Ernst. *Reisebriefe aus Paraguay.* Wansbeck, 1882.

Molins, Wenceslao Jaime. *Paraguay.* Crónicas Americanas. Buenos Aires, 1915.

Moreno, Fulgencio R. *Diplomacia paraguayo-boliviana: antecedentes de los tratados de límites y causas de su fracaso.* Asunción, 1904.

Moscarda, Andrés. *Un caso de prescripción contra el fisco—las tierras de Madama Lynch, 1865–1920.* 2d. ed. Asunción, 1920.

Mulhall, M. G., and E. T. Mulhall. *Handbook of the River Plate Comprising the Argentine Republic, Uruguay, and Paraguay.* 5th ed. Buenos Aires, 1885; 6th ed. Buenos Aires, 1892.

Mulhall, M. G., and P. A. Freund, *Letters from Paraguay Extracted from "The Standard."* Buenos Aires, 1888.

Pastore, Carlos. *La lucha por la tierra en el Paraguay: proceso histórico y legislativo.* Montevideo, 1949.

Paternó, Giuseppe de Stéfano. *Relazione sulla colonizzazione nel Paraguay de D. Giuseppe De Stefano Paternó, presidente della Societá Colonizzatrice Italo-Americana: Fondazionde dell Trinacria.* Catania, 1899.

Pérez Acosta, Juan. F. *Carlos Antonio López, obrero máximo: labor administrativa y constructiva.* Asunción, 1948.

Pincus, Joseph. *The Economy of Paraguay.* Praeger Special Studies in International Economics and Development, New York, 1968.

Pinheiro Guimarães, Francisco. *Um voluntário da pátria.* Coleção Documentos Brasileiras, No. 943, Rio de Janeiro, 1958.

Pitaud, Henri. *Les Français au Paraguay.* Bordeaux and Paris, 1955.

————. *El General Caballero: relato novelado de cuarenta y dos años de historia del Paraguay.* Traducido del francés por Gabriela de Ceviny. Asunción, 1976.

Quistorp, Henry. *Paraguay. "What place is that, Sir?" "Can you settle me there?" "What am I waiting here for, please?" Three questions answered.* 2d ed. London, 1884.

Reclamación temeraria: las pretendidas 3,105 leguas de tierras públicas en el Paraguay de Madama Linch y de sus subrogantes, consideradas ante la razón y el derecho: artículos jurídicos publicados en "La Nación" sobre esta cuestión. Asunción, 1888.

Resquín, Francisco Isidoro. *Datos históricos de la guerra del Paraguay con la Triple Alianza.* Buenos Aires, 1896.

Rey de Castro, Carlos. *La clase rural paraguaya: con un prólogo del Doctor Manuel Domínguez.* Asunción, 1903.

Rio-Branco, Barão do. *Efemérides brasileiras.* Rio de Janeiro, 1946.

Riquelme García, Benigno. *Cumbre en soldedad: vida de Manuel Gondra.* Buenos Aires, 1951.

Rodríguez Alcalá, José. *El Paraguay en marcha.* Asunción, 1907.

Salum-Flecha, Antonio. *Historia diplomática del Paraguay de 1869 a 1938.* Asunción, 1972.

Sánchez Quell, Hipólito. *Falando do Paraguai ao Brasil*. Rio de Janeiro, 1958.

―――. *Proyección del General Caballero en la ruta de la patria*. Asunción, 1970.

Schurz, W. L. *Paraguay: A Commercial Handbook*. Washington, 1920.

Schuster, Adolf N. *Paraguay: Land, Volk, Geschichte, Wirtschaftsleben und Kolonisation*. Stuttgart, 1929.

Service, Elman R., and Helen S. Service. *Tobatí: A Paraguayan Town*. Chicago, 1954.

Société Générale Paraguayo-Argentina, Buenos Aires. *Colonies de Villa Sana créés en 1889 par J. Valentin*. Paris, 1891.

Sosa Escalada, Gustavo. *Revolución del Paraguay 1904: el buque fantasma, diario de un tripulante del "Libertad, ex-"Sajonia."* Asunción, 1982.

Stewart, Guillermo. *La peste*. Asunción, 1899.

Stewart, Norman R. *Japanese Colonization in Eastern Paraguay*. Washington, 1967.

[Taboada, Antonio], *Memoria*. Centro Democrático. Asunción, 1890.

Tasso Fragoso, Augusto. *A paz com o Paraguai depois da guerra da Tríplice Aliança*. Rio de Janeiro, 1941.

Taunay, Affonso de E. *História das bandeiras paulistas*. 2 vols. São Paulo, 1951.

Terrero, Máximo, and Francisco Wisner de Morgenstern. *Paraguay: A Note as to Its Position and Prospects*. London, 1871.

Valle, Florentino del. *Cartilla cívica: proceso político del Paraguay 1870–1950; el Partido Liberal y la Asociación Nacional Republicana (Partido Colorado) en la balanza de la verdad histórica*. Buenos Aires, 1951.

Valpy, Henry. *Paraguay Land Warrants: Report to the Council of Foreign Bondholders on the Selection of Lands*. London, 1888.

Veneroso, Angel M. *Guía general de la República del Paraguay*. Asunción, 1894.

―――. *Guía general de la República del Paraguay*. Asunción, 1895.

Warren, Harris Gaylord. *Paraguay: An Informal History*. Norman, 1959.

―――. *Paraguay and the Triple Alliance: the Postwar Decade, 1869–1878*. Austin, 1978.

Washburn, Charles A. *The History of Paraguay, with Notes of Personal Observations and Reminiscences of Diplomacy under Difficulties*. 2 vols. Boston, 1871.

White, Richard Alan. *Paraguay's Autonomous Revolution, 1810–1840*. Albuquerque, 1978.

Williams, John Hoyt. *The Rise and Fall of the Paraguayan Republic, 1800–1870*. Austin, 1979.

Ynsfran, Pablo Max. *La expedición norteamericana contra el Paraguay, 1858–1859*. 2 vols. Mexico and Buenos Aires, 1954–1958.

Zinny, Antonio. *Historia de los gobernantes del Paraguay, 1535–1887*. Buenos Aires, 1887.

Zubizarreta, Ramón. *Dictamen del doctor Ramón Zubizarreta sobre el valor legal de los títulos de Ma. Lynch en la reclamación de las tres mil y pico de leguas*. Asunción, 1888.

Articles

Ayala, Eusebio. "La significaión del laudo arbitral del Presidente Ruther-ford Hayes." In *El Paraguay en el primer cincuentenario del fallo arbitral del Presidente hayes*, comp. Eduardo Amarilla Fretes, pp. 53–64, Asunción, 1932.

Báez, Cecilio, and Juan D. Centurión. "Límites con Bolivia: capítulos del informe encomendado por el congreso de la nación para el estudio del tratado Benítez-Ichazo." RIP, Año II, tomo III, No. 15 (1879), 81–105.

Baker, E. L. "Report on Yerba Mate or Paraguay Tea." Bureau of American Republics, *Bulletin* 54 (Washington, 1984), 96–104.

Carpenter, Frank G. "Sarmiento en Paraguay." *Humanidades* 37 (1961), 27–58.

Corvalán, Grazziella. "Ideologías y origen social de los grupos políticos en el Paraguay." *RPS*, Año 9, No. 23 (Jan.–April, 1972), 106–17.

Dahl, Victor C. "The Paraguayan 'Jewel Box'." *The Americas* 21 (Jan., 1965), 223–42.

Elchibegoff, Ivan M. "The Forest Resources and Timber Trade of Latin America." *The Inter-American Quarterly*, 3, No. 2 (April, 1941), 75–81.

Forgues, M. L. "Le Paraguay: fragments de journal et de correspondances, 1872–1873." *Le Tour du Monde: Nouvelle Journal des Voyages*, 27, Nos. 701, 702, 703 (Paris, 1874), 369–416.

Galeano, Luis A. "Dos alternativas históricas del campesino paraguayo: migración y colonización (1870–1950)." *RPS*, Año 15, No. 41 (Jan.–April, 1978), 115–42.

González Erico, Miguel Angel. "Desarrollo de la banca en el Paraguay (1870–1900). *RPS*, Año 9, No. 25 (Sept.–Dec., 1972), 133–54.

————. "Estructura y desarrollo del comercio exterior del Paraguay: 1870–1918." *RPS*, Año 12 (No. 34, Sept.–Dec., 1975), 125–55.

Herken Krauer, Juan Carlos, "La revolución liberal de 1904 en el Paraguay: el trasfondo socio-económico y la perspectiva britannica." *RPS*, Año 20, No. 56 (Jan.–April, 1983).

Hicks, Frederic. "Interpersonal Relationships and Caudillismo in Para-guay." *JIASW* 13 (Jan., 1971), 89–111.

Livermore, Harold V. "New Australia." *HAHR* 30 (Aug. 1950), 290–313.

M. M. [Miguel Macías], "Paraguay, 25 de noviembre de 1882." *RP* 2 (1892), 270–313, 422–27, 506–11; 3 (1893), 9–15, 33–53.

Mendonça, Juan Carlos. "La cronología de las generaciones paraguayas." *El Paraguayo* (Asunción), Aug. 15, 1963, pp. 3–5.

Parodi, Enrique de. "La prensa." *RP* 1, Nos. 8, 9, 10 (1891), 341–48, 389–96, 441–53.

Paternó, Giuseppe de Stéfano. "Colonización italiana en el Paraguay." *RM* 3, No. 26 (April, 1898), 36–48.

————. "La obra del Dr. Paternó." *RM* 3, Nos. 27, 28 (May–June, 1898), 65–137.

Peña, Enrique. "Monedas y medallas paraguayas." *RIP* 3 No. 24 (1900), 51–99.

Peterson, Harold F. "Edward A. Hopkins, a Pioneer Promoter in Paraguay." *HAHR* 22 (May, 1942), 243–61.

Pidoux de Drachenberg, Lyra. "Inmigración y colonización en el Paraguay, 1870–1970." *RPS*, Año 12 No. 34 (Sept.–Dec., 1975), 65–123.

"La producción del algodón en El Paraguay." *RM* 2 (1897), 358.

Rolón, Francisco. "El Paraguay y Bolivia." *RIP* 9 (1903), 337–70.

Ruffin, John N. "The Temerario at Asunción." *The American Foreign Service Journal* 21 (Nov. 1944), 612–13, 636–44.

Warren, Harris Gaylord. "Banks and Banking in Paraguay, 1871–1904. *IAEA* 32 (Autumn, 1978), 39–57.

———. "Brazil and the Cavalcanti Coup of 1894 in Paraguay." *Luso-Brazilian Review* 19, No. 2 (Winter, 1982), 221–36.

———. "The Golden Fleecing: The Paraguayan Loans of 1871 and 1872." *IAEA* 26 (Summer, 1972), 3–24.

———. "The Hopkins Claim Against Paraguay and the Case of the Missing Jewels." *IAEA* 21 (Summer, 1968), 23–44.

———. "The 'Lincolnshire Farmers' in Paraguay." *The Americas* 21 (Jan., 1965), 243–69.

———. "Litigation in English Courts and Claims Against Paraguay Resulting from the War of the Triple Alliance." *IAEA* 22 (Spring, 1969), 31–46.

———. "The Paraguay Central Railway, 1856–1889." *IAEA* 21 (Spring, 1967), 3–22.

———. "The Paraguay Central Railway, 1889–1907." *IAEA* 21 (Summer, 1967), 31–48.

———. "The Paraguayan Revolution of 1904." *The Americas* 36 (Jan., 1980), 365–80.

———. "Journalism in Asunción under the Allies and the Colorados, 1869–1904," *The Americas* 39 (April, 1983), 483–98.

Williams, John Hoyt. "Note on Blas Garay." *The Americas* 35 (July, 1978), 123–24.

———. "Observations on the Paraguayan Census of 1846." *HAHR* 56 (Aug., 1976), 429–37.

———. "Paraguay's Nineteenth-Century *Estancias de la República*." *Agricultural History* 47 (July, 1973), 206–15.

Wisner de Morgenstern, Francisco. "El Paraguay de 1871, según Wisner." *RIP* 8 (1903), 763–72.

Ynsfran, Pablo Max. "Sam Ward's Bargain with President López of Paraguay." *HAHR* 24 (Aug., 1954), 313–31.

Zubizarreta, Ramón. "La cuestión de la moneda." *RIP* 11 (1904), 113–64.

Newspapers

Titles marked with an asterisk were found as enclosures in diplomatic despatches. Unless otherwise noted, place of publication was Asunción.

La Bastilla
El Centenela
El Cívico
El Comercio
*La Constitución (Pilar)
La Cotorra
La Democracia

El Diario
El Diario (Buenos Aires)
El Eco del Paraguay
El Ecónomista
El Estudiante
El Grito del Pueblo
El Heraldo
El Independiente
El Látigo
El Látigo Inmortal
La Libertad
La Nación
La Nación (Buenos Aires)
Nación Paraguaya
El Nacional
*New Australia
La Opinión
El Orden
El País
*La Palabra (Montevideo)
*La Pampa (Buenos Aires)
El Paraguay
El Paraguayo
La Patria
La Patria Paraguaya
La Prensa
La Prensa (Buenos Aires)
El Pueblo
El Rayo
La Razón
*A Reacção
La Reforma
La Regeneración
La República
La República (Buenos Aires)
El Semanario
*El Siglo (Montevideo)
The Stanard (Buenos Aires)
El Sud-Americano (Buenos Aires)
El Tiempo
Tribuna Nacional (Buenos Aires)
El Triunfo

Index

PITT LATIN AMERICAN SERIES
Cole Blasier, Editor